Workers on Strike
France 1871–1890

Michelle Perrot

Workers on Strike
France 1871–1890

Translated from the French by
Chris Turner
with the assistance of
Erica Carter and Claire Laudet

Yale University Press
New Haven and London

Originally published as *Jeunesse de la Grève: France 1871–1890*,
Editions du Seuil, Paris, 1984
Translated from the French by permission of the author
First published in Great Britain 1987 by **Berg Publishers Limited**
First published in the United States 1987 by **Yale University Press**

English translation © Berg Publishers 1987

Printed in Great Britain.

Library of Congress Cataloging-in-Publication Data
Perrot, Michelle.
    Workers on strike.
    Translation of: Jeunesse de la grève.
    Bibliography: p.
    Includes index.
    1. Strikes and lockouts—France—History—19th
century.   I. Title.
HD5374.P4613   1987   331.89′2944   86–26753
ISBN 0–300–03849–6

10 9 8 7 6 5 4 3 2 1

Contents

Tables

Figures

Introduction

Every thesis and indeed every book takes so long to research and to write that it develops its own history. This would be of no interest if the author alone were involved, but in spite of the cloistered nature of academic research, such histories cannot help but assume some of the colouring of their own time. First of all, no choice can be said to be completely free or wholly without consequences. In choosing the topic of the present book, I was indeed prey to a twofold obsession, being imbued with that slightly ingenuous seriousness typical of the student generation of the 1950s, an obsession with the working class and with the possibility of writing a 'scientific' history. The France in which we had grown up was an old country; indeed, it belonged fundamentally to the nineteenth century, to a past age which was only then finally dying away. There were times when we had a presentiment of the huge economic and social upheavals which were around the corner — growth and underdevelopment, the consumer society and technocracy, the Third World and the 'new social strata', the crisis of socialism and of culture — but we did not grasp the full extent of these phenomena. Though we did not realise it at the time, we were on the brink of experiencing a kind of Baroque 'Renaissance'; yet our vision of the world remained a soberly classical one.

We had no doubts whatsoever of the existence in our country of a classical capitalism and, under its yoke, of a classical proletariat, which was both exploited and politically aware. That proletariat was our model and our hope, the key to our own destiny and to that of the world. After all, the leading lights of the period — from André Breton to Jean-Paul Sartre and Maurice Merleau-Ponty to Emmanuel Mounier — paid homage to it.

Our purpose, however, was not to identify with the working class. We were not content to adopt the approach put forward by Simone Weil; it was too individualist and ethical for our tastes. As the respectful heirs of humanism, we believed in the power of books and the labour of scholars. Taking the working class as the object of

1

our research seemed to us the best way of becoming part of it; it was our way of 'going to the people' and thereby making contact with the present.

There were, however, many risks involved in telling this history. It was a field laden down with romantic tales and full of conflicting passions, and it is one where the temptation to indulge in hagiography, excommunication or lyricism is still strong today. We rejected the easy formulas of the epic and the false certainties of Zdhanovite schematism. We wanted a warm and open history, one that was both rigorous and all-embracing. We also believed in 'Science'. Under the influence of a diffuse neo-positivism (despite all the sarcasm we heaped upon Seignobos), we dreamed confusedly of a 'social physics', of historical laboratories staffed by researchers in white coats, constructing the 'facts'.

On a quite different level, the work of Ernest Labrousse encouraged us to look at economic series, at statistics and surveys; to work at establishing constants and correlations, all of which seemed capable of rescuing history from its uncertain fate. By that route, we rediscovered the tradition of the French sociologists of the early part of the century, of Durkheim and of Simiand, Halbwachs, Mauss and the Année sociologique group, which, though curiously forgotten by a sociology tormented by the fiendish complexities of language, found a new lease of life within a history that was anxious to become a sociology of the past.

We were wary of a history that was 'literary' or ideological. Every text and every idea aroused our suspicions and had to be carefully sifted. We were haunted by the idea of measurement and by numbers which were pure and solid, whose metallic cutting edge could tear through the soft fabric of a historical discourse which seemed merely the pleasant reverie of some solitary wanderer.

This was, then, a time when quantitative methods were becoming more and more popular. The various stages in this process are not difficult to trace. Quantitative methods were first finely honed within the field of economics, where the mere amassing of series of isolated facts without their being given some integrated structure was rejected as inadequate. From there, they extended their reach to all aspects of social reality. Only what could be counted seemed to us solid and worthy material: registrations and solicitors' records, tolls and fiscal archives, parish registers and records of wine-growing, lists of notables, copyright records, prison registers and criminal records, voting statistics and figures for religious observance, and so on. The domain of the measurable stretched out as far as the eye could see, and we were discovering the extent to which societies were made up of interlocking patterns of repeated acts. We were in the grip of a statistical madness. We thought in terms of curves and cross-sections, secretly convinced that at the end of our patiently accumulated statistical work, reality would stand before us as imposing as the statue of the Commander in Don Juan.

When, at the beginning of the 1960s, mechanical data-processing — from the most humble and most inconvenient systems of cards and rods to the most complicated of machines — and the computer made their belated entry into historical research, researchers were often already staggering under the weight of their statistics. These new methods provided effective support and though sometimes below a certain threshold of complexity, they acted as an encumbrance, they also gave a stimulus to further work. The computer brought quantitative perspectives to a fine point, extended and systematised them. It made possible all sorts of operations that could not be performed manually. For some time, a sort of punch-card mania and a computer 'philosophy' held sway. However, these are now happily behind us, for, remarkable as this instrument was, it could not replace the outlining of a problematic. Its influence on the method of organisation of work, the conduct and even the initial formulation of research, is, however, undeniable, and we are still far from having felt its final effects.

My choice of the strike as a research object is explained by the perspectives, outlined above. It is an object that provides rich and dense material, its roots plunging deep into the life of the working class; it is at the same time eminently quantifiable. It stands at the crossroads of two preoccupations. Before choosing it, however, I meandered for some time around other possible topics. I first considered the possibility of producing a more wide-ranging study, taking in the whole of the late-nineteenth-century working-class universe — structures and movements, conditions and ideologies. I spent quite some researching into socialism, but before 1893 the various socialist 'schools' tempted the working class very little. It was not among Brousse's people, nor Guesde's or Vaillant's, nor even Alleman's that I would find them. The working class spilled over on all sides from these categories. Moreover, in the absence of preliminary partial studies, the field was too large. Everything still remained to be done from scratch: figures for wages and employment, demography, levels of skill and class stratification, trades and techniques, language and attitudes to life. On all these points, in spite of the research that has been carried out, much still remains to

be done today. Finally, I was wary of a temptation to conflate levels
— economy, social structures, attitudes — and equally of the trap of
presenting these merely as juxtaposed panels, with their mutual
connections likely to disappear into the binding of the book.

Concentrating on the strike seemed a way of avoiding these
various pitfalls. The time has now come to list the merits of that
decision, which are almost the only absolute certainty I still possess
now that my explorations are completed. A strike is an event which
speaks and which is spoken about. It is a subject which looses
tongues and makes ink flow freely. And not only the ink of the
guardians of order, but that of chroniclers and story-tellers, of the
journalists whom strikes attract out into the working-class areas,
along with novelists and artists. Strikes grasp the attention, fuel a
climate of disquiet and demand investigation. They generate an
abundance of documentary material. Above all, they break down
that dumbness to which the guardians of culture habitually condemn the popular classes — those inhabitants of a 'world beneath a
world' (the Goncourts) — consigning them, as soon as they disappear from view, to the trivial whisperings of oral tradition or to
nocturnal silence. Demands, protests, petitions, graffiti, discussions,
harangues, slogans, shouts, cheers and insults are so many links in a
chain of discourse that can give us a great deal of information about
the aspirations, desires and conceptions of the workers. And they
can tell us about them at the most humble levels. Figures hitherto
unknown, surface momentarily, taking the stage for an instant, only
to be submerged once again seconds after. These are precious,
fleeting forms, the skeleton of a movement in which too often we
know only the principal actors. Silent sufferings, desires buried
beneath the exhausting monotony of everyday life, rise up here and
find expression. Full of sound and gestures, a strike is an outpouring
of words, a psycho-drama in which repressed drives are liberated. It
plunges down into the heart of the unknown masses.

Complex in its origins and implications, the strike straddles
classifications and defies terminological divisions. In a strike we find
articulated together a variety of 'instances' which all too often are
merely presented layer by layer, piled one upon the other like a
house of cards. The strike forces us to enquire into the connections
between them; it compels us to wrestle with the details of multiple
correlations and imbrications. As a site of conflict, it multiplies the
relations between classes and social groups, which we are accustomed to seeing confined in their own separate compartments. It is
not only the worker that it presents to us, but the employer class,

the state and public opinion as they appear in the mirror held up to them by the workers. A strike is a dynamic relationship.

Strikes reproduce themselves. They escape from the class of accidental phenomena to acquire the status of 'social facts', facts possessed of a constraining power in the Durkheimian sense. By their frequency they lend themselves to the establishment of series and to analysis along economic lines. Where immediate perception, which is dissociative because it focuses on the exceptional and the sensational, finds only the episodic and discontinuous ('upsurges' and 'outbursts' as they are commonly known), Anglo-Saxon and, more recently, French economists are beginning to attempt to discern tendencies and regularities. Identifying the general growth of the strike, its distribution over time — year, month, week — and fluctuations, and locating the relations of these latter with the diverse dimensions of the economic situation offers a means of escape from the apparent incoherence of day-to-day development.

However determined we may be here to flush out the element of chance, we shall, nonetheless, take care to avoid the trap of pre-judging or imposing an illusory order on objects and events. We shall be as attentive to troubling discordances as to reassuring concordances, for these discordances are both a source of fresh questions and an invitation to different readings of the strike phenomenon. Indeed, in spite of a certain autonomy of structure, which confers on the strike an existence relatively independent of that of its participants, it should not be seen as an abstraction but as a locus of 'human' decision-making which has complex roots, as a process in which external realities are mediated through the consciousness of the actors. In the following, therefore, we shall have to sound out that consciousness by ceaselessly measuring acts against words, seeking to grasp zones of sensibility and indifference, to track down lasting or transient representations, hidden thoughts and even, if possible, what remains unthought. On this difficult path, which research has marked out before us, the guides who will come rushing to our aid will be precious few in number.

Since, however, the strike is a quantifiable phenomenon, there are a large number of points where quantitative methods can gain a purchase — whether direct or indirect — upon it. As the basic unit to be dealt with, each strike (defined according to the unity of the participants, a matter to which I shall return) presents several dimensions: extension (the number of strikers, but also the number of workplaces and *communes* affected), length, and intensity (number of days 'lost'), which give a summary measure of its impact in time and (both geographical and social) space.

Conforming to a regular pattern in its fundamental characteristics, every strike behaves as an ensemble constituted by a variable combination of identical elements. These may be listed here. Briefly, they include:

> *Stable components*:
> — location, date
> — nature of workers on strike
> — nature of strike
> — types of demand
> *Dynamic components*:
> — type of outbreak
> — course of the strike: organisations
>   meetings, demonstrations
>   violence
>   negotiations
>   arbitration attempts
>   repression
> — outcome

A questionnaire may therefore be made out for every strike to produce an inventory of these elements. Once these have been counted, they allow us to identify the dominant characteristics and the types of strike within a chosen historical space. Moreover, these elements may serve as a basis for establishing a whole range of correlations (e.g. between strikes by women, skilled workers or miners, etc, and the length and nature of the strike, demands, demonstrations, violence, arbitration, outcome, etc). So many types of correlation are possible, that it has in fact only been possible to use the most classical coordinates in this operation (a point which is doubtless open to criticism). Overall, then, the strike lends itself to highly detailed internal investigation.

These possibilities dictate a particular method and demand certain means to carry it out. First of all, they impose a need to accumulate a large quantity of statistical data (in the present study, almost 3,000 cases), without which any attempt at establishing correlations would be derisory, since this demands the identification of smaller subsets. We had also to conform to the rule of exhaustivity, not only to establish complete series of strikes but also to enumerate all their aspects. The information had not only to be indicative of the succession of events but to be dense and detailed about their content. For want of homogeneous and complete sources, we had to set up overlapping networks of information, so that material from one source could complement what was provided by another. Fortunately, there was no lack of sources: the novelty of the phenomenon and the interest or fear it aroused provided additional information to supplement the detailed accounts of the administrative services. The combined contributions of the National Archives, the Paris Prefecture of Police, the Department Archives (sifted through systematically) and the inexhaustible newspaper sources provided extensive documentation, even if it was not always of the type one might have wished for.

All this allowed me to establish a file for each of the strikes identified (2,923 from 1 June 1871 to 31 December 1890) or, at least, a file card containing the largest possible amount of the desired data. The move to processing this data on the computer, which had not originally been intended, was therefore relatively straightforward. Having obtained a grant of 10,000 francs (1965) from the National Centre for Scientific Research (CNRS), with the aid of the advice of programmers from SODAM, to whom the work was entrusted, I established a code which was a systematisation and transcription of the questionnaire I had gradually worked out by trial and error. It occupied almost all of the 80 columns available on each card. We had also had to decide on using a system of multiple punching, which was complicated and which I was later to regret having chosen as it made certain correlations impossible. Each strike was therefore transformed into a punched card. This was done in two stages: firstly, I produced a coded matrix (more than six months' work) and then the punching was done. As will be evident, these were the early days of data processing; I shall not go any further into this aspect of the procedure, which already has an old-fashioned ring to it. I shall simply, and briefly, indicate in what respects the technique seems to me to have influenced the work itself.

First of all, it considerably reinforced the demand for precise information. Cards containing too many unknown factors jeopardised the whole experiment. The need to reduce the number of such factors, to obtain information that was always complete, made me go back to my sources on many occasions. It also put the emphasis on the structural analysis of the object, since, apart from simply adding up the elements, the tables provided by the computer mapped these diverse constituents against each other. The object was thus subjected to a rigorous internal analysis which augmented its solidity, autonomy and coherence, but at the same time isolated it from its environment, about which, as a result, we have much less precise information. The contrast between this brilliantly illuminated area and the surrounding 'darkness' is so great that at first one hardly dares to venture out again into those outer reaches. Contact with the computer (however limited) puts the imprecisions of literary language to the test. But that is perhaps no bad thing.

Thus the method adopted, far from overriding my original preoccupations, contributed to reinforcing them. My work was getting further and further away from a history of strikes presented in merely narrative form or as a succession of exemplary monogaphs; it was tending more and more in the direction of historical sociology, towards a description of strikes as a social phenomenon at a given moment in time.

Now, the reader will doubtless ask why I chose the particular moment that I did. In the first instance, I was dealing with a period which, though located at the heart of a relatively densely populated research terrain was itself more or less uninhabited — and not by chance. It was an obscure period, that had no clear outlines and was seemingly of little interest. Opinion had it that the labour movement was so demoralised after the Commune, that it was rendered totally inactive. The scattered nature of the sources — the Office du Travail only began issuing strike statistics in 1890 — seemed to confirm this impression. It is curious to note that the great strike waves from 1878 to 1880 and from 1888 to 1890 are not mentioned in the classic histories of the workers' movement. In their instinctive attachment to institutional frameworks, they are unable to come to grips with a period in which there was no centralised trade-union organisation.

I was attracted to the subject by these very reasons. Already certain of not being tied down by other people's interpretations, I was also secure in the knowledge that I was dealing with a brand-new subject about which there was no shortage of historical questions, properly so called. What had become of the labour movement after the Commune? Had it been marked by the experience and, if so, how? How had it greeted the nascent republic? Was the law of 1884 solely a product of Waldeck-Rousseau's benevolence? How was the birth of revolutionary syndicalism, which was soon to step into the breach left by the Commune, to be explained? Quite clearly, something had disappeared here and needed to be rediscovered.

To the attraction of the unknown was added that of origins. To grasp a phenomenon not at source but in its emergence into society has always (and often in a very fallacious manner) fascinated historians! Certainly, strikes were not by this time in their cradle; but the law of 1864, by freeing them from legal fetters, had given them new life. I wanted to know how the workers had used this weapon, how society had reacted and whether, in fact, it had become adapted to strikes. The use of a weapon blunts it and wears it out. Nowadays a strike is a relatively routine occurrence, which only rarely captures our attention. We neglect the sprinkling of little disputes, which are just as revealing as others of life's many trials and tribulations. As a decision made by union leaderships, as part of a broader strategy, strikes have become more a way of applying pressure than a means of expression.

Another factor which attracted me was the very absence of central organisations (the Guesdiste Fédération Nationale of 1886 was of little real significance) and, perhaps, the opportunity this afforded to get at the more obscure factors, at that infrastructure of social movements which most often remains hidden from us. Not that the unorganised have any special claim to creativity. They are no more able than others to escape the conceptions, vocabulary and stereotypes of their times, by which they, as much as organisations, are surrounded. These latter, however, also secrete a language of their own, which doubtless reveals something of the class they represent, but which can also, on occasion, be an impenetrable mask. This phenomenon of 'superimposition' occurs in all organisations. Would one judge the psychology of the faithful on the basis of liturgical texts alone? Studies in the sociology and ethnology of religion have taught us to compare and contrast the text of a commandment or the words of a prayer with the actions and behaviour of the majority of believers.

Finally, I must justify my precise choice of dates. The absence of any geographical limitations, which would have been incompatible with the desire to study a social phenomenon in its entirety and to escape the constraints imposed by the historico-geographical monograph, obliged me to set temporal limits upon my work. A twenty-year period gave me a sufficient number of cases; with the means at my disposal I could hardly go beyond that: the weight of documentation available to the historian of the modern period rules out vast canvasses centuries long and pushes us towards the close exploration of precisely defined 'moments'. The year 1871 offered an acceptable starting point; but 1890 will seem more surprising, in that it corresponds to no great economic or political watershed. But why should we impose a political or economic periodisation on a phenomenon which these forces do not necessarily govern? Is not the underlying idea behind such a procedure — the idea that all orders of events bend to the same general pressures — open to question? It seems to me that we must seek breaks that are inherent in the subject itself and that have a meaning within its own history before we accord significance to the other phenomena with which it may be connected. May Day 1890, the first attempt at creating a general movement on a national scale, marks a new stage in the history of strikes; it has a very appreciable effect on the graph representing strikes, which suddenly rises to new levels at this point. When the general strike takes on substance for the first time, and when, by its very failure, it leads to the formation of a central organisation, we are, surely, led on to a new terrain of investigation.

These then were the reasons for my choice; they have become more precise and also more nuanced as a result of my research. The somewhat simple object I first perceived in the illusory light of a first encounter — 'one knows clearly what one knows crudely' (Bachelard) — has become more substantial, richer, more complicated. My fine initial certainties have given way to new lines of questioning, prompted both by the ceaselessly reactivated demands of present observation — the strike is once again ablaze on our horizon — and by the resistance of the material. Quantified and enumerated, strikes still lie beyond our reach, just as they elude all the skilful ruses deployed to try to capture them in writing. The strike is a multi-faceted object and requires the application of a wide variety of approaches which are beyond the scope of a single individual.

At the same time, however, as the strike was taking on more substance as a research object, my text was becoming heavier. And the reader will doubtless interject here in some surprise: 'Why all this defence of numerical methods? You have made too little use of the certainty and conciseness they provide. Your book is very long and, when all is said and done, very "literary"'. This is true and I can suggest why it has come about. There is, firstly, the opacity of things; if words are to penetrate them, they have to strain all their resources. Then there is the inadequacy of a training which has left me unable to take advantage of all that my statistical sources had to offer. And lastly, there is the taste the historian retains for writing, even if she is not — alas — a 'writer', but just someone who writes.

All this reflects the — uncomfortable — situation in which the whole discipline of history finds itself: uncertain and divided, historians are being pulled in different directions by the various languages available to us. Tempted by a variety of methods and plagued by an enormous range of questions, we are engaged in the infernal pursuit of a reality which haunts us and yet escapes our grasp.

Assuredly, ours is a difficult discipline.

The Unfolding of a Strike

Only the dictionary definition of a strike, which is heavily influenced by political economy, makes it seem a simple phenomenon: a stopping of work, a holiday, a void, a 'blank' in the continuous line of production. It is only simple if you consider it in terms of a crude perspective which defines it as the monotonous repetition of a scenario which is always begun again from the beginning. In fact, each strike consists of a complex set of elements whose combination and mode of operation one must seek to identify, and from which, if one had a better mathematical training, one would undoubtedly be able to deduce the appropriate models.

Rather than start by sketching out, at this necessarily static, external and simplificative level, a typology of strikes, which would result in an arbitrary series of isolated and self-contained studies, I have chosen instead to investigate their genesis, not so as to lose myself in labyrinthine detail but in order to apprehend their unfolding from within, to learn how the relations of force were consolidated and dissolved, to attempt, in short, to produce a morphology of stages.

The birth, life and death of a strike could be said to be a classic piece of urban theatre, but it would be a bare stageset without the actors. The strikers' actions and cries bring the stage alive; sometimes they even obscure the mechanism and architecture that their great numbers reveal to our dazzled eyes. The strikers do not move at random, however; their playing obeys rules whose code it is up to us to recover.

The subject of the following pages is therefore that of workers making and unmaking the strike, but at the same time being fashioned and led by it, in that, whilst it cannot exist without them, it nevertheless, as a 'social fact', exceeds their individual personalities and their particular trajectories.

1
How Strikes Broke Out

Strikes break out much as wars do; sometimes they are a result of parleys which have not worked, of negotiations breaking down. These kinds of strike are at least preceded by a warning; sometimes, however, strikes break out quite suddenly, with no preliminaries. These are all-out, wildcat strikes which our French contemporaries, rediscovering them after decades of union discipline, sometimes call 'thrombosis strikes'.[1]

General Survey

The following statistics show how strikes in France broke out between 1871 and 1890:

Origin unknown	1,228	42.0%
Strikes preceded by negotiations or by warnings	834	28.5%
Sudden strikes	861	29.4%

Out of the 1,695 strikes whose origin we can be reasonably certain of, almost 51 per cent were sudden strikes.[2] These figures show that the French working class in this period was very turbulent.

The factors favouring such a turbulent approach, and militating against caution, were the sex of the strikers (82 per cent of women's strikes were sudden), age (80 per cent of young people's strikes were sudden), and the nature of the conflict (78 per cent of defensive strikes were sudden). The industries which feature the highest rates of sudden strikes are, in descending order:

1. *Le Monde*, 25 March 1969.
2. The percentage would certainly be higher than this; it is simply that when there is advance notice, more people tend to know about it. When the manner in which a strike declaration was made remains a little obscure, there is a strong chance that it was 'sudden'.

Chemical industries	82%
Mines	70%
Transportation, storage and handling	69%
Agricultural industries	68%
Textiles, clothing	64%

Those industries in which prior notice prevails are:

Timber industry	91%
Food industries	62%
Metals	60%
Construction industry (stone)	54%
Leather and hides	50%

The figure for the food industries may seem a little surprising here, but this category includes the bakers, a highly organised profession and one which preferred negotiation to stoppage; by contrast, in the sugar and bottling/canning industries, the rate of sudden strikes goes as high as 94 per cent. Conversely, the figure for the construction industry would be much higher if the navvies, 95 per cent of whose strikes are sudden, were not included in that category. Other discrepancies are worth pointing out; thus in the textiles and clothing group, in particular, strikes with prior notice were as follows:

Dyers	72%
Cutters	53%
Weavers, spinners	28%

The disadvantage of a technical classification is, obviously, that it lumps together, solely on the basis of a given raw material, quite heterogeneous social groups.

Thus the sites most suitable for sudden strikes were building-sites, spinning-mills and cloth-mills, sugar refineries, gas-works, forests, quays and docks, and mines; all in all, we should expect to find such strikes in heavy rather than in light industry. Sudden strikes are also much more frequent in joint-stock companies than in family businesses, for management was more accessible in the latter, and discussion was therefore more direct. Thus:

	Strikes with prior notice	Sudden strikes
Family management	55%	45%
Joint-stock companies, limited companies	31%	69%

The geographical distribution of sudden strikes by and large reflects these conditions. Wherever strike action involves the building industry, metals or hides, the proportions of strikes with prior notice rises; that is to say, paradoxically enough, in those departments with fairly scattered industry and with infrequent strikes (e.g. Maine-et-Loire, Gironde, Loire-Atlantique, Haute-Garonne, Ardennes, Oise, Alpes-Maritimes). When, on the other hand, textiles or mining are dominant in an area, it is the other way round (e.g. in Marne, Aisne, Vosges, Pas-de-Calais, Nord, Somme). Particular departments do, however, have their own traditions of regional organisation. Thus strikes with prior notice are the rule in the Bouches-du-Rhône, in the Rhône and in the Loire.[3]

Chronologically (Fig. 1) the picture unfolds as follows:

	Strikes with prior notice	Sudden strikes
1871–80	42%	58% (out of 508 strikes)
1881–90	52%	48% (out of 1,187 strikes)

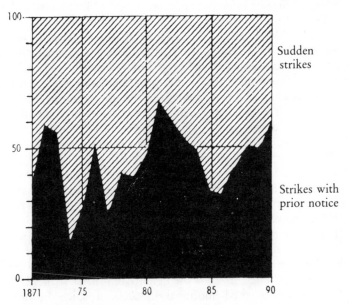

Figure 1: Sudden strikes and strikes with prior notice, 1871–90

3. The case of the Seine department is more curious, since here sudden strikes amounted to 51 per cent of the total. One would have expected less turbulence in the capital of unionism. Several factors may, however, be invoked to explain this situation: firstly, the fact that many of the *coalitions*, being restricted to one

The documentation itself gradually becomes more precise, as the percentage of strikes whose origin is known rises from 55 per cent for the decade 1871–80 to 58 per cent for the subsequent decade, whilst the rise in strikes with prior notice is, as the above figures show, still more marked from one decade to the next. Examination of annual rates also reveals the role played by the economic crisis in checking the impulse to come out on strike, with the percentage of sudden strikes being above average for the years 1884 to 1887.

Sudden Strikes

By sudden strike, I mean an interruption of work which is at once abrupt and unforeseen, with the grievances and demands only being formulated at the moment of stoppage or, indeed, as often as not, afterwards. At the Vogel spinning-mill, Beauvois (in the Nord), 'around eight o'clock in the morning, the workers and a large number of children came out on strike, singing "La Marseillais"'; it was only on the following day that they sent a letter listing their demands to the boss. At Saint-Quentin, on 18 March 1889, 'a number of workers came out on strike, without apparent motive, and without canvassing their bosses'; they waited five days before sending a delegation, armed with a programme, to the Town Hall. Such approaches, common enough in the mines and in the textile mills suggest a worsening social climate and an underlying discontent, which had very probably been long repressed and which it was no longer possible to express peacefully within the enterprise itself. In assessing the spontaneity of these actions, which is always relative, we are often simply admitting our own ignorance. We only apprehend them at the moment of their existence; they may take an observer or an employer by surprise, but a worker may to a certain extent be expecting them or, indeed, have prepared them.

It is possible to distinguish between three main types of sudden strikes, each of which is perceptibly different from the others.

1. The first, and most common type (60 per cent of recorded instances) of sudden strike is the defensive, protest strike. It flares up as a kind of shocked emotional response, in which the 'how' —

---

establishment in particular, eluded the control of the unions and were nothing more than the expression of brief episodes of ill-humour amongst groups of workers, who were quite able to speak up for themselves; secondly, the influence of the anarchists, who tended to use surprise as a tactic; and thirdly, the turbulent role played by the big factories in the suburbs.

manner and tone — counts for as much as the 'why' of the ostensible grievance, which is often the most minor of irritations, but which unleashes a whole series of accumulated resentments; it is related to the mass walk-out. 'Last Wednesday, pay day, Messers. Franquebalme informed their workers that their wages would be cut by 2 francs a month', with this cut also applying to the previous fortnight; 'offended by this way of going about things, the workers walked out of the workshop at 11 o'clock, singing'. At the Rogelet factory, in Reims, when they entered the workshop the weavers saw some posters announcing a cut in wages; the manager, upon being questioned about this measure, disclaimed any responsibility for it, whereupon 'the workers took up their red handkerchiefs and made a flag. One of them raised this flag and, placed himself at the head of the workers, who paraded around the workshops, singing "La Marseillaise", "La Carmagnole"', and then continued the demonstration outside. An indignant mood of this sort encourages the kind of brutality and violence which are characteristic of the strike-uprising.

Such expressions of anger occur on particular kinds of day, at certain hours and in certain seasons — on pay-days, when the wage packet is disappointing, or on days when workers return to find upsetting innovations in the workplace; in the morning, when workers still have some energy, rather than in the evening, when they are exhausted; and in spring, a particularly explosive time of year. Particular conjunctures also favour sudden outbursts, such as recessions, for instance, which make management more aggressive, and mining accidents, which create a nervous mood conducive to stoppages. Innumerable strikes flared up as a response to fire-damp explosions or to deadly landslips. The day after the burial of the victims the miners would refuse to go down the pit, not so much out of anxiety at the thought of dying as out of a desire, more or less conscious and more or less calculated, to profit from a situation in which the family of workers was gathered together and public opinion sensitive to the perils of that dark hell. It is at any rate remarkable that claims made on these sorts of occasion were much less concerned with security down the mines (although the problem of safety helmets is often mentioned) than with the classic demand for a rise.

2. Secondly, there are eruptive strikes, which burst like bubbles of magma at boiling point, and which spread like an epidemic. Thus, at the time of the great strike wave of May 1880 and May 1890, the workers abandoned their workshops abruptly, as if impelled by an

external and irresistible force. 'Hardly had the strike broken out in two establishments and the rumour spread, than it spread like wildfire. Without prior warning, without a clear statement of their demands, and without any attempt at coming to terms, the workers walked out of their workshops'. We could perhaps regard this reaction as contagion by example or as a feverish desire to participate for, when questioned as to their motives, 'they present as a motive for stopping work their wish to do what the others are doing'. It may even happen that the workers made no claim and went back into the factory without having demanded anything at all, so that the strike was in effect a pure communion, an unspecified hope that something would happen. May Day 1890 generated a veritable flood of unanticipated strikes, whose number and size took the organisers themselves by surprise and which may be thought of as the flaring-up of hidden discontents, as the expression of repressed desires, of a desire long repressed and all of a sudden unbridled; or an almost parousic expectation of something grandiose: 'The miners (from the Gard) did not really know just why they had come out on strike nor what they could really hope to gain. "Be united, brothers", they said, "and we will be victorious". Just what victory they had in mind no one was quite sure but at the back of their minds there was undoubtedly the victory of labour over capital, *the Social Revolution*'. This is clearly an expression of the Socialist Millennium, which in the modern world has taken over from the Promised Lands, and the delivered Jerusalems of the past. The persistence of such movements, related as they are to millenarianism, and to the eschatological or 'panic' impulses described by so many historians,[4] has confounded the attempts of the human sciences to formulate the laws of social behaviour. How is one to explain May 1968? Such movements serve to show how industrial societies, which are founded upon the principle of calculation, and which are so normative and rule-governed, do nevertheless generate dissatisfaction, and are traversed by desire and steeped in irrationality.

3. There was, however, a third kind of strike, which only appeared to be spontaneous. Such strikes were orchestrated in secret, through a hidden connivance. The tactic of the surprise strike was very dear to the anarchists in the years of unrest, because its effect was at once to shock, to excite and to confound, as some outrage — an explosion or assassination — might do. It was hardly compatible

4. H. Sinay, 1966, p. 300–1.

with the slow and cumbersome working of a union apparatus, which was always committed to consultation and therefore to publicity. But, in this period, institutions counted for less than active minorities, or for 'leaders' who were ever ready to sense a latent discontent, to mould and to express it. There were thus genuine instigators of strikes, whose energy and ascendancy over their work-mates, was sufficient to unleash a conflict. In a workshop of forty zinc-workers in Paris, a certain Chambon, 'upon arriving at the workshop, urged them to leave their work-benches upon a signal, which he would give by taking off his hat. At the prearranged signal, all the workers left their benches and blew out their lamps.' At Cholet, in the Pellaumail mill, when it was announced that Biton, an active and respected militant, had been dismissed, 'upon a signal given by one of his comrades, all the looms stopped and the workers left the mill'. At Anzin in 1878 the miners demanded a rise: 'one of the miners, whom the others seemed to obey, cut the cage ropes, began to make threats and urged his companions to follow him . . . In under an hour, 500 persons, men, women and children, had assembled and paraded around the Anzin coalfield, singing.' At the la Beaume mines (in Aveyron), 'the strike broke out suddenly . . . though nothing had happened which might lead one to expect it. The workers left off without a word, at the instigation of six miners, led by Mr Philippe Laprade, who, the following day, had himself been nominated as president of the strike at a public meeting which he had organised in order to settle upon a claim'. In every one of these cases the workers obeyed an agreed signal, responding to the expected gesture from the clandestine conductor of the orchestra. An elementary tactic of this sort, which throws a lot of light upon the processes of decision-making at grassroots level, can only succeed if a restricted area (a single enterprise) or a homogeneous milieu is involved. The strong group cohesion of the miners favoured rapid initiatives of this kind. Indeed, prior to the advent of unionism, this was how most strikes began. Many strikes broke out at dawn, and on Monday in particular (this is the case in the strike represented in Zola's novel, *Germinal*), having ripened overnight; militants passed from one mining village to another, knocking on doors, slipping leaflets into people's hands, arranging places to assemble; at daybreak the miners slipped out silently to the woods or tracks where they had agreed to meet; sometimes they paraded around the village singing; or, gathered around the pits, silent and still, they simply refused to go down. Strike action tended to begin at one particular pit which, because of the composition of the workforce (unruly elements were sometimes concentrated at a single point) or because of the greater independence of that pit from the mining companies, was particularly susceptible. For instance, in the Allier coalfield, the miners from Ferrières, whose housing was not provided by the company, were much more ready to rebel; in the Gard field, the miners from Lalle, galvanised by Henri Marius, were a kind of leaven between 1882 and 1890. These epicentres apart, the strikes simply spread, thus giving rise to the classic image of mining *coalitions* advancing by leaps and bounds.

With the rise of the unions, the use of surprise as a means of disrupting production was to become a very effective weapon; in our own time, warning strikes and improvised stoppages are particularly dreaded by management. We already find some trace of this in blacklisting procedures: the workshop which is blacklisted is chosen secretly or by the drawing of lots; on the chosen day the delegates present themselves, and while they are parleying the workers stop work. If negotiations are successful, they begin work again; if they fail, they stage a walk-out. This is what the Parisian cabinet-makers did in 1881. The only person to be surprised here is the boss, but it is a tactic that requires careful planning, tacit agreement and discipline.

But at a time when the unions had no real strength, sudden strikes were less the result of calculation than of emotion or of anger. They were stormy and dramatic in form, often marked by violence, and sometimes consisting of nothing but violence. Born of anger, such actions were naturally short-sighted and ill-prepared; they lasted only a short time and often failed (61.7 per cent of the time, whereas planned strikes only failed 30 per cent of the time). It is for this reason that unionists, only too aware of the defeatism occasioned by a failed strike, strove to transform strikes into something willed and carefully thought out.

Openly Announced Strikes

When a strike was preconceived and openly declared, the claim, like a herald, preceded the suspension of work, by a longer or shorter period of time. Such a strike was therefore not an act of impulsive anger but one of calculated pressure, which was generally offensive rather than defensive (67 per cent of offensive strikes, whose origin is known to us, were thus preceded by advance warning, or indeed by pre-negotiations). It presupposed preliminary organisation (meetings, consultation, a drafting of grievances, delegations, etc) whose influence continued to make itself felt throughout the course of the strike, so that it would be less tumultuous, more sober in tone, longer and larger (these disputes were more extensive than the previous type), sometimes a little meandering but with a better chance of arriving at a felicitous conclusion (almost 70 per cent ended successfully). It may be helpful to give several examples here:

1. Sometimes a strike was only embarked upon as a last resort, after genuine pre-negotiations had been conducted, sometimes for a good few months: 'We are not unaware of the fact that strikes represent a blow to both work and workers, and we have therefore had recourse to this means only when every attempt at reconciliation between us and our bosses had failed', wrote the joiners of Bordeaux. This kind of attitude prevailed in small industries, in small workshops, where the boss was visible and dialogue easy to establish, and in professions that were well rewarded and could afford to wait and in trades where the *compagnonnages* held sway. In the letters that carpenters, joiners, cabinet-makers, masons, bakers, and so on, addressed to their employers, there was still a muffled echo of the deference, of the imploring tone, of former days; workers described themselves as 'regretfully obliged to ask'; 'it is therefore because they are altogether obliged, Sirs, that they have resorted to begging you to cast an eye' over the demands 'which the unfortunate exigencies of the period in which they live have forced them to make'. They declared that it was not their wish 'to disturb in any way the industrial interests of their trade and to trouble the good relations which exist between bosses and workers'. If the bosses acceded to their requests, they lauded them for it as if they were their benefactors: 'You may rest assured that, if you comply with our demands, our gratitude will cause us to redouble our efforts to lighten the weight of the sacrifices that you have taken upon yourself on our behalf'. This conciliatory and benignly diplomatic tone is mainly to be found prior to 1880, when militants tended to feel a degree of pessimism about 'this great scourge called the strike'. They did not accommodate themselves very readily to the rise of more combative conceptions, or to the sentiment of class struggle. Nevertheless, amongst these professions the practice was to persist of giving sufficient advance notice for discussion to be broached.

2. The length of the advance notice in fact enables us to shed some light on its meaning. Sometimes it is simply an ultimatum, an abrupt

formal notice demanding an immediate response, and therefore an act of defiance. Thus, at Bohain in 1871: 'A large number of weavers congregated before various manufacturers . . . declaring that if a wage rise was not accorded to them, they would stop work and go on strike that very moment.' Indeed, their impatience would sometimes be so great that they would come out on strike without even waiting for a reply.

Sometimes, by contrast, the bosses were allowed more time to consider: twenty-four, forty-eight hours, eight days (these latter two periods were the most common), sometimes a fortnight and, in exceptional circumstances, a month (e.g. glass-makers, joiners, carpenters). Professional or local customs tended to determine the length of advance notice given. At Roubaix, 'courtesy delays' were generally forty-eight hours, from Saturday to Monday: 'Last Saturday, all the dyers gave their bosses a courtesy delay'. Likewise with the mechanics who, when accused of disruption, protested: 'The Roubaix strike followed all the rules; we presented ourselves to our bosses with two delegates for each workshop, we stated the reasons for our claims quite honestly, we gave our bosses forty-eight hours to give us the answer we had demanded.' The bosses strove, moreover, to make these customary delays the rule. Those at Rouen, in 1871, attempted to take out an action against the weavers before the *conseil des prud'hommes*, on the grounds that they had walked out 'without observing the delays prescribed by the law'. The use of the term 'law' here, though mistaken, is significant: French legislation nowhere dictates that one must give advance notice; even today it is only required in the public sector. However, the Rouen *conseil des prud'hommes* forced the strikers to pay their bosses a fine of 3 francs a day. At Flers in 1881 the *prud'hommes* forced the dyers, who had abruptly walked out, to finish their eight hours. Weavers from Lyon in 1883 and glass-makers from the Nord in 1890 also had to pay fines in recompense for damage caused by their sudden walk-outs. The bosses thus sought, like all those of the liberal school of economics, to conflate the collectivity with a simple collection of individuals, to consider a strike as simply the aggregate of a series of individual breaches of contract, which is tantamount to denying it. An interpretation of this kind has occasioned a huge and still growing jurisprudence. It is only very recently (between 1957 and 1960) that it has at last been admitted that 'a strike does not represent a breach of a work contract' and that 'every condemnation of waged employees to damage payments for sudden breach should be rejected'. On the other hand, before 1914, for want of legislation respecting advance notice — which the parliamentary majority had always opposed — the bosses had sometimes tried to regulate strikes within the framework of their enterprise. This was always done with some reticence and caution, because the advantages ensuing from it were not all on one side; there was, for instance, some reciprocity (a commitment to maintain wages stable for a given period, for instance), and the effect of this restriction was to lead in the end to genuine collective contracts, thus implying an acknowledgement of union power. There were all developments to which the bosses were deeply hostile.

In some cases, and in the first decade in particular, the workers gave advance warning both to the bosses and to the authorities. Sometimes, for instance, they would rather timidly 'request authorisation to come out on strike', a formula which suggests that they were still far from certain as to their rights. Sometimes, somewhat more boldly, they would solemnly give warning of their intention to 'come out on strike', in order to pre-empt any charges of clandestinity, and in order to call the authorities and public opinion as witnesses of the justice of their claims and of the propriety of their actions. The wood-cutters of la Guerche, for instance, sent the Mayor their declaration to come out on strike, signed with twenty names and thirty-eight crosses; the weavers of Moirans, in a procession, 'made their way to the Town Hall . . . where they signed their strike declaration, the claims that they proposed to make and their decision to form a *chambre syndicale*'. This approach, which is diametrically opposed to that of the wildcat strike, is informed by a concern with legality but also by a desire to invoke, if the occasion demanded it, the arbitration of the state.

In the light of these distinctions one is tempted to enquire further into the meaning of the developments that took place in this period: less sudden strikes, as we have noted, and the disruptive effects of the crisis notwithstanding, an increase in the number of precalculated strikes, with a corresponding tendency for the gradual development of advance notice (with this practice being introduced into what were, so to speak, the angry professions, the textile industry and the mine. Consider, for instance, two blanket-weavers' strikes, fourteen years apart, at Cours (Rhône), affecting in both cases all the factories. The first strike, in 1875, erupted in an uncontrolled manner, with no precise demands being formulated; the second, in 1889, led by a *chambre syndicale*, involved the preliminary communication of a new wages schedule to the bosses, with the latter being invited to a joint meeting and with a stoppage occurring only in the event of their abstaining and refusing to speak. The change is still more dramatic in the case of the colliers. In 1890 at Firminy, Carvin and Lens the unions were in charge of operations, made their claims in written form (Firminy) or through a delegation (Carvin, Lens) and only declared a strike after their demands had been rejected. The start of the strike at Lens in January 1890 shows how union practice was grafted on to former custom: the company having sent away several militants, amongst them the delegate Bonnel, the workers informed the union committee, which in turn called a meeting of the delegates at eight o'clock in the evening; one last approach was made to the chief engineer, which failed; a further meeting, a general one this time, was held at eleven o'clock at night, at which the decision to strike was taken: 'the motion was passed and, this morning, barely ten workers turned up at the pit'. This meant, moreover, that the strike assumed a different pattern, the stoppage being general and immediate rather than occurring by stages. With the development of the unions, this scenario became more and more common. The structuring effect of the unions, even the revolutionary ones, was in fact considerable. Not that they necessarily preached reconciliation; they rather advocated reflection before taking the decision to come out on strike and discipline in the launching of it.

Union action did not, as certain economists and politicians expected, reduce the number of strikes, but it did undoubtedly transform strike procedure and rationalise the opening stages.

It remains for us to discover, however — and this is a great problem and one which still concerns us today — whether it is possible to harness the energy of spontaneity without the source running dry. Does taming a wild animal necessarily mean domesticating it?

2
The Running of a Strike: the Organisations

Nowadays union and strike constitute an indissoluble and unequal pair.[1] The union has the initiative and the ultimate control: action taken outside of it seems if not suspect, at any rate disturbing, a sign of malaise rather than an indication of health. In the context of the now extended scale of its activities, amongst which the functions of representation, negotiation and bargaining have become fundamental, the strike has come to seem secondary, subordinate and, as some would claim, of lesser importance. May 1968, an irruption of the 'rank and file' and an insurrection of desire, represents a provisional disturbance of the equilibrium whose ultimate significance is still difficult to gauge. Was it a resurgence that was to have no further consequences or a signpost pointing towards new practices? For the time being, unionism is in control.

When unions first emerged, the situation was quite different. The strike reigned supreme. It was the major form of expression of the workers' movement, a direct, unmediated expression of discontent and hope, originating from below. But not all strikes were linked to a particular organisation: 41 per cent of the disputes studied here bear no trace of such a connection, being for the most part sudden strikes, brief flare-ups too immediate in their effect to allow of any planning. In their flickering light we can just make out silhouettes as they flit past, lending their faces and voices to the workers' revolt, to their own revolt. This was the era of 'agitators', ardent but ephemeral, quickly worn out and as quickly replaced, with neither

1. Initiatives of this sort are, of course, not arbitrary and I make no claims here to study the process whereby the decision to strike is taken in the present period, a highly complicated question in which many different sorts of consideration are involved; the choice of the precise 'moment' at which to come out on strike has become an increasingly more onerous responsibility, so much so that there is a risk of the workers becoming paralysed by it. It seems to me that sociologists of labour would do well to devote a great deal of attention to these processes, about which we possess too little information.

long-term design nor prudence, the polar opposite of 'full-time officials'.

In the case of organised strikes, which were nevertheless in the majority (59 per cent), the strike could be said to have dominated the organisation, generating its own forms. The union itself was often merely its creature, born through and for it, living off its success and being killed off by its failure; and if it tended to free itself from its guardianship, in order to assert itself more fully, this was only the better to serve the needs occasioned by its assumption in a general strike.

General Characteristics

From a picture that necessarily is now somewhat fragmentary, I shall isolate a number of key features:

1. The relatively frequent coexistence of several forms of organisation, a fact that is borne out by the presence of more than 2,000 for 1,707 organised strikes, the most common form of association being that of a strike committee alongside the union.
2. The increase in the number of organised strikes (Fig. 2): though they represent less than 50 per cent of the total number before 1880 (except in 1872), there is always a higher proportion of them from then on, even during the crisis, which is however marked by a regression and one which is more apparent still if one looks at unions alone. The most spectacular leaps occur from 1877 to 1881 (+ 28 per cent) and from 1886 to 1890 (+ 19 per cent). In 1890 three-quarters of the disputes were supported by at least one organisation.
3. Within the permanent organisations, certain ancient forms disappear almost totally after 1880 (notably, the *compagnonnage*, seven out of ten of whose interventions take place prior to this date). At the same time, new types of organisation emerge: under the heading 'socialist organisations' I have in the main listed the 'social study circles', which were set up after the Marseilles Congress and which sometimes, as in the case of the Défense des Travailleurs group at Reims in 1880, played a significant inspirational role.
4. Of all strikes 72 per cent were free of any union influence. Nevertheless, unions constituted the pilot organisations, lead-

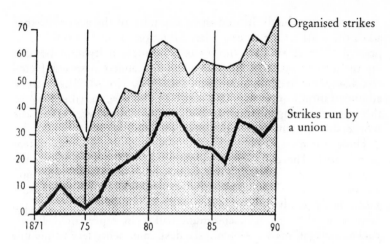

Figure 2:   Organised strikes and strikes run by a union, 1871–90

ing 46 per cent of organised strikes. Their involvement increased in a spectacular manner from 1877–8 onwards, reaching its height in 1881–2 (39 per cent of conflicts had a union leadership), falling back a little because of the crisis but recovering rapidly from 1887 onwards.

It is indisputable that the strike was becoming unionised.

Forms of Temporary Organisation

The most simple, elementary form of organisation consisted in the appointment of delegates. This was something that the bosses loathed; they dreaded encouraging the initiative of ringleaders, 'disruptive elements and genuine enemies of the workers', and entering into the dreaded machinery of representative power. All in all, they still preferred to talk with the mass of their workers: 'I wish henceforth to treat with whoever has the actual power, and the mass of the workers are the only ones in possession of this power', wrote Martin, a manufacturer from Tarare, in a printed letter addressed to his weavers in which he proposed 'a general meeting, with all outsiders excluded'. The delegates were very often dismissed, either on the spot or at the end of the strike, with their *livrets de travail* being marked with distinctive signs. The workers also hesitated before offering 'victims tailor-made to suffer from the bosses' spite'.

27

They strove to shelter behind the anonymity of the group, so that all of the workers, or at least a large fraction of them, would go to present their claim. But this system of mass delegation became impracticable once, with the strike being extended or several factories being involved, one entered into negotiations. The factory administration, or even the bosses themselves, terrified at the thought of having to deal with some outside power, urged the workers to appoint their representatives.

There was no procedure or principle governing an appointment of this sort. The delegates were chosen by lot, appointed on the spot, or elected in workers' assemblies, most often 'by acclamation', a consensus as to the most suitable personalities emerging, it would seem, fairly easily. In the case of long-drawn-out strikes, each factory, workshop, pit or commune had to be represented. Large, packed delegations were obviously desirable, being less vulnerable and less easily impressed once in the manager's or prefect's office. These delegates were chosen for their ardour, for their gift of the gab, sometimes for their age. In one place, the miners appointed young men of twenty or twenty-five 'so as to deflect the suspicions of the company; in another, by contrast, they prefer to have recourse to the oldest workers. The delegates did not enjoy any special privileges; they were almost never remunerated, except in Paris, where provisions were occasionally made to pay them for such work. They might be recalled if their approach was too lukewarm: at Montceau, on 1 March 1878, at the end of an interview with the prefect, the delegates were greeted with jeers when they proposed a return to work; they were replaced that same evening. At Armentières, the delegates were met with boos and with the cry of 'down with the Bazaines' and had to return to the ranks.

A second level of organisation involved 'strike committees', which were still called 'executive commissions' so as to underline that they were nothing more than organs of execution, with the powers of decision belonging to the general, sovereign assembly of strikers. A strike committee united the strike delegates, on a federative basis (neighbourhoods, factories, communes); or else it united these with the union members; or again it might gather together the representatives of the various corporative organisations of the town, or of the trade: thus, in the case of the joiners of Bordeaux in 1877, the committee was formed at the request of the union branch and its control extended over mandated representatives, unionised and non-unionised workers and trade societies.

The committee was given a structure: an executive in which titles and duties were shared out, there being a president (called 'president of the strike'), a secretary and a treasurer. Where necessary, it was further subdivided or additional commissions were added. Thus the Lyonnais locksmiths in 1881 set up a 'grand claims commission', consisting of delegates elected by their workshops and divided into four sub-commissions (finance, propaganda, correspondence and records).

The function of the strike committee was not only to govern but also to mobilise energies and to encourage workers to participate. With this aim in mind, the Lyonnais glass-workers set up 'watch committees' for each factory, which reported back on the situation each evening. The Paris shoemakers, imbued with libertarian ideas, drafted a 'federative pact', much vaunted by Paul Lafargue, which was a veritable pyramid of different committees: each workshop with ten or more workers constituted a branch; this group would appoint a delegate to a 'neighbourhood commission', which would mandate two members to a 'commission of administration' and two to a 'control commission'. These latter supported the 'executive commission of the strike', elected directly by a general assembly and the supreme organ of the strike.

At any rate, the executive committee of the strike remained the key to power. Committees and delegates were answerable to it; it supervised their handling of affairs in an often haughty manner, particularly where finances were concerned, and it took the crucial decisions.

In short, if the workers borrowed some of bourgeois democracy's terms and characteristics, their basic model was that of Rousseau's *Social Contract*: sovereignty resided in the body of workers gathered together in a general assembly, and they had no intention of being robbed of this sovereignty.

Forms of Permanent Organisation

Organisations of the Old Type

Compagnonnage only played a fairly insignificant role in struggles over wages and conditions; they were involved in only ten strikes during the period under consideration, all prior to 1883, and were confined, as one might expect, to the building trade and to a handful of large towns. They still featured predominantly as a brake on struggle, of a fairly regressive kind. One can follow the decline of this form of organisation in Paris between 1876 and 1881. It was still the dominant form of organisation during the carpenter's strike of 1876, but it did not function well, being undermined by antagonisms between the various categories (employees and foremen belonged to it and opposed the claim) and by disagreements between the societies which continued to express rivalries between different quarters, the so-called 'Mothers', which were no longer anything more than *restaurateurs* competing for the custom of migrant workers, and which served to perpetuate corporative festivals now drained of all meaning. Harsh criticisms were thus levelled against *compagnon* organisations which had turned into sects. At the end of the strike, in June 1876, a commission composed of young people was set up with the aim of forming a union with a fighting fund. In 1879 this union relaunched the strike and ran foul of the old societies which, furious at being ousted, took their revenge in 1881 by breaking a new *coalition*: 'We will not march at the head of the strike,' declared the president of the Compagnons Passants at a meeting, 'we will follow on behind it, and we will not provide any member for the commission which is to treat with the bosses'.[2]

The guilds at Lyons continued to be more forceful and more ardent. The Compagnons du Devoir provided a serious leadership for the carpenters' strikes (1872, 1880), and for those of the roofers and the farriers (1876); they organised the departure of labourers to other localities and, so as to boycott Lyons, they placed a watch on the building-sites and stations. The guild societies were sufficiently effective to keep their members on the fringes of the wider movement. 'The guild members are more able to resist the action of the International', the prefect reckoned, 'because guild membership yields more or less the same results as would affiliation to that association.'

Not only does guild organisation survive as something more than a folk memory, it also has a broader legacy. We have already noted that it serves to impart a particular style to workers' relations with management (use of letters and of advance warning); the boycott, which has become the modern strike-by-rota (*grève tournante*) is also a part of the legacy of *compagnonnage*. It undoubtedly influenced the manner in which claims were made in the timber and building corporations.

---

2. Arch. préf. pol., B A 174, pièce 37. This dossier contains more than a million items on the *coalitions* of the Parisian carpenters. We cannot, however, enter here into the detail of these tedious quarrels, which the police, for their part, followed so closely.

Mutual aid societies (called *sociétes civiles de prévoyance* or *sociétés de crédit mutuel*, etc.) continued to play a part, albeit a shrinking one, in strikes, their names often serving to conceal forms of organised resistance, a legacy of the time in which, combination being a crime, the organisational structure for it had to be hidden. Seventeen of the twenty-four occasions upon which such societies were involved are prior to 1877; eleven refer to the Rhône, and to Lyon in particular, the capital of mutual aid. Such societies were usually established at the end of the Second Empire. Thus, in Lyon at the head of the strike movement there was the Société de Prévoyance et de Solidarité des Ouvriers Tanneurs et Corroyeurs, the Société de Prévoyance et de Renseignements des Travailleurs de la Teinturerie Lyonnaise, the Cercle de l'Union Fraternelle des Ouvriers Apprêteurs, and so on.

Likewise, there were a number of cooperatives (twelve were involved, seven of them prior to 1876) which served as a cover for resistance funds, such as that of the Lyonnais hat-makers. They were often locally based, with several different trades participating in them: at Roanne, in 1872–3, Solidarité, Association Coopérative pour l'Alimentation, served as a camouflaged form of resistance whose statutes provided for solidarity strikes and which supported every form of combination.

Organisations of this sort served to prolong the existence, up until around 1876, of forms of social struggle originating in the closing years of the Second Empire but, being of necessity pluri-functional (a hypothetical function serving to conceal a real one), they more and more yielded to forms concerned specifically with defence of workers' interests; namely, the *chambre syndicale*, which was first tolerated and then, thanks to the law of 1884, authorised by the government.

The Role of the Unions

It is worth emphasising once again the limited role played by the unions: they had no part in 72 per cent of disputes. During this period the strike may be said to have transcended unionism inasmuch as, in 1879–80, remarkably enough, the number of strikers exceeded that of union members, an exceptional situation which did not recur for a long time (not even in 1936). This was only to be repeated in May 1968, whose originality and importance stands out each time we compare it with earlier episodes.

Nevertheless, union involvement was growing. Though weak between 1871 and 1876, the level of unionisation rose suddenly in 1877 (17 per cent), reached a peak in 1881–2 (39 per cent), but tailed off during the depression, with only 20 per cent of strikes having a union leadership in 1886. Yet from 1887 onwards, a third at least of all conflicts again involve unionist as leaders. During this same period, from 1877 on, the union tends to become the major form of organisation.

If unions play a larger role, this is, on the one hand, attributable to the development of unionism itself and, on the other, to its progressive 'conversion' to strike action, which, having been at first despised and feared, again becomes a front-rank method. We must now present a sketch of this growth and describe this conversion.

The Rise of the Unions

I do not intend to retrace the history of unionism here, for the classic accounts have covered the major episodes of a somewhat lack-lustre narrative. I want rather, by bringing out a number of curves and cross-sections, to identify the main stages and components. This is by no means an easy task for, whilst there is an abundance of descriptive accounts, there is a distinct lack of information of a quantitative nature. Only the archives provide us with the kind of material that will allow us to establish statistical runs; the history of statistical studies of unionism may in fact be compared with that of strikes, and is almost parallel to it, there being however a delay which reflects the doubts of the government and administration of the day, which were more hesitant about combination than about strikes: twenty years separate the laws of 1864 from those of 1884, and there is a gap of sixteen years between the instructions establishing statistics on strikes (1860) and those on unions (1876).

The statistics of 1876, 1880 and 1883, and the cross-sections of 1876 and 1880, have been established using archive material. From 1884 onwards, however, good information on the different occupations is provided by the tables drawn up by the Labour Office, in *Les Associations professionnelles ouvrières*, which gives the annual figure of unions and unionised members for each of the industries and sub-groups identified.

During this period, unions and strikes had overall rates of growth that were more nearly comparable than they would ever be again, both in volume and in variation; over a period of fourteen years, between 1876 and 1890, there were eleven cases of parallel growth and only three where there was any divergence.

The take-off of the unions, at the end of the Second Empire, which a tolerant administrative regime favoured, seems to have been a fairly vigorous one, above all after 1867–8, and in Paris in particular. However, union involvement in strikes remains at an extremely modest level. I have only managed to identify nine for the years from 1868 to 1870.

War and the repression following the Commune effectively silenced the movement, yet its reconstitution in the following years was remarkably rapid. In Paris, where *Le Rappel* enables us to follow the history of the workers' organisations step by step, forty-five associations of which thirty-five were union branches, were reconstituted between January and October 1872. By the end of 1874 there were sixty. In the provinces, or at any rate in the large centres, which already had an embryonic union organisation (e.g. Lyon, Marseille, Bordeaux and Limoges), similar developments occurred, although they were impeded by the harassment of a watchful administration. The Parisian prefects of police, whilst keeping everything under close surveillance, were in the end more tolerant than their colleagues in the departments. In Paris, as in the provinces, it is the continuity in both organisation and membership which is striking. There were very few new organisations in these years; most of the associations were reconstitutions of the old ones, with the original statutes coming into effect again, and with the same men reassuming the leadership.[3] But these revived organisations lacked staying power and when the 1873–4 crisis added its depressive effects to the political situation they found it hard to re-establish their former level of involvement. They displayed, in

---

3. In Paris we find Pastoureau, one of the leaders of the 1865 strike, amongst the leather-workers; Aulu, president of the society of roofers in 1870 is once again among their number; Payan, an 1870 militant, is back among the chair-makers; the mechanics' *chambre syndicale*, founded in 1868, was reconstituted at the beginning of 1873; the meeting of 18 May was presided over by an individual who had been a member of the *conseil des prud'hommes* for thirteen years; on 15 June Antoine, treasurer of the old trade union, presented the accounts: André Murat, delegate to London in 1862, and later to various congresses of the International, continued to play a prominent role and led a delegation to Philadelphia in 1876. (Very detailed information on the mechanics' *chambre syndicale* can be found in the Arch. préf. pol., B A 161.) The situation was identical in Lyon, Marseilles, Rouen, and Roubaix, where the principal figure, Charles Bonne, was the 'ringleader' of the strikes of 1867 and so on.

addition, an extreme caution and, either out of diplomacy or conviction, repudiated the strike weapon.

In 1875–6, the easing of the economic and political situation,
which found expression in a wave of *coalitions*, was also the occasion for the establishment of new organisations; these began as early
as 1875 in Paris, where the first attempts at founding a union press
were made, and in 1876 in the provinces (e.g. at Rennes, Reims,
Troyes, Grenoble, Armentières). Thanks to the answers given by
the prefects to the Teisserenc de Bort circular, it is possible to
construct a fairly accurate picture of conditions at the end of 1876,
and from this one can isolate the main characteristics of the situation.

The total number of unions was still small: eighty-two unions
were identified in the provinces, with 12,000 to 15,000 members
between them; there were about a hundred in Paris, with perhaps
25,000 members altogether. The capital thus continued to enjoy a
startling primacy over the provinces. Unionisation was by and large
urban, and tended to have little to do with the actual distribution of
industry. Twenty-six towns, scattered over twenty-two departments (of which, if we except the Seine, only three had more than
eight organisations: Bouches-du-Rhône, with fifteen; Rhône, with
fifteen; and the Gironde, with nine), *chefs-lieux* (county towns) for
the most part provided the headquarters for organisations grafted
on to the old occupational structures. The building industry trades,
which derived their habitual forms of association from the experience of guild organisation, often played the leading role: carpenters,
cabinet-makers, masons and painters tended to form the core
around which the unions formed, together with the shoemakers,
printers, bakers, and the more skilled and extremely diversified
categories of metal-worker. Heavy industry was hardly represented
at all. A single branch existed among the miners of Saint-Etienne,
which in 1876 had been grafted on to a very old 'fraternal fund'. In
the vast textiles industry, there were eight associations, most of
them Lyonnais and of a very particular kind: the weavers' *chambres
syndicales*, with almost 3,000 members, divided into seventy-eight
different cells, were mainly concerned with defending the interests
of the head foremen. There was no unionisation in the chemical or
transport industries. With 180 members on average in each union,
membership was invariably very modest. The statutes tended to
draw their inspiration from the mutual aid societies, expressing
much the same sense of propriety and the same moralism. Thus the
chambre syndicale of the weavers at Tours proposed to settle disputes by avoiding strikes by 'moral and intellectual means'; to gain

admittance one had 'to fulfil its conditions of apprenticeship, to be an honest man and to be presented to the commission by two paid-up members'. Nevertheless, approximately half of the unions for which there are records were prepared to provide strike aid.

At the end of 1880, a suitable date for effecting a new cross-section, the situation has changed. The first difference is a quantitative one. There are now 478 unions, with 65,000 members, which represents an increase, for the years 1876–80, of 162 per cent and 94 per cent, respectively, and therefore a notable rise in unionisation, at the level of organisation in particular. It was in fact more a question of new unions being founded than of a massive increase in membership, hence the drop in the average size of the unions (133 members per union). This wave of unionisation was therefore marked by the new level of prestige enjoyed by the institution itself. Unions sprang up everywhere, with thirty-six departments and sixty-two localities now having one, and these were no longer just the *chefs-lieux* but small places with factories as well (e.g. Lodève, Saint-Junien, Bolbec, Lisieux). Some departments, which had been very weak before, underwent a marked increase in this period (e.g. Marne, Nord, Alpes-Maritimes, Isère, Bouches-du Rhône), whilst former front-runners, such as the Seine or the Rhône, played a correspondingly smaller part. By comparison with 1876, the number of unionised persons actually fell in Lyon, a fact attributable in part to the intensity of the crisis and of the unemployment which was then affecting the metropolis of the silk trade. Paris, meanwhile, was stagnating, with growth of unions at only 47 per cent, which was much lower than the overall rate of growth in the country; the capital thus lost its primacy. The fourteen departments featuring for the first time in the statistics tended to be in the south of the country, mainly on the edge of the Massif Central (Allier, Cher, Gard, Hérault, Puy-de-Dôme, Tarn). The building industry continued to play an important role in getting things going, but other types of plant also began to appear, under the impact of heavy industry, and textiles in particular.

The first step towards a unionisation of textiles indeed represents another notable change. In this sector the number of unions rose from fifteen to sixty-eight and its proportion of the total increased from 8 per cent to 14 per cent. The other occupational sectors grew in ratios with no significant effect on the overall balance.

Qualitative alterations also occurred, affecting institutions, language and men. The unions provided a better definition of their own functions; namely, defence of professional interests and of wages in particular. The classic rule-book would open with a preliminary declaration affirming that the union 'will take care to ensure that wages never suffer illegitimate reductions and that they always follow the rises in price of basic commodities, and finally that they correspond as nearly as possible to the real value of the labour so that they be in constant relation to the progress of civilisation'. Some rule-books, drawing their inspiration from models which were to be found in various places, a fact which helped to disseminate a new language, employed a bolder tone: 'The emancipation of the workers can only be the work of the workers themselves; the subjection of the workers to capital is the source of all moral and material servitude'. The above statement may be read in the statutes of various metal-workers' union branches, in the south-east in particular. Whilst arguing in favour of a new regulation, the mechanics of Paris denounced 'a social condition which must disappear and give way to collectivism'. The old federative principle, proclaimed an important instrument of liberation at the Marseilles Congress, inspired several attempts at founding local and occupational organisations. In this same period, the first union press was established.

Almost everywhere, new and younger men (between the ages twenty-five and thirty-five) who were sceptical of the virtues of cooperation and who were more combative, assumed the leadership of the organisations. Apart from their attitude, which was more violent and more challenging, what marked these new men out was the range of activities in which they were involved, both on the political and on the social front, so that the same militants were to be found urging on both the *chambres syndicales*, the social study circles and the socialist groups. It is tempting to regard this development as 'infiltration', as a subordination of unionism to politics, but this is not in fact the case. For the generation active at the time of the Marseilles Congress, the workers' party should not be anything else but the 'federation of union branches, of social study groups, of consumption and production groups, on condition that they are composed exclusively of workers'; in other words, a confederation of labour. Within this definition there was nurtured the profound misunderstanding which would lead to the workers' movement and political parties being opposed.

It is important, however, not to exaggerate. The majority of unions would have found it hard to isolate their own specific function. Many continued to combine the defence of their professional interests with obligations inherited from the old societies, so that they sought to be at once mutual aid societies, retirement funds, cooperatives, libraries, funeral associations,[4] and so on. Their statutes were still imbued with a moral tone, demanding that members be of 'upright morality', and refusing aid on occasion, to those who had been guilty of misconduct or of drunkenness,[5] and itemising a whole range of fines to be paid by defaulting unionists.[6]

The outstanding characteristic of this newly emergent unionism (58 per cent of the unions in existence at the end of 1880 in the provinces had only been in existence for two years, a proportion which falls to 24 per cent in Paris, more deeply marked by the foundation of new unions in the years (from 1871 to 1876) is its fragility. The associations were essentially ephemeral and did not stand up well to the crisis, which caused members' subscriptions to dry up and which brought down attendances dramatically. Membership collapsed and many unions were in the end forced to dissolve. The overall statistics, although they should be handled with caution, reflect these difficulties: a slowed-down rate of growth is followed in 1884 by a distinct fall, more pronounced in the case of unionists (−23 per cent), than in the case of the unions (−18 per cent), for the weight of the institution served to check complete disintegration.

This downturn in the workers' movement made it extremely vulnerable to various sorts of seduction, so that it succumbed to xenophobia and to the in part overlapping phenomenon of Boulangism. J. Néré, in her analysis of the elections of 1889, has shown how in Paris the organised workers — in light rather than in heavy industry — were better able to resist. In many places, however, the Boulangists attempted to infiltrate the unions and, temporarily at any rate, succeeded, notably by exploiting, as in Marseilles and Bordeaux (where they had won over the dockers' unions), conflicts with foreign workers, and by representing themselves as the apostles

---

4. The obligation to attend the funerals of deceased members figures in a large number of the rule-books, even those of unions that were, in other respects, quite modern: the honours to be bestowed were set out in great deal and the prerogatives of seniority were not neglected: the union of the workers of the Avre valley, founded in 1888, laid down that fifteen should attend for an ordinary member, thirty for an official.

5. Thus the copper boiler-makers of Marseilles (1878) and the shoemakers of that same city 'did not give aid to workers who had lost their income as a result of misconduct' (Arch. dép. Bouches-du-Rhône, M6 2453).

6. Like the *chambre syndicale* of the Cannes joiners, which imposed fines for missing general meetings, for lateness, for those who disturbed the meetings by arriving drunk, or who smoked or who made offensive remarks to a member present, and so on (see Arch. dép. Aples-Maritimes, VI M (9)).

of national labour. In the Vosges, Laguerre, a committed Boulangist, helped to set up a union in the building industry; the hosiers' union, founded in 1882 and the main inspiration behind the strike of 1885, was exploited by the Boulangist candidate in the elections of 1889–90. This was also the case at Carcassonne with the Union Syndicale des Ouvriers Tailleurs de Pierre et Maçons. In other places, this hold on the workers' movement was effected by a somewhat ambiguous complicity between Blanquist militants and Boulangists. This is how it was at Lyon, where the weavers of Thizy invested all their hopes, during the long strike of 1889–90, in Lachize, whom the prefect had described as a 'Blanquist–Boulangist', and where the combative union branch of glass-makers 'belonged in the main to the Blanquist–Boulangist Party', as did that of the blacksmiths. In Paris, the stone-cutters' union, led by the dynamic Boulé, one of the leaders of the navvies' strike, was at least for some time overtaken by this development. These examples, which might readily be extended, testify at any rate to a lack of union autonomy and indicate a real fragility. Furthermore, it is well known how fascinated the most revolutionary socialist groups were with Boulangism, thanks to its popular content and its combative character.

However, the unions recovered fairly quickly, in quantitative terms, with 1886 levels returning to, and then surpassing those of 1883. From 1888 onwards growth accelerated (in the case of the unions, +17 per cent for 1888, +33 per cent for 1889) and, as in 1877–80, first of all at the level of organisation. In 1889, whilst the target of a thousand unions was reached and passed, the average membership of each one fell to 136. Then memberships swelled in their turn. This represented the beginning of a significant upsurge (1888–93), which brought unionism to a higher level than ever before, and which was a manifestation of the multiform vitality of the workers' movement, also reflected in strikes and in the socialist success at the 1893 elections.

Heavy industry played a large part in this change. In 1888–90, the chemical, mining, food and textile industries experienced rates of growth which were much above the average. In 1890 forty-eight weavers' unions were founded, thereby adding 16,000 more unionists to the 1888 total for that industry. Things were particularly lively in the north, the Aisne, the Somme and in Rhône, Loire, Isère in the south-east. A regional federation constituted at Lyon in 1890 held its congress there on 5 October; the idea of a general strike was strongly supported and a national federation proposed, whose first congress took place the following year. In the chemical industry, some gas-workers' unions were founded (three in Paris in 1890), as were unions for tobacco workers (eleven between 1888 and 1890), and in 1890 a federation showed signs of emerging. In the transport industry the union of railway workers and employees, born after a strike at the end of 1889, in the workshops of the Western Company, underwent a rapid process of growth; at 8,000 members strong it was able to organise a national congress in April 1891. The number of miners' unions went from eighteen (1889) to twenty-five (1890) and the number of paid-up members from 8,700 to 22,500, a remarkable growth due above all to that of the Pas-de-Calais union. Finally, these years saw the introduction of federative structures (twenty or so large professional federations were founded between 1890 and 1893), which led in 1895 — after the unfortunate experience of the Fédération Nationale des Syndicats (1886) — to the constitution of the Confédération Générale des Travailleurs (CGT).

This unionism, however, remains small in scale (with 188 unionists per union the highest membership in 1893). If, furthermore, the number of unionists is measured against the total number of workers in France, the ratio is still very low. An enquiry published by the national Secretariat of the Bourge du Travail in 1893 put it at a tenth. According to my own statistics, there were in fact 300,600 unionists on 31 December 1891 as against 3,303,000 industrial workers recorded in the 1891 census; that is, 9.1 per cent.

Once a union exists it has the power to attract more members. The brochure written by the Secretariat, which I quoted above, provides details, for 200 unions, of the number of members belonging to the various occupational categories involved: the percentages range from 6 to 100 per cent. Yet, even where the percentage is 100 per cent one cannot speak of mass unions in the strict sense, for the associations mentioned (which would today constitute 'sections' of larger wholes) rarely exceeded 500, and might exceptionally reach 1,000 members. The only union deserving this description is the union of miners of the Pas-de-Calais: out of 26,000 miners, 21,000 were unionised in 1890; at Lens, 'in each shop a placard was displayed which read: "You can join the Miners' Union and receive your membership card here" '. It is worth emphasising that this first mass union was resolutely reformist, in the style of British trade unionism: its strikes were 'political'; that is, strikes were a means of exerting pressure with precisely defined ends in mind. Thus the great *coalition* of 1891 culminated in the signing of the first collective contract in France, the famous Arras

Convention.

Let me conclude by noting that this period represents the first stage and acclimatisation process of unions as institutions; checked for a time by the depression, they quickly recovered a vigorous rate of growth, affecting both heavy and light industry, but in both cases their influence was in general restricted to the most highly skilled occupational categories.

The Union Theory of the Strike

In his *Coutume ouvrière*, Maxime Leroy has described the spectacular manner in which the unions were won over to the use of the strike. Without harking back to this study, which is very richly documented for the end of the Second Empire and the end of the century but provides a far more summary account for the period with which we are concerned here, there are two points I would like to comment upon further. As regards chronology, Maxime Leroy locates the revival almost at the very end of the century, presuming it to be contemporary with the birth of the CGT. This, to my mind, is to date it too late. I would place the shift a good decade earlier and would argue that Leroy's judgement rests upon a conception of change effected from above: 'Strikes were not the workers' foremost preoccupation until they came under the influence of the unions.' It would seem to me, however, that precisely the opposite was the case. Experience of strikes preceded the theory; their success preceded their official adoption and glorification. It was the choice of the grass-roots that came first and was the determining factor. I have already emphasised this fact; I will return to it when we come to consider the general strike. The whole interest of this history lies, in fact, in the process by which this change occurred.

For the time being, we merely have to grasp the different stages as they are reflected in the kinds of statements issued by unions. The reports presented by delegated workers to exhibitions (Lyon, 1872; Vienna, 1873; Philadelphia, 1876), and then to the congresses, constitute a relatively homogeneous 'corpus', not so much in its content, which rapidly altered, but in its nature. The delegates of the workers' organisations may be considered to be the leaders of the workers' movement, and their reports may therefore be treated as an expression of the line of thought dominant at the time. A sociological study of these militants would anyway be very necessary, especially in order to assess how stable their presence was. Of those sent to the Paris Congress (1876), very few are to be found again at the Lyon Congress in 1886. The notion of a 'full-time official', so characteristic of modern associations, would have seemed alien both in theory and in practice. A rapid changeover in men went hand in hand with as rapid a change in ideas. Such shifts are particularly obvious in the case of strikes.

During the years from 1871 to 1879, the strike, commonly termed a 'scourge', was in general condemned. The planning committee for the delegation to the Lyon exhibition included in its programme the following: 'To look into ways of maintaining wages at the level of labourers' needs without having recourse to strikes.' No one presenting a report actually challenged this initial proposition; with varying emphases, each and everyone of them criticised strikes as 'always burdensome to the bosses and fatal to the workers'. The spokesman for the leather and hide workers was adamant in his proscription of them: 'They are harmful, one rarely obtains good results from them; even when they succeed, they only provide a temporary relief.' Others reckoned that, given contemporary conditions, 'it is difficult to arrive at anything solid without having recourse' to them. Both camps regarded the strike as a primitive and 'barbarous instrument' and thought the development of associations would make it possible to supersede it: 'The strike represents an enforced way forward at the present time, the only remedy available until the day dawns when larger institutions enable us to implement the principles of the Association, which alone meet the just aspirations of the workers.' The work most often quoted is the *Histoire des classes ouvrières en Angleterre*, by Martin Nadaud, and the example generally chosen is that of the British trades unions. Federation was regarded as the great alternative: 'Strikes, about which people complain so much, and with reason, would no longer happen if this double organisation (by trade and by region) could be put into practice.' In effect, they argued, the fear of having to confront solid resistance from the workers would force the bosses to modify their practice in relation to wages.

The report of the workers' delegation to Vienna says in effect much the same thing: 'Strikes are a violent, and consequently unjust means . . . We should strive, through preventative organisation, to stop them recurring.' According to the mechanics, 'in France [the strike] only has a very small number of partisans now, and the vast majority of workers consider its time is past, and only intend to employ it in very extreme and rare cases'. Furthermore, their Paris *chambre syndicale* ruled out the solidarity strike. In 1874 Murat, a long-standing internationalist, who was standing as a candidate for the *conseil des prud' hommes* was asked a series of questions: 'Do you accept emancipation by means of cooperation? — Yes. — Do you accept strikes as a means of emancipation? — Yes. — In that case, said Donnay, your principles are not ours and we will not vote for you.' 'We will reject a strike, even if it should be to our advantage', declared another person present (Platner), 'for it is to strikes and to those that fashion them that we owe recent events in France, and we have paid dearly for the good that they have done us.'

The kind of attitudes expressed at the congresses at Paris and Lyon are identical. On all these points, the workers' leaders invariably found common ground with Radicals such as Pauliat and Barberet, editors in turn of *Le Rappel*, who never tired of contrasting the disastrous nature of strikes with the redeeming qualities of unions.

The reasons put forward for opposing strikes were not only moral (and imbued with a Proudhonian concern with respectability) and strategic but also economic. A strike, it was argued, served no purpose. First of all, it rarely succeeded: 'Out of ten attempts, we do not believe that we are mistaken in stating that only two or three succeed.' Even though the statistics, particularly for these years, show it to have been based on an entirely erroneous assessment, this pessimism was very widely shared. Secondly, a strike was thought costly, because it emptied the corporative coffers and placed the workers' families in debt: 'It always undermines the strength of the corporation and sometimes brings about the total ruin of its funds.' 'It would be much better to spend the money thrown away on a strike on the founding of a cooperative society.'

Even if the strike was won, they said, the gains were ephemeral and undermined by management once it had survived the crisis. They were also illusory because the rise in wages brought about a rise in prices: 'The prices of the products produced in the industries supporting the strike rise, so that the worker must give back with one hand what he receives with the other.' Whether one raised wages by amicable agreement or by economic war, — that is, by striking — the proletarians' budgets would be affected to precisely the same degree by the rise in basic living costs; their painful sacrifices will have been to no avail. To the ideas inherited from Proudhon, which, according to Marx, 'can only have blossomed in the brain of an uncomprehending poet', there was added a tenacious belief in an 'iron law of wages', conveyed by the Guesdists, who were still infected by Lassallism; still discernible at the end of the century amongst the leaders of the CGT, this doctrine led to a kind of discouragement in advance.

Finally, strike reduced production, upon which the standard of living depended. Many endorsed Barberet's opinion: 'It is clear as day that strikes halt production and paralyse commercial activity, which alone is able to make a country wealthy and upon which everybody depends.' 'Never to interrupt work for a single moment, to produce,' Barberet felt, 'this and this alone is our salvation.' And to those who hesitated before displaying such solidarity with capital, the image of a national industry, wounded by 'our disasters', threatened by 'our powerful neighbours', was sufficient to counter any scruples. Workers' literature is riddled with declarations of industrial patriotism. Nothing negates class-consciousness more thoroughly than does the ideology of reconstruction, which serves to represent strikes as a kind of treason.

However, within this general harmony several dissonant notes can be heard. There is a current tendency which, without extolling strikes, considers them justified, emphasising their inevitability: a strike is something which one cannot decree, something which one undergoes. Defensive strikes are seen as just and necessary, while offensive strikes are justified by the rise in prices which precedes them and sets them in motion. Offensive strikes are regarded as nothing but an expression of 'the necessity of balancing wages and expenditure', an interpretation which reverses the wages–prices relation invoked by those who opposed combination.

Finally, there are those who place the emphasis upon the educative and uplifting aspects of this form of struggle, a position which foreshadows the championing of 'revolutionary gymnastics' by writers like Pouget or Griffuelhes.[7] When Murat declared that one 'owes to strikes the little achieved in the way of emancipation', he was admittedly disowned by his union, but we learn from the police report that a section of those present 'applauded' him.

Theoretical disapproval anyway did not prevent workers from coming out on strike. In 1875–6, there were several disputes in which strike committees were opposed to the reticent *chambres syndicales*. This was the case with the mechanics, the carpenters and the leather workers. Upon each occasion the driving force behind the strike was provided by young people, aged twenty-five to thirty-five mindful of the importance of organisation, they sought

---

7. Jacques Julliard, 'Théorie syndicaliste révolutionnaire et pratique gréviste', *Mouvement social*, Oct.–Dec. 1968, p. 59.

to imbue the unions with a more aggressive approach. In the case of the polished-leather curriers. Toussaint, aged twenty-seven, and Cuzin, aged twenty-five, organised a resistance fund against the instructions of a hostile union. The same thing happened among the tawers, who were spurred on by two young men, both twenty-seven, Magnard, the son of a man who had fought in the Commune, and Vergne. Amongst the tanners, the militants won their case and in September 1874 their union's rules made provision for strike pay of 2 francs a day. In 1876, during another curriers' strike, the workers' commission (Pastoureau, Bellemcontre, Gahon), winning support from the collective kitchen of the curriers of Rue La Fayette, held a series of well-attended meetings in which they launched a specialist breakaway union in opposition to the main leather and hides union. Amongst the mechanics, the current which drew its inspiration from Murat, by now an old man, gained in strength and, at the end of 1876, succeeded in having a clause allocating funds for fighting strikes added to the union's rules. In the course of the preparation for the Philadelphia Exhibition, along with that for the Paris Congress, there were numerous meetings at which more combative conceptions were expressed. Judging the sums of money devoted to the journey to America — a prestige venture — to be excessive, several unions withdrew their contribution and set up fighting funds instead. This was the case with the roofers and porcelain-workers. Defence and agitation in favour of wages 'by the most vigorous means possible came to the forefront of union tasks', whilst the mists of cooperativist illusion were beginning to be dispelled.

But it was the large-scale social upheaval between 1878 and 1880, at first defensive then, from spring 1879, resolutely offensive, which brought the strike to the forefront of the stage, where it was to remain from then on. A theoretical reversal took place at this time, the strike being reassessed and all the arguments which had previously been employed against it now being reversed: 'We are told that our strikes will have the result of increasing rents, the price of foodstuffs and of the basic necessities of life, and that these rises will invariably rebound upon us. Not at all,' said Jules Cazelles, the leader of the Parisian joiners in 1879, 'this is an error; in fact they will fall upon those who do not work, upon the capitalists alone, for when these rises begin to affect us we will simply force the entrepreneurs to increase our wages yet again.' This shift is reflected in the change of tone of *Le Prolétaire*. In April 1879, it treated the Vienne weavers' combination as a hopeless venture. At the beginning of

August, however, stirred by the general strike of the Paris weavers, *Le Prolétaire* published the statutes of a 'permanent support committee for strikers, present and future', 'seeing that the effect of strikes is to sharpen the antagonism between classes by arousing in workers a consciousness of their interests'. At the end of August, Prudent Dervillers, a member of the editorial committee, condemned the defeatism of the period which had just ended: 'Owing to the moral and intellectual depression following the bloody triumph of order, the strike is no longer accorded its true value.' He then proceeded to set about rehabilitating it. At the Marseilles Congress, various orators — Isidore Finance, Prat, a number of tanners from Marseille and others — sang its praises: 'We must accord due honour to the strike, which we have too much disdained, not realising that to ignore its value is to undermine our moral strength.' The following resolution was adopted: 'Whilst acknowledging that the strike is only a palliative, this being nonetheless the sole weapon we possess with which to resist the exigencies of capital, we propose that workers lend each other mutual support in the conflicts which may arise between labour and capital.'

The following congresses, which were dominated by disputes between the socialist factions, ceased to have a typically unionist character. The strike was still, however, the object of extensive debates, in which the positions of the various members of the divided 'family' were expressed. Absent until then, from the congress agendas, the strike featured as an issue for the first time at the Reims Congress (1881). The rival congresses of Saint-Etienne (possibilist) and of Roanne (Guesdist) in 1882 devoted long discussions to it and both affirmed their commitment to prepared and organised strikes. Curiously enough, the possibilists seemed a little more reserved, re-emphasising the priority of the political path, whilst the Guesdists were more enthusiastic, presenting a report which was in fact a rapturous eulogy of the strike, with hardly any reservations. The Guesdists were seeking at that time to identify themselves with the workers' struggle; their leaders, according to Marx and Engels, had not wholly turned their backs on Bakuninism and, their militants played a part in all the major conflicts. Nevertheless, the plan of action which they recommended involved channelling such disputes in far too rigid a manner for a working class that had always been jealous of its autonomy. At any rate, this plan never worked and, later on, the (Guesdist) National Federation of Unions gave up all hope of planning activities in this area.

From then on, the terms of the debate shifted a little. It was no longer a question of choosing between cooperative and strike, between union and strike, but between partial and general strikes, between reformist and revolutionary strikes. A reformist strike, being subordinated and limited, was favoured by all those who held that party politics provided the royal road to power. The revolutionary strike was already the major option of direct-action syndicalists. Once again this problem was raised at the grass-roots level before being posed at the top. The question of the general strike only emerged at the union leadership level for the first time in 1887 at the National Federation of Unions Congress at Montluçon, and then only very tentatively. It emerged into the full light of day only at the Bordeaux Congress (1888). This discussion split the Federation and confirmed the division between socialists and unions (*syndicaux*). For the latter the triumph of the doctrine of the general strike, around the years 1890 to 1900, placed the partial strike in shadow, although it in turn was re-established and rehabilitated into the everyday struggle by militants concerned with day-to-day practice, such as Pouget and Griffuelhes.

This theory does of course follow a meandering path, and inevitably disparities and discontinuities have been encountered. No theory proceeds along a continuous curve. Its destiny would rather be like the 'staggered structure' of which Michel Foucault speaks in relation to the history of 'discursive formations', with the statement at the top always lagging behind the experience at the base. Like Rosa Luxemburg, I think that 'far from being invented by the leadership, every new form of struggle is born of the creative initiative of the masses'.

3
The Running of a Strike:
the Ringleaders

In a period in which the workers' movement was still not particularly institutionalised, 'ringleaders' were very important, as much for setting strikes in motion as for running them. I would have loved to have known those unruly elements, those rabble-rousers, and what a host of fascinating questions they could have been asked — to penetrate their minds, their conscious and subconscious motives, to grasp the essential nature of their revolt and the secret of their influence. I would have liked to have sketched out a psycho-sociological – indeed, a psycho-analytic — profile of the strike leaders.

Methodological Difficulties

Unfortunately, we have no choice but to lower our sights a little, for our sources are far too meagre to measure up to these demands. On my table there are more than 2,000 file cards (whilst some strikes are completely anonymous, others supply us with the names of several leaders), but the information that they bear is for the most part summary: a name, often the age (in 924 cases, i.e. almost half the total), frequently a geographical origin as well, sometimes also a note of a person's civil status (168 cases), a comment on their morality or education, the salient details of a person's criminal record, at best a *curriculum vitae*, but of a utilitarian sort, detailing militant activities and, very rarely, describing a face or, exceptionally, giving a biography.

The quality of the information depends on several factors. First of all we have to take into account the nature of the sources, the two principal kinds being police and judicial records, the nature of which I have explained above. The style in which any given militant action is conducted will determine the point at which either of these makes its entrance. If an action is of the ephemeral and episodic kind, we will be granted a short, dry police report, precise but entirely external. If, on the other hand, the action is a livelier one, it may occasion police-station minutes, which have the inestimable advantage of letting us hear the suspect speak. If the action is a violent one, it will set the whole judicial machinery in motion, with its ceremonial procession of written documents. But even here, the contribution is out of proportion to the event: a police-court will simply dispatch the accused, the magistrate's court will deal with them quickly, confining itself strictly to the present, to acts rather than to persons, limiting itself to assembling the half-dozen or so classic items of information concerning the civil status of the accused. The records of the assizes alone provide us with a more satisfyingly dense account, thanks to the exigencies of the examining magistrate. But of the strike cases in the period under consideration, very few went as far as the assizes. The vast majority of cases of 'offences against the right to work' were under the jurisdiction of the magistrate's courts.

No matter how succinct their reports may have been, I would like to have been able to have made use of them. For the 1,179 cases tried between 1871 and 1890, according to the *Comptes de la justice criminelle*, with 3,303 accused and 2,705 found guilty, would have constituted, because of their relative homogeneity, valuable raw material. Here too I must scale down my ambitions a little, for there is not, unfortunately, a complete run of national judicial records for the period; furthermore, at the departmental level, judicial archives have not always been maintained; having remained in the charge of the clerks of the court, they are generally inaccessible. Also, since it is only very recently that they have been deposited in departmental archives, they have only rarely been included in inventories, and it is barely possible to use the 'U' series to which they belong. Finally, wholesale destruction has mutilated them, affecting above all the magistrates' courts' records, in which at best only the registers containing the sentences have been kept. My attempts to use the judicial archives have therefore usually been in vain.

Apart from material constraints of this kind, a whole series of factors serve to limit the richness or scope of these documents. Firstly, there are historical factors. As strikes become routine events and less violent in nature, and as repression diminishes a little, we are given less information about them. Furthermore, the changes in the nature of the institutions within the workers' movement helps to mask the faces of the men involved, so that the reports speak to us more and more of groups, unions and strike committees, without allowing us to see beyond the basically anonymous front which is presented. Only when fear re-emerges, thanks to the operations of the anarchists, will the police become more inquisitorial again and justice become committed to intervening more actively. It is the fear of revolutionaries which prompts the setting up of a systematic filing system, such as the very revealing one at Bessèges-La-Grand-Combe.

Secondly, there are psychological factors, which render these documents still more opaque, falsifying the tone of voice of the actors involved or serving to make those involved in enforcing the law less perceptive. The hard benches of the police-station, like those of the magistrates' court, hardly have much in common with the psychoanalyst's couch. Legitimate defence and mutual defiance are the rule here, for each is provoked by the other. When confronted with the rule of justice, a strike leader will either repent or seek to justify his actions, express regrets or further his claims. Eugène Ratton, aged seventeen, a journeyman at Courcelles gas factory, pleaded: 'I had been drinking and I didn't know what I was doing.' Pierre Meubry, aged thirty-three, accused of attempted murder against the person of a foreman at the Malétra factory (Saint-Denis, chemical products), pleaded 'three glasses of absinthe drunk this morning on an empty stomach'. The woman Marie Perrot, aged forty-five, guilty of acts of violence against the non-strikers of Commentry: 'I acted without thinking and I have been well and truly punished for what I have done, for my son who used to work down the mine has been laid off.' Young Fournier, aged nineteen, wished his failed attack on Brechard, a manufacturer from Roanne, to be regarded as youthful folly; it was, he said, 'plain foolishness'. These declarations should not be taken at face value. Pleading guilty is quite fair, for what would be the good of playing the hero before a judge?

Some, however, preferred to strike up a defiant attitude. Thus, at Villefranche, Mlle Lapierre boasted that her demonstrating helped to consolidate the strike. 'Yes, I was sent to Nouméa and I'm proud of it', proclaims Pruneyre, a stove-setter, age thirty-two, 'an amnestied person who has not been mindful of the grace accorded him'. Morever, from 1880 on, the revolutionary militants, the libertarians especially, would often transform the course into a public tribunal. Whether victim or apostle, the leader would at any rate offer little explanation for his actions, still less would he confess anything. If such a confession were forthcoming, it would involve testifying to an unfortunate, and therefore exemplary life: 'I will certainly be reproached for having four times been sentenced for theft. . . . It should be borne in mind that I am the son of a poor girl seduced by a bourgeois, then abandoned by her seducer; that I have long known the agonies of poverty and of hunger. It should be borne in mind that these sentences involved thefts of fruit, of potatoes.' These autobiographies, formulated quite deliberately, refer to an implicit and latent model; they thus resemble each other in much the same way as, for an outsider, do people of another colour, or the portraits of a particular period or artist. The individual melts into the social, the particular features melt into overall schema.

The painter's gaze is no more liberated either, for he is inspired by a particular conception of man and of the strike leader. In the eyes of this self-satisfied and puritan society, the person whom it accuses is guilty; his present act simply sums him up and characterizes him definitively.[1] There is singularly little concern with enquiring into his past, to discern the gradual entanglement of the threads of social responsibility, which theories of heredity or of 'cerebrality' are one more way of obscuring; it is as if he had risen up, all of a sudden, solitary and revealed in a present moment which is then annihilated along with him, as if he had neither ancestors nor youth. The occasional description of someone as an 'illegitimate child' alone allows us to glimpse into a suspect world of cheap hotels, or of wild goings-on during the haymaking, but the door is soon drawn shut again. This does little to satisfy the curiosity that sociology and psycho-analysis have rendered well-high insatiable, for nowadays we have no sense of knowing someone unless we know his or her childhood or milieu. Triumphant moralism, always the dominant note in the nineteenth century, yields by contrast an abundance of summary judgements: drunkenness and dissolute morals will ordinarily feature on the record of the male strike leaders, and even more on that of the female leaders. We hear, for instance, that 'the worst possible reports have been transmitted to us concerning each of the defendants, whose easy morals are a matter of public knowledge'. You would gather from the judgment of the court at Vienne that an outline sketch of a strike leader would ideally have him be a bad son, a bad husband and a bad father. This, at any rate, is how the person of comrade Tennevin was described:

1. It is, moreover, significant to see how low the percentage of acquittals was. Between 1864 and 1896, this was never above 30 per cent and, most of the time, was below 10 per cent. The judges' sympathies lay with the established order. They had little doubt what their verdicts should be.

'*Déclassé*, living off his hate-filled preaching, but abandoning his mother, wife and sick daughter to the pity of the charitable boards and of the sisters of Saint-Vincent-de-Paul. His mother reassumed her maiden name so as to bear that of her son no longer.'

There is undoubtedly some truth in this picture. In effecting a breach with the dominant order, these bold spirits would undoubtedly have neglected, if not rejected, its morality. But we should also bear in mind that, in tracing these lines, the hands of our witnesses are guided by the ancient image that bourgeois society has of the 'ringleader'. He is seen as a crude brute, an alcoholic and a formidable figure, a man belonging to the dangerous classes. Traces of this kind of representation survive in the few physical portraits that we are given of the strike leaders, who are always said to be endowed with a 'disturbing gaze'.

What is most interesting, however, is the fact that this image become blurred and that, time and time again, the authorities and the observers emphasise, not without some astonishment, the good qualities of these leaders; namely, their intelligence, their professionalism, their coolness of temperament, their charm even. More and more often we hear descriptions such as 'a very good worker, remarkably intelligent' and 'passionate, active, intelligent, a quite talented public speaker'. At Bordeaux, the tram company strike was prepared 'in a mysterious fashion by the most intelligent employees of the company, who wielded a kind of authority over the others'. At Fourmies, 'I observed a fairly curious fact', wrote the prefect of the Nord, 'namely, that the delegates were in general the most intelligent workers; there was not a single one amongst them who did not declare himself personally satisfied with his wage'. Presenting an outline sketch of the typical Parisian leader, which was anyway heavily influenced by Denis Poulot's *Le Sublime*, the newspaper *La France* wrote: 'A bad worker of this kind is not always a clumsy worker, he works quickly and well, he enjoys amongst his work-mates a deserved reputation for professional skill, and he is proud of it.' Envy, incompetence and professional or social maladjustment were not therefore the sole motives behind militant action. There were others, which could be said perhaps to be more refined, more 'bourgeois' even, such as the taste for action and for power. De Plet, the leader of the Fourmies strike (1886), who was young, lively and well-off (with his wife, he earned 13 francs a day) was said by Paul Cambon to have 'begun to develop a taste for the blandishments of popularity. One could feel the kind of self-esteem developing in him which creates the Baslys of this world'. 'The leader writer triumphs', notes *La France*, 'as is clear from the newspapers which carry his contributions ... The strike produces him, brings him into the limelight and establishes his popularity.' A new representation thus replaces the earlier one so that, in the eyes of the bourgeois world, the fast-talking and hard-fighting leader, from the dregs of the lower classes, is transformed into someone who is ambitious, conscious, organised and, according to the formula which will become classic in the police files, 'all the more dangerous for his great intelligence'.[2]

The striker thus begins to be looked at in a different way. But his physiognomy may also be said to change and the range of profiles offered increases. We derive commonplace reassurance from the notion that it is the object that determines our field of vision, but the truth of the matter is that several types co-exist. Before describing this diversity, I shall attempt, as far as is possible given the lacunae and the nature of the sources, to isolate the general features.

Identikit Picture of the Strike Leader

For a good 2,000 names, the state, or rather, the clerk of the court, records only a hundred or so nicknames. This is a fact worth noting. These nicknames, being for the most part geographical, emphasise the 'incomer' origin of the individual concerned, who thus stands out against a background of general stability: Vincent, known as the Spaniard, Raoux, the Marseillais, Sarrazin, the Parisian, the mysterious leader of the Roubaix textiles strikes of 1880, the Auvergnat, the Bourguignon, the Nantais and so on. Or they may refer to some physical peculiarity, an infirmity perhaps: Curly, Lame (the most common), the Hunchback, the Round-Shouldered, Wooden-Leg. Some of these nicknames might refer to a person's manner, so that Levet, a smelter, was called the Marquis because of his 'comfortable, well-groomed' manner. We hear of Speed and Greed, young piecers involved in the troubles at Lisieux (1873); Auclerc, an ex-communard, a weaver at Cours, called Massacre, on account of his violent language; Bruno Manifacier, from Bessèges, known as the

2. I have two examples of such remarks in the records: of Marquet, a Roanne mechanic, 'powerful in stature, with regular features and a remarkably intelligent countenance, he is certainly one of the most remarkable and, consequently, one of the most dangerous figures in the anarchist groups' (Arch. dép. Loire, M82, pièce 215). The police report on Paul Reclus, an engineer at Bessèges and the nephew of Élisée, described him as 'the more to be feared for being one of the most intelligent' (Arch. dép. Gard, 6M 1414 [1]).

Chopper. Actors who follow a more mediocre course earn titles such as Purée, Eat-Sugar, Little-Gain. Finally, there are the political nicknames, such as Jules Simon, Gambetta, Garibaldi and also Mohammed.

These nicknames pertain to individuals and therefore have nothing in common with the ones we find transmitted from person to person in the eighteenth-century army, as it is described by A. Carvisier. What does a practice of this kind, which lasted until the last part of the nineteenth century, signify? It is undoubtedly a survival, and today's workers, who are better integrated into the world, hardly give each other any nicknames at all; such shopfloor appellations as do exist are certainly never accorded civil status. Is it perhaps an inheritance from the days of *compagnonnage*, the laicised rite of a religious society in which a baptism is the mark of an initiation and mystery the law appropriate to a situation of clandestinity? Or is it rather a relic of what was an old necessity for the dangerous classes, where the proletarian, ever spied upon and under suspicion, bordered upon being a cut-throat, even if he did not look like one, and needed to develop his own secret code. 'The language that one speaks there', writes Louis Blanc of the Parisian lower depths, 'is a baneful language, invented in order to conceal thought.' The characters who inhabit Eugène Sue's world use nicknames, and it is highly significant that Delvau, in his *Dictionnaire de la langue verte*, mixes up robbers' and workers' slang. More profoundly, perhaps, this usage demonstrates the importance attributed to vocabulary, such that the name marks the beginning of the existence of something or someone. We are witness here to a need for a language of one's own, which one invents and appropriates, on the margins of the language in common use, which is experienced as a foreign, uncomfortable, if not hermetic and hostile language. This sense of maladjustment and of ill-ease, combined with a thirst for spontaneity and for creation, seems to me to be highly revealing, but we must, I think, approach the study of slang — trades slang, popular slang — from an ethnological perspective. School and the spread of education have killed all this off, just as they have killed off *patois*. As the main instruments for effecting an integration into society, they have relegated slang to the level of the 'badly brought up', or the picturesque. There can be no doubt whatsoever that it was once much more than that, that it in fact comprised the communication network of a whole social group.

Physical Portraits

There are very few physical descriptions. This scarcity does not so much reflect the indifference of a class as the paucity of actual, in-the-flesh encounters. It was not common for the authorities and the strike leaders to meet face to face, and the portrait, an essentially bourgeois form of art, demands and confers a distinction that these physiognomies are not held to deserve. The small number of sketches that have come to hand — descriptive files, interview profiles — once again bear the mark of their authors, who emphasise if not what strikes them, at any rate what they believe they are seeing. Muscular strength inspires them with fear, so that Blanié, a puddler at Decazeville, accused of having struck Watrin a mortal blow, is described as being 'a terrible man, at least six feet tall, built like a Hercules and as strong as a bull'. Likewise, the police at Bessèges, when confronted with a number of strapping young men, with a degree of foresight which is also somewhat archaic, note that they are 'to be feared in case of revolution'. Sloppiness tends to provoke disgust: 'An indolent air, the bearing of a worker who is negligent and takes little care of her person.' But what comes across still more forcefully is the unease engendered amongst the well-fed by the always disturbing sight of bodily misery: 'Small, puny, lame, bilious, capable of hatching the worst of plans' is a typical outline sketch of a strike leader, in this instance, of Fauviaux, leader of the strike at Anzin. This shows how suspicious the authorities were of deformity, with thinness necessarily being a sign of envy and infirmity a mark of perversity. Thus for every Voidier, 'a big, handsome boy, in his thirties', highly valued by his boss for his skill as a glass-maker, there is a host of the *popolo minuto*, of small, rachitic, bandy-legged, stooped men, with tanned faces and troubling expressions. Henri Marius, the hero of Bessèges, has the height of a child, a mere five feet tall; Pruneyre 'is a small man, well below the size of a foot-soldier, but whose tanned face and burning eye could not be less reassuring'. Pierre Martin, the anarchist from Vienne, known as the Hunchback, is described as a 'small man, with a sickly, stunted air'; Meunier is said to be 'small, somewhat deformed; he has long arms and thin hands, with tapering fingers'; Jourdan, public scrivener at Bessèges, suffers from a 'general atrophy of the right leg, walks on crutches'. Upon these undernourished, underdeveloped bodies, which are a true image of the poor physical condition of the working class, as medical reports and conscription statistics bear out, the brutal industry of the nineteenth century imprints its stigmata: 'various blue blast marks on the forehead, the nose and the left cheekbone'; 'serious blast scars below the left eye; powder stains on the left side of the forehead'. These features cannot easily be reconciled with the canons of bourgeois beauty.

The workers, however, were not at all shocked by ugliness and thinness, which, for them were familiar and fraternal, representing a kind of closeness and serving as a guarantee of honesty. Fat is a sign that one is a bourgeois, and it smells of treason ('you don't get fat by scraping out the bottom of the pan'); a club orator in 1869 could be heard fulminating against 'this obese and bourgeois democracy, with its unhealthy rolls of fat, which has turned its guns on the people'; the capitalists are always represented as 'satiated' and 'big-bellied', and a fat strike leader would be a cause for astonishment. Workerism thus even extends as far as physical appearances.

When it comes to dress, however, there is some hesitation. Workers are in fact divided, it seems, between two sets of contrary aspirations. Some choose to distrust the 'nobs', expressing their appreciation for simple dress. Thus Christou Thivrier, the 'deputy in the smock', owed a large part of his popularity to his choice of attire. But since the majority of workers wore their best clothes on the first days of a strike, they did not hate their leaders for dressing well. Tortelier, it is true, 'always dressed sloppily', but Ludovic Ménard, who was as much an anarchist as he was, when he was to speak at meetings, would 'swop his working clothes for his wedding jacket'. According to the clerk of the court at Vienne, and to his astonishment, Tennevin and Martin were 'dressed in the latest fashion and wore white silk cravates'. Furthermore, the photos of delegates at congresses show them to be very much in their Sunday best, their watch-chains being displayed with some satisfaction on their neat waistcoats. This is another image, and just as real a one, of a working class concerned to bring 'honour to its own affairs' and greedy for respectability.

The Gift of the Gab

A strike leader must thus have some style if he is to make headway but, above all else, it is the gift of the gab which will win him his prestige. There is no end to the number of leaders I could mention who owe their ascendancy to this talent. Some of the common terms of praise run as follows: 'His ready tongue gave him a certain hold over his comrades'; 'possesses a certain gift for language. Very resolute'. Charles Bonne, at Roubaix, showed his colours at the burial of Deputy Derégnaucourt: 'He made a violent speech which won him the admiration of the workers.' Tortelier was well liked for his modulated voice, which was at once sweet and raw. The influence of Basly, 'active, turbulent and a fine speaker', who was contrasted with the more distant 'Monsieur Rondet', was attributed to the fact that he 'uses familiar terms when speaking, employing the very turns of phrase and words of the miners themselves . . . so that he is interrupted after every sentence by frenetic applause'. At the other end of France, Jarlier, leader of the dock-workers at Marseilles, 'endowed with a certain style of public speaking, was able, in spite of his use of a slightly whimsical French, to win over the workers' milieu'. 'People listened to this man as if, within him, there was the salvation of men.' Marseillais such as Jules Cazelles, the joiner, and Raoux, the shoemaker, had a 'thoroughly southern flair' which guaranteed their success in Paris.

The kind of eloquence that the workers valued was a popular one: 'The miners distrust orators who are not unpolished, as they are themselves, and who are not involved in the dispute.' Armandine Vernet, speaking in the woods of the Cévennes, was warm, prepared to be lyrical and sometimes tender, and it was 'her speciality to make a part of her audience weep'. Speeches were often emphatic in their form but simple as to the themes chosen (the destiny of workers and bosses would be compared, proletarian unity would be exalted, and so on). Their vocabulary would be a limited one. Above all, speeches would be violent. Tortelier, 'with brusque gestures and a hoarse voice, . . . perhaps harmless, had a rough and slightly frightening air'; Basly 'speaks only of the scaffold . . . Citizens, let us unite in order to make the capitalists yield up their wealth'. Raoux 'makes the bosses tremble'. Finally, this was a discourse which held out the promise of a better lot; it readily assumes a prophetic and a messianic tone.

Along with a smooth tongue, a sense of initiative and pluck in the presence of the bosses — what admiration there is for someone who stands his ground, risking his neck for all the downtrodden — boldness, spirit, guts, rather than knowledge, experience or presence, are the qualities which make a strike leader. These qualities, which are existential in nature, reflect the kinds of struggle in which workers were engaged. The increasing unionisation of the workers' movement, the complexity of the problems which it had to confront, would in time require different kinds of men, who were not so much tribunes of the people, and who were more concerned with studying, with files and with written texts. Such shifts are exemp-

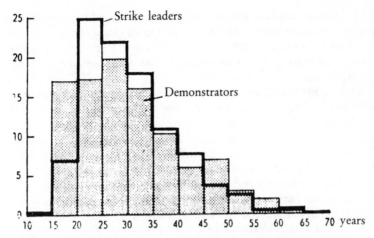

Figure 3: Distribution of demonstrators and strike leaders arrested, according to age

lified by Merrheim's personality and the controversies which it provoked.

The Relative Youth of the Leaders

In the early days, however, the spoken word ruled. Youth ruled too, as the statistics quite startlingly show. Age being the item of information most consistently recorded (924 files include a mention of it), I was able to draw up two bar-charts (Fig. 3): one representing the strikers designated as 'leaders' (445); another representing the strikers arrested during demonstrations, a category that is obviously wider than that of 'leaders' in the strict sense.

These two charts differ in a fairly predictable manner, above all for the fifteen to nineteen year olds, being larger in the case of the demonstrators (16 per cent of the whole) than in the case of the others (6 per cent). This apart, they have many points in common and also bring out the important contribution made by the young: 71 per cent are fifteen to thirty-four years old or, more precisely, 42 per cent are between twenty and twenty-nine years old. There is a significant drop at the thirty-five-year mark. There are thus few apprentices, but few old men too. René Michaud recalled that 'for many young people, old age was a horrifying thing'.

At meetings, the old had no special privileges. Age conferred no special power nor, on the other hand, did it constitute an obstacle.

In 1884 Paul Cambon was astonished to find the old miners speaking of Basly, a young man of twenty-nine as their 'father'. Coalitions needed men who were young and fresh to lead them, men who were in their prime, who had not been eroded by time or worn out by repression.

Men needed to be unattached too. Age was regarded not only in terms of its virtues but also in terms of the marital status it implied. In the absence of any institutional protection, militants had to have loose moorings. The bachelor, in his furnished lodgings, fancy free, footloose, solitary, irreverent, would gradually put down roots and become the head of the family, fearful and feltered by a concern for his brood, his hungry children and his reproachful wife. Along with the weight of family responsibilities there were, in heavy industry at any rate, advantages to be derived from age. Management, fully aware of the moderating influence of kinship, sought by every means possible to fashion for itself a stable and familial workforce: lodgings, bonuses and retirement pensions are each and every one obstacles to rebellion. In the large concerns, dismissal amounted not only to loss of employment but also to the abandonment of hard-won positions. For all these reasons, heads of families proved unwilling to stop work and prompt to start up again. So exceptional was it for leaders to have children that it was considered an especial distinction. Thus a comrade of Blanchard, leader of the Paris union of box-makers and packers, blacklisted in every workshop and the father of seven children, proposed that a medal be struck in recognition of his dedication and the resolution was thereupon passed.

Age and Profession

The capacity of young people to create a disturbance was not the same in every branch of industry. It was most developed in the less skilled industries, where sheer output — a matter of strength, agility and speed — prevailed over professional worth. Feeling themselves to be vulnerable, an old weaver or an old miner (Father Bonnemort in Zola's *Germinal* springs to mind here) would lie low, whilst the young would press their claims. This is how it was at Montceau, at Bézenet, in 1878, and at Commentry in 1881, to name but a few instances. In the textile industry, there were several occasions upon which the young — indeed the very young — played a key role in setting a strike in motion. They succeeded in drawing their elders along behind them because no qualitative difference separated them; no technical barrier existed to halt the shock wave which their actions had unleashed. The fragmented nature of the work itself was a factor serving to establish social homogeneity, for it rendered the factories uniform, suppressing grades and levels of ability.

In the skilled trades (glass-making, porcelain, metals, wood-working, artistic industries, and so on), those who were older continued to act as mentors. Skill, which cannot be acquired without experience, and seniority are qualities which serve to win one independence and prestige. Whilst the workers may admire the prowess of a good workman, for the boss he is an investment and, as such, a good number of indiscretions may be forgiven him. The leader will have a different style in this sort of industry. He will have knowhow, high earnings and will be in the prime of life; he will be a personality. Pasquet, a cutter working in bronze, a very good workman, forty-four years old, the best-paid man in the workshop (earning 10 francs a day), led the Paris engravers in a strike. Consider Eugène Cinquin, a cardboard-maker, and foreman for three years for a boss who 'showers him with advances'; Guyon, an excellent team leader with Krieger, the furniture king; Joseph Denis, a metal-worker so skilled that the boss considered taking him on again in spite of his rebellious spirit; Lisoni, forty-one years old, the instigator of several strikes at the Vieillard faincerie at Bordeaux, 'kept on because he is a very good workman'; Louis Voidier, a wonderfully gifted glass-maker at the crystal-glassworks of Sèvres, earning 400 francs a month and who, it was said, had 20,000 francs or so in savings; the president of the union of glass-makers of Bas-Meudon, able to halt production whenever he saw fit. Each of these men was approaching forty or more. As a consequence, the young people did not get a hearing. As for the apprentices, who were forever being dressed down and who were sometimes persecuted, no one would dream of following them. If the feeders at the printworks, the hammermen at the foundries or the boys at the glass-works came out on strike, they would be spurned by their elders and scolded by their parents, as if they were school-children. In trades such as these, where age established stratification and hierarchies, traditions weighed more heavily. This explains why the choice of a new direction might assume the guise of a conflict between the generations, as was the case in the Paris strike of 1879, when the young organisers of carpenters' union were ranged against the old men in the *compagnon* organisations.

No matter how many sociological differences of this kind there may have been, there can be no doubting the influence of the young strike leaders. Knowledge of the demographic structures of an enterprise, an industry or an industrial zone would certainly shed further light upon the nature of the disputes and the degree of combativeness. If we are unable to pursue this research any further, it is for want of the means to do so rather than for lack of motivation. Such a study would not, moreover, answer all the questions one might raise about the role of age in social movements; it would refer us, rather, to other factors, which might well explain the variations in this influence.

During the period under consideration, the very nature of the workers' movement, which had very few reliable cadres and which was still largely informal, made it well suited to the young. Indeed, the young represented a factor which served to encourage change and innovation. The rapid conversion in the late 1880s of the workers to strikes was undoubtedly related to the absence of any leadership offering and established strategy. Men and movement alike were young.

The Mobility of Strike Leaders

As well as being young, strike leaders tended to be mobile. Quite a number of them were men who moved around the country systematically. These men were undoubtedly condemned a priori by the authorities, who tended to exaggerate their role, because by the same token it would clear them from any blame. Rebellion, in this respect, was always seen as coming from elsewhere. It is always a source of comfort and reassurance to management to be able to draw a contrast between the calm satisfaction of 'our own workers' and sowers of discord, and to attribute responsibility for a conflict to some professional agitator, perhaps a mysterious agent of occult powers. 'The most dangerous, by all accounts, are those nomadic workers who appear to have no other aim but that of sowing discord wherever they go.' Just after the Commune, this sense of mistrust reached fever pitch. So it was that at Saint-Etienne, two carpenters, Vidot and Dubot, were regarded as shifty simply because they had come fom Lyon, and indeed, they would have been arrested had they not set out again, in the revered tradition of journeymen passing through in search of a job. Amongst the leaders charged at the time of the strike at the Anzin coalfield in 1872, much was made of the presence of Jules Broutin, twenty-eight years old, who had already 'done' seventeen pits; of Louis Thomas, thirty-five years old, born at Strasbourg; and above all, of Saleski. Saleski was a master-overman, about thirty-five years old, who had roughed it a lot, who had undoubtedly participated in the Borinage strikes and, because he had just returned from America, the press launched a campaign against him, dubbing him 'the agent from Chicago'. Because Jules Pobe, aged twenty-two, a tawer, born at Lunéville, had already worked in seven different towns, the chief constable concluded that 'he was probably a member of the International'. A migrant is by definition suspect; being unsettled smacks of immorality.

Representations of this sort, which became a genuine psychosis in times of fear, and which was underpinned by an ideal of sedentary existence, involving disapproval of the exodus from the rural areas and a phobia about the bustling and dissolute towns, were however not entirely imaginary. There are many facts which suggest that they were in fact founded on reality. Thus the part played by outsiders in triggering a large number of strikes is not in doubt. We have already seen the disruptive influence of foreigners, Belgiass above all, on industry in the north of France; in Paris, among the cabinet-makers and tailors in particular — they always had an explosive impact. Incomers[3] are hardly any better, for, being displaced, they bring with them a whiff of contention, of comparison and sometimes of revenge. Many strikes explode under the influence of intractable newcomers. Thus, at Cransac, in 1880, seven recently employed people provoked unrest; at Troyes, amongst striking cardboard-makers, 'it was evident what part was played by eight workers, from Paris and from Lyon, only recently employed by the bosses and who had already come out on strike in Paris'; at Montagny, the weavers from Roanne, who had been brought in especially to supervise an inexperienced workforce, lost no time in urging their work-mates to make wage claims; Koska, a wool-weaver, and Trieur, a wool-sorter, had no sooner arrived from Reims than they caused unrest in Roubaix and in Croix. In the Alais coalfield the *gavots*, people who had come down from the mountains around Cévennes, often on a temporary basis, were the most combative of all. In Paris 'the organiser and spreader of strikes never remained for very long in the same firm; he would go from one to the other without ever putting down roots'. These itinerant workers, ever prompt to take up their tools, the possession of which conferred on them real independence, along with a great sense of freedom, brought to the small 'shops' an atmosphere of insurrection

3. The expression, 'incomers' (*horsains*) is applied here to Frenchmen, but to ones who were born outside the area where they worked, men who came from another department or region.

that one would encounter nowhere else.

The roots of this instability are both individual and social. The former, unfortunately, cannot help but elude us. Familial antecedents and 'temperament' undoubtedly play a part. Age, as we have seen, is also significant, in that the strike leaders travel light and have not yet put down roots. Repression, whose main weapon is dismissal, serves to perpetuate mobility, chasing rebels from workshop to workshop and from town to town. Resentment itself makes them recidivist, so that the miners, driven out of Le Creusot after the 1869 strike, played a leading part in the one at Montceau in 1878; in the Haute-Loire, the spirit of unruliness was sustained by the colliers who had come from Allier; this was also the case at Prades (Ardèche), which had been quiet up until then, but which was disturbed by disruptive elements from Bessèges. No sooner had they registered for work at the glass-works of Saint-Léger than Lazare Fouchet, former president of the Montluçon strike committee, and his comrades, tried to stir up unrest amongst their new work-mates. This is how things were until the time when these wandering protesters became worn out by their efforts.

Mobility and Occupation

Mobility varied with the occupations involved. It was low amongst textile workers, who were content to go from one establishment to another. Thus Charles Bonne at Roubaix changed cloth-mill seventeen times; Baudelot at Reims, who was forever being sacked, was in the end unable to find work anywhere. Miners tended to restrict their movements to a single coalfield and within fairly modest limits; anyway, colliery people distrusted those whom they did not know. Conversely, the skilled workers, with all the self-confidence that possession of a trade gives, had no hesitation in covering the larger or smaller areas known to their profession. Millau, Annonay, Grenoble, Chaumont and Paris would be the typical stopping-off points in the itinerary of a disruptive tawer. Thus Pobé, at the age of twenty-two, had already 'done' seven localities. Claude Cartalier, 'a very good workman, remarkably intelligent, travels from town to town'; it is he who leads the strike of the Paris tawers in 1882, as well as the one in Grenoble in 1883. Indeed, all the leaders of the latter came from elsewhere: Joannès, aged twenty-six had been in Paris just a few days before; Fouillon, thirty-five years old, born in Romans, had arrived from Lyon: Herset, Sabatier and Desroches (twenty-six, thirty-six and thirty years old, respectively) had come from Annonay, where their activities had led to their dismissal. In 1889 Brun, sacked by Burdan's in Fontaine, for coming out on strike, had committed the same offence six months later in Grenoble. In Paris the agitation of the leather-workers, which was very intense between 1874 and 1876, was maintained by young workers aged eighteen to twenty-five, who would rarely stay more than a fortnight in the same place.

Yet the most mobile of all the militants were the metal-workers, who were also inveterate recidivists. Whichever town he passed through, be it Grenoble, Saint-Etienne, Le Creusot, the caster Saulnier, whom we know from his correspondence with Jean-Baptiste Dumay, organised union branches; in 1880, at the head of the Grenoble metal-workers' branch, he struggled for the ten-hour day; in 1882 we find him at Mâcon, where he founded the Union des Travailleurs. The mechanic Loenger, born at Montpellier in 1838, was politically militant from 1872 to 1882 in Lyon, which he left at the end of a strike, proceeding then to Firminy, where he supported the Libre Pensée; he was arrested there and sentenced to six months in prison in 1883. Henri Tricot, likewise a mechanic, born in Haute-Marne in 1852, turns up for the first time in Paris, in 1875, in a strike in Belleville which results in his dismissal; we come across him again in Lyon in 1882, in Saint-Etienne in 1883; employed in a workshop there, he was shown the door at the end of five days, 'as they didn't like his looks'. Feuillade was politically active in Lyon, then in Saint-Etienne, then in Bayonne; he returned to Saint-Etienne in March 1883, where his wife died, leaving him with two children; being no longer able to find work in Saint-Etienne, he left for Marseilles, where he played an active part in the dock-workers' strike there, before abandoning the militant life altogether. Jean Renaud, yet another mechanic, born in Lons-le-Saunier in 1841, worked at Lons, Saint-Julien, Paris, Saint-Denis, Lyon, Bessèges, where the police superintendant noted in his file that he had 'a very excitable temperament, concerning himself with revolutionary politics as well as with strike movements, which he seeks to instigate in the localities through which he passes'. Sacked by the factory where he was working in Bessèges, on 17 May 1886, he headed, for Marseille, 'saying that if he did not find work in that great city, he would cross the sea to Algeria'.

These leaders, of an above-average mobility and leading a relatively free and rootless existence, brought a breath of fresh air to the sedentarised working class, providing a yardstick against which to measure their own lives. Yet, in spite of everything, very few of these men ever strayed outside the relatively narrow limits of France itself. The astonishment of the workers delegates at the exhibition at Philadelphia, when they came across the sea for the first time, can only have been equalled by the wonderment of the Toulouse labourers, as described by Jaurès, at their first glimpse of Paris. The French workers' movement could not help having a slightly provincial air about it.

Good or Bad Workers?

Were the leaders good or bad workers? Did they have outstanding skills or did they rather belong to that 'envious mediocracy' which, according to Balzac (in *The Peasants*), constituted the mainspring of all the social movements? The prefect of Nice wrote as follows of the leaders of the *coalition* of masons, who were in fact young: 'The delegates who are at the head of the strikers ... are mediocre workers, conceited and boastful, who are intoxicated by their role and who regard the strike simply as a means to bring themselves to the fore.' At Roanne, in 1889, the dyers' strike was led 'by a hundred or so individuals whose notoriously bad conduct, whose incompetence and whose violent character caused them to be sacked from every factory'. Here too, of course, we have to depend on trial records. However, if we had to do a statistical count, our juridical sources would outnumber any other. For every Marçais ('idle and drunken'), the leader of the strike at Le Mans in 1882, for every Charlet ('cut-rate whitewasher'), for every Raoux ('hardly capable of doing the simplest repairs'), for everyone of the handful of 'bawlers at public meetings', how many good workers, described as the most capable and the best paid, do we hear of? I have already made the point that for skilled workers (and in truth the question I have asked is applicable only to them), professional skill, permanence even — consider the passionate contest held in the forge in Zola's *L'Assommoir*, in which Bec-Salé and Goujet competed to make the best bolts — are undeniably important elements in social prestige. In these milieux there will be strong resistance to both the theory and the practice of sabotage.

The Leader's 'Morality'

In trying to draw a 'moral' portrait of a strike leader, where the evidence to hand presents a still more awkward combination of truth and opinion, examination of the police record will supply us with some basic factual elements. The balance-sheet of previous convictions for the strike leaders in our sample is as follows: twenty-five had been convicted (thirty-nine times) for militant activities (i.e. impeding the right to work, assaulting a police officer, rebellion, and so on), of which twelve were for affiliation to the International, at the end of the Second Empire, or for participation in the Commune. Twenty-three had been convicted, generally in magistrates' courts for drunkenness, assault and battery, theft, filching food, trespassing, vagrancy, assaulting a rural policeman, and so on.

Some of the militants in our sample feature in both of these lists and pile up convictions, so that one has the impression of a rebellion against all forms of social order — rebellion of a kind that the present-day workers' movement neither wants nor remembers. Finally, in both categories, recidivism is common: Lescure, thirty-six years old in 1886, mucking-roll at the forge at Decazeville, had eight convictions for drunkenness, affray, hunting offences, and so on, before earning at the assize court seven years' imprisonment for participating in the murder of Watrin. Ferdinand Vivien, aged forty-four, a native of the Orne, nicknamed 'the strikers' captain' during the Paris navvies' *coalition* (August 1888), where he was sent down for six months by the Saint-Denis magistrates' court had already had seven previous convictions.

Even if one grants the incomplete nature of our sources, this collective police record still seems quite slim if one considers that from 1871 to 1890 there were 2,705 workers convicted for combination, and thousands for vagrancy. This suggests, on the one hand, that, apart from a small, passionate but restricted group of recidivists, of out-and-out firebrands, the great majority of our leaders are men who were quite new to dealings with the judiciary — and the same can be said of each new wave of leaders. This underlines once more, the discontinuity and 'spontaneity' of this epoch, as well as the fact that the strike was, relatively speaking, something out of the ordinary in the life of a worker.

On the other hand, these statistics, whilst they indicate a more or less equal division between convictions for militancy and those for 'common law' offences, thereby implying a definite overlap between the strike leader and the criminal, also suggest that there is a significant distance between the two. It would be interesting to compare these men with the Communards, whose police records, according to Jacques Rougerie, were particularly long. A strike, admittedly, is not an insurrection; it does not descend so far into the depths of society. But this recognition of the strike leaders' innocence brings out, if not a rupture, at any rate a distancing between the labouring and the 'dangerous' classes. As a phenomenon of an industrial society, a strike was more and more becoming part of a game with its own rules, and less and less of a revolt, or *rebelle*, to use the miners' term. And, from a more general perspective, one cannot help but wonder whether the anarchist celebration of theft as a revolutionary act, or the glorification of bandits as heroic models, were the sign of an increasing liberation or whether, on the contrary, they were not a backward-looking and desperate refusal of a morality which was in the course of being constructed, and whose triumph was made quite apparent in May 1968. The libertarian and surrealist aspects of the movement deeply shocked working-class militants, who no longer admitted that property was theft or that violence was a virtue.

The Different Types of Leaders

The characteristics presented above, which are wholly external in nature, tell almost nothing about a strike leader's state of mind, so that his motivations, representations and 'consciousness' elude us. At best they delineate a crude morphology, and one which in fact conceals a broad diversity. Indeed, we may differentiate between leaders in terms of the level of their commitment to the dispute, in terms of the nature, style and extent of their action and, above all, in terms of the length of time during which they continue to be militant.

1. Firstly, there was a Pleiad of fireflies, leaders for a brief episode, rebels for a day, making a single, unforgettable and possibly regretted outburst, a startling gesture which could perhaps crush them. These leaders were young and violent, they made no calculations and they had no plans; they emerged suddenly from out of the night for one brief moment, they made a gesture or uttered a cry, but their barely glimpsed faces were a mere blur. 'Ah! You think you are going to give us our marching orders', says Laplanche, a joiner, to the boss who is showing him the door, 'but it will soon be our turn to give you yours', he goes on, taking his colleagues out with him. Another cabinet-maker, Léon Gilbert, who was twenty-four years old, and who had been dismissed for insulting a comrade who was working overtime, went into a wine-shop, climbed up on to a stool and urged the workers to desert the

workshop. These hotheads, always ready to answer back, tend to be found in the small workshops, where the boss is near to hand and where a strike is easy to arrange. In the textile industry, with its grey, anonymous throngs, which are hardly conducive to individuality, the leaders tended to present themselves in clusters, often corresponding to work-teams or areas within the workshops, and forming around an original kernel, such as a young person, a foreigner (in the factories of the north, it is striking how often Belgians would play an instigating role) and, more rarely, a known union militant.

The groups would dissolve and disappear after a strike, for the law of the weaving-shops was hard on the leaders, and they had either to give in to it or leave. Thus, at Gisors, the four leading lights were two men and two women, the most passionate of them, Jean-Pierre Amps, twenty-two years old, Alsatian in origin. At Moreau's, in Le Cateau, there were five instigators of the strike, aged between sixteen and thirty-three; the oldest, Ernest Leplage, sent round a card requesting everyone to stop work; the youngest, Henri Duchesne, who went with him to the management office, explained: 'For a long time my father had been complaining that I was not making enough and, seeing that people here wanted a rise, I joined together with the workers to protest that we would not work after eight o'clock any more.' In a factory at Lille, there were three prepared to challenge things; namely, Plouvier, an ex-convict, his mistress, widow Cagniard, aged thirty-two, and their comrade, Hiroux, all of whom were taken before the magistrate court and charged with violence. Their manoeuvres were rudimentary, their strategies threadbare. Nineteen miners at Noeux, from twenty-five to thirty-six years old, were simply accused of having shouted out: 'Down with Aniel, we should fling him down the pit'; the special envoy of the Prefecture of Police, sent there in June 1877, when the authorities were jumpy about everything, was clearly upset to have discovered so little and wrote that 'they were not at all intelligent and by no means interesting from the political point of view'. We obviously share his disappointment.

Only when there was serious violence or when something turned out badly do we learn any more. Consider, for instance, the ten people charged at the time of the Watrin affair,[4] of whom, further-

4. After some considerable efforts, I managed to find the dossier on this affair. All the information and quotations which follow are taken from this. Watrin, an engineer at the Decazeville mines (Aveyron) was hated by the workers, who blamed him for their difficulties. He was defenestrated in the course of a demonstration at

67

more, only four were ultimately convicted: eight men, two women, from the ages of nineteen to thirty-eight (with an average age of twenty seven); six of them were married, with eight children between them; four were unmarried; several were reputed to be 'of easy morals', the women in particular: Eulalie Phalip, 'flighty and course mouthed when talking to her work-mates'; Marie Cayla, the wife of Pendariès, twenty-eight years old, whom her husband at the same time denounced and excused: 'Poverty', he said, drove her to sell herself'; she, for her part, bridled at this and said, 'he is jealous because he's old'. As labourers, they earned very little, particularly the younger ones. Adolphe Caussanel, who was nineteen, earned 50 sous doing piece-work, employed as a chaser at the forge. These people would often have to improvise. Lescure, for instance, worked as a strong man at the fair, whilst Marie Cayla, as we have seen, turned to prostitution. Impoverished existences of this kind were always dogged by illness and death: Lescure was already a widower at the age of thirty-six, and with two children to care for; Chapsal, a shoemaker, lost his first wife in childbirth, most of Marie Cayla's children died when very young, so that she was only left with a four-year-old daughter. Souquière's brother, a chauffeur at Decazeville, died in 1878; Bedel's father was the victim of a mining accident, for which his widow, who was employed in screening coal, had been awarded a pension of 300 francs a year by the company. There is nothing out of the ordinary about our sample, for many other biographies of militants would provide us with similar instances. The demographic study of workers' families, using family files based on state records, would enable one to arrive at mortality statistics, not only for the various occupations but for the proletariat as a whole. A project of this sort would, I think, be of great interest.

Of the ten who had been charged, five had had previous convictions, a relatively high proportion by comparison with what we have noted above. Lescure, a trimmer at the forge, and a positive bundle of energy, was a notorious recidivist and a born fighter, but a very good workman nevertheless; he had had eight previous convictions, one of which was a forty-day sentence for rebellion, the rest being for brawling, drunkenness, theft or petty larceny, for which he had received heavy sentences. Antoine Souquières was given a fortnight in gaol for stealing a litre of wine!

Decazeville town hall. There followed a six-month strike which had immense repercussions (in 1886).

Six out of the ten were illiterate, and Eulalie Phalip did not even know how to sign her name. Seven were originally from Decazeville itself, or thereabouts; three came from regions adjacent to it; namely, Lot and Cantal. Only two of them had 'travelled': Lescure had worked for three months in the Biétrix factory at Saint-Etienne in 1878; Antoine Souquières, who was twenty-nine, had done his military service at Briançon and had then tried his luck in Paris; he worked there from 1881 to 1885 as a waiter in a restaurant, but this can hardly be described as a very lucrative adventure for in July 1885 he returned to Decazeville from Paris on foot, registering as a labourer in the mines. Of those charged only one was 'organised'; namely, Auguste Granier, twenty-six years old, the site foreman at Paleyret, a unionised worker who furthermore wrote to his wife: 'Long live the strike! Long live the social revolution!'

It is not hard to grasp from all this the suffering, humiliation and bitterness that had built up in these men and women who were in the avenging band that had killed Watrin. No doubt a large proportion of those who were 'leaders' for just one day were led in this way to take action, through resentment, repressed hatred and even lassitude, habitually timid people perhaps, who would very probably be astonished the following day at their own audacity. Yet no matter how primitive and fleeting this obscure sense of being exploited may have been, it is surely the necessary mainspring of every accession to political awareness.

2. The recidivists constitute a second type of leader, and their more frequent appearances before the guardians of law and order make them better known to us. These hard-fighting, hard-drinking, travellers, who reap and sow strikes wherever they go, are rebels who make no secret of their grudge against society. Their actions, wholly individual, are rarely organised but are intermittent and repeated. This type would seem to stem from two separate sources, which thus serve to perpetuate two different varieties.

The first type, which was still very common in those periods when the proletariat was expanding, and when peasant emigration provided a limitless number of labourers who were quite unaccustomed to industrial discipline, was restricted to the dangerous classes. Recent immigrants of this kind, with no roots and no family, unstable both by temperament and by situation, were 'primitive rebels' whose criminal record represents a mingling of infractions of every code, both to do with morality and to do with the workplace. Since they were very quickly eliminated from the big provincial factories, where selection of the labour force and surveillance were stricter, these intractable elements took refuge in situations that were more open; namely, in the ports, in building sites, in the suburbs of the big cities and in those of Paris in particular. They created a climate of violence in these places, where the class struggle was settled with ones' fists. Here are a few outline sketches of a number of leaders from the suburbs. Eugène Ratton, a journeyman, who was seventeen years old and a fiercely committed architect of the strike in the gas factory of Courcelles, was sentenced to six months in prison for a brawl with a non-striker; a difficult child, he had been sent to La Roquette as a young offender subsequently dismissed from a workshop for insubordination, and later imprisoned for theft. A small uprising occurred at Aubervillers, in a factory making chemical products, when the workers there were forbidden to go and have a drink; three young labourers, aged eighteen, nineteen and twenty-one, respectively, were the leaders of it, one of them being originally from Metz, the second from a village in Loir-et-Cher, and the third being from Paris. 'I'll drink if I want to', said the first, 'and as for you others, we'll have you drinking out of the sea itself'; his comrade, Gessien, said: 'I don't give a damn about the police; I am the terrible dark man of La Villette.'

The biographies which follow also present us with examples of out-and-out brawlers, but ones whose rebellion assumes a more developed character. Pierre Capelli, born in 1863 at Cavaso, in the province of Treviso, arrived in France when he was seventeen, to work as a navvy; he stayed first of all in Die, where he was sentenced in January 1883 to a fortnight in prison for assault and battery. He then went to Lyon, changed his lodgings three times, doing a moonlight flit each time. Dismissed yet again from a site for brawling with some French workers, he had barely registered somewhere else before he went with a French comrade to request the contractor to give them a rise; he walked about with a flag upon which he had inscribed 'Long live Italy!', he insulted the contractor, he fought like a madman in his attempts to resist being arrested by policemen, calling his fellow countrymen to come to his aid, some fifty of whom did in fact attempt to rescue him. Once brought before the magistrates court, he was sent down for three months. The prefect who had written to the minister of the interior, requesting Capelli's expulsion, described him as 'a quarrelsome fellow, always spoiling for a fight, with a very violent character; people even say that he is a dangerous man'.

What a life Prosper Bourguet lived! He was a powerful figure in the port of Marseilles, leader of the strikes of 1871 and 1883, and was an old salt on the Cendrars model. Born in Alais in 1841, while still an adolescent he organised the Cercle des Enfants du Gard there; when it was closed down, on the grounds that it was politically suspect, he made a profit out of selling off its library. He secured his first conviction at the age of fifteen (in 1856), which was eight days in prison for theft. Six other convictions followed, amounting altogether to four years, ten months and fourteen days in prison. Six months later we hear of Bourguet in Marseilles; a fraud (about which I know nothing) cost him another three months. He then boarded ship as a sailor, but being unable to resist the lures of smuggling, he won another year's imprisonment. He was again released, and we next hear of him aboard the *Asmodée*, where he rebelled against a superior. This was in August 1860, and it earned him two more years of prison. In 1864 the court on board the *Gazelle* sentenced him to a year's imprisonment for smuggling brandy onto the ship. He gave up being a sailor and became a docker again. He took an active part in the Marseilles Commune, was a member of the International,[5] was at the head of the coalition of port workers, and his authority and passion won him the reputation of being a 'formidable leader'; arrested on 24 April, the court martial of the Sixth Military Division gave him six months imprisonment and deprived him of his civil rights for five years. Upon his release, the newspaper *L'Egalité* employed him as an odd-jobman, but . . . he was fired for bad conduct two months later. During this same period, he left his wife for another companion, with whom he was still living, moreover, twelve years later. In 1883 he was again to be found at the head of the striking dockers, still very influential and active, giving of his all both with his voice and his fists. He was then forty-two years old.

He had to appear one more time in court, for impeding the right to work. His trial made quite a noise, for his lawyer was Maglione, the ex-mayor of Marseilles, and there numbered amongst the defence witnesses two general councillors, one deputy mayor and the president of the district council. It was a political matter, the republicans on the municipal council being ranged against the maritime companies and the prefecture. Bourguet, addressing the court, invoked Gambetta: 'If he who now lies in Nice were not dead, I would never have been summoned before the magistrates court.' Furthermore, he was acquitted, perhaps for the first time in the whole of his eventful life. From then on he 'settled down', and when some two

5. On Bouguet's participation in the International, see J. Maitron, *Dictionnaire biographique*, vol. IV, p. 388.

years later some unemployed workers came to ask him if he would assume the leadership of their movement, he refused, 'saying that he no longer wished to have anything to do with questions of this kind'. He was forty-four years old.

In the case of Chaussivert, a maker of wood-working tools in Paris, and Réal, a weaver and public letter-writer in Roanne, the forms that their disputes took were more consistent still, since, opting for organisation, the former became the secretary of the union branch, the other of an anarchist group. Born in the 1840s, each of these men remained in the thick of the struggle and, even when they were over forty years old, paid little heed, or so it would seem, to private, or at any rate to family, life. Thus Chaussivert offered the union meetings the protection of his bachelor's lodgings; Réal, who had married late, had no children. Their early years had not been easy, and they had had frequent brushes with the law. Chaussivert (1846–1912), a native of Autun, was convicted of assault and battery in 1886 at Aix, and in 1868 of bankruptcy at Autun. He took part in the Paris Commune, as a gunner and then as a police commissioner. When the Commune was suppressed, he was locked up for five years in Clairvaux, but he escaped. 'Taking refuge in Germany, he committed a burglary, for which he was extradited from Geneva, where he had fled and was earning a living making pieces of joinery. The German authorities sentenced him to three and a half years in prison for theft and handed him over to the French authorities, who took him back to Clairvaux.'[6]

Réal had had eleven convictions in the magistrates courts for theft, breach of a court order and vagrancy (one of these sentences, for theft, was for five years in prison). One day he would explain what a complicated mesh of circumstances his life had been, with the first conviction having given rise to all the others. Once it became publicly known that he had been a convict, 'he became the object of public scorn; he found that the doors of all the workshops were barred and bolted against him. This accounted for his numerous breaches of court orders. But in his conscience he had had nothing to reproach himself with . . . if he had not been rehabilitated in the eyes of the world, he had been so in his own, through the efforts he had made to work and through the sufferings which he had endured'. In 1876 at Roanne, where had come to settle at the age of thirty-five, he made the acquaintance of Marius Rausch, twenty-one years old and a chair-maker, a wanderer like himself, whose father

6. Maitron, vol. V, p. 86.

was believed to have died on a barricade during the Commune. Rausch was a diligent reader of Proudhon, whose ideas he did his utmost to spread: 'One Sunday of Corpus-Christi, he took the liberty of forcefully reproaching his boss because he was working on a temporary altar. Upon another occasion, he declared that he would never fight for France.' Rausch won Réal over, initiating him into the work of Proudhon. So it is that, one night in February 1876, we find both of them sticking up posters — some thirty in number — which Réal had copied out in his fine public letter-writer's hand, from a text dictated to him by Rausch. These posters celebrated the Commune, preached the abolition of authority and of property: 'Long live the social revolution! Down with all those who produce nothing and who merely consume! Long live the Social Republic!' The assize court in the Loire sentenced them to four years in prison and to a 50-franc fine. I do not know what became of Rausch, but Réal crops up again in Roanne, described as a public letter-writer and weaver, and a fiercely committed militant at the time of the strike of 1882. By this time Réal was definitively won over to the cause of anarchy; he was secretary to the group known as 'the Revolver' and was charged with exploding a bomb of dynamite in 1884 but was released for want of any solid evidence. Described as 'very intelligent', he drafted numerous reports and pamphlets for the revolutionary groups.

These biographies, and the last one in particular, demonstrate how forms of insubordination which are at first quite crude and individual may in time be transformed into a genuinely militant consciousness and commitment; they cast light, no matter how incompletely, on the shift from rebel to revolutionary. In every one of these cases we see an example of a libertarian, free spirit or outlaw. These men invariably came into conflict with society when very young, but repression and confrontation with the law, far from stifling them, simply served as a stimulant.

The other kind of established leader was typically Parisian. Such men are painted in less sombre colours and are reminiscent not so much of the world of Eugène Sue or of Zola as of that of Sébastien Mercier or of Monsieur Nicolas. We find ourselves in the cheerier world of the small Parisian workshops. Indeed, the capital is the domain of the worker who is just 'passing through', a plotter who earns a lot and spends still more, a wag who will celebrate Holy Monday, a loud-mouth and a hothead, who will go from one shop to the next, always making trouble and raising demands, picking up his tools and leaving at the slightest pretext. It was invariably the young itinerant workers — unmarried, rarely born in Paris and relative newcomers to the workshop — who led the *coalitions* of the leather-workers, the shoemakers, the saddlers, the tailors and also, to a lesser extent, the cabinet-makers. If they were sacked, these men simply started up again somewhere else. Thus between 1874 and 1889 we find Bergès, first a tanner and then a saddler, involved in half a dozen strikes in succession: 'He was always in the forefront of these sorts of thing'; around 1887, together with Lemaitre and Mauras, like him fierce enemies of the 'exploiters', he went on to found a revolutionary group, which was anarchist in tendency, called the Military Saddlers. One of the leaders of the metal-workers' strike at the Cail company, in 1881, was a genuine *Sublime*. His name was Jules Conrad; he was born in Metz, was forty-seven years old and a fitter; a widower, and the father of three children, he lived in furnished lodgings, and in the space of a single year he moved three times, each time leaving unpaid debts behind him. 'This individual, who only works four or five days a week, is an incorrigible drunkard who has left ... numerous debts behind him, in almost every place he has passed through ... one would have said that he was prepared to do almost anything, provided that one supplied him with money to buy drink.' In 1888 the cabinet-makers' strike was led at Jeanselme's by 'fifteen or so new men, who had only been on the premises for about three weeks', and at Lincke's, by Midy, a Belgian who had registered for work on the first of the month, and by Pira, his cousin, an old hand of three month's standing. At Krieger's, the strike was led by Guyon, an excellent workman who had become the leader of a work-team within a year on account of his talent, and who was very popular in the Parisian faubourg of Saint-Antoine. Guyon was a supporter of the tactic of general strike, a member of the group known as the Equals, and he had filled the 'Citadel' (as the Krieger company was called) with anarchists known as the Flat-foots, uproarious comrades who were 'in the habit of robbing the wine merchants who gave them credit'.The wine merchants took their complaints to Guyon, who, the management insisted, should either pay up or be gone. Guyon chose to go.

Réne Michaud, whom Denis Poulot describes as 'the heart and soul of the workshop, with a fierce energy for everything touching upon the question of rights', was a leader of this type, which inherits many of the features of *Le Sublime* or of *Le Fils de Dieu*, and whose behaviour and psychology are graphically described in Michaud's own autobiography, a priceless account of working-class

Paris at the beginning of the century.[7] A child of the *cité Jeanne d'Arc*, Michaud started out by making shoes in countless shops, in the thirteenth *arrondissement* in particular: 'We had not yet arrived at a period of security, when one could put down some roots. The very idea of long service filled the young people of that period with horror. For us, the old-timers were just a bunch of faint-hearted mediocrities, the boss's lapdogs. We ourselves were the last nomads of industrial labour and the number of shops through which I passed, my turnover, as it were, would lead some learned psycho-sociologist to describe me as a pathologically unstable individual . . . But since there was no regulation of apprenticeship, one simply had to use one's initiative instead.' Michaud also remarked: 'I was always amongst the first to preach revolt in the shops through which I passed.'

Jacques Valdour was to run across this type of leader again, after the war, 'from la Popinque to Ménilmuch', but more settled and stable. He has survived even into our own times, in the workshops of Belleville, where Louis Chevalier describes the sort of worker 'who claims the right to define his task, his labour, his timetable and indeed his life in his own time, and who regards the big factory, with its clocking-in, its regimentation, its assembly-lines, its work-team leaders, its noise, as a fall from grace and a kind of prison'. This type of worker, the timeless and stubborn bearer of a distant and deep-rooted tradition of independence, represents one of the pillars of the libertarian spirit.

3. With the type of leader who has a more long-standing commitment, we draw near to the *militant* in the modern sense. Three features may be said to characterise this type; namely, continuity of action[8], stress laid upon the importance of organisation and assertion of class-consciousness. For him a strike is simply an episode — albeit often a fundamental one, in terms of his initiation or as a way

---

7. *J'avais vingt ans. Un jeune ouvrier au début du siècle* (Paris, Éditions Syndicalistes, 1967).
8. The *Littré* dictionary only recognises the term *militant* as an adjective. 'Today', it observes, 'this is employed in the lay sense to mean "struggling", "aggressive".' *Robert* gives two examples of its usage as a noun, one of them taken from Malraux, the other from Aragon. Our dictionaries are, however, behind the times. The term was employed regularly at the end of the nineteenth century and the beginning of the twentieth. To appreciate this, one only has to leaf through Maxime Leroy's work of 1913. The *Dictionnaire biographique du mouvement ouvrier français* (vol. I, p. 23), emphasises the importance of duration in the definition of the militant: 'Thus slowly and painfully there emerges in the columns of this dictionary the notion of a working-class *militant*. A *militant* is not the worker who takes part in a movement occasionally nor who accepts temporary functions once only in a more or less stable organisation. *Militantisme* is synonymous with continuity.'

of proving himself — a means to an end, which will be more or less prized depending upon whether it is the economic or political path which is stressed the more, in a much wider and more multiform struggle. The domain covered here would be very extensive indeed, such that it would no longer be a question simply of 'strike leaders' but of the whole human armature of the workers' movement across a period of some twenty years. So as to avoid straying outside the boundaries of our present topic, I shall not describe this domain for its own sake but only insofar as it interferes with strikes. Nevertheless, every workers' leader has had to confront it at one time or another.

To remain a militant over a long period of time was a difficult business, given the absence or, at any rate, the weakness of an institutional framework, and of structures offering some sort of protection or welcome. Neither the unions nor the emergent parties were yet able to provide much of a loophole. Imbued with the ideal of direct democracy and haunted by a fear of despotism, the unions found the notion of full-time staff repugnant; they were always careful to restrict mandates to a limited span of time, and reflection was often forbidden. The expenses which were allowed for were modest to say the least; namely, 100 to 120 francs a year at the maximum, save in the case of the miners, who had very early on made their leaders salaried officials. Likewise, the socialists, whilst they handed out some fairly meagre stipends to the party faithful, in the municipal fiefs in particular (Commentry, Vierzon, and Roubaix above all), hardly ever allowed proletarians to stand for Parliament. It made no sense to talk of a 'career as a militant' before 1914 (and still less before 1890).

Under these conditions the real persecution suffered by the leaders rapidly wore them down. Five years or at best a decade of the activist life would represent a good run, at the end of which one would have to knuckle under or quit. Thus one finds some of the workers who for several years had led the struggle, disappearing without trace. There are, however, several instances of long service.

To last as a militant one would need, apart from an exceptional temperament and sense of conviction, a degree of economic independence. If the metal-workers, glass-workers, porcelain-makers, and the workers in wood, leather and books, and so on, were so persistent, it was because the highly skilled nature of their work together with a high level of geographical mobility generally gave them some security. Most of those who, having been born into lives of militancy at the end of the Second Empire, reassumed control of the workers' movement once the terrible days of the Commune had passed, and inspired the workers' movement up until the relief brought by the new wave of 1878–80, and sometimes beyond it, were people with a trade and an education, free-thinkers, enthusiasts for both organisation and writing, and often advocates of working-class candidature to Parliament. I have in mind here metal-workers like Loenger, Brosse, Robertson, Victor Delahaye and so on, porcelain-makers like Baudin (in Vierzon), Boudard (in Limoges), and in Paris, Chausse, a cabinet-maker and a militant up until the day of his death (1850–1935), Loth, a wood-worker, and Brébant, a piano-maker, and so on. Many of the long-standing anarchists were highly skilled professionals, such as Tortelier, a joiner; Bernard, a locksmith; and Willems, Couchot and Duprat, who were all tailors. Furthermore, if Ludovic Ménard was able, up until the day of his death, to combine with the exercise of his trade the militant activities described by François Lebrun, it was because the profession of slate-cutter was carried out as piece-work, in a very independent manner, with no fixed hours and sheltered by a work-team which was protective and had a strong sense of solidarity.

Heavy industry could hardly allow such a division of one's time. Indeed, it was quick to smoke out any rebels and to bolt its doors against them since it was so easy to find replacements. The only solution for a militant was to leave heavy industry altogether and head for a small shop or small business, the worker's refuge. Once they had been driven out of the factories, the die-hard militants became newspaper sellers (e.g. Basly, Fevez, Fauviaux),[9] pedlars (e.g. Dormoy, Mélin and Baudelot, Sourdeau),[10] artisans, shoemakers

9. Etienne Basly (born at Valenciennes in 1854), a miner, dismissed as a result of a strike at Denain in 1880, thrown out of the miner's cottage he occupied with his wife and four children, took refuge in modest lodgings 'to which poverty soon reduced him. To make a living, he turned to selling newspapers in the mining villages; the miners — even those who could not read — bought them from him out of kindness, but in the long run sales fell off and his poverty again became acute' (Arch. dép. Nord, M626/11, pièce 105, com. pol., 8 April 1883). Clément Fevez, born in 1845 in the Meuse, was a locksmith stove-maker at Roubaix. A socialist militant and later an anarchist and the leader of a strike in December 1882, he became a hawker after being sacked. Selling needles and thread, for many years, he also distributed socialist books and pamphlets around the countryside on his travels (Arch. dép. Nord, M 154/59, pièce 24). Élisée Fauviaux, born in Belgium in 1852, began as a school-teacher in a Bully-Grenay company school; dismissed as a troublemaker, he took to selling newspapers on the public highway. He was later thrown out of Anzin after the 1884 strike.

10. Jean Dormoy (1851–98), who began as a metal-worker at the St-Jacques factory in Montlucon, 'was sacked for making politics in the workshops. From that point on, he turned to selling oil, on a handcart, which he pushed from street to street' (Arch. dép. Allier, U, affaire Dormoy, 1883, pièce 71, Proc. Rép. 8 February

for the most part of hairdressers, whose booths remained genuine political clubs,[11] small traders, in the mining country in particular[12] and in the north especially, inn-keepers (e.g. Charles Bonne, Basly, Carrette, Lepers, Delory, Lefèbvre at Amiens, Deparis at Roanne, Treich at Limoges, Yzamblin at Paris, and so on). The inn, as well as being the 'people's parliament' (Balzac), was also its salvation.

In all of these cases what counted was the cohesion of the milieu, which offered protection and moral support to those leaders who were recognised as such, and which helped them to live. These might be professional milieu, but more often they would be local communities, and they would be less likely to be big towns, where an individual might waver and lose himself, than isolated industrial sites, where resistance to the factory would assume quasi-feudal forms of struggle. The leaders, who were prestigious figures, relied upon permanent structures, which would always be there to catch them on the rebound. Each strike would set in motion a primary and a secondary level of struggle, linking together close economic

---

and 26 April 1883). See also the letter from Lafargue to Engels, in *Correspondence Engels-Lafargue*, vol. I, pp. 112–13. After having served six months in Sainte-Pélagie prison, where he had been sent by the Moulins Assizes, he set up as a cobbler. Charles Mélin, born in 1854 and Léon Baudelot, born in 1835, both of them weavers at Reims, leaders of the collectivist La Défense des Travailleurs group, sacked from all the weaving mills after the great strikes of 1880, joined forces and became vegetable sellers and rabbit-skin dealers, whilst continuing propaganda activities in their new situation. Having sunk into poverty, however, they left Reims for Paris. Mélin first became a waiter; it was said that, in his bitterness, he planned to assassinate Jules Ferry; very troubled by this, the socialist group of Reims pleaded with him not to do so and sent him some money. He took a job on *Le Cri du peuple*, but then fell gravely ill with typhoid fever. His wife joined him and later Baudelot followed, having himself been reduced to poverty. Thereafter we lose track of them (the sources here include Arch. dép. Marne, 30 M 39 and 30 M 72). On Sourdeau, see Daniel Halévy, 1901, pp. 40–41. Dismissed for his role in the 1882 strikes at Montceau, he set up as a cutler and wine merchant. 'The company blacklisted his shop and no one dared enter it. Sourdeau lived as a pariah in that town where he had so many friends . . . To earn a crust, he travelled around selling his knives at country fairs, but he came back home every evening. That was the time when the boldest of the inhabitants would slip along to his shop to read newspapers and talk about the factory.'

11. In small-scale industry the militants sought to set up on their own account, like Boudin who became a potter at Vierzon. But the two major sources of refuge were hairdressing and cobbling, which seem to have required little training. It is in no way fortuitous that cobblers had a reputation for being notorious 'revolutionaries'; the explanation was that they were often rebels for whom their awls and lasts were keys to independence. In all the industrial towns, their workshops were socialist reading rooms and discussion centres. We may cite the examples of Georges Féline at Vierzon, Léon Lefèbvre at Dorignies (an inveterate conspirator) and Henri Mercier at Trélazé, who christened his shop the 'Anarchist Noah's Ark'.

12. At Decazeville, Jean-Pierre Blanc, born in 1847, an ex-miner who had become a commercial traveller, was secretary of the mine-workers' *chambre syndicale* in 1885, and in 1886 the workers asked him to lead the strikers' delegation.

— one has to bear in mind here the part played by the management's shops — and familial solidarities. Sometimes the real leaders would actually be outside the factory, men who had been thrown out of it and who, setting up anew in the tertiary sector, would often cut something of a figure and would lead a struggle which in some respects is reminiscent of that so stubbornly waged by Balzac's *Peasants* against the new proprietors who had emerged in the course of the Revolution.

Such militant nuclei existed around the mines and enjoyed a stability altogether rural in nature, in southern, republican France in particular, where the political tradition still betrayed its oppositional character. At Bézenet in 1878 the main pillars of the coalition were Gidel-Parent, a foreman in the mines, whose wife kept an inn; Cluze, a bootmaker; Gazet, a shoemaker; Philippon, a baker. The first three let their shops be used for meetings, whilst the last handed out bread to the strikers. At Doyet it was the deputy mayor, Fonlard, a retired school-master who had taken to dealing in coal, who would pass the hat around. At Decazeville, Establi, a shop-keeper, and Barbès, whose wine-shop served as a meeting place for the blacksmiths, played a similar role. At Montceau-les-Mines (1878), the young miners, who were the real force behind the movement, were supported by Guenot, a manufacturer of liqueurs; Baudier, a hatter, thirty-nine years old, a former employee of the Lyon railway who had been 'dismissed for his lack of discipline and for his incessant wage claims'; Robin, forty years old, a blacksmith; Petitgras, thirty-eight years old and a book canvasser; Boyeau, a hairdresser in the Rue Centrale; and Palat, twenty-five years old, a wine merchant at Blanzy, gave over their shops to the strike committees, watched over by busts of the Republic with Phrygian caps. At Sainte-Florinne (Haute-Loire), Fombel, who was a news-agent, gave the secretariat of the miners' union his financial backing and ran the strike of 1884. Apart from him, the general staff consisted of Retoret, an innkeeper; Boubon, who dealt in safety matches; and a municipal councillor by the name of Gasquet. At Noeux-les-Mines, Charles Demiselle, also known as Jules Simon, a publican, was regarded as the main inspiration behind the conflict which took place there, and he was sentenced to eighteen months in prison. An identical situation arose in Tarare, at the time of the velvet-workers' strike (from 12 October 1871 to 3 January 1872), whose committee met in the house of a man called Serre, who ran a café: 'It served as a refuge for all those individuals who, in the name of liberty, advocate those ideas which are most opposed to the public good.' Much the same thing happened at Cours, too, where in 1889 Brivet, the grocer, performed the functions of union treasurer. The police files in Bessèges (1886) allow us to analyse the various strata of the activist milieu, and it turns out that 35 per cent were tradesmen and artisans. Furthermore, I think it can be safely assumed that this cross-section is typical.

Beneath such ramparts, powerfully individual figures, with a flair for leadership and even for heroism, might well flourish. Consider, for instance, Maillard, who set in motion the action against piecework in the La Sentinelle mines in 1883, whom his comrades cheered and protected from the gendarmes. Consider, as a particularly striking example, Henri Marius, who inspired the miners of the Gard in the years between 1880 and 1890 and very probably beyond that date too. Born at Bessèges in 1859, his father unknown, Marius returned to his native town after military service, married a young widow aged twenty-one and had two children by her. He was not very well educated; the letters we have that are in his hand, scattered amongst the archives, are awkward in composition. He made good this deficiency through his native intelligence, his daring and his tireless activity. Although a small man — 'just five feet tall, with a slight tan, a thin face, drinking very little, cool in action' — his influence spread far and wide. He transformed the mines in Lalle, where he worked, into a centre of resistance, organising all the debarred men there. He was secretary of the joint *chambre syndicale* of Bessèges workers, and later of that of the miners, which was founded in 1887, and he organised numerous revolutionary meetings. An observation in the police records for 1887 has it that Marius 'recommended both strikes and social revolution, advocating any and every violent means. An active, enterprising man with a kind of ascendancy over a large proportion of the workers'. He led the 1887 strike, putting out propaganda in favour of the eight-day week. In the spring of 1890 he organised the May Day shutdown in the coalfield; he presented the workers' claims in very vivid terms, threatening to 'blow the boss's head off'. He was sacked; but, upon hearing the news, the mines in Lalle, then the coalfield, ground to a halt. The strike spread to the metalworkers and even to the spinners in Alaise, thus affecting more than 6,000 workers. A warrant ordering Marius to appear before the authorities was issued but he lay low: 'The guilty party must have hidden in the wooded mountain which overlooks Lalle; there he received the newspapers and gave orders. A number of strikers were responsible for ensuring that he was safe and, when any danger whatsoever threatened, Marius took refuge in one of the old mine shafts, where he went to ground like a rabbit. When night fell, he would retire to a friend's house to sleep, taking care never to sleep in the same house two nights running. Sometimes he would venture out on to the paths and even into the streets, but he would then be preceded and followed by his own "guard" and by messengers who would scour the terrain; he was even said to have worn a false beard and to have dressed so as to make himself unrecognisable.' He kept the police at bay, and finally they resorted to offering a reward for his arrest. Whether or not he was betrayed we cannot say, but he was arrested in the streets of Alais a few days later. Upon his leaving prison, a procession awaited and escorted him, with everyone singing the 'La Marseillaise'. It is difficult not to be reminded here of Jean Cavalier, of the Soubeyran farmhouse. The Cevennes region has a tradition of rebellion and of resistance to oppression in every shape or form, which is here incarnated in someone who is clearly an heir of the Camisards, and who opts quite spontaneously for the 'desert' road.

Whilst having none of the flair of maquisards of this sort, Rondet in the Loire, Basly, Lamendin in the Nord, Calvignac at Carmaux and Ludovic Ménard at Trélazé each ruled unchallenged for years. The union as an institution, adding its weight to the protection offered by the milieu, was soon to generate the sort of permanent official that the revolutionary syndicalists execrated and who, with the triumph of the second age of unionism, would entirely transform the nature and function of the strike.

The leaders' ideology still remains to be described. But it is difficult to separate this from a study of the movement in its entirety, which it informs as much as it serves as an expression of it. We find every tendency represented here. Reformist unionists advocated association, negotiation and legality — amongst their number, 'Monsieur' Rondet, the leaders in the mines (Basly and Lamendin) or metal-works (Criquelion, Doyet and Lagache) of the north, and a number of leaders in Paris, won over by possibilism. Their behaviour, their measured language, their well-groomed air, their ease in discussion, as much with the bosses as with the authorities (Rondet had 'good relations with the Prefecture' and was not cowed by government ministers), marked them out as men of order and of administration; they prefigured the leaders of the future. They would go on to become public figures to whom statues would be created and streets dedicated.

The 'political' leaders, for whom a strike was often nothing more than a means to promote the party, were to be found amongst the first members of the socialist parties, concerned above all to let a new language be heard. This was the case with the Guesdist militants from the Nord, from Roanne, from Allier (Dormoy is a typical example), the Blanquists, such as Lachize (from Lyon) Baudin, who was based at Vierzon and Boulé. One should also mention Emile Chausse, who belonged to the First International and who was later, from 1938 to 1935, a Socialist municipal councillor. For all of these men the strike represented an initial episode at the dawn of an existence that was to become increasingly bound up with political structures.

But the dominant ideology of these leaders — crude and instinctive amongst those who were only episodically involved, more developed amongst those who openly advocated anarchy — was resolutely libertarian. The greater number of them shared a common language, at certainly after 1882, in which the main themes were hatred of the exploiters, apologias for violence, a refusal to be duped politically, a celebration of strictly working-class forms of struggle, and of the strike in particular, and a belief in an approaching revolution. The militants of Lyon, a centre of anarchism, speak this new language with a particular intensity: men like Bernard, a locksmith; Bordat, Baguet, Dejoux, Courtois, who were all shoemakers; Crestin and Tricot, who were mechanics; and so on. In Paris there were Raoux and Leboucher, who were shoemakers; Bergès, Lemaître, Mauras and Mercier, who were saddlers; tailors such as Willems, Couchot and Duprat; joiners like Tortelier, Raimond, Franchet; and so on. There were also the militants of the Gard, those of Trélazé, and many others too. All of these men played a crucial part in strikes, which they held to be a crucial instrument of education, and in the development of the project of a general strike. Direct-action unionism did not yet constitute the 'official doctrine' of the French workers' movement, but already that movement lived it and breathed it.

4
Strike Methods

The workers of today have at their disposal a relatively varied arsenal of strike methods, which have been perfected over the years and which seek to achieve maximum results at a minimum cost to those involved. The weapons in that arsenal include warning strikes, strike-by-rota (grèves tournantes), go-slows, sit-ins, wildcat stoppages, and so on — and, very recently,'thrombosis' strikes. The workers carefully limit the amount of working hours lost (hence the very short average length of present-day strikes) and only use the general strike weapon with extreme caution. The general strike of May 1968 in France seems largely to have got out of the control of the strategic planning of the major trade-union confederations, even if they subsequently used their authority to ratify the desires expressed at the 'grass-roots'. Strikes today are seen as a means of applying pressure rather than as a mode of expression. As such, they are subject to strategic calculations involving economic, political and social considerations.

Around 1880 strikes were an infinitely plainer, simpler matter. They involved, above all, the collective desertion of the workplace for an indefinite period. Of the conflicts recorded between 1871 and 1890, 63 per cent belong to this category and only concern one single establishment. The reasons for this are twofold. Firstly, sudden strikes, whose importance in this period we have already seen, could not in any way be predicted. Secondly, strategic thinking on the various forms work stoppages could take was not as yet very advanced. Where such thinking existed, it concerned itself more with space than with time. Yet if the moment chosen for going on strike was determined not by a reasoned assessment of the likely outcome, as some were already advocating that it should be, but nonetheless by an empirical feel for the 'right moment', refined by many years of experience, its length was the chance product of the circumstances and the powers of resistance shown on each side.

Only a small number of strikes (around 10 to 15 per cent) involved any kind of choice, and this was itself restricted to two basic options, which were frequently debated and put to the vote at this time. The choice was between partial (and successive) strikes and a general (and simultaneous) one. For reasons of economy, efficacy and security, the former route was sometimes preferred. But the workers' fighting spirit, their desire to register their protest and their need to feel a sense of collective solidarity combined with a range of psychological, ethical and ideological motives to make them favour the latter solution. This was an age when the 'general strike' was in the air.

The Strike by Rota

The 'blacking' of enterprises one after another derives from the old *compagnon* practice of 'damnation', still very much in force in Lyon, which involved the 'blacklisting' or boycotting of a recalcitrant firm that was unwilling to comply with established agreements. Yet it differs from that practice in being offensive and multiple in character. It leads, in fact, in the direction of the modern strike-by-rota.

The prefect for the Nord noting the novelty of the practice in his own region, defined it as follows: 'Only some of the firms would be "blacked", whilst the workers in the other establishments would club together to maintain their comrades who were on strike. In this fashion, short of their being an understanding between all the employers, each of them would by turns be forced to agree to the workers' conditions.' This form of action was therefore economical for the worker, who always received substantial strike assistance from well-stocked fighting funds, kept up by the contributions of those who were still working. It required, however, very firm agreement and very strict discipline. It was always led by a trade-union organisation, and a rich one at that, and was narrowly limited to the cities (twenty-five cities in the period under consideration, chief among them Paris, which made up some 30 per cent of the total, and Lyon, which accounted for 27 per cent). 'The Parisian proletarians, better organised for struggle than those in the provinces, only call general strikes as a last resort. They proceed in a more methodical fashion and almost always achieve good results by the blacklisting of firms which will not keep to the rates set by the *chambres syndicales*.' This is the favourite weapon of the craft workers (e.g. cabinet-makers, tailors, tanners, Lyon silk-workers), working in small workshops that are easy to locate and keep a watch over. It is not a model suited to large-scale industry, where there are no known examples of it. Consequently, the strike-by-rota only mobilised small numbers of people, yet might stretch out over a long period.

These strikes which involved no risk were basically instrumental in character. They were not seeking to stir up emotions or to make a great show of numbers. They were aimed at getting results. Moreover, they were extremely effective and had the remarkably high success rate of 72 per cent. Their effectiveness was clearly based on the successful exploitation of inter-employer rivalry. This explains the tactics involved in the choice of enterprises to be blacklisted. If the list was sometimes arrived at by drawing lots, much more often a deliberate decision was made to isolate the large firms, whose unpopularity among the smaller ones is well known. These latter were always ready, whether out of necessity or by calculation, to let the big firms go under. Against these 'poor-makers', as the Lyon expression had it, a united front was easily cemented. The employers' only means of retaliation was the lock-out. This occurred in 19 per cent of such strikes, if one leaves out of account a larger number of failed attempts. But it too proved ineffective in cases where the small enterprises broke ranks. At Lille in 1881, during the lock-out in which the Compagnie de Fives-Lille was the prime mover, the small firms refused to lay off their workers and, in fact, took advantage of the situation to increase their sales and poach a number of clients. In the faubourg of Saint-Antoine in Paris, the small employers in the cabinet-making trade turned a deaf ear to calls for help from the Krieger company (the 'Citadel', as it was known), which they wished to see go under. It is even reported that some contributed to the strikers' funds. And finally, some wage-labourers seized on this temporary eclipse of the 'big concerns' to set up on their own account and run their own businesses. At such moments, the age-old dream of production cooperatives was born again, reflecting a long-standing spirit of craft rebellion against the monopolies and a deep-seated refusal of concentration which one finds at so many moments in French industrial history.

The authorities were very happy with this form of strike, which was infinitely more peaceful and restrained than the stormy mass walk-out: 'Thanks to this intelligent, reasoned form of organisation, which gives the workers hope and provides them with a means of earning a living, public order has not been disturbed for one moment', wrote the prefect for the Nord. On another occasion, when called upon to instigate proceedings against the workers by blacklisted employers, he refused on the grounds that the new system seemed to him preferable to the violence that had prevailed in the past and the minister supported his decision.

The employers, by contrast, feared this method like the plague, since it left them powerless. They too were forced to organise in their turn and such strikes gave birth to employers' associations, fighting funds and financial solidarity pacts. In retaliation at the strike-by-rota called by the cotton-twisters, Lille employers formed the Cotton-Producers' Committee. Each member had to pay 25 centimes per spindle per week and, when there was a strike, they received 15 centimes. At Armentières the formation of an employers' association in the weaving industry came about as a response to a succession of *coalitions*. In the end the factory-owners tried to have the authorities admit that the procedure was illegal. It is interesting to note that on 31 July 1963 a law was enacted which prohibited the strike-by-rota (in the public sector only), condemning it as particularly harmful and disruptive.

From the Generalised to the General Strike

In spite of the material advantages of the strike-by-rota, the workers tended increasingly to prefer the method of the simultaneous downing of tools. The former type was prudent and ordered, progressing by stages in a piecemeal fashion. Yet not only did it reproduce the division of the workshops instead of breaking it down, it was also without prestige, without warmth, without pageantry and therefore deprived the strikers of psychological satisfactions that were as important to them as success. It robbed them of the exhilarating feeling, which stemmed from sheer strength of numbers, that they were a force to be reckoned with; it frustrated their desire to be together, their need for a festival, which could not be had without the crowds and noise that were a part of so many industrial conflicts at the time. And we must also remember that the libertarian conception of the strike was less concerned with the immediate results of the action than with its revolutionising, revolutionary power. Lastly, the emergence of large-scale industry rendered obsolete those strategies that were conceived on too small a scale. For all these reasons, in practice as well as in theory — indeed both were interwoven — the 'general strike' gained ground whilst its meaning, which was in fact still rather vague and open to a variety of interpretations, was modified. It is this change in meaning which we now have to attempt to describe and understand.

There is a first period, marked by scepticism about the usefulness of strikes, in which the expression 'general strike' simply refers to a technique of stopping work characterised by simultaneity ('the same day at the same time'). In theory the workers' organisations declared their hostility to it: 'Emphasise all the progress that the *chambres syndicales* have brought about in terms of workers' rights without having recourse to strikes', wrote the Paris tailors' union in 1872; 'combat general strikes and accept only partial ones — and these latter only as a last resort'. Since the strike was an evil — 'the augmentation of misery', as Bonnal, the Paris tanners' delegate at the Lyon Congress called it — it was only right that it should be limited.

However, in practice, the tactic was widely used, most notably by the corporations in the building trades — the masons, carpenters, roofers and so on — who needed to hit hard and swiftly at the beginning of each campaign. In 1872, when the wood and stone-workers were between them responsible for 46 per cent of the conflicts, what were called 'general' strikes made up 13 per cent of total stoppages. It was the same in 1876. In that year, a rumour went round Paris that there was going to be a general strike in the building industry, brought on by the euphoria over the Exposition Universelle and the loan the city had taken out for that purpose. What was in fact about to take place were carefully planned general strikes, reformist in their objectives and narrow in scope, each affecting a single trade in a single locality. Hence their relatively modest dimensions, the maximum number involved being 2,500 at the time of the carpenters' strike.

Outside the building trade, contagion was more the order of the day than conscious decision, and it provoked *generalised* rather than *general* strikes. Such strikes varied in their profiles and had boundaries that were vague since they were, in part, accidental. One strike in 1871, which had started in a weaving mill in Rouen, spread to twenty others in six neighbouring communes, and also affected some spinning mills, growing tenfold in four days (350 strikers on the morning of 4 November, 3,600 on the evening of 8 November). This is a classic scenario, found to a greater or lesser degree in all the strikes in large-scale industry (mines, textiles), which at the time lacked any decision-making body to give them a solid structure. The best example of this is the great strike wave from 1878 to 1880, which had a markedly epidemic character.

Whether by conscious decision or by contagion, the tendency

towards generalisation was, in fact, the most notable feature of this particular upsurge; everywhere the rank and file got out of the leaders' control. In Paris in October 1897 the joiners left their workshops four days before the date officially set, as if they could not hold out any longer. At Roubaix in April 1880 the *chambre syndicale* of which Charles Bonne, an advocate of the partial strike, was secretary, began by 'blacking' two establishments, but the action developed into a veritable whirlwind, sweeping 40,000 workers in fourteen communes and 325 separate establishments before it. The prefect, who was at this very same time so concerned to emphasise the progress which the 'blacklisting' method represented, noted that the conflict had passed out of the control of the *chambre syndicale*: 'The contagion of example has caught up a great number of workers in its sweep and the strike has become generalised.' Often young people were the driving force within such upsurges, as at Reims, for example, where the 'reachers in' were the first to come out or at Troyes, where 'it was the children who set an example'. At Lillebonne, the women and children were the first to rise up against a concerted reduction in wages by the factory-owners of the valley. It is as though sensitivity and intuition were in this case factors which helped to spread a resonating wave among the other workers.

The barriers between groups of workers were also becoming less important. Not only did workers in different trades come out on strike in rapid succession, one trade following in the wake of another — which was of course quite common — but they also attempted to coordinate their actions. In Reims, a single *chambre syndicale* brought together all the various trades in the building industry. The same happened in Grenoble within the metal-working industry and in that city the Workers' Federal Association was also set up, which was to have the *Révolution Sociale* as its organ. The Paris joiners launched a plan to set up a federation of building-workers. In Marseille, to support the striking marble-workers a committee was formed that brought together delegates from all the unions in the city. At Troyes, breaking down the sectional loyalties of the crafts, the workers called a 'General Meeting of the Corporations on Strike'; according to the prefect, they even 'went so far as to speak of a general strike'. Whilst the fine old idea of federation was winning out at the Marseilles Congress, the militants took advantage of the conflicts that were going on to stress the 'generality' of the struggle: 'There is a general movement in France. Everywhere the workers are raising the same demands as you.' The spontaneous movement of the masses and the carefully thought-out activity of the militants who had issued from their ranks came together to broaden the consciousness of the workers and give their struggles wider dimensions.

The idea of the general strike actually emerged in two separate milieus, which were subsequently to be hotbeds of its development: the mines and the Paris building industry. The joiner Tortelier is sometimes credited with a sort of paternity in respect of the idea, but he did in fact have a number of precursors. As early as 1879 Jules Cazelle, the chairman of the joiners' strike committee, was advocating the idea of a corporative general strike: 'We shall make the whole of France rise up if we have to . . . It is possible, even probable that our fellow building-workers will take a decision to stop work. The strike would then cover all the workers in the building trade: masons, stone-cutters and sawyers, brick-makers, tilers, roofers, painters, plumbers, and so on.' At the same time, Cazelle formulated the conception which provided the basis for the general strike idea, the power of the producers: 'The masters will give in to us because we are the producers, and when hands are not put to work, capital falls.'

In 1880 in the mines of the Loire, where there was a certain amount of unrest (2,000 workers in the Firminy coalfield had gone on strike), the miners were contemplating 'an agreement between all the miners in the Loire fields and even with the Belgian miners, and calling a general strike if the companies do not accede to the demands put to them'. In both cases what was involved was a general strike within a corporation, the scale of the action being variable, but always capable of being extended. In each case the objectives of the strike were predominantly concerned with wages and conditions.

However, if strikes were undergoing an overall re-evaluation, as we have described above, the partial form was still favoured in the higher echelons of the workers' movement. The Reims Congress reaffirmed its preference for 'blacklisting'. The rival congresses at St Etienne and Roanne both concluded, in more or less the same vein, that in spite of all its virtues, the strike remained of secondary importance in the workers' struggle for emancipation. For the possibilists, too, 'Salvation and emancipation can only come about by our uniting under the banner of the Workers' Party'. The Guesdists did perceive the revolutionary possibilities of the general strike in this period, and in *L'Egalité* of 2 June 1880, we read: 'General strikes will remain fruitless so long as they remain limited to one locality and one industry. Not until they take on a general character and make all the working masses of the country rise up will they bring positive results'. But, preoccupied as they were with avoiding 'libertarian and therefore liberticide' practices, they hedged the workers' initiatives about with so many preliminaries as to render them impossible. Moreover, party-building and electoral matters would very soon absorb all their efforts.

The anarchists too seemed hesitant. At the regional congress in St Etienne, which had strong libertarian leanings, Rodary, a metal-worker, advocated 'the system of general solidarity strikes' as an alternative to the ballot box. The theme found hardly any echo among the other speakers. Emile Gauthier declared to the Lyon shoemakers 'that strikes were not considered an effective means of achieving emancipation by the anarchist revolutionaries, but that while waiting for the moment at which to liberate ourselves by seizing hold of the means of production... there were good grounds for encouraging strikes which prepared workers for struggle and spread hatred of the bourgeoisie and the masters among the masses, together with the spirit of revolt against ex-ploiters'. At Lyon, the notoriously libertarian Bernard sketched out before the locksmiths a plan for a rational strike, which involved gathering together information and funds and then 'beginning a partial strike by "blacklisting" several of the large workshops'. In 1882 and 1883, the strike-by-rota was considered more effective than the general strike in all the trades most impregnated with revolutionary fervour, both in Lyon and in Paris. And when, at the end of one of these conflicts, Bayet, an anarchist shoemaker from Lyon, announced that the workers 'have to organise for revolution because a strike cannot achieve our goal', the opposition of the two terms 'strike' and 'revolution' shows that the two were not yet classed together in the minds of the workers.

In the years which followed, however, the general-strike idea gained ground in the milieus where it had first emerged; it began at the same time to find its way into other sectors, notably the textile industries and pass into general awareness there. Among miners, the Anzin strikes (1884) and, to a lesser degree, the strike at Decazeville (1886) produced new advances in corporate consciousness. The first had hardly begun when the union of the Loire miners attempted, by way of the prefect, to put pressure on the minister for public works to mediate, arguing 'that if the company (Anzin) would not be reasonable in its demands, the other coalfields might well take up the cause of their fellow-workers in the Nord.' This hope sustained the Anzin strikers and, at the beginning of March, Basly declared

that 'if we are unsuccessful, it is very possible that the Miners'
Congress, meeting at St Etienne . . . will declare a general strike of
all French miners'. On 24 March the delegates from the coalfields'
thirteen divisions meeting at Denain made 'an urgent appeal to all
their brothers in the mining regions, inviting them to take the
measures necessary for a general strike as quickly as possible'. There
were the beginnings of an attempt to put this plan into operation
when, on 30 March, 400 miners at Sainte-Florinne, a remote corner
of the Haute-Loire, voted to strike out of solidarity, arguing that 'if
the strike were general throughout France, the miners would address themselves to the Chambre des Députés'; as for detailed
demands, the workers only presented these some days later. But this
was as far as any spreading of the action went: the meeting of the
miners' delegates in St Etienne on 10 April was content simply to
send off an ineffectual telegram to the minister of the interior. For
his part, the prefect for the Nord judged that this failure would have
the effect of 'preventing any attempt to call a general strike from
succeeding for some years, . . . which is no small benefit'. In fact,
the Decazeville strike, which had much more impact upon public
opinion than the Anzin strikes, aroused only a faint echo among
other miners, an echo deadened by the resentments inherited from
the previous dispute. In the years which followed, the National
Miners' Federation of France, itself undermined by dissensions
between the Nord and Loire regions, maintained only a precarious
existence; the period saw a general withdrawal into the individual
coalfields, as can be seen in the disputes of 1889 (Nord and Pas-de-
Calais) and of 1890 (Loire). Moreover, the miners' general strike
was resolutely reformist; it was 'an exceptional means for applying
pressure, directed as much against the companies as it was against
the authorities and Parliament'.[1]

By contrast, in Parisian working-class circles it took on an
increasingly revolutionary shade. Amongst the tailors, for example,
the executive committee, in conflict with the *chambre syndicale* (or
the 'senate', as the strikers mockingly called it) which favoured
'blacklisting', hailed the general strike as an instrument of proletarian emancipation. In 1887 a variety of corporations, foremost
among them all the different trades in the building industry, called a
public meeting 'against unemployment' in the Salle Favié. They
considered a number of different actions and announced: 'If these

1. R. Trempé, 'Le réformisme des mineurs français à la fin du XIXe siècle', *Le
Mouvement social*, Oct.–Dec. 1968, p. 95.

fail, measures are to be taken to bring about a general stoppage of work in Paris.' According to *La Révolte*, 2,000 people were in favour of the idea.

In the same year, Combomoreil, a stone-cutter, and Berger, a sawyer, both of them Parisians, presented a resolution to the Second Congress of the National Federation of Trade Unions in Montluçon, to the effect that the corporations should be called upon to 'look into the question of a general halting of work, . . . in view of the fact that partial strikes have not as yet been able to achieve complete success in forcing the exploiters to respect the just demands of the workers'. The resolution was adopted.

The expression 'general strike' now spread into diverse sectors of industry. In 1883 the dockers of Marseille closed a meeting with cries of 'Long live fraternity! Long live wisdom! Long live the general strike!' In 1884 the shoemakers of Tours heard its merits vaunted by a foundry-worker called Gauthier. At Voiron, during a *coalition* of weavers in February 1884, 'men went through the streets moving from factory to factory shouting "general strike!"'

Finally, the appearance of the term in the textile regions of the Nord was a sign that the idea had passed into popular consciousness. 'We want the strike to be general', said Langrand at St Quentin. 'We want our demands to be accepted first of all by the industrialists of St Quentin, then beyond St Quentin and even abroad. It is a general movement, and it may as well begin here as anywhere else. Others will follow our example.' In the streets of Fourmies, the weavers chanted: 'Poverty. Bread or lead . . . Long live 93! Long live the Social Republic! Long live the general strike!'

From 1888 onwards the economic upswing, stimulated by the Exposition Universelle, the revival of international relations between workers and a new, large-scale strike wave both in France and abroad, produced yet another leap forward for the idea: the general strike ceased to be a tactic, a technique, and became instead a priority. For some it even came to be considered the great means of achieving emancipation, even the revolution itself. The strikes in the Paris building industry in the summer of 1888 played a considerable orchestrating role in this phase of development. The navvies were joined in that action by contingents of carters, demolition workers, joiners, painters, masons, cabinet-makers and also, curiously, café-owners and hairdressers in revolt against the employment agencies. Some of the latter formed the General Strike Committee, whilst Tortelier, Franchet and Raimond made efforts to promote a general movement in the building trades. Not a day passed without the subject being raised at public meetings, some of which were called especially to debate this issue. The expression passed into everyday parlance and increasingly became associated with the idea of 'revolt' and even of 'revolution'. Tennevin advocated 'the general strike, a revolt of all workers', Boicervoise spoke of it as 'a precursor of revolution' and the cabinet-maker Lamothe announced that he was a 'supporter of the general strike, which would be the beginning of revolutionary agitation'. A motion passed at a public meeting in Marseilles committed the navvies to 'stay firm to the end, so that they may bring about the general strike, which will lead the people to social and economic revolution and the suppression of the employer class.' In all these texts the general strike appears as the trigger to a revolutionary process whose subsequent course still remains obscure.

The anarchist militants in particular, along with the Blanquists, became staunch advocates of the idea. Their role in the crystallisation and rise of the term is of the utmost importance. At the Congress of the National Federation of Trade Unions at Bordeaux in October 1888 it was Boule, a Blanquist whom we have already met in the navvies' strike, who, supported by Raimond, a joiner comrade of Tortelier's, proposed 'the sudden stoppage of production for only twenty-four or forty-eight hours, in a branch of industry chosen at random, throughout the length and breadth of France as a means to whipping up a formidable reaction within the working class, sweeping it along and making it overturn the whole capitalist social edifice'. The resolution adopted by this congress illustrates the amazing rise of the strike concept, so disparagingly treated only some ten years before: 'In view of the fact that capital . . . is nothing if it is not set in motion by labour, and that therefore by refusing to work, the labourers would be annihilating at a stroke the power of their masters and in view of the fact that the partial strike can be nothing more than an instrument of agitation and organisation, this congress declares that only a general strike, that is *the complete cessation of all work, or the Revolution*, can set the workers on the road to their emancipation.' It seems astonishing that a congress with a Guesdiste majority should have passed such a resolution. There were, admittedly, some objections, which revealed sources of future conflict in embryonic form. For example, Jourde, a Guesdiste from Bordeaux, argued that, 'if a general strike could be called, it would be the Revolution that was being accomplished. The workers are not, however, well enough organised as yet to declare the Revolution . . .; the question of its organisation is a very serious matter'. The POF, which had not as yet made its position clear, was about to do so. At the Lille Congress of 1890 it condemned the general strike and went on to condemn the Federation of Trade Unions that was meeting at Calais. Henceforth, as is well known, this question was to become the main bone of contention between socialists and syndicalists. In 1894, at Nantes, it led to the definitive break-up of the Federation of Trade Unions, the collapse of the Guesdiste attempt to secure domination of the workers' organisations and the end of the process begun at the Marseilles Congress with its project for a 'Workers' Party', which now shown to have been based on a misunderstanding.

The idea of a general, concerted stoppage throughout the whole of France found concrete expression in the demonstrations of February 1889 and, particularly, in the May Day marches of 1890. This latter may be considered a dry run for a first national general strike. By taking the initiative in what they announced simply to be a 'day off work' (but what was a voluntary day off work for the workers if it was not a strike? — and this indeed was what the majority of them understood it to be), the Guesdiste and Blanquist revolutionary socialists seem to have been seeking to respond to the fighting spirit of the workers and also to channel it in a certain direction. Hence the suspicions aroused among the anarchists, who were hostile to what they judged to be an exercise in recuperation, and the anarchists' repudiation of measures they believed to be the beginnings of a dialogue with the authorities and the setting in place of the dreaded machinery of reformism. They acted vigorously to ensure that the masses, who had descended on the streets, kept the initiative and that the return to work did not take place in an ordered, slave-like fashion, but in the kind of confusion properly reflecting a state of rebellious, unappeased desire.

Whatever its limitations may have been, May Day 1890 projected the image of the national general strike. It showed that it was possible and at the same time aroused in some the hope and in others the fear that it might take place. It is a very important date, and it gave powerful impetus to the idea of the general strike both in the sphere of language and that of imagery. The list of references to the idea from this point on would be very long indeed and, since it began to proliferate at a great rate, such a list would inevitably be incomplete. Some fifty localities would be on it, as would most trades, particularly the miners and slate quarrymen, the workers in the glass and gas industries, the wood-workers, the building workers and even the textile workers, who, before returning to the

Guesdiste fold, were powerfully attracted to the general strike: as early as 1884 the weavers of Roanne were publicly advocating the idea. 'Strikes', they said, 'will only really be serious when they become general strikes.' In 1890, at the regional congress of the Lyon textile workers, the following proposal was adopted by eleven votes in favour to sixteen abstentions: 'This congress . . . resolves that it is necessary to organise a general strike using all the means at its disposal.' By contrast, the metal- and leather-workers and those in the book-printing trade, distanced themselves from the movement for the time being.

Now that we see it on the way to becoming banal, at least as an expression, the phenomenon will be of less interest to us here. From this point on, however, two things will claim our attention. The first is the diversity of contents given to that expression; these clearly vary according to the different speakers, who give it neither the same temporal nor spatial extension, nor the same ultimate goal. The second is the resistance the idea meets with, the way this idea, apparently so simple and grandiose that it should have set the whole world alight, merely marks time; in short, then, the extreme difficulty which was encountered when proceeding from concept to execution. There was no successful general strike before 1914. As is well known, 1920 was to be a tragic failure. In June 1936 the great festivities which accompanied the arrival to power of the first socialist government in France, gave birth to a different sort of model. When all is said and done, the general strike that was closest to the revolutionary syndicalist plan was, in many ways, that of May 1968.

In this chapter it has been our aim to locate a transformation process, in which strikes moved from being seen as marginal and much-disparaged phenomena to assume a supreme, central position. This is why we have described the strike phenomenon in the somewhat fastidious detail of a history of small, individual events, striving to trace out the everyday course of development both of language and actions. But to describe something is not to explain it. It is this fact which constitutes the historian's drama: when the patient work of reconstruction is over, the question still remains just as it was; the *how* is not the *why*. It is hardly even possible to discern what is cause and what effect; in this case, it seems, however, that practice precedes theory. The experience of the generalised strike precedes the theory of the general strike; a glimpse at the power of the strike gives rise to the thinking about all its possibilities. But, in its turn, this thinking gives the strike its impetus, its breadth and power; it transforms spontaneity into will, empiricism into a plan. The strike would be nothing without its theory. From this stage onward, this theory will make a prodigious leap forward, to the point where it will come to seem utopian.

The prior, precedent character of practice leads us to consider the role of spontaneity in history and in the workers' movement in particular. The retrospective influence of Leninist voluntarism has sometimes caused this to be, if not denied, then at least underestimated. It seems, however, that in the case under consideration here, the impulsion does not come from a central organisation, which simply did not exist, but from below, from the depths of a collective psychology whose undercurrents are, to be sure, very difficult for us to discern. We have neither the historical material nor the methods to perform such a task. By definition, we know only events, those things that have happened, that have entered history.

But how does change come about? How are new social developments born? In describing the various changes the strike phenomenon goes through, I am aware that it is just such questions that are raised; I am, however, less sure that I can provide any clear answers.

5
Participation in Strikes: Strikers and 'Loafers'

The effectiveness of a strike depends in part on the unanimous commitment of those involved and on that commitment lasting over a long period. Such commitment is the product of conditions that are as much material as psychological. Without doubt, holding out is a question of money, but it is not a question of money alone. Why are there splits and weak points in every strike, people who do not feel involved or do not wish to be? Why do some choose not to strike? The question of the non-strikers, the militants' great bugbear, raises the question of the limits of solidarity, of the cracks in the collective consciousness. The study of absences, attitudes of passivity and resistance is an indispensable complement to the study of any social or political movement.

An Overall Assessment

The precise measurement, in figures, of participation in strikes is not easy. Our sources often omit to mention the total number of workers in a factory or the total in the particular category involved, especially where short disputes are concerned. I have nonetheless tried to make such a measurement wherever possible, by dividing the highest figure for the strikers into the number of workers in the corresponding category. In only 24 per cent of the strikes (710) is it possible to arrive at a percentage figure; these are in general small-scale actions which are easy to gauge. Forty-two per cent can be qualitatively assessed, without exact figures being possible, as either total or partial strikes. Finally, in 34 per cent of cases, no classification of any sort is possible. Our analysis of levels of participation will therefore necessarily be rather rough and ready.

The first clear finding is that partial participation is more common than total participation (by 52 per cent to 48 per cent, respectively). Absolute unanimity is difficult to achieve; more often than not there is a part of the workforce that is undecided or will not go along. Yet, on the other hand, where they can be measured, levels of participation are high. Strikes may, in the first instance, be made by minorities; when they do break out, however, they produce a strong knock-on effect and display a great power to draw others along or force them to join in. It is, then, the non-strikers who appear to be in a minority; they form a residual fringe, the nature of which it would seem we ought to investigate. However, this second remark must be tempered by the consideration that the participation rates we possess are, for the most part, figures for small disputes, where unity is easier to achieve. Strikes within a single establishment or a single category of workers involve many less defections than generalised strikes, whose extended nature multiplies the risk of workers pulling out of the action or of manoeuvres on the part of the employers. In terms of immediate effectiveness alone, general strikes are always something of an adventure.

We must also note that defensive strikes come nearest to achieving full participation: protest mobilises people more effectively than making fresh demands on an employer. It is moreover the case that semi-skilled workers display greater unity than skilled workers and much more than unskilled labourers, but also that participation rates are highest at the lowest salary levels: above 3 francs per day, partial strikes are the most common form. These latter are at their highest levels in the chemical and food industries (which are not highly skilled) and in the wood and (stone) construction industries, where there were a lot of prolonged strikes. Total strikes are most common (in descending order) in the printing, glass, porcelain, textile and metallurgical industries.

Too many interwoven factors come into this distribution pattern for it to be easily explicable, and it would not be possible to draw any conclusions from it as regards the psychological make-up of the different trades. The forms of total participation among the book-printing workers are not the same as they are among the textile workers, nor are the underlying reasons for unity. In the former case we are talking about strikes within a single category of worker, which are limited in scope but totally solid; in the latter case, of strikes involving a whole establishment in which the very structures of the industry make for uniformity. In textiles, low wages that were all more or less equally mediocre and working conditions that had a levelling effect, conspired to produce an undifferentiated mass of workers, quick to rise in collective anger, following like sheep once any movement was under way. These remarks apply to an overall level of participation which we have assumed to be static over time. However, this is rarely the case. When a strike goes on for any length of time, the level of participation in it necessarily fluctuates.

Strike Profiles

These fluctuations can be seen in the profiles we have been able to draw up with the help of police records.[1] Several examples of these are shown here (Fig. 4).

Let us examine the phenomenon schematically. We see first that solid, perfectly rectangular profiles, reflecting a perfect unity from beginning to end, are extremely rare (see, for example, Fig. 5, no. 1). More often we encounter two rectangles side by side, either in descending or ascending steps, depending on whether there was unity at the beginning of a strike or in the return to work. The first type is characteristic of sudden, defensive strikes, in which the enraged workers staged a mass walk-out, even though they might simply return to their workshops the next day in defeat and disorder. The second type is indicative of a different process: when a more compact group of workers forms around the initial protesting group, the employer may decide to cut his losses by coming to an agreement with them; this ordered return to work is then sometimes a sign that a strike has had a satisfactory outcome.

These simple profiles are produced in disputes that are narrowly circumscribed both in time and space (they are generally limited to a single establishment). The longer and more drawn out the disputes, the more their profiles are complicated and uneven. The graphs then vary in the number of 'steps' involved. Each will have a different surface area and there will be uneven jumps between the levels, revealing moments of hesitancy and multiple splits within a strike. It is possible for there to be a large number of steps. The compact profile of the Anzin strike (Fig. 4 no. 9) — in which the distance between the minimum and maximum number of strikers is only 49 per cent and which, after some tentative beginnings, remained absolutely stable for some twenty-five days — may be considered

1. When a strike lasted for any length of time, the variation in the number of strikers was often followed with a great deal of attention, as a matter of symptomatic significance; police commissioners carefully collected the details from the employers' clocking-in cards. As a result, we are quite well informed of the pattern of the major strikes, especially in the mines, where the figures for the number of men going down are easy to check.

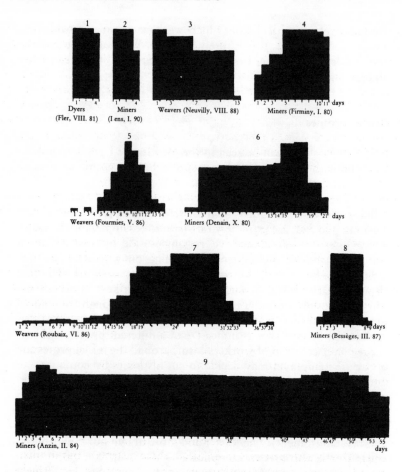

Figure 4: Strike profiles (for each strike, I have taken the number of strikers on the most successful day of the strike as a base figure — i.e. as 100 per cent — and calculated the percentage figures for the other days on this basis)

rather exceptional. After a very small drop in the level of participation, this strike even showed some evidence, towards the end, of a rise to an even higher level. This was a mark of uncommon doggedness, which in fact made a great impression at the time. The profile of the Decazeville strike of 1886, which the lack of continuous daily statistics prevents us from constructing, would be of the same type and would stretch over six months.

By contrast, no. 5 in Figure 4 shows the slim, soaring profile of a wool-weavers strike at Fourmies, where the number of strikers varied daily and there was a difference of 96 per cent between the highest and lowest participation levels. In passing, it should be noted that there was all the difference in the world between the Anzin and Fourmies actions. Whereas in the former there was strong trade-union organisation, in the latter there was none. And at Anzin, where a single company dominated the twenty villages and pits affected, the economic space was a unified one, whilst at Fourmies it was fragmented. There were fourteen employers of various sizes at Fourmies, and though they were in fact in the course of coming to an economic agreement among themselves, they refused to enter into any common negotiations with the workers. This explains the staggered return to work. Generally, for reasons identical to those discussed here, strikes in the mines have more compact profiles than those in the textile industry. Though that point need not greatly concern us now, this example certainly shows the complexity of the processes concealed beneath the word 'strike'. It would be quite wrong to regard strikes as always involving the same scenarios and processes. Each one has its own particular history, and a strike profile is one way of revealing it.

Several things have to be taken into account in analysing these profiles, the most important being the distance between the maximum and minimum number of strikers. Where this is insignificant, it suggests the existence of a group that has some coherence, whether it be from a common sense of resentment or from internal discipline; where it is very marked, it suggests by contrast a heterogeneous mass, more or less responsive to the initiatives of a minority. Union activity tends to eradicate these distances, but in this period it rarely does so with total success. A second fact which requires study is the respective length and rhythm of the phases which make up the strike profiles (onset — peak — final stage). A perfect equilibrium between the three is very rarely met with. In most cases, the stationary state is precarious and fleeting, except in some miners' strikes (Fig. 4, nos. 6, 9); the other two phases are generally dissymmetrical: sometimes there is a rapid take-off and a slow return to work, indicating a high level of discontent and a high degree of combativeness; at other times there is a slow take-off and a rapid return to work, which is a sign of uncertain conviction (Fig. 4, nos. 4, 7). All this reveals very clearly that the bloc of strikers is not monolithic but always to some degree fissured.

The Non-strikers

We now have to turn our attention to those splits which in every strike indicate zones of weakness, areas that are liable to subsidence, if not total collapse. What are these splits? How are we to explain them? In the ranks of the non-strikers, or the uncertain strikers whose reticence is always likely to turn into outright defection, we find all the economically weak or threatened categories. These were people without resources to whom stopping work may have meant privation and even hunger. They were the labourers, the provincials who had come to Paris, the country-folk who had come into the city for a few months with the sole aim of building up a little nest-egg to feed the families they had left behind or buy a little piece of land. They are the home-workers squeezed by the jobbing tailors, reduced to poverty by competition from the factories, who chose to break a strike rather than join it. And finally they are the family men bearing a burden of daily domestic pressures.

Let us take a closer look at some of these categories. The family men rarely take the initiative in making claims against the employer. They are, moreover, a dead weight which the strike committees make every effort to carry along: aid distributed is proportional to the number of children a striker has. In spite of all this, they are often the ones who give the signal for the return to work. During a masons' strike at Alençon, 'only one section of the workers on strike . . . [went] back to work and that portion comprise[d] the married men. The other part, which was not very large, was made up of the bachelors; many of them [had] already left the area'. At Bézenet in 1878, the first to go back down the mines were 'family men or old workers who [had] only chose[n] to go on strike reluctantly, fearing physical attack from the young miners who [were] very turbulent'. During the Paris carpenters' strike of 1876, 'some of the married men with families announced that they could not stay out any longer as their resources were exhausted. They seemed disposed to return to their building-sites', and certain of them dared to say so. During a meeting, 'Etienne, speaking for the family men, urged them to accept [the masters' offers]'. On the fifteenth day of the navvies' strike (Paris, 1888), a striker rose to announce, 'if we do not get 5 francs a day to stay out, I shall start work again tomorrow . . . I have a wife and four children. I haven't a penny left to my name. Are we going to spend a whole year doing nothing?' An overcharged hall does not receive such defeatist words well: Etienne was howled down, while the other was 'thrown out, though without being struck. A chorus of groans gave clear evidence of the indignation felt by those present'. Reduced to silence in this way, the family men, fearing reprisals, returned to the workshops in silence, hugging the walls and hiding themselves, a little more crushed, a little more bowed down with each year that passed leaving them all the more vulnerable: old workers could also be frightened strikers.[2]

The economic situation of the family men easily explains such an attitude; but it is an attitude which also finds expression in anxious, scowling women's faces. As workers, women often showed themselves very combative.[3] As housewives running households, they became sullen grumblers. We certainly have to make an exception here for the miners' wives. In their case the cohesive character of the family environment and the very structure of the habitat made domination by the mine such an ever-present, daily affair — for all the women in the mining village had also worked at the pit in their youth — that a strike was a matter for the whole tribe.[4] When they were convinced of the rightness of the cause, the women showed a peerless tenacity, collecting for the strike funds, eking out what little food there was, keeping up the men's flagging morale and ensuring the policing of the strike. Before each shift, they would post themselves by the paths and entrances to the pits; at Commentry in 1881, several of them lay down on the mine railway track, where 'the engine only came to a halt a few yards from them'. And woe betide any traitors! The women whipped up all the inhabitants of the village against them, shouting and banging on their pans; they shouted insults at these treacherous characters, chased after them and hit them. At Commentry, they used stinging nettles;[5] at Molières, they took a worker's trousers down and publicly whipped him. It was their presence at the head of the marches, singing,

2. Like the opposition between married men and bachelors, that between young and old is also frequent. Cf. above at Bézenet in 1878 and at Valenciennes in 1872: 'All the miners are on strike except for fifteen old overseers and their children' (Arch. dép. Nord, M 626/5, pièce 157, sub-prefecture/prefecture, 23 May 1872. Zola provides a consummate depiction of such a situation in *Germinal*.
3. Women's strikes and specific forms of action are analysed in the first part of my *Ouvriers en grève*.
4. Though after the second decade of the Second Empire, one no longer finds women working underground, they were nonetheless employed in all the surface operations, as sifters, sorters, crushers, and so on.
5. Archives nationales, F12 4650, gendarmerie report, 24 June 1881: 'The women who stood . . . day and night in appointed positions had an aggressive . . . attitude. Several of them struck and insulted workers on their way to work. By their violent acts, the women often caused very large crowds to gather; as a result, there were nearly some serious incidents, especially on the evening of the 11th, when two women were hitting a miner with nettles as he made his way to work.'

carrying flags and dragging their children in train, that gave miners' demonstrations that tribal air evoked in the paintings of Roll or Adler and in Zola's narratives. They knew better than anyone how to hate. Though these women were accustomed to a life of subjection, once they were angered, they could be terrifying; they were capable of the most extreme violence. One observer in Anzin noted: 'The women are beginning to stir up their husbands; they are saying out loud in the streets that the miners should take revenge on the company and blow up the pits. They are even saying the men would be cowards if they did not shoot someone within the next few days.' At Decazeville, they harassed Watrin: 'He must sign', they screamed as they stood in front of the town hall, where the engineer had taken refuge and which the crowd would soon take by storm. The judicial record gives us portraits of some of these impassioned women, worthy in the eyes of the public to stand alongside the *pétroleuses* of the Commune. They were generally matrons loaded down with children, like La Maheude in Zola's *Germinal*. They were women who had stood by their men-folk in the struggle and had been roused to action by some final injustice. For example, Marie Charvillat, née Bidet, aged fifty and Françoise Decorps, née Michard, aged fifty-one, both of them illiterate and blessed with five children, who led the campaign against the strike-breakers at Commentry, rebelled because their husbands, who had worked down the mine for twenty-five and thirty-one years, respectively, had been dismissed shortly before the strike with derisory compensation. Amongst their nine co-defendants, five were over forty; between them they had thirty children.

One can certainly find other examples of the positive role of women elsewhere than in the mines. The textile industry is a particularly good source. At Castres in 1872, 'a number of women — veritable harridans — entered a factory and forced the male and female workers to abandon their posts, cut the yarn on the looms with knives and completely cleared the workshop'. Furthermore, out of twenty-three accused at the criminal court on 10 May, twenty were women. Most of them were mothers and the court doubtless took into consideration their previous good conduct and the good impression they made during the proceedings. In 1879 at Vienne the mothers and housewives formed a delegation to ask the mayor, among other things, to create municipal works schemes. Whether the women's attitude was positive or negative depended ultimately on their relationship to their husbands' working environment, on the proximity of the factory and the immediate character of the oppression it represented. Feminine revolt was not fed by figures or distant images, but by concrete facts, by daily grudges kept alive in conversations in the local neighbourhood and at the local marketplace. In the industrial towns, a community of house-wives formed which constituted a backdrop to social conflicts and conditioned their tone and their duration. The leaders knew this well and weighed up the situation on the basis of the number of women at meetings, a number which the police commissioner, for his part, always noted very carefully for its symptomatic value. 'The women are getting involved', wrote one, 'whereas ordinarily they are a restraining influence. The ringleaders could seek to take advantage of this to spread the action wider.'

More often, however, women exerted a negative influence. Far removed from the workshops, whose imagined freedom they en-vied, and ignorant of the problems that went along with their husbands' jobs, which in fact only increased their dependency, they were concerned with one thing alone: the wages. For them, strikes were suspect because they saw them as a festival to which they were not invited, a costly revelry. They were not therefore very under-standing and were even downright hostile at times.[6] The wives of the Lille casters 'went to the police stations and the local charity offices to get aid; they freely expressed their discontent at their husbands' stubbornness'; similarly, the wives of the Meudon glass-workers 'seem[ed] to want to involve themselves in the movement to force the men back to work'.

Thus the nodal point of many disputes is to be found in the heart of the workers' households, which were veritable decision-making centres, a fact which doubtless explains many other aspects of the workers' lives besides strikes.

The labourers, whom the lack of a skill made easily replaceable, constitute a second zone of weakness, if not of outright dissidence. For example, they torpedoed the boiler-men's strike in the gas-works, though it must be said that the boiler-men rarely came out on strike for them. In spite of a certain awakening of consciousness, there was still a great deal of inertia among the pithead workers in

6. Report of Ducarre, 1877, p. 306: 'Every time French resistance organizations have decided upon a strike, it has been the wives of French workers who have refused to go along with it'; and he quotes Rigal's report to the Paris Workers' Congress: 'The housewives forbid their husbands to join the unions. They understand nothing of the social question or of the good that can come from our organisations. This is solely due to the poor education they have received'. See also Arch. nat. F12 4653, préf Tarn-min. Com., 3 April 1872: 'the loom-hands are almost all married, and the influence of their wives plays a considerable part in preventing them from going on strike.'

the mines, where there was all the difference in the world between those who worked above ground and those toiling below. They were divided by age (many young men began at the pithead and many old ones finished there), sex, wages (which were on a daily basis at the pithead and piece rates below ground), working hours and, lastly, prestige: the face-worker, though he had none of the characteristics of the skilled worker in the modern sense, was considered the only truly productive worker in the pit: he was the king of the mine, 'the soldier of the abyss'. Around him, the underground workers formed a solid bloc, sometimes, when they came to make demands on their employers, forgetting the workers above ground. Thus in the Nord coalfield it was not until 1900 that the bonus granted to workers below ground by the Arras conventions, was extended to cover those above ground. However, to be fair, we must also note that clauses relating to the pithead labourers figured increasingly on strikers' agendas. We should also stress that a great number of strikes involved both categories of pit workers in a united front. This was the case in 1883 at Carmaux (in spite of the fact that the whole policy of the company consisted in setting them against each other), in 1884 at Anzin, and in 1886 at Decazeville, to name but a few. Furthermore, the continuation of work above ground could be used as a stratagem, as a means for families to keep up what was normally an 'extra' income, but had, as a result of the strike become their basic one. However, in spite of this possibility, in many cases, the pithead workers' refusal to join a strike was a sign of indifference, if not of a silent hostility towards those below ground.

More serious difficulties existed in the potteries and the glassworks, with their very hierarchical workforces. At the Vieillard de Bacalan factory in 1887, out of 1,200 workers, the only ones to go on strike were the 300 *ouvriers* 'properly so called' (i.e. the moulders and polishers). At no point did they present any demands for the 900 labourers, a category which included many women and children who were not members of the union. At socialist Vierzon, in spite of a much greater degree of solidarity, which was reflected in the holding of joint meetings, the pottery workers and the labourers had two separate unions. At Lyon in 1886 a dispute turned sour when the glass-workers' *chambre syndicale*, made up solely of skilled workers, refused to give assistance to the labourers. The latter, reduced to poverty, called on the employers to reopen the factories from which they had been locked out. Their comrades reproached them vehemently for doing this and, during a tense meeting to explain their action, Petit, the president of the Labourers' Committee, riposted by saying, 'as the *chambre syndicale* did not come to our aid, we had to turn to someone. If you had shown good sense and a good heart, you would have let us share in the benefits of the contributions you gathered from the small traders'. Similar conflicts recurred in 1887 and 1888; on this occasion they almost came to blows.

This selfishness shown by the better-off is reminiscent of attitudes prevailing within British trade unionism in this same period, where the skilled and the unskilled formed separate and often divergent unions. There the disdain of the former found its counterpart in the resentment of the latter. In a society based on money, it is inevitable that the hierarchy of wages will have an effect on the workers' own outlook on society.

Besides wage levels, the mode of remuneration created other divisions; the fact that some workers were paid by the job and others by the hour, some by piece-work and others by the day also prevented them from joining together to go on strike. As for those who received a monthly salary, they were regarded as being outside the working class. To be paid by the month was to leave behind the proletarian condition and its inherent insecurity.

The particularism which set the various different trades against each other and the rivalries between types of worker which subdivided these trades produced more subtle distinctions in which economic and psychological motivations were involved in a complex interplay. The rarity of inter-union strikes is evidence of the reality of the boundaries between trades. The initiatives that other workers *were* most likely to respond to were those coming from the building trade. I have several times emphasised their role in sparking off disputes, as they did, for example, in the autumn of 1879 and the summer of 1888. We must now ask why this should have been the case. No doubt the reason was that, with a greater or lesser degree of conscious awareness, the workers saw the lads in the building trade as good barometers of the economic climate. That industry being considered the keystone of the economy, it fell to them to give the go-ahead for industrial action. They had a tried-and-tested sense of the right moment. The symptomatic position which Renault and the car industry have today in the French economic and social landscape was in those days filled by the construction industry. It is, moreover, significant that the earliest conceptions of the general strike sought to bring this sector to a halt first; as late as 1912, in Pataud and Pouget's utopia, the revolution was to begin with a strike in the building industry. No other trade had the same motive force. The miners enjoyed the esteem and sympathy of the other workers; they could stir them emotionally, but they could not pull them along. And the iron and steel industry was even less capable of doing so. Most trades went on strike alone, with their own particular objectives. Even in May 1890 each one presented its own demands, thus fragmenting the general strike into a series of individual ones.

Sometimes *coalitions* even brought hidden rivalries out into the open, such as those between the miners and metal-workers, who were as different in skills, life-style, culture and mobility as country dwellers were from townspeople. In 1886 at Decazeville bitter arguments over strike relief divided them, to the point where the metal-workers, judging themselves badly wronged, organised their own independent fund, spoke at an early stage of a return to work and were only dissuaded from organising a demonstration to that effect at the eleventh hour. At Bessèges in 1887 the metal-workers only joined in the strike called by the miners long enough to obtain payment of the back-pay owed them by the ailing Terrenoire Company. They advocated reaching a negotiated settlement with the employer and took the initiative in organising a secret ballot for a return to work, which was restricted to metal-workers alone. In 1890 it was with very little conviction that they followed the May Day movement in which the Lalle miners — the *enragés* of the Marius group — went on the offensive. Even today the iron-and-steel men are sometimes seen as a rather selfish, privileged group. During the May 1968 strike I heard construction workers criticising them for fighting only for their own ends. There is, then, a difference between corporate spirit and class-consciousness.

There is an even greater difference between the latter and the spirit of sectional loyalty born of the division of labour and still strong in the old trades where mechanisation had not exerted its unifying influence. Far from helping each other in disputes, they ignored or even condemned one another in their eagerness to keep their distance and show their superiority. At Le Mans, as at Tours, the cutters in the shoemaking trade did not follow the less well-paid *déformeurs* out on strike. In hat-making, the *approprieurs*, those 'aristocrats who wore black coats and silk hats', as the *Ouvrier chapelier* put it, acted separately from the fullers, the plebeians of the trade. In the tailoring trade the cutters ('big wigs' on a yearly salary), the alteration hands who were paid by the hour, and the piece-workers who often worked together as a family at home, hardly ever made common cause. The alteration hands, who were workshop men, unmarried, nomadic and cosmopolitan — including many men from Germany, Luxemburg, Belgium, England and Italy — formed a motley crew in Paris. They were a highly dynamic group, and their little world was a hotbed of anarchism and a place where the idea of the general strike took root. They were responsible for numerous disputes in which they were generally disavowed by the haughty cutters and deserted by the needy piece-workers. The leather-workers were even more fragmented; not only did tawers, curriers, dressers of chamois leather and tanners form obscure specialist groups, each with its own separate association, which pulled in all directions during *coalitions*, but each one of these was divided into an infinite number of sub-groups, originally based on the variety of technical operations involved in the preparation of the raw material. Amongst the curriers, the *noireux* (workers of black leather) did not mix with the cow-hide workers or smoothers who were 'the dregs of the leather trade, and men ignored by their fellow workers'. Solidarity, which was nonetheless very highly developed amongst leather-workers, worked horizontally within a narrowly limited stratum. Vertically, they did not want to know each other. During a strike of chamois leather dressers in 1874, the tawers made no move ('they live in constant hostility towards them'); in 1876, during the strike of the smooth leather curriers, it was reported that 'the heavy-leather workers fraternally support the strikers, but the fine-leather tawers hardly make any contribution to their funds . . . And so the strikers promise to do the same for them one day, i.e. to give them not the slightest support'.

The threat of rapidly advancing mechanisation in this industry did, however, contribute towards bringing these hostile categories together: in 1882 the support of the tanners and chamois leather men for the tawers' strike was reported as a novel occurrence; even the unskilled labourers joined in the action, demanding that they should in exchange be 'shown the trade' (a symptomatic development).

In heavy industry the social structure was simpler and collective action easier. This was the case for example in the textile industry. Among that homogeneous mass, strike movements spread easily; hence their magnitude and rapid expansion. Here, where there were differences, they were between different establishments rather than between the various categories of worker. However, differences of behaviour do show up between tenters, finishers, combers, twisters, and so on (the 'cream' of the workforce) and the doffers and reachers-in (youngsters and women who were merely 'helpers') and all the mass of spinners and weavers in-between. These latter, who were both more skilled and more independent, formed the active hard-core element in disputes.

This feeling of sectional loyalty is complex. It has economic and technical foundations which are sublimated into value judgements and social images. It apes solidarity, but in a profoundly mystificatory way. It is one of the great working-class 'alienations'.

The same can be said of geographic particularisms, loyalty to the village or to the firm. In the coalfields tenacious local rivalries of the village-pump variety make nonsense of the notion of a common economic space. Denain and Anzin, for example, though both vassals of the 'Grande Compagnie', never came out on strike together. In 1878 Denain stayed at work: 'Miners themselves arrested an agitator, whom they took to their manager'. In 1880 Anzin repaid the compliment. Except for 1884, the story was almost always the same. Moreover, until the turn of the century, Anzin almost always went its own way, resisting the strike calls that came from neighbouring concessions. As a result, general strikes in the Nord Pas-de-Calais area were very rare. Even in 1889, in very favourable economic circumstances, Anzin refused to come out with Lens, and 'it was noted in Lens itself that almost all the miners who did not take part in the present strike action were former workers of the Anzin company sacked after the strike'. Similar difficulties prevented the spreading of disputes in the Gard or the Loire. In the former, La Grand-Combe — where, incidentally, the miners enjoyed higher wages — left Bessèges in the lurch; in the latter, Firminy refused to join St Etienne, going so far as to welcome the strikers with cries of 'Long live work! Down with strikes!' As a result, when the Firminy workers themselves came out four weeks later, St. Etienne refused to assist them.

These few examples, which by no means exhaust the study of the refusal to strike, reveal the lack of unity among the workers, the diversity of antagonisms and contradictions within their world, the enormous number of obstacles to class-consciousness and to one of its most modest but most tangible manifestations, unity within a strike. Under the influence of an ideology we have inherited from the Enlightenment, we are too prone to represent the history of the workers' movement as one of continued progress, to see it as a march of conquest and, as a result, to chart only the territories that have emerged into the light. What is quite striking, however, is the extent of the dark reaches beneath the surface and of the weight of resistance. It is just as necessary to identify and understand the reasons for the absence of class-consciousness as the reasons for its presence.

Keeping Order in Strikes

It is sometimes necessary, then, to use force and seek to maintain order within a strike. The methods employed to this end were still rudimentary in this period. The workers had not yet discovered the potential of the occupation tactic, which was only rarely used (I have found only six examples in the twenty years covered). When they did occupy, they generally did so without any conviction. Most occupations were abandoned before it became necessary to call in the police. In actual fact the workers — particularly the men — did not know what to do in the factories; they felt like intruders. The idea of 'the factory for the workers' had no concrete meaning for them. Hence their embarrassment and awkwardness. In one occupation, for example, they remained, silent and motionless, at their workbenches. In another, they drank and sang, walked around and 'knock[ed] over the factory equipment, though they [did] not break anything'. The women do not seem to have been at quite such a loss: at Roubaix, 'they spent their time sewing or knitting'; at Marseilles the women tobacco-workers 'stayed in the factory for two whole days on end with their arms folded'. It would be interesting to know what the role of women was in the June 1936 occupations in France. Let us also note in passing how little material damage was done. Whether this is to be explained by fear, respect for private property or superstition is difficult to say, but the worker's instinct to look after his tools has ancient roots. In any case, the workers eventually tired of the game and abandoned the occupation of their own accord: the street was the place where they could feel free again.

Keeping a watch on the deserted factory premises, when it was done at all, was a job for the strike committee and for itinerant lookout committees — which were particularly common in Paris on account of the distances involved — or for strike pickets, though these were still a somewhat novel idea at this time and were only used rather half-heartedly. When in 1882 Pochet proposed to the Paris carpenters 'that they should employ the shoemakers' system; that is, place a sentry at the gates of firms that had been "black-listed" in order to be able to report the traitors who were still working and expose them to the scorn of the union', his suggestion was rejected. Moreover, the term 'picket' (*piquet*) did not yet exist; the terms used were the very military ones of 'sentry', 'orderly' and, most commonly, 'posts' (*postes*). Fearing reprisals, the workers sometimes apportioned this task to union officials from outside the establishment in question; they also employed their wives for the job, as was the case, for example, with the Lyon glass-workers in 1886. Moreover, they avoided the actual entrances to the factories and posted themselves at the corners of the roads leading up to them. Or they wore masks. In Paris the tawers 'covered their faces with a piece of linen with a slit cut out at eye level, so as not to be recognised'. However, the practice of putting pickets on the factory gates grew more and more widespread in the years between 1888 and 1890. This even tended to become the first job that was handed out, the union's first reflex reaction.

Tracking down blacklegs was not a simple task in the larger-scale disputes. In 1888 the Paris navvies even had the idea of using photography: they took snapshots with little cameras called *détectives*, stating that 'there will then be irrefutable pictures of people, and it will not be possible for anyone to bring false accusations'. But this practice remained quite isolated. More often, lists of those joining the strike were passed around, and woe betide anyone who refused to add their signature or who subsequently broke their word.

All means were considered fair for bringing the blacklegs round to the strikers' way of thinking. They would begin with gentle persuasion, especially where newcomers who were not yet well integrated into the group were involved. They would discuss the matter over a drink, offering to reimburse the person's travel expenses. Or they called the recalcitrant to meetings where they sometimes admitted the error of their ways; if they did not comply, their tools were confiscated.[7] Or they were sent written warnings: 'Citizens', wrote the tawers' *chambre syndicale*, 'a majority of the

7. Arch. dép. Gironde, M1188, pièce 209, police report, 10 August 1885, minutes of a meeting of coach-builders at which two non-strikers engaged in self-criticism. The account reveals a whole morality built on solidarity. 'I accepted the master putting me on piece-work', said one of the 'accused'. Brun (the chairman of the session) then told him: 'When you are on strike, you must not accept anything which does not conform with the decisions taken, and with the example set by the other workers. I was offered the same as you and I did not accept it'. Box then rose and said, 'Citizens, I have done wrong, but I swear that I shall not work again until the masters have reduced the day from eleven hours to ten'. 'Citizens', said Brun, 'Citizen Box was in the wrong, but he has now made amends'. By contrast, the other recalcitrant, Lescarra, refused to admit his guilt, and they gave him until Tuesday to think it over.

members of the corporative assembly have decided, by a unanimous vote, to summon you to quit your work. If you do not, you will be put on the "blacklist".'

This blacklisting, which was also known as 'putting in the pillory', constituted in effect the second stage in the escalation process. The names of the blacklegs were posted up, published in the local press and spread about on printed lists. These dissidents were truly ostracised. In one place in the Ardennes we read that 'the publicans are forbidden to serve them with a drink, upon pain of being blacklisted. The barbers are forbidden to shave their beards or cut their hair, and they are generally sent to Coventry . . . they are treated with contempt, even struck, and live hunted like pariahs'. And when the trade union had a closed shop, as was the case in the Lyon glass-works in 1888 and 1889, it was impossible for them to find a job after the dispute, for hatred felt against non-strikers — and even more against strike-breakers, later to be called *jaunes* — was inextinguishable. Where strikes were successful, their dismissal was often demanded. If it was not granted, their lives were made not worth living by continual harassment. At the Paris saddle-maker Herrenschmidt's, this reached such a degree as to cause criminal proceedings to be instigated: a certain Monsieur Salomon 'was said to have been thrown into a trough full of dirty water, and it was alleged that in his fall he had injured his forearm and been unable to work again for two days. His clothes had apparently been torn and his hat trampled under foot. A gentleman by the name of Delaplace was also said to have been molested; his tools had been hidden from him and he had had dirty cloths thrown in his face . . . Finally, the strikers were said to have threatened all the workers with "being thrown in the canal"'. These feuding brothers even came to blows at times. At Doyet in 1878 a brawl would have ended with knives being drawn had it not been for the intervention of the innkeeper.

Numerous trade unions, particularly those with craft-guild traditions, gave out certificates at the end of disputes. These were awarded to good strikers at solemn meetings or fraternal banquets, in order to 'distinguish those who took part in the strike from those who did not stop work, and to do this with the aim of putting the latter on the blacklist in the workshops'. In this way, a morality, a code of honour, was built up, the first article of which was solidarity. This was the workers' patriotism, and it is not merely by chance that these cards were often coloured red, white and blue.

In these practices, which usually began in the more organised trades, pressure was channelled and institutionalised. In large-scale industry, where strikes involved large numbers of people, it took on more brutal forms, ranging from verbal threats to physical confrontation. The strikers would go as a body to the workshop entrances or to the pitheads travelling along the roads in groups, heaping abuse upon the renegades, chasing them (this was known as the 'foxhunt') or beating them up. Zola has provided us with an epic description of these festivals of cruelty. The actual historical ones were, however, more modest in our period. The most spectacular demonstrations occurred at Mehun-sur-Yèvre in 1887 against four workers who had given up the strike. For eight days in a row, a crowd of between 300 and 400 people awaited their appearance morning and night. They were met with jeers and shouts of 'let's get them' and serenaded to the strains of 'La Carmagnole'. Finally, quaking with fear, they ended up living night and day in the factory. After the strike, they doubtless had to leave the area. At Lyon in 1886 matters took a more tragic turn. Having returned to work, a certain Leynneer, who claimed to be of Alsatian origin, but whom the workers knew only as 'the Prussian deserter', had all his furniture transported to the Allouard glass-works. The workers, tipped off by the women on the picket line, boarded the wagon, manhandled the driver and threw his load into the river. They then lay siege to the factory. At that point, shots were fired from inside the glass-works, where the employer had issued revolvers to his faithful workers and had opened fire with them on his besiegers. A young man of fifteen was hit in the eye.

There are reports of brawls — of varying degrees of seriousness — in 165 strikes (6.5 per cent of the total). There are marked irregularities in these figures between one year and the next, but no clear pattern emerges. As one might expect, the proportion of fights increases as a function of the dimensions (size, extent and length) of the dispute: the longer the strike, the greater the tension. At Anzin in March 1884 the strikers were happy simply to boo the renegades. Yet on the 4 April a crowd of about 1,000 people attacked mines where men were still working in an attempt to cut the cables and trap the traitors down in the mine or at least stone them as they left. The highest rates for fighting are found in the least skilled trades: 33 per cent among the coach-drivers, 25 per cent among the dockers, 22 per cent among the gas-workers, 14 per cent among the navvies, 13 per cent among workers in the food industry and 12 per cent in the chemical industry. They fall to 6 per cent for the miners and 2 per cent for the textile workers. These brawls varied both in intensity and the degree of collective participation. They only really became brutal when the fighting was against foreigners: xenophobia overrode all scruples. A strike then provided an opportunity to work off pent-up frustrations. In all other cases it seems that workers were quite restrained in their fighting. There were, admittedly, a few broken ribs here and there, men put in hospital for a few weeks, but these were really few and far between. The aim was not so much to injure as to seek to frighten and particularly to shame and humiliate, whether by an enforced ducking or a public thrashing, the latter being the favourite weapon of the women, among whom the age-old image of the castrating female was still alive, as was the maternal custom of inflicting a spanking. A violence that is so restrained and carefully measured as this is no longer a primitive impulse; it has become a ritual.

In the sphere of language, the vocabulary of insults is particularly rich. There are, first of all, the great classic terms: 'traitor', 'renegade', 'swine', but, above all 'loafer' (*fainéant*), which was by far the most commonly used. '"Loafer"', wrote the prefect of Arras at the time of the great miners' strike of 1889, 'is the insult currently addressed to anyone who does not go on strike. There is a general desire not be seen to be inferior to one's fellows.' Thus 'going on strike' is the very opposite here of 'doing nothing'; strikes are not laziness, as the bourgeois like to insinuate, but action, and in certain circumstances the worker's true occupation. The striker is, indeed, a man of action. Let us also note in passing that the popular doublet of *fainéant*, the word *feignant*, is, according to the Littré's Dictionary, thought to derive from the verb *feindre* (to feign) and according to Delvau, 'also means poltroon, coward and is an insult of the highest order'.

Certain terms drawn from the jargon of particular trades passed into general use, like the hatters' *macchabée* and the printers' *sarrazin*. Professional pride plays a role here. Moreover, strike breakers were also called *gamin*, the term for a glass-worker's helper, and *renard*, which, according to Delvau was the name for an apprentice *compagnon*, as though they could only be considered half-workers, worthless individuals.

Professional and economic scorn rub shoulders in *galvaudeux*, which was also widely employed and which the Robert dictionary defines as 'a vagabond, a good-for-nothing, living from hand to mouth', indicating 1865 as the earliest known occurrence. According to Delvau, it is the equivalent of *fainéant* and *bambocheur* (reveller), whilst Littré's Dictionary, which has no entry for *galvaudeux*, gives us *galvadaire*, meaning 'vagabond' and translates *gal-*

vauder as 'doing quick, slipshod work'. The coach-drivers in the Paris City Transport Company reproached non-strikers with 'not being honourable in their dealings': 'You're so hard up you'll do anything, you bloody paupers!' Thus, paradoxically, what comes out of insults is a series of implicit models of the workers' universe.

Finally, alongside such varied epithets as *rossard, caffard, figure de capucin* and *magot*, a whole set of insults give expression to a latent xenophobia. Though the word 'Cossack' was becoming less popular, 'Uhlan' was found, as, more often, was 'Italian'. Colonial expeditions had left their mark on popular slang: the old compositors' *sarrazin* began to give way to *Bédouin, Pavillon noir* and, above all, *Kroumir* (Krouman). Regarding this latter, *Le Temps* wrote: 'A year ago, the Kroumen were absolutely unknown in France; today, like the Cossacks and Bedouins, they have taken their place in the popular vocabulary. "Krouman" has become a common expression of scorn.' And the word figures in the Supplement added by Fustier to the third edition of Delvau's Dictionary (1883): 'Since the Tunisian expedition, this word is employed amongst the people as a synonym for "dirty fellow". It is also applied to ragpickers who have fallen into the most abject poverty.' How the promiscuities of language can reveal our attitudes!

6
The Material Circumstances of Strikers:
the Question of Assistance

'How was it possible to live without working?' This simple question, which contains within it a complete social destiny, lies at the heart of strikes. The study of domestic budgets has shown us how working-class life bordered constantly on penury. The brief duration of many disputes can be explained by the lack of savings, for prolonged resistance could mean hunger raising its ugly head once again. How then could strikers 'hold out'?

When economic conditions were favourable they could try to find work elsewhere, by changing their jobs or places of residence. But this supposes mobility and flexibility, both of which, it seems to me, are notions that mean something very different in times of recession. French workers settled down in one place and became specialised in one trade; they therefore acquired a double rootedness, which rendered them all the more vulnerable. Besides, in an emergency like a strike, job flexibility became a mere caricature: a sliding back into unskilled work. Apart from stores and handling work — a classic possibility that was available in the cities, where docks, stations and wharves could be havens of salvation for the jobless — there were two major refuges: navvying and working on the land.[1]

The railway building sites, which the Freycinet Plan had scattered over the whole country, were decisive factors in creating full employment. There can be no doubt that they acted as a stimulus to wage claims. The police commissioner of Castres expressly noted

---

1. In *La Bohême du travail* (Paris, no date), Barberet gives a description of the *galvauds* who waited around the Paris stations in the hope of finding 'odd jobs'. It is an interesting description, though marred by a distorting moralism. My mother remembers similar poor wretches before 1914, running between the Gare St-Lazare and the Place d'Italie behind the omnibuses and cabs, in the hope of receiving a few coppers for unloading luggage.

117

that the building of railway lines in the surrounding areas encouraged *coalitions* among the building-workers, who were always sure they could find employment there. Such a conversion may have been easy for these men, but even the potters of Aubagne, the tawers of Grenoble, the metal-moulders of Bordeaux and, of all people, the Chazelles hatters — none of them used to handling a pick — showed no hesitation in turning to the railways. It is easy to grasp why a slowing down of the Plan, and then its complete collapse, should have brought about a real fall in industrial tension. In these years, employment remained dependent upon large-scale public works: Great Exhibitions and state building works played a stimulating and regulatory role.

More traditional in nature, work on the land presupposed that the countryside was quite near — that it was at least within easy walking distance. Hence the concentration of such work in little rural market towns, where, until relatively recently, the inhabitants had combined agricultural and industrial occupations. This 'mixed' work continued to survive in certain isolated areas, where the main occupation was weaving to order and working in some mines bordering on the Massif Central region, where the companies still had difficulty struggling against absenteeism in summer. At Boismoreau (Creuse), 'at certain times of year, almost all the workers abandon the coal-mines to do the sowing, the harvest or the haymaking in their own fields and meadows'. It was the same in the Puy-de-Dôme and the Haute-Loire, at Graissessac and Fuveau. At Carmaux, as at Decazeville, there were little plots belonging to peasant-miners, for whom hewing coal constituted only a secondary income. For all of them, a strike was a pretext for a long absence; it was like taking time off for personal reasons: 'The miners of Saint-Eloy are almost all landowners. In demanding a shortening of the working day, they were seeking to gain time for their agricultural work.' Generally, however, half-time work was in its dying stages, though it had left some habits behind, such as the tendency to consider summer as the opportune moment for making a wage claim. The quarrymen of Loches 'chose for their protest and their strike a time of year when they were sure to find harvesting work of one kind or another'. Whether by calculation or simply out of ingrained habit, the same thing was quite clearly visible in the mines. There the frequency of strikes reached its highest point in the May–July period, a time of year when unemployment figures were rising. And 10 per cent of mining *coalitions* were accompanied by a return to the land. Not only did they retreat to their own gardens, which played a classic background role in pit strikes, but they also went to work in 'the fields'. In the north this meant labouring in the cornfields or harvesting sugar beets and potatoes; in the south it meant work in the vineyards, which remained of considerable importance in maintaining full employment. At Decazeville, digging over the vineyards was a useful source of work in springtime: 'You can see [the miners] on most of the hillsides from here to Cransac and Aubin. You can easily tell them by their black clothes and their wide-brimmed hats.'

Taking all strikes together, however, agricultural work is only involved in 1 per cent. The countryside which was some distance away and very often hostile, could not feed the strikers. It was from the towns they were walled up in that they had to find ways to maintain themselves.[2]

Hence the importance of the question of assistance. This interests us here on two counts, both as an aspect of material life during strikes and an index of the resonances and solidarity that strikes produced.

Assistance

The number of strikes that received financial assistance (for brevity's sake, we shall call them 'assisted strikes') is the relatively small figure of 653 or 22.3 per cent. But it must be remembered that only 39 per cent of *coalitions* lasted more than a week. Generally, after 1880 the proportion of assisted strikes increases and becomes more regular (Fig. 5); the highest figures are found in between 1880 and 1882 (maximum 32 per cent in 1881) and between 1887 and 1888; these correspond to the years in which support from trade unions, the major source of financial aid, was at its height.[3] Being prepared and planned in advance, offensive strikes are better financed than defensive ones (23 per cent as against 18 per cent). The influence of job status and wage levels is patent, the poorest workers being the least assisted. An industry-by-industry breakdown reveals great differences, ranging from 10 per cent for strikes in the food industries to 48 per cent in glass and porcelain. If the position of the textile industry (17 per cent) is not surprising, one would, however,

2. Of the unemployed workers of Paris in 1848, Flaubert writes: 'For many of them, moreover, being accustomed to more delicate work, agricultural labour seemed degrading' (*L'Éducation sentimentale*, La Pléiade, Paris, p. 350).
3. In 1881–2, 39 per cent of strikes were led by a union.

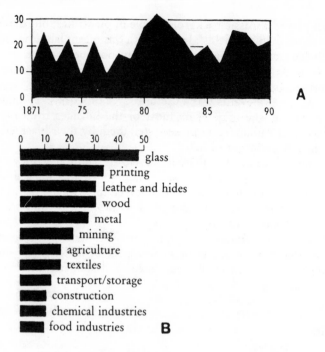

Figure 5: Strikes enjoying financial support (per 100 strikes)
A By year B By industry

have expected better for mines and quarries. Only 17 per cent of miners' *coalitions* received assistance, but it is in this industry that the growth of such assistance over time is most appreciable.

Furthermore, there are once again a large number of disparities hidden within these industrial groups. The figure for textiles, for example, includes the hatters, who reached the exceptional rate of 71 per cent whilst the building industry (average rate 11 per cent) groups together navvies (3 per cent) and painters (52 per cent), and so on. All this shows once again that the groups of workers within an industry, though we give figures for them here to make necessary comparisons with *La Statistique des grèves* were not socially homogeneous. In the present case one has to assess matters at the level of specific trades or even of specialisms within them: hatters (71 per cent), moulders (54 per cent), painters (50 per cent), stand at the head of the league table for assisted strikes. At the other end, sugar refinery workers, oil-men, salt-workers and navvies had almost no experience of strike assistance.

The table for the different departments does not really require extensive commentary. We shall only deal here with departments where there were more than twenty strikes. Generally, the south, richer in assisted strikes, stands in quite marked opposition to the north and north-west (the Ardennes being a spectacular exception). This can doubtless be explained to some extent in terms of 'southern sociability', but it is mainly due to the industries concerned and their traditions. The contrast which divides the Rhône (38 per cent) and the Seine (34 per cent) from the Nord (14 per cent) clearly suggests workers' movements that were of quite different types.

Sources of Assistance

Where did the money come from? Table 1 groups assistance received by source. Unfortunately, it is impossible to put exact figures on the particular sums concerned.

This table shows three dominant characteristics emerging, along lines of class, trade and geographical location. In 75 per cent of cases the assistance was of working-class origin (and this figure should almost certainly be higher, as the workers provided the largest part of the assistance locally). More than half the total came from within the strikers' own trades. Lastly, 66 per cent of strike aid was gathered in the locality; that is, in the places where the strikes were taking place. So much then for the factors circumscribing the rather narrow limits of financial solidarity. Socialists tried to break these down, notably by the newspaper fighting funds that were set up, and the success of these in any particular case is the best indicator of the wider impact of a strike; overall, however, the results of their efforts were unimpressive.

Trade Solidarity

Aid from workers was most often channelled through trade-union organisations, both within a single trade and between different ones (Table 1). After 1879–80 most union rule-books made provision for strike aid, sometimes specifying its rate and duration. Some trade unions were nothing but contingency-fund management bodies formed for the purpose of fighting a strike at some point before it was declared. The idea that it was necessary to build up reserves, an idea much disputed later in the name of revolutionary

Table 1: Sources of strike aid

1. *Aid from workers belonging to the strikers' own occupation*:		
From union funds	374	
From levying funds from workers still at work	80	
Aid from workers in the same trade within the locality	67	
Aid from workers in the same trade outside the locality	110	
Total		631
2. *Aid from workers in other trades (essentially organisations) belonging to*:		
The same locality as the strikers	85	
The same department	46	
Different departments	59	
Workers' organisations abroad	32	
Total		222
3. *Aid that was not specifically from workers*:		
Political aid (parties)	79	
Raffles, lectures, concerts and dances, etc	41	
Collections, donations	88	
Subscriptions organised by newspapers	61	
Help from traders	23	
Assistance from local authorities	19	
Miscellaneous	10	
Total		321
Grand total		1,174
Assisted strikes		653
As a percentage of all strikes		22.3%

spontaneity — poverty being, according to Proudhon, 'the providence of the human race' — did not at that period encounter any theoretical osbtacle. On the contrary, it was one of the practical conclusions drawn from strikes that had failed: 'Go back to work all of you', said Anscelle, a Socialist from Ghent, to the weavers of the Nord: 'You were wrong to leave the workshops without having the necessary funds for resistance. Besides, you will never be able to win your rights, nor raise your wages, unless you form yourselves into one single Provident Association and each pay a contribution of 25 francs every week into a special fund.' *Le Citoyen* drew the following lesson from the failure of the Bessèges miners: 'You need money, a fighting fund . . . Force yourselves to set up an obligatory subscription.' Socialists of all tendencies advocated the Anglo-Saxon type of union, with large subscriptions and substantial reserves of money. And a significant proportion of workers — the most skilled — was inclined to favour the British trade-union model, which, after a short period of hesitancy, won out within the CGT on the eve of the First World War.

There did in fact exist in certain occupations (in the book-print, porcelain, and hat trades) some very well-off trade unions, particularly in Paris. The Paris Association of Piano-Makers had 12,300 francs in its coffers when it called a strike, while the Grenoble tawers had 6,000 francs, the Lyon glass-workers 15,000 francs, *L'Initiative*, the porcelain-workers union in Limoges 16,000 francs, the Paris copper foundry workers 23,000 francs and the Society of Parisian Typographers, the Société de Savoie, which was both a Friendly Society and a trade union, had funds of 102,000 francs and was able to hold out for forty days paying a daily strike indemnity of between 3 and 5 francs. Moreover, these unions, being highly skilled in financial dealings (they generally put their funds into state bonds like the rest of French small investors), took out loans when the situation demanded it. The copper foundry workers owed some 100,000 francs to various *chambres syndicales*, whilst the Société de Savoie raised a loan by issuing 50,000 bonds at 2 francs each, though it only managed to find investors for 12,000 of them. Trade unions like these handled funds of considerable magnitude and had to present detailed accounts to their vigilant 'shareholders'. In effect, a strike was now no longer an adventure, but a business to be properly managed; the striker was becoming something like a member of an 'insurance scheme' with a critical attitude towards the administrators of that scheme and little awareness of running any great risk.

It must, however, be said that in the unstable trade unionism of the period, these cases were exceptional. We must note that only 47 per cent of the trade unions involved in strikes managed to give strike aid from existing reserves. Most of the time they had to improvise and find expedients.

The main advantage afforded by partial strikes was that they allowed the organisers to tax those who were still at work: these latter paid a fixed sum or a percentage of their daily wages (generally between 5 per cent and 20 per cent) or even the amount of the wage rise obtained. This contribution was most often left to the goodwill of the workers and was almost always restricted to one locality. It did occasionally spread spontaneously to neighbouring towns, as in 1882, when the weavers of Tarare and Thizy decided to raise a levy of 2 sous a day for their comrades in Roanne. In 1872 the Société de Savoie made plans for an obligatory 5 per cent levy 'in all the printing works of France', though this was not in fact collected. In subsequent years this form of taxation would become increasingly more necessary and would be extended to cover all the members of a trade. The decline of the *compagnon* tradition and the fact that federative organisation was still in its infancy, explains the limited nature of the geographical area from which assistance came. In only 3 per cent (or 110) of the disputes did workers enjoy assistance from members of their own trade collected outside their locality. Intra-corporative links were best in the metal-working industries (5 per cent in general; 11 per cent for the moulders), the wood industry (5 per cent) and, above all, the leather industries (11 per cent for the group; 14 per cent for tanners, tawers and curriers) and glass-working and porcelain (17 per cent for the whole group; 20 per cent for the glass-workers alone). These last two groups were concentrated in sites which were not far removed from one another. The workers travelled between these sites, establishing links that came into play in time of need. Thus we find Claude Cantalier, who is at Chaumont in 1874, in Paris in 1881 and at Grenoble in 1882, writing to his 'brothers' to ask them for aid. Between Annonay, Grenoble, Chaumont and Paris, the centres of the tawing world, and Me-hun-sur-Yèvre, Limoges, Bordeaux and Paris, the porcelain capitals of France, and the great glass-works of central France and the Paris suburbs, there were smoothly functioning lines of communication. An industrial geography, perceived as such, makes for a strong corporate consciousness. In cases of strikes of any great size there were exchanges of information, funds and representatives. The federations, when they were formed, would build on what was already a solid framework. By contrast, the miners were not very willing to give money to help their comrades in the other coalfields (only 2 per cent of miners' strikes received help from other mining centres). Even Decazeville only aroused among them a limited generosity: 'Our miners', wrote Rondet to Calvignac of Carmaux, 'are hardly falling over themselves to raise money for the Decazeville strikers. At a meeting of 200 people at Firminy, we took 2.5 francs. In other coalfields, not a penny was raised. This is disgusting and the Decazeville miners are not very happy about it.' These

Table 2: Trades benefiting from outside aid

	Total number of strikes	Strikes receiving aid from outside strikers' trades	%
Porcelain-workers	46	12	38
Moulders	42	11	26
Glass-workers	62	10	16
Carpenters, cabinet-makers	136	17	12
Stonemasons, slaters	80	9	10
Leather-workers	219	20	9
Miners	165	12	7
Weavers	857	38	4

semi-peasants had a limited geographical horizon. And this was even more true of the weavers, only 0.5 per cent of whose strikes received assistance from within the trade.

Solidarity between Trades

Similar remarks apply to solidarity between different trades. This found pecuniary expression in 6 per cent of strikes. In percentage terms it was principally the trades shown in Table 2 which benefited.

Apart from weavers and miners, who received more from other trades than from their own, all the others were in more or less the same position. In other words, solidarity was much more a question of organisation than emotion or sympathy. Help was given to whoever could provide it in return. It was not a question of free handouts but one of reciprocity between established and solvent *chambres syndicales*. Here as elsewhere the adage that people only lent to the rich was confirmed; the workers' trade unions managed their finances like bourgeois.

Private Assistance

The appeal to individual generosity was most commonly made by way of lists of contributions. These were usually printed and prefaced with preambles exalting solidarity, some of which constitute genuine manifestoes. These lists were distributed in the workshops or left with small traders such as bar-keepers, cobblers, barbers, or alternatively, cards were sold in aid of the strikers.

Lastly, strike committees organised events where an admission fee was charged, such as dances, fencing or singing competitions, raffles, public meetings with an entrance fee or a collection, plays, of which Félix Pyat's *Paris Ragpicker* remains a great classic, and most important of all, lecture concerts which, as much as being a way of obtaining money, were a means of making propaganda and an aspect of the festival which a strike represented in the workers' dreary round. A lecturer, sometimes a Radical, but increasingly a Socialist, would speak on an edifying topic, either historical or political, which local singing groups would interlard with bursts of harmony. For the weavers of Lyon (1879), the Chanteurs du Grand-Théâtre and the Harmonie du Rhône performed the Trio di Lombardi, Romances and the Cavatine de Cinq-Mars, before an orator gave a complete account of the life of Danton from his birth to 'the scaffold on which the head of the illustrious orator fell'. At Charleville, the programme included a talk by J.-B. Clément, then a grand concert with the participation of a group from the Lyre Ardennaise and amateurs. Sentimental, burlesque or street-corner romances alternated according to the taste of the day with patriotic and revolutionary songs. At this 'family festival', there was 'free admission for female citizens'. At Marseilles, between 'La Marseillaise' of the opening and the 'Le Chant du Départ' which closed proceedings, the audience, summoned to help striking tanners, applauded the curiously named vocal ensemble, the Touristes de la Méditerrannée, together with a number of local artists, including Mademoiselle Jane, lyrical artiste, and 'Bienfait, the little hunchback of the south, eccentric comedian' in *Le Grand Air de la favorite*, *Pour avoir la paix*, *Si j'étais roi*, *Alice mignonne*, *Ca s'alourdit*, *Les Moissonneurs*, *La Dent de sagesse*, *Négro burlesque*, and *Le Grand Air du Trouvaire*. From these programmes there emerges an aesthetics which ought not to be left out of account in the discussion of what is known as 'popular culture'. However, in the decade beginning 1880, these lecture-concerts tended to take a more political, militant turn especially in Paris. There was a meeting of this type at the Alcazar d'Italie on the occasion of a strike of leather dyers at Thissier's in the Boulevard Arago (thirteenth *arrondissement*). A hundred people were present, of whom forty were women. On the platform were Rollin, from the group Les Egaux du Treizième, two women, Georges Féline, a Blanquiste who was at the time a journalist on *Le Cri du peuple*. They spoke in praise of strikes, which they called 'a prelude to the revolution which will destroy the masters and the bourgeoisie', and this was followed by poems and songs. We read that 'several women sang inoffensive romances. The men did not, however, follow suit. Their songs were revolutionary and, amongst other songs, "La Carmagnole" was sung in unison, and was followed by various shouts of Down with Floquet! Down with the Boulangists! We'll string up Floquet! and Boulanger will hang!' Then they drew the raffle.

Assistance from Abroad

In spite of the rantings of a hostile press, financial support from foreign countries was minuscule in this period, when the International was in abeyance. Thirty-two strikes (barely 1 per cent) received such aid, all but one of them (in 1874) occurring after 1878. Table 3 lists the beneficiaries.

Table 3: Beneficiaries of overseas aid

Trade	Strikes	Department	Strikes
Wood	8	Seine	15
Textiles	9	Nord	5
Glass & porcelain	5	Rhône	2
Leather	4	Gironde	2
Metal	4	Isère	2
Printing	1	Ain	1
Tobacco	1	Ardennes	1
Navvies	1	Aveyron	1
		Cher	1
		Loire	1
		Haute-Vienne	1

The countries from which the donations came for the strikes shown in Table 3 were as follows:

Britain	14
Belgium	13
Switzerland	5
Italy	4
Germany	2
Austria	1
USA	1

The donors were, for the most part, workers' organisations and, more rarely, socialist groups (Belgian or German). The British trade unions came out top of the list both in terms of numbers and size of sums loaned — 52,000 francs to the Parish copper foundry workers, 12,000 francs to the Limoges porcelain-workers, 13,000 francs to the Calais tulle-weavers. They were also top for amounts given: in 1885 the London tailors, bound to their French colleagues by fraternal links and shared experiences (there were many Englishmen in the trade in Paris) sent them 625 francs a week and formed 'a solidarity committee with the striking Paris tailors'. It is clear, here again, that solidarity existed between highly skilled trades. It was rarely spontaneous and most often came at the request of French and, particularly Parisian workers, who turned willingly towards London, which to them was both a source of aid and a model. 'We address ourselves to you', wrote Charles Fouilland, a weaver and secretary of the Roanne strike committee of 1882, 'because your trade unions and the long and courageous struggles they have sustained against capital, are admired by the workers of France, who, since the beginning of this century, have been too oppressed by bourgeois governments to be able to organise themselves power-fully in defence of their wages'. On several occasions French delegates were despatched to London, which still retained a genuine prestige. By contrast, the break with the German workers seems to have been complete and one can see how lacking in foundation were the efforts of the Second International to impose the leadership of German Social Democracy on the movement. Exchanges with the United States were very rare indeed. As it was for the whole of French diplomacy, for the workers' movement this was also a time of isolation and withdrawal within national boundaries.

Newspaper Fighting Funds

Did the newspapers, which started funds for around 100 strikes in this period, break this narrow circle? A study of the lists of con-tributors shows that they did succeed in overcoming geographical barriers, at least within France's national frontiers. This is illustrated by one admittedly particularly favourable example, the fund opened by *Le Cri du peuple*, in which the geographical distribution of the donors has been analysed by Henri Feller. Social boundaries were only rarely broken down. The lists in fact carry a mention of the contributors — ascribed precisely to a particular locality — opposite the sums given. For the most part, the donors were groups. There were trade-union organisations (put at the head of the list) or political ones (social study circles, free-thinkers, electoral committees, etc.), but there were also workplace communities (e.g. gangs, workshops, factories) or people brought together on social occasions (collections were made in the local café, during a civil funeral, at the end of a public meeting or dance and, most frequently of all, 'after a singsong'). Individual donors, though almost always anonymous, sometimes mentioned their jobs: 'A publican, a shoemaker, a revolutionary cobbler, a packer with a few ideas about this Parliament to unpack.' In other cases they described themselves in such a way as to leave little room for doubt: 'A man ground down by the factory', 'a man who loves the bottle', 'down your pint and enjoy it'. This slang and impish humour are a signature, and it is that of a public which is definitely working-class and urban. The few rare bourgeois sympathisers who appear there strike a discordant note: 'a trader who demands that house-owners be compelled to have the shutters completely sealed up in rooms occupied by women of easy virtue', or 'revolutionary socialist students of the Ecole Centrale'. The modest nature of the contributions confirms this diagnosis. Donations exceeding a few francs came from convinced socialists or left-wing politicians, who, concerned for their popularity, willingly gave their names. But there were not very many of these. In little offerings of a few centimes (10, 20, 50 . . . only rarely as much as one franc), these funds drew on workers' money or at least that of the lower classes.

There is nothing very surprising in this. The newspapers which were collecting funds were, in the main, socialist ones. In this ambiguous period, ushered in by the Marseilles Congress, in which the Socialist Party merged with the Workers' Party and even with the Workers' Federation, this means they were newspapers with a working-class audience. They included, in Paris, such daily papers as *Le Citoyen*, Lissagaray's *La Bataille* and, in particular, *Le Cri du peuple*, which identified with all the major strikes in the years between 1884 and 1888 together with weeklies like *Le Prolétaire*, *L'Egalité*, *Le Socialiste* and *L'Homme libre*. In the provinces there were the little local sheets like *La Défense des travailleurs* (Reims) and, above all, *L'Emancipation* (Ardennes), which was always in the thick of things on account of a large number of disputes (nine fighting funds between 1888 and 1890). The Radical papers (especially, *L'Intransigeant*, *La Marseillaise* and even *Le Radical* and *Le Petit Lyonnais*, which collected money from 1871–2 onwards) also launched a

129

number of fighting funds, which generally raised less money than those of the socialist papers as well as being of a slightly different financial complexion. One finds larger individual donations there, indicating a better-off readership. The fighting funds run by *L'Intransigeant*, which had become Boulangist, are worthy of some attention. In the fund launched in aid of the Paris glass-workers, which was closed at a figure of 3,371 francs, there were offerings of 5 or 10 francs and more, sometimes accompanied by the words, 'a Boulangist'.

Yet, in overall terms, these funds brought in relatively small sums. *Le Petit Lyonnais* collected 284 francs for the plush-weavers of Tarare in 1872 and 854 francs for the copper foundry workers in the same year. In 1882 the sugar refinery workers received 1,204 francs *La Bataille* and 194 francs from *Le Citoyen*, 101 francs from *Le Prolétaire* and 20 francs from *Le Radical*. In the same year, *Le Citoyen* sent 854 francs to the Paris shoemakers, 395 francs to the miners of La Grand-Combe and, largest of all, 10,335 francs to the weavers of Roanne, a figure higher than any attained before. In 1890 the Ardennes paper, *L'Emancipation*, which was continually collecting money, raised 5,000 francs for the Revin casters alone. *L'Intransigeant* gathered 3,371 francs for the Pantin glass-workers in 1888. No newspaper, however, did so much as *Le Cri du peuple* (twenty-two fighting funds), which amassed 12,000 francs for the Anzin miners in 1884 and in 1886, a great year of social struggles which was also the paper's high-water mark, collected 33,000 francs for the metal-workers of Vierzon and more than 70,000 francs for the Decazeville miners, for whom the fund was kept open six months. In 1887–8 *Le Cri* was constantly running a fund of one kind or another. *Le Cri* was the first socialist newspaper to acquire national standing, and succeeded in breaking down the workers' isolation.

The magnitude of the funds depended on the size of the newspaper's readership, of which it was, conversely, an indicator, and on the interest aroused by disputes. Defensive strikes in particular won sympathy. Public opinion was somewhat lukewarm towards workers making demands and inclined to regard any claim for a wage increase as excessive (one had to learn to be happy with one's lot). But it was more easily stirred to anger by injustices on the part of the bosses, especially the big industrialists, whose faceless power it feared. The monopolies did not enjoy a good press in France. At Anzin, as at Decazeville, at Roanne as at Vierzon, the workers, up against limited companies, were regarded as acting in justifiable self-defence; they seemed the kind of resistance fighters with whom one could identify: 'For the Children of the Fighters for Justice' ran *Le Cri du peuple's* headline on the Aveyron strikers. This sense of injustice, within which there lurked an obscure awareness of being similarly under threat, aroused solidarity, as did the spectacle of a long, heroic struggle. Lastly, some trades attracted more solidarity than others. These were the poorest trades (especially textiles) and the most dangerous. Public opinion was favourably predisposed towards the miners both on account of the risks they ran and the socially useful work they did. Heroes of the black hell, celebrated in an extensive literature, of which Zola's *Germinal* is the finest flower, these 'pioneers of the underground world' sustained industry by providing the coal which was its 'daily bread'.

However, the principal interest of the contributions to the funds lies in their form, which makes them a singularly fascinating means of popular expression. The individual gifts were very widely accompanied by statements from the contributors in which in lapidary fashion, 'set down on paper as though direct from their lips' (Montaigne), they introduced themselves, declared their support for something or denounced it, gave vent to their anger, howled their hatred or proclaimed their hopes. This was not done without humour. Irony prevails over any tragic tones in these little texts, in which the pleasure of saying one's piece, of 'getting one's oar in' shines out visibly from the page. It was a pleasure dear to those common folk, whose outspokenness was almost legendary. Here is a collective sketch of a detested female overseer from *L'Emancipation*: 'So Mme X, known as *Boule-de-Suif*, overseer, 20c — shall not go to the market in her veil any more, 20c — and shall not say her neighbours are beneath her, 20c — Oh my! Just you watch out for me, 20c — I'll drown you!' Racy or vulgar banter took up a large part of these pieces: 'for P.D., known as *sans fesse* ['no buttocks'] to listen to the advice of a mother; for a young lady of Montuy to be modest in her speech and for Mr M. of Charleville to spend less time kissing the young female citizens in the dance halls; Marie, who is sweet on Alexandre, the little lathe operator, Don Juan of the Rue Mercoeur.'

But the most insistent themes are of a political and social nature. They are the hatred of tyrants, bosses, priests or political schemers and the hope of revenge. Like a kind of prose poem, this popular litany unfolds in the columns of *Le Cri du peuple* from February to June 1886. Here are a few small extracts from it: from Saint-Bérain-sur-Theune, 'one who would like to see Baihaut [minister of public works] down in the pit when it's 40 degrees centigrade, a friend of Basly who would like to see all the mines revert to the state, a socialist who wants to see the Social Revolution . . . a descendant of Cabet who would like to see the Nouvelle Icarie in France, a penniless miner, a man who would like to see the resignation of the Radical deputies who do not keep their election promises, the wife of a socialist who would gladly see all the capitalists strung up, a female citizen wishing for the downfall of all tyrants; her two kids who will grow up good revolutionaries.' From Troyes, 'a packer who would like Ferry's head so he can put his stamp on it; another packer who can't keep his feelings about all the deputies wrapped up, a cobbler, an anonymous footslogger, an enemy of the proper-tied classes, a democrat'. And there are more: 'An internationalist; a café-owner; a man who would like to see Jules Ferry stuffed; Gaspardo, who longs to see an exploiter hanging from every gas-lamp; little Mimi, thinking not of her communion but of the strikers; a family of revolutionary atheists; a repentant follower of Gambetta; a friend to Robespierre; one awaiting revenge; a *cami-sard*, an enemy of the monopolies.'

The study of these texts, like the study of any others of the same nature, certainly poses a variety of problems and demands a prior reflection. To what degree is this language spontaneous? Are we dealing here with 'automatic writing', which liberates unconscious material or are these simply the splendid borrowed clothes the poor are forced to put on if they wish to impress. Stereotypes lay their snares around all forms of speech, even those which seem the most innocent.

I have simply felt it necessary here to stress the interests of these contributions as a means of expression. As forms of opposition and protest, they elevate what might be scrawled on walls or shouted in the street to the dignified status of writing; they are a chance to speak out. They illustrate what, in my view, constitutes the appeal of strikes, or at least of certain strikes, which is their liberating power.

The Role of the Small Traders

Amongst the assistance which came from outside the working class, we must mention the aid given by small traders (found in twenty-three cases) and by municipalities (found in nineteen). There was generally nothing altruistic about this generosity. It rested on

132

quite patent economic or political foundations and, in both cases, it reflected a need on the donors' part to preserve their clienteles. We have already mentioned, on several occasions, the role small business played in certain industrial communities as a refuge, or as a source of support and even of social discipline. Being itself a by-product of the world of wage-labour and closely reliant upon the income of that sector, it had a symbiotic relationship with its working-class clientele, siding with it entirely — especially when the threat of company shops was hanging over a village. At such times the struggle took on an anti-feudal aspect in which the proletariat was merged into the broader notion of 'the people', as celebrated by Michelet.

The forms of assistance the small traders gave to strikers varied widely in degree. Sometimes they simply gave extended credit, which could in fact on occasion be nothing more than disguised usury, exacerbating the workers' dependent situation *vis-à-vis* the tradesmen to whom they owed money. Maigrat in *Germinal* is the embodiment of a type of all-powerful grocer who grows fat from the strike, until his tragic end. Sometimes the traders accorded the *chambre syndicale* or the strike committee the right to function as a bank, accepting the bread coupons or grocery coupons issued by them as a mode of payment, repayable after the strike. Sometimes they went further, participating in the collection of funds or granting permission for lists of strike-fund contributors to be posted on their counters and calling upon their colleagues to support the workers' cause: 'It is your interests that the strikers are defending along with their own', declared Jourdan, a grocer, and Bracourt, a watch-maker, at Bessèges. At Commentry the retailers themselves organised a solidarity fund against which they issued bills of exchange. At Lyon in 1884, during the long Barral and Gacogne strike, traders from the Croix-Rousse quarter organised meetings on their own initiative to study 'what means could be employed to support the weavers' demands'. Under the chairmanship of a local butcher, 200 retailers decided to split into groups and carry out a city-wide collection. A watch-maker proposed that the shopkeepers and craftsmen of the first and fourth *arrondissements* set up a permanent body, whose declared objective would be to come to the weavers' aid 'when they were forced to have recourse to a strike in furtherance of a wage claim'. The solidarity of the shopkeepers' at Roanne in 1882 was intense, made all the stronger by the high-handed attitude of the Manufacturers' Union and by their decision to resort to the unpopular 'lockout' tactic.

Rarely whole hearted.

The aid the traders gave to strikers was, however, rarely absolutely wholehearted. They were prone to turnabouts, either pulling out once their own interests had been satisfied (with, for example, the removal of a company grocer's) or deciding, where strikes had become protracted, that it was not in their best interests to continue to afford further, dangerous credit. At such moments their withdrawal could bring about the collapse of a strike. At Firminy in 1880, 'it is said that the tradesmen have agreed between themselves to refuse the striking miners credit'. At Villefranche, 'all credit having been denied them at a stroke by their bakers and other shopkeepers, who had grown weary of the situation, the strikers (dye-workers) turned up *en masse* at the . . . factories'. In towns where the clientele was mixed, the traders took a cautious line and were even downright hostile at times. At Vierzon in 1886 they got up a petition calling for the troops to be kept on.

These facts show that a strike was not simply a duel between bosses and workers, but a complex confrontation in which diverse pressure groups played a role. They do, moreover, illustrate the subject status of the workers and the fragility of the alliance between wage-labourers and 'middle strata'. They would seem likely to reinforce workerism among workers, since the latter found they were only able to rely upon their own kind.

Workers only able to rely on their own kind.

Municipal Interventions

Financial intervention in disputes by local councils began to occur after 1879. This was a new development and one met with essentially in industrial areas where the workers made up a considerable proportion of the electorate. It was in reality the effect of a concern for popularity which was reinforced by the presence of representatives of proletarian origin — some of them elected as Radicals, but many more as Socialists — who were a thorn in the flesh of what in some cases were rather somnolent local councils.

The style of this aid varied from charitable donations to strike relief, from patronage to class struggle, according to the political colour of the councillors. In the Conservative boroughs, 'charity' was the order of the day. It could be used by the Right to remind the workers who their 'real' friends were. At Reims, the sub-prefect was alarmed to see the archbishop opening the soup-kitchen organised by the town council at the Convent of the Sisters of Mercy and the haste displayed in Catholic circles to contribute to the strikers' collections. Such charity was not always to the workers' tastes. At Vienne in 1879 the town council, pressured by the striking weavers' wives to open municipal workshops, decided to grant 5,000 francs to be distributed to the 'needy' by 'a group of ladies chosen from outside the families of the strikers'. This the strikers themselves rejected in terms worthy of their interlocutors: 'The honest and industrious worker lives only from the product of his labour and not from alms which degrade a man, whereas work ennobles and improves him, leaving him that modicum of freedom which the many tyrants of this world have not been able to take away.' During the weavers' strike at Cholet (1887) the local council, put under some duress by the example of the Paris City Council, whose generosity — much appreciated locally — had shown up their own miserliness, voted to make a donation of 3,000 francs. To avoid any misunderstanding, however, it stipulated that this sum would be distributed after the resumption of work. At Decazeville, to dampen the psychological impact of the assistance voted by the Paris City Council, the mayor, Dr Cayrade, a moderate Republican, decided to have the 10,000 francs distributed by the local charities board.

At Commentry, which in 1881 became the first Socialist local authority in France, the tone was as far removed from this as possible: the Council pronounced in favour of a 15,000 francs grant 'to the miners, who have been forced out on strike by the dismissal of 152 of their comrades'. They went on to say that they considered it 'the duty of society to ensure the survival of all ... and ... so long as the state shirks that duty, it falls to the municipal authorities to fulfil it'. These are extreme cases. More often, a more discreet formulation was found, such as 'aid to strikers' families', a compromise formula which did not offend the sensibilities of the moderate voters and gave protection from the wrath of central government. Thus, in 1886 the Paris City Council rejected Edouard Vaillant's motion that 10,000 francs should be given to the mayor of Decazeville for the strikers, but accepted Cernesson's, which named the same sum but specified that it was to be given 'to relieve the miseries of the inhabitants of the town, who are victims of the stoppage of work in the mines'. What was being accepted here was, it must be said, an unprecedented type of action. For the first time, a local authority was providing funds for a strike situated outside its own boundaries. This represented an extension of the town council's field of action, and it also gave that action a much more political coloration. On several occasions the Socialists, a sizeable minority within the Paris Assembly, manifested their opposition to the Opportunist governments in this way. If they wished to denounce the class character of these latter, they were also seeking to show up the social moderation of their Radical colleagues.[4]

The various local authority initiatives gave rise to impassioned debates. Whilst the Socialists considered the action of the Commentry Council a justification of their electoral strategy, the Right denounced it as 'just as illegal as it is outrageous and threatening'. They saw in such actions the fearful spectre of workers' power: 'The employers can do nothing but capitulate.' And how far could a local authority go in spending taxpayers' money to support a strike? That was what Paul Leroy-Beaulieu wanted to know on the occasion of the Limoges porcelain-workers' strike (1882). 'We have arrived at the extraordinary state of affairs', he said, 'in which public authority, represented by the town council, takes money from the masters in the form of taxes and gives it to the men. And why? So that they may triumph over the masters? These unfortunate bourgeois are being made war on, and it is being done with their own money.' He concluded: 'It is the duty of the government to annul a decision that is as unjustifiable in a court of law as this and as harmful to the interests of the country.' The polemic came to a head over the decisions made by the Paris City Council to give aid to strikes outside its boundaries. The Conservative press loosed all its fury on them, particularly at the time of the Pantin glass-workers' strike of 1888 because of what the strike was about. The issue was not, as at Decazeville and Cholet one of wages, in which the low levels of pay involved might give rise to some justifiable sympathy, but one of trade-union power and the employer's authority in his factory.

The government's hesitancy, particularly in the period of Boulangism, made these polemics even more impassioned. To tolerate the grants to the strikers meant siding against capital, or at any rate engaging in dangerous demagogy; to annul them meant denying municipal autonomy. The government flitted continually back and forth between these two attitudes. The sub-prefect of the Allier annulled the resolution of the Commentry Council, on the pretext

4. The Radicals, who had aspirations to form a government, found themselves in a particularly difficult situation and tried to distance themselves from the Socialists either by mitigating the effects of the latter's proclamations or blocking them altogether. Thus in 1888 Edouard Vaillant's proposal of assistance to the navvies (20,000 francs) was ultimately rejected after a stormy discussion in which the Radicals denounced the Boulangist demagogy lurking behind the call for a general strike and warned of the subversion that was threatening the Republic.

that it had been made at an unofficial meeting, though the real reason for his action was the anti-capitalist tone of that resolution. After consultations with the Ministry of the Interior, the prefect of the Aube forbade the allocation of 5,000 francs to the Decazeville miners that had been voted by the Troyes Council, arguing that 'it is a cardinal principle that the resources of municipal budgets may not be used for any purpose other than the financing of expenditure relevant to the locality'. Similarly, the donations of the Paris City Council to the weavers of Cholet, and of the Lyon City Council to the blanket-makers of Cours (amongst others), were annulled on the same grounds. Many others were, however, allowed, the Decazeville strike receiving the fruits of the generosity of at least twenty towns. No clear legal position was therefore established, nor was any general rule followed. Everything depended upon local or national circumstances; that is, upon what seemed expedient at a given moment. During the Pantin glass-workers' strike of 1888, within a matter of a few days Floquet first blocked the Paris City Council's vote of 10,000 francs assistance to the strikers and then allowed it. His turnabout was said to have been due to Boulanger joining the list of donors. According to *Le Petit national*, because the General sent 500 francs 'of his modest pension . . . all the clowns in politics are performing charitable somersaults'.

In this way, these grants from local authorities, which were not in themselves of any great significance, brought the question of strikes to public attention, forced statesmen and political parties to reveal their true colours, and thus had the effect of exploding the myth of neutrality.

The Distribution of Strike Relief

The strike committees did on occasion, then, dispose of considerable amounts of money. The budget of the Decazeville strike has been estimated at more than 300,000 francs; the expenditure of the Paris typographers (1878) reached 268,000 francs, and that of the copper foundry workers 150,000; for the cabinet-makers the figure was more than 100,000, and the Graulhet tawers' *chambre syndicale* distributed 60,000 francs to 1,100 striking workers over a 77-day period. Most of the time, the amounts distributed barely exceeded a few tens of thousands of francs and indeed were generally around a few thousand. Moreover, these figures have only a limited social significance. Set against the number of strike days, they reveal wide disparities in the amounts of money per head made available. For example, the chair-makers' trade union, which, like many Parish trade unions presented a detailed balance sheet of the strike had 5,511 francs in its coffers, to which were added 6,440 francs, giving a total of 11,951 francs. It spent 10,798 francs; that is, 3,599 days at 3 francs. The navvies had some 25,000 to 30,000 francs to hand out for 240,000 days lost, which gives an average of 12 centimes per head per day.

In these conditions, the distribution of assistance posed some delicate problems, both technical and social. To whom should strike relief be given? The general rule was that it should go to whoever went on strike. Here, improvisation guaranteed egalitarianism. The strikers had to take pot-luck, receiving help only where the 'pot' had been hurriedly topped up. Discriminatory measures were rare. There were three types of discrimination, along lines of trade, union membership and nationality. At Lille, only the unionised metal-workers were given assistance: 'Those who are not in the union get nothing and are discontented.' But was it fair to pay for these improvident individuals? Corporate coffers — which were assidu-ously topped up — frequently engendered a blinkered selfishness among those who saw themselves as hardworking and thrifty.

The quarrels over assistance which set miners and metal-workers against each other at Decazeville and opposed labourers to glass-workers at Lyon were of the same order. But there was an added problem here in the form of underlying job and status rivalries, which, as we have pointed out above, represented fault lines in the workers' solidarity. As for discrimination on national lines, this once again revealed a latent xenophobia. During the Paris refinery workers' strike, 'the Italians [said] that if they were not given strike relief, they [would] resume work in two or three days' time. As for the German workers, it was said that they had still been given no strike pay'.

How was the rate for a daily allowance to be fixed? Should it be a flat rate or progressive, according to the real needs of each individ-ual. The well-off unions willingly opted for the former solution, which was more discreet and avoided embarrassment, and they gave their 'members' 'strike pay', which varied in size, though the most common rate was 3 francs a day. This was a sort of comprehensive insurance and anyone was free to do with it as they pleased. This system suited the anonymity of cities, where the individual alone counts and where work-based relationships are accorded more importance than those of family or neighbourhood. By contrast, in villages or when it came to organising for an indefinite period of hardship, levels of assistance were determined that took into account the strikers' resources and overall situation. Criteria were not always well defined and the vague and humiliating term 'needy' still appeared from time to time. And yet the deep-seated language of pauperism was fading away. It is at this point that the 'great adventurer of the modern world', the family man, steps forward, with his brood of children, whose number determines his rights. The Reims strike committee gave 2 francs to weavers with two children and 2.5 francs to those with more. The allowance made to the Parish glovers ranged from 3.5 francs to 5.25 francs, according to the number of dependents. The chair-makers gave 3 francs to each man, plus 50 centimes per child. The carpenters gave assistance only to workers with three children or more, to whom they accorded between 10 and 15 francs a day. And the weavers' delegates of Roubaix proceeded in the same manner: 'After completing the list of married men with three children or more, the widowers and men with two children were called. They received . . . 4.5 francs each.' Let us note what little importance is attached to women, who always received less than the men, as though they could never be heads of households. At Mazamet in 1887, for example, the men received 1.25 francs across the board, the women 75 centimes.

Strike relief was distributed in cash, in kind (especially bread) and, more often — the delegates being wary of the temptations of the local tavern — in the form of coupons made out in money values or in quantities of goods (bread or groceries and also meat). The strike committee or, on some occasions (as at Decazeville in 1886), the town hall served as banks to which the traders went to be reimbursed. The Roanne committee and that at Graulhet, who were prudent treasurers, took great care not to put more coupons into circulation than they could cover from their funds. At Montrouge the unmarried mushroom growers, 'following the arrangements decided upon at the General Meeting, [had] their meals paid for by the *chambre syndicale*'. At Reims, the women organised soup-kitchens, the precursors of the *soupes communistes* seen at the beginning of the century, but this was still something relatively unusual. Little tempted, it seems, by collective dining, the French worker preferred to take advantage of the opportunity to eat at home.

Money as a Source of Argument

The distribution of strike relief was done at the strike committee's headquarters, in a cafe, in the open air or, in the case of a mass strike, through factory or local delegates. It often gave rise to arguments, to suggestions that such and such a factory was being favoured or that the delegates were giving themselves excessive allowances. There were rumblings of discontent at Decazeville over the 5 francs a day. On this point, the workers were suspicious and always had the feeling they were being cheated. In the wake of disputes, there were some painful recriminations, especially where the strike had failed. Among the Paris carpenters, where the strike ended with losses of 14,000 francs, a pernickety meeting went over the books with a fine-tooth comb: 'Jenty asks Vilon to explain why a sum of 83 francs received between 1 and 17 December 1881 does not figure in the accounts of the relief committee. Vilon demonstrates that this sum was entered in full under Miscellaneous Expenses, together with his delegate's allowance.' It was the same story among the pit sawyers. There, a 'stormy discussion' ended in an exchange of insults: 'The former members of the committee were called opportunists and responded with the epithets "Socialists" and "Commune-ites" [*Communeux*].' Similarly, Basly, who, to reassure the miners, had gone about throughout the strike with a purse on his belt was pressed to explain the disappearance of this fabulous pile of money. At Bruary 'the audience, very dissatisfied with his explanations, ... howled him down', and he left the meeting amid jeers and shouts. For Balsy as for Etienne Lantier, to whom he served as a model, failure made a guilty man out of the hero. In actual fact, certain delegates could not resist the attraction of money and did put their hands in the till. Proceedings were instigated against such people for embezzlement, and the workers in their disgust would usually abandon the organisation. Money, 'poisonous and destructive' (Zola), can wreak its havoc anywhere.

Hardship and Poverty within Strikes

With no money coming in, however, the workers simply grew more and more destitute. Every strike which lasted any length of time inevitably brought intense misery in its train. After the joy of the early days — for the strike was, in the first instance, a liberating festival — poverty inevitably followed, to the point where the strikers could be reduced to begging desperately for bread.

Unfortunately, there is a dearth of documents relating to the private lives of workers during strikes. The police chiefs kept a watchful eye on public meetings and demonstrations; the journalists' curiosity was also becoming sharper, but in this period the 'reporter' was still a bourgeois, whose world ended at the doorstep of working-class households. There is, in general, a certain decline in the amount of literature with poverty as its theme. As the workers became organised and entered into struggle, society ceased to regard them as 'deserving of pity'. It was, after all, their own fault if they were hungry. Silences can be very eloquent repudiations. As for the workers, if they perhaps complained, they did not talk about their experiences very much. And hunger is incommunicable.

One thing is sure, however, and that is that strikes brought the question of subsistence back into the foreground of workers' lives, as is shown by the kind of aid distributed, which took the form of provisions (as coupons or in kind) of the most elementary sort. Meat was a luxury which they hardly dared touch any more. At Decazeville, on the thirtieth day of the strike, *Le Figaro's* correspondent was astonished at the miners' restraint: 'These unfortunates are always easily satisfied with what they are given and one has to wonder if they are not in fact suffering starvation since what they are given is so little. Out of nearly 800 who turned up yesterday, there were only five who asked for beef or mutton. All the others were content just to have bread, bacon or vegetables.' Bread, the staple of the handouts, regained the pre-eminence it now no longer held in normal life. The mine-workers rushed to the Ermitage tavern at Anzin or the Salon de l'Usine cafe at Denain to receive it as though it were the most precious of commodities. In every town and village they jealously demanded their share. Certainly, today we would not see the socialists of Ghent sending a goods wagon full of bread to the weavers of the Nord. As with those days of heavy snowfall, which are capable of plunging our towns — suddenly jammed and paralysed — into a long-dead pre-industrial age, strikes produced a regression to an earlier level of civilisation and to a dietary regime considered the barest minimum capable of supporting life.

Was there in fact worse? Was there complete destitution or absolute famine? Did people die of hunger during strikes as in *Germinal*? In some unforgettable pages, Zola has described the advance of penury, the insidious and then acute, agonising, excruciating march of hunger. The historian always has some qualms about enquiring into the meaning of works of art. He remembers André Breton's anger at the efforts of 'petty scribblers' to give Lautréamont's writings the stature of a biography: 'All this so we may wear our hearts out on the doorsteps, and yet the doors will remain closed to us and we will merely end up scraping our tongues along the top of the walls.' She feels petty, like the man weighing gold in Quentin Metsys' picture who, stooping over his balance, sees the world only in the narrow image of a mirror. Hers is assuredly a grey task, by comparison with the colourful activity of the story-teller, and yet she still has to do it — or give up altogether.

The cruellest scenes that are painted come largely from the Nord and principally from the great mining (in Anzin, 1878) and textile strikes (1880), movements that were largely spontaneous and lacking in any system of food provision. Left to their own devices, many in number and without assistance, the workers were pushed to the very limit. At Anzin, feeling hunted, the miners lived in small bands in the woods. There they camped, bivouacked and cooked: 'They stay there, living as they can, whilst the women and children go off begging almost as far as Valenciennes.' As the correspondent of *La Marseillaise* wrote, 'half-naked children with no shoes or stockings, some of them without shirts, their bodies covered only by a torn smock or half a pair of trousers made of patches and pieces go from door to door or shyly approach passers-by for money to buy bread. Some are still so young and so small that they have to lift each other up to reach the doorbell. Nowhere have I seen a poverty so dark, so truly distressing'. It was the kind of spectacle one might find in the underdeveloped countries today or in poverty-stricken Mediterranean areas. This spectacle directly inspired Zola, who carefully annotated Yves Guyot's reports in *Le Voltaire*. Similar scenes recurred in 1880, when the distribution of dispute pay was rudimentary. At Wattrelos, 'some strikers are entirely without money. Yesterday an unidentified group entered a farmhouse at Bonté-Picavet . . . and forced the servant to give them slices of bread and butter. They left saying "that's how you can eat when you've no money left and no work"'. In 1889 the weavers of Cambrésis, in a state of perpetual undernourishment, experienced such total deprivation that they were reduced to eating grass.

Not all disputes reached this critical pitch. Such situations were relatively few and far between. The recrudescence of begging in the 1880s, a significant social phenomenon and one that has not been accorded due note, must not, I think, be put down to strikes, but to the 'Great Depression'. Furthermore, the workers took pains to set this activity apart from real begging. To avoid any confusion, they applied for official authorisation for their collections and carefully marked this activity off from any other. On a deeper level, they found begging particularly repugnant. When la Maheude (in Zola's *Germinal*) pushed her children into begging, she did so as a result of unbearable necessity. 'In the past, she had threatened to kill them if she ever caught them begging. Today, she herself was sending them out onto the highways and by-ways. She even spoke of them all going, the 10,000 coal-mining folk of Montsou, taking up the old beggar's stick and bag and scouring the terrified countryside.' The Anzin children's shyness about begging provides an eloquent revelation of their confusion when faced with having to do something so unfamiliar. This revulsion derives in part from the puritan scorn for the mire of poverty, the idea that it was shameful to be poor. One can begin to detect here a growing concern for respectability, which conceals an obscure dream of upward social mobility and therefore of social integration.

7
The Collective Life of Strikers: Actions

Nowadays a strike is, very often, an act of evacuation, of flight. The factory is abandoned to a few pickets and the workers withdraw into themselves. This is partly explained by workers living at some distance from their places of work, as the greater concentration of enterprises typically means that they do in our society. It is also partly explained by the workers leaving it to trade-union leaderships to initiate action. Disciplined and ordered, and in many ways more effective, strikes today are usually less animated than in the period we are studying here. It took May 1968 to remind us for a brief moment that a strike can be something other than a well-run economic scenario, that it can in fact be an expression of latent desires and repressed dreams, a freeing of both word and action, a festival of the assembled populace.

I should like now to evoke these aspects which make up the full richness of nineteenth-century strikes, though I shall not be closing my eyes to the difficulties of an undertaking which is doomed, for several reasons, to remain superficial. In the first instance, there is a problem regarding the nature of historical sources. For the purposes of such an enquiry, these sources are particularly unhelpful. Consisting generally of descriptions by observers who were, by definition, outsiders,[1] they provide us with a summary morphology of the gatherings, seen as a single mass, as if from a balcony whose great elevation effaces the differences to leave only an undoubtedly artificial impression of uniformity. That equality, which Elias Canetti sees as the very basis of the crowd-state, is perhaps, primarily, an effect of the position of the narrator.[2] At best, the latter seizes on some external elements, such as the number and nature of the

---

1. It is rare that one finds the participants' own stories, especially for demonstrations as humble as those held by strikers. Accounts of political demonstrations are more frequent; see, for example, the extensive reporting by Jules Vallès's *L'Insurgé* of the funeral of Victor Noir, or of 31 October 1870.
2. *'Within the crowd there is equality.* This is absolute and indisputable and never

144

demonstrators, shapes, colours, noises, and so on. He cannot take us into the heart of these gatherings, whose internal life remains for us a closed book. We cannot see the secondary groupings — the product of voluntary organisation or, possibly, of hierarchy — or hear the conversations and the remarks exchanged by the participants which are sometimes so revealing of their intentions, hesitations and conceptions.

The second deficiency arises from the inadequacy of the methods that have been developed for treating data of this type, an inadequacy which cannot simply be put down to the obvious weaknesses of my personal training in the field of social psychology. Georges Lefebvre's article on this subject is particularly insightful, but it dates from 1934. Georges Rudé's works reflect preoccupations that are fundamentally sociological. A more detailed approach to the study of collective forms of behaviour is, thankfully, finding its way into historical practice, via the work of historians like A. Dupront and E. Le Roy Ladurie, and so on, but their studies provide us with no guidelines for tackling the urban masses in the industrial era. The same must be said of Canetti's fine book, whose early chapters are bristling with suggestive ideas, but which becomes too much embroiled for my taste — and for my purposes here — in descriptions borrowed from mythology and ethnography. And yet, admittedly, a multidisciplinary approach is needed. It appears, however, that after their infatuation with the crowd theme in the early years of this century, psycho-sociologists have now deserted the field altogether. They have, it seems, abandoned crowds to the bestial condition and trance-like states in which Le Bon, Tarde, de Felice and their ilk believed they had found them. For the moment, therefore, one is compelled to practice a regrettable empiricism, which sadly limits the significance of studies of collective mentality. These are reduced to being merely intuitive — if occasionally poetic — interpretations.

The Strike as a Festival

Before outlining the main forms the strikers' collective life took (i.e. meetings and demonstrations), it is important to stress something which is consubstantial with these, namely the element of festival. If

---

questioned by the crowd itself. It is of fundamental importance and one might even define a crowd as a state of absolute equality' (E. Canetti, *Crowds and Power*, p. 32).

revolutions are 'life's great holidays', then strikes are the proletarians' great holiday. They bring release from the stranglehold of rigid hours and the insistent pace of work; they introduce the freedom of leisure time into an unremittingly exhausting existence. This aspiration goes some way towards explaining why they are so commonly concentrated in spring. In May the factory seems unbearable. Even today a thrill runs through it at the first sight of sun. Claire Etcherelli has given a striking description of this phenomenon, bringing out the contrast between French workers, who are now relatively well adapted to the implacability of industry's rhythms, and their comrades of Mediterranean origin, who find it simply unbearable.[3] If some incident should occur, perhaps an over-sarcastic remark from one of the foremen, they will down tools and flee towards the freedom of the street in one of those 'mass factory exoduses' — a classic picture-postcard theme — that have impressed so many observers with their almost childlike joyousness. 'They come out looking as though they are escaping. They burst noisily into the suburb, talking, jumping about, gesticulating, and slip away in little groups towards the outer boulevards. You might take them for school-children just let out of class.'[4] Similarly, strikes are, initially, a happy escape.

The beginnings of a strike give an impression of happy people, people relieved, relaxed and pleased to be back among their families, indulging in their favourite pastimes, be it some game or other, or just pottering about. In winter the cafés are brimming with people; they are drinking, talking, playing. The carpenters, in the *compagnon* lodging-houses, 'spend their time playing cards or billiards'. The miners lounge about among their families: in the sleepy mining villages, they lie in until as late as . . . 8 o'clock! At Anzin, 'you see them playing with their children', or at Bézenet they are seen 'out walking in their Sunday best, playing marbles or else busying themselves at home with their vegetable growing', digging over their little gardens again and again.

In summer, particularly in Paris, there was a wild rush out into the countryside. The cabinet-makers 'went to Charenton to enjoy themselves'. The glass-workers 'spent their time mainly in the woods at Meudon'. The weavers of Flers and the Givors glass-

3. *Élise ou la vraie vie*, Paris, 1967. The setting is a large factory in the Paris region during the Algerian War.
4. 'L'ouvrier fondeur', *Le Cri du peuple*, 23 May 1888. This is a description of a foundry at Belleville: 'In summer, especially, the spectacle of the factory turn-out is particularly curious . . . You should see these hundreds of men escaping, suddenly let out into the street and the open air after twelve hours of incarceration.'

workers arranged to meet for meals in the neighbouring villages. They returned home gaily, a little drunk, some in little groups, others in procession singing 'La Marseillaise'. In the hills of the Lyonnais, the home-working weavers organised an open-air banquet at Lagresle and went off there in little bands.

If it was fine, the strikers' outdoor get-togethers took on an air of family picnics. At the Champ de Grève in Reims, 'the women bring their sewing or knitting, the children play leapfrog, and the men chat together and tell each other the news'. The women loved dancing. Their strikes took on the outward appearance of dances. At Céton (Orne), where the Neyret glove factory employed a large female labour force (100 in the workshop, 600 in their own homes), 'the day following the strike declaration, the whole population went to a meadow ... and they danced there until dusk'. At Ablain-Saint-Nazaire the strikers, female flint gatherers, went through the village streets led by a band, singing and dancing. They waved their pocket handkerchiefs and aprons attached to long poles as banners ... The day ended in an open-air dance.[5] Many a lecture-concert, the utilitarian aspects of which we have already noted, ended in a noisy tombola or a party. And many a street demonstration was simply a joyous parade to the music of a brass band. Such events were an opportunity for the workers to sing, stretch their legs and get some air into their lungs.

The putting on of Sunday clothes was another sign of this strikers' 'festival' in the first days of the strike (and the symbolic function fulfilled by costume in popular milieux is well known). At Le Ballon, a frontier village near Roubaix, the weavers 'are 500 or 600 in number, stretched out on the grass, proud of their inviolability, in their corduroy trousers, their blue or grey smocks or else their black Sunday waistcoats, and with their caps and pipes'. At Firminy on the day the strike was called, 'the miners went to the café at La Malfolie; they ate and drank; they acted as they would on a Sunday'. This was, however, only a brief respite. The next day found them standing 'at their doors or by their windows and they were in their working clothes'. At Saint-Quentin, as at Vierzon, to welcome their comrades who were leaving prison, the workers put on their finest clothes: 'The men who had been released passed in triumph through the faubourg in an open carriage; in the evening, a grand banquet was given by the weavers, who had been victims of

---

5. *Le Combat*, 31 March 1890: 'What makes this women's strike even odder is the fact that it is one of the most cheerful.' The paper refers, further on, to 'these joyous strikers'.

the magistrates.' During the dockers' general strike of 1883, the city of Marseilles had a jubilant air: 'The quaysides, La Joliette, the Rue de la République and the Canebière, together with the Cours Belzunce and the Place d'Aix were crowded with people out strolling in their Sunday best, walking or standing about in groups, discussing the burning questions of the day, grumbling about the rapacity of the employers.'

May Day 1890, the first festival of labour and, perhaps, the first general strike, raised this joyous atmosphere among the people to a new pitch. Numerous observers speak of a relaxed atmosphere — indeed, they labour the point, for they had feared it might be otherwise — and conjure up images of happy workers on a magnificent spring day. In Paris, 'the workers are dressed in their Sunday best. They meet in the streets with smiles on their faces. "Here it is, then, May Day, and no need to work". "That's right", replies a work-mate, "we're on holiday"'. At Saint-Quentin, 'a majestic sun smiles down upon the workers and, in the faubourgs, they talk about the events which will be going on during the day. Most have only sandals on their feet and are in shirt-sleeves, stretching their limbs, as if after a hard week's work'.[6] At 10 a.m. they went off to the Circus to hear Massey, Renard and Langrand who spoke to them of new days to come. 'The old world will pass away. The old world has passed away.' Then they picnicked all around: 'The garden, refreshment room, café and corridors of the vast establishment were filled to overflowing. Everywhere you could hear singing, shouts of joy and bursts of laughter intermingling. You would have thought you were in the land of Cockaigne ... happiness and hope were imprinted on the wildest of faces.' In the evening, after the delegations had been to the sub-prefecture, it was back to the Circus for a concert, at which 'everyone [might] sing ballads, socialist or comic songs, according to what [suited] them best'. And once again, it was a dance which brought to an end this day that

6. Account taken from the *Défense des travailleurs* of Saint-Quentin, 11 May 1890. But there are plenty of others. At Narbonne there was a 'monster' party at the union's premises, (*Le Combat*, 5 May 1890); at Troyes, red Chinese lanterns in the suburb of Saint-Savinien; illuminations at Montluçon, at Roanne, 'in most of the mechanised weaving mills, they pass round membership lists ... and everyone who joins has to pay 2 francs to attend the dinner and dance that is to be held', according to Arch. dép. Loire, 10M87, pièce 104. In Paris the workers went off into the woods: 'The demonstration took on a rustic air; it was a spring-time event', according to *Le Petit Parisien*, 3 May 1890, or else they ventured into the wealthier quarters, as far as the Champs-Elysées, where they created a scandal: 'Some of them, for amusement, sat down next to the most elegant ladies amid theatrical gestures and laughter', wrote *Le Figaro* of 3 May, which was on the whole relieved that nothing more serious had occurred.

was, in its extraordinary mingling of village fête and church mass, so typical of what was happening all over France. For here are the beginnings of the ritual through which the new ascendancy of institutions is registered, institutions which are so adept at transforming the rapid, spontaneous, disordered movement of the masses into that procession whose slowness is proportional to its distance from the proposed goal.[7] The anarchists had appreciated very clearly the threat posed by ceremonial — hence their rebellion against it.

Times of leisure, sometimes of pleasure, and always 'events', strikes were festivals for another, even more important reason. They created that 'being together', which, according to Rousseau, constituted the very essence of the festival: 'What show will they put on there? None if they so choose. When there is freedom, then everywhere people throng together, there is well-being.'[8] Meetings and demonstrations, which make up the fabric of the strikers' collective life, do not simply have a utilitarian function of communication and decision-making. They bring about the union of the *membra disjecta*. Industrial organisation, by means of the division of labour — that drama of technological progress — isolates the workers, tied as he or she is to the little individual task. It produces that sense of disgust, solitude and despair which Charlie Chaplin has so masterfully portrayed on film. A strike goes beyond levels of skill or wage differentials to bring out that common denominator which is simply the condition of being a wage-labourer, of being exploited. It dissolves differences in an equality of refusal.[9] The spectacle of well-filled halls and well-attended demonstrations cements unity and tends to produce the comforting feeling that 'We are many'. A strike is a festival because it is a gathering and, therefore, also a communion.

Strike Demonstrations

In France today, as no doubt in most industrialised countries, a

7. Canetti has produced a remarkable analysis of the transformation of the crowd under the influence of organisations, in *Crowds and Power*, especially pp. 22 and 44.

8. *Lettre à d'Alembert*, quoted by Starobinski, *La Transparence et l'obstacle*, p. 117. This admirable text has so many points of application to popular movements: 'Plant a stake topped with flowers in the middle of a square, gather the populace there and you will have a festival. Or do yet more: present the spectators as a spectacle; make them creators themselves; make each see and love himself in the others, that they may all be the better united.'

9. See Canetti's analysis of a strike as a 'prohibition crowd', pp. 63–6.

demonstration by workers is a premeditated act of will, planned and organised by the trade unions. Nothing is left to chance, be it the day, time and place — all of which are carefully weighed up, having regard to the specific objectives of the action and to a particular symbolism — or the banners, slogans and songs.[10] When the demonstration takes place, a powerful, high-profile group of stewards sees to it that things go smoothly and that directives are obeyed and also ensures the rapid dispersal of the participants. Enthusiasm counts for less than numbers, which are the crucial factor in a demonstration, as is shown indeed by the controversies which surround the various figures that are given. All this explains the extent of the preparations and of the material means put to work to ensure a massive turn-out. Demonstrations in fact serve a dual purpose. As ritual, they meet the psychological needs of the demonstrators. As a means of exerting power, they seek to impress public opinion and the powers-that-be. Within a perpetually on-going negotiation process, they constitute an additional degree of escalation. It is a question of showing one's strength at the opportune moment in order in fact to avoid having to use it. Most often there is no place for violence, which is indeed rejected and condemned. It arises only by accident or by treachery. The successful demonstration attracts large numbers but passes off in a calm, orderly fashion.

The strike demonstrations which concern us here had neither the size, intention, nor organisation of these modern ones. They were born of an anger or fervour coming 'from below', particularly from the most emotional or the most combative elements, namely women and youths. Largely spontaneous and improvised in their form, they expressed feelings rather than any specific intentions. They were less an attempt to convince than a way of letting off steam. This explains why so little importance was attached to numbers. Fifty workers could easily form up into a procession in the streets of a town and feel triumphant. Indeed, 20 per cent of demonstrations brought together less than 100 participants. However, what they lacked in numbers, they made up in movement. These rudimentary demonstrations were outside the control of the unions, who were often wary of such activities and sought to channel the crowds towards meetings behind closed doors, conferring on disputes a parliamentary style, the emergence of which has already been

10. It is well known what lengthy negotiations the demonstration of the 13 May caused in 1968 and what concessions to the students' struggles the substitution of a République to Denfert-Rochereau route for the classic République to Bastille represented.

highlighted. Street demonstrations were on the decline, and public meetings were taking their place. Labour's forward march was coming to a halt, and action was giving way to words.

Some 304 strikes (10.5 per cent) gave rise to one or more demonstrations.[11] The figure rises to 17 per cent for purely female actions, is 13 per cent for defensive strikes, which were quite stormy, and only 8 per cent for offensive strikes, which were better controlled. In disputes affecting joint-stock companies, the figure is 15 per cent, as opposed to 8 per cent in family businesses. The trades which held most demonstrations were (the figures are for the percentage of strikes accompanied by demonstrations):

Miners	25%
Agricultural industries	20%
Spinning, weaving	15%
Chemical industries	14%
Glass and porcelain	12%

The trades which held least were:

Bookprinting and binding	2%
Wood	3%
Metals	6%
Leather	6%
Building (stone)	7%
Transport	6%

This latter list spans a range of conditions that are not easily comparable. The book, wood, metal and leather trades were highly organised and preferred meetings to demonstrations. Workers in the building and transport industries, where there were frequently quite turbulent strikes, were more noted for bitter internal clashes than for collective shows of force. Overall, then, demonstrations seem to tie in with a certain level of skill and concentration: they were the prerogative of the unskilled workers in heavy industry.

Types of Demonstration

Uncomplicated in the forms they took, demonstrations differed according to the ends they were seeking to achieve. These ends conferred varying degrees of stability on the gatherings and im-

11. At Decazeville and Vierzon in 1886, demonstrations were held daily when the strike reached a certain stage. Something of the order of 1,000 individual items of information, most of them brief, were examined in this case.

parted differences in density, duration and style to them. The most basic type was the 'mass walk-out', typical of defensive strikes. When a wage reduction was declared or a notice spotted announcing one for the future or introducing harsher working conditions, the workers stopped the machines and protested. They did so first within the factory, either in the workshop or the yard. Then, if their complaint achieved no results, they continued outside, almost always in procession, singing. This was the classic scenario of numerous sudden strikes. I have cited several cases of this type when looking at how strikes break out, and I shall not go back over these here. But let us nonetheless note the significant features of this action, namely the procession and the singing. These are almost instinctive forms of demonstration. They are a way of staying together and making a noise.

These 'prohibition crowds' (Canetti) break up rapidly. But their elements, as if in suspension, were always ready to crystallise. Hence the ease with which gatherings formed, particularly in the smaller localities where the workers, with time on their hands, were always on the look-out. It only needed some affront to their feelings to whip them up into an angry crowd. The sight of the bosses or of some 'traitor' passing by (however furtively), not to mention the repressive action of the forces of order, could cause crowds to gather in a flash, crowds all the stormier in nature for being so sudden in appearance. We read for example at Cours of 'a crowd of 200 people . . . outside the Sarrazin café, where several manufacturers were gathered . . . All the employers were subjected to more or less direct abuse from the crowd'. Cormouls, a rich industrialist from Mazamet, which was the centre of the dispute, was spotted in a café. More than a thousand weavers surrounded the building, pelting him with stones. The notorious tyrant, Testart, was rumoured to be in his factory, and 500 people, 'of whom many were not from that factory', gathered in front of the establishment to prevent him from leaving. The physical presence of the masters, who avoided showing themselves most of the time, was for the crowd as a red rag to a bull. It was the same with strike-breakers. At Lavaveix, crowds of men, women and children, the women with stones in their aprons, formed outside the pit gates, uttering threats against the workers who had gone in that morning. At Lyon the women who had been given the job of keeping watch on the Allouard glass-works while their husbands were holding a meeting, came running to say that Leynner, 'the Prussian deserter', was in the process of moving his furniture into the factory. Five hundred strikers immediately rushed the wagon, throwing its load into the water 'at the point where the rivers meet'.

Interventions by the police or the gendarmerie to coerce the strikers had the effect of making them the more united. At Gisors, three workers sacked from a sheet-making factory did not succeed in bringing their fellow-workers out in sympathy. They rioted and were arrested, at which point 'the gendarmes were very soon surrounded by a number of Alsatian workers employed in the same factory'. At Neuvilly the weavers arrived at the double to release one of the strike leaders whom the authorities had thought they could imprison, given that the strike was fading, and forced the gendarmes to retreat to the town hall 'beneath a hail of stones and cries of rage in which hatred for the gendarmes was every bit as discernible as hatred for the masters'. Similar scenes occurred during the Anzin strike, as they did generally among the miners, who were always quick to rise in defence of their own people. Everywhere, repression was a powerful engine of unification.

The employers' refusals often had the same effect. At Lyon a rumour went around that a master-manufacturer was not going to apply the new rates. Between 400 and 500 weavers went down from La Croix-Rousse to the Place Tolozan where this recalcitrant individual had his premises. The mayor of Avesnez-les-Aubert denied the weavers the authorisation they had requested to demonstrate on the public highway, and 'the working people, fired by suffering and also perhaps spurred on by a few agitators, suddenly streamed out into the streets, bearing a flag . . . In an instant, there were 1,500 demonstrators outside the town hall'. These reactive demonstrations have affinities with the 'mass walk-outs' seen in defensive strikes. They share with such walk-outs the characteristics of immediate, sharp protest, and being generally unorganised and unled, they are also most often short and violent.

The formation of 'gangs', who went from one cloth-mill to another, or, more frequently, from one pit to another, bearing news of a strike and striving to spread the action — veritable 'increase packs', in Canetti's sense — were still semi-spontaneous forms of demonstration, their decisions being taken by the members and their destinations chosen in the street. Someone would shout out the name of a pit or factory they were to go to, and the whole troop would set off towards it. In the absence of trade-union leadership, it was by this kind of direct contact that communication was established. The spreading of most of the miners' strikes in the Nord happened in this way: in 1872, as later in 1878, the Anzin coalfield

153

was riddled with groups which started out peacefully but became exasperated as they encountered more and more obstacles. They were continually being dispersed, and continually they formed up again, until they either broke up in exhaustion or violence. In his superb description of the exhausted but vociferous parade of strikers wandering over the Flemish plains, Zola was drawing both on classical and recent models. Union organisation tended to make such wandering bands less common. They are still found at Denain in 1880, but they were absent from the Anzin strike of 1884 and that of 1889 in the Pas-de-Calais and at Douai. The trade-union officials in these cases (Basly and Lamendin) preached moderation and, at their urging, the miners stayed at home or went along to indoor meeting places to obtain news and discuss the situation. The Loire coalfield, the first to be unionised and, it must be said, traumatised by the terrible memory of La Ricamarie, seemed almost to completely renounce the use of wandering bands. In twenty years they appeared in only a tiny number of cases. By contrast, in Saône-et-Loire, where an aggressive mine-owning class opposed the formation of a trade union, such bands swept through the countryside every time there was conflict. They were indispensable transmission-belts. They were the messengers.

Most other demonstrations involved only a minimum of organisation, such as deciding on a meeting-place. Sometimes this was decided by active minorities who summoned their work-mates to a meeting, as was the case with the miners' so-called *rebelles*, which sprang up in the dead of the night and imposed their authority in sudden, early morning gatherings. Sometimes, by contrast, decided on by all the workers together, it was the product of men working in unison. On occasion detailed scenarios were produced by such groups. Among the weavers of the Thizy district, whose actions were remarkably well orchestrated, 'the workers of several communes [met] on an appointed day and proceed[ed] to the commune where they wish[ed] to incite their comrades . . . to strike'. Once they had reached the town, they proceeded in precisely the same fashion on each occasion. They would request a place where they could meet and, upon receiving the inevitable refusal, they would occupy the public square. On 11 May, to support their delegates, who were negotiating with the employers, it was with military precision that the bands of workers who had come down from some twenty mountain villages joined up at 1 p.m. at the intersection of two roads. In a similar vein, the weavers of Avesnes, meeting at night out in the fields, decided which of the employers' residences would be their target the next day and at what precise moment they would act.

However, such instances of planning remained the exception; a broad margin of improvisation continued to exist. Generally, a time and a place were all that were given, and they were passed on in confidential whispers in that daily conversation which constitutes the fabric — now, alas, lost to us — of every popular movement. Written notice of a meeting, which was both unusual and inefficient, aroused mistrust, raising fears of a possible trap. To succeed, a demonstration had to retain its conspiratorial air. It was therefore the antithesis of the English-style meeting, which was both legal and publicly advertised; it perpetuated the tradition of a certain clandestinity — that of *compagnonnage*, Blanquism, and all the 'resistance' movements.

The timing and location of the gatherings, which were dictated by circumstances, cast some light upon their objectives. Factories were the major assembly points; the workers massed there at the beginning of the working-day and, more especially, at its end — a better time for such vast gatherings than the mornings when they were in a hurry — to put the 'loafers' (*fainéants*) to shame; almost one-fifth of the demonstrations were directed against these latter. Or else they went there to keep a watch on the industrialists, whose homes, in the smaller localities, also constituted a necessary stopping-off point on the strikers' marches. The town squares offered a convenient place to come together, not only for practical reasons but because they were the site of official buildings and seats of power. Outside the law courts the workers declared their solidarity with the accused. In front of the prefectures and town halls they waited for their delegates, both in order to give them support and to keep them on the right lines, ever ready to acclaim them if they won a victory or to disown them if they should yield. These stagnant gatherings, continually growing in size as new people arrived, brought together the largest numbers. Five thousand people gathered outside the town hall at Lisieux to press the claims of the weavers at the Méry-Samson mills who had rebelled against wage reductions; there were between 5,000 and 6,000 at Thizy, where the crowd was swelled at 7 p.m. by the wave of workers leaving the workshops, and between 12,000 and 15,000 thousand at Roubaix on 13 May 1880. These gatherings were also the most likely to produce trouble. And this never failed to occur when the disappointment of failure was added to the tension of waiting.

Railway stations provided another quite different site for demonstrations. They were symbols of an opening out on to the world, and joyous and often victorious crowds turned out there in their Sunday best to welcome comrades released from prison or Socialist orators newly arrived from the capital. At Anzin on 4 April 1884, 3,000 miners cheered Roche to the strains of 'La Marseillaise'; the comings and goings of Duc-Quercy, Gaullé, Roche, Basly, and so on, at Decazeville were a pretext for innumerable parades. The Vierzon strike of 1886 was punctuated by noisy receptions, as for example when, on 27 October, 2,000 people gathered to await the arrival of a certain Bardiot, who had just served fifteen days in prison: 'He was cheered by the crowd which accompanied him as far as the parade ground, bearing lanterns on the end of poles and singing "La Marsellaise" and "La Carmagnole".' On the way, they hooted at the gendarmes and heaped abuse on the 'loafers'. This was repeated on a dozen or so other occasions, observing a ritual that was always identical — bouquets and red lanterns, songs and shouts, processions, meetings and sometimes parties — the turn-out varying according to the notoriety of the militants involved.[12]

Here demonstration becomes ceremonial. The converse can also happen, and certain festivals may serve as a pretext for demonstrations. Or they serve as quite literal disguises for demonstrations, as for example when the Anzin miners took advantage of the subterfuges that were made available to them by carnival. Since a number of masked workers armed with staves had attempted to prevent workers doing their jobs, the mayor of Denain had issued a decree forbidding the use of masks: 'Art. 1: the wearing of fancy dress is only authorised this year on carnival days.' At the mid-Lent cavalcade, which was in fact a rather staid and 'respectable' event (one float represented the Republic and Alsace-Lorraine), a horseman carried a sign which read 'An old warhorse from 1884'. The chief constable had it removed. Generally, the Socialists of the Nord were to use these popular celebrations for propaganda purposes.[13] At

12. Between 2,000 and 6,000 people turned out on 20 November for Citizen Toussat, nicknamed the 'Louise Michel of Vierzon'. There were between 4,000 and 12,000 for Baudin, the popular porcelain-worker, who was a Blanquist municipal councillor, but a mere 300 for young Alfred Janvier, aged eighteen, whom his friends, almost all of them aged between twelve and sixteen, adorned with a Phrygian cap. Accounts of these various demonstrations can be found in Arch. dép. Cher M23.
13. Arch. dép. Nord, M 154/61, pièce 170, com. pol. Roubaix, 20 March 1882: one float was organised by a group from the Catrice café (run by a socialist activist) on the theme 'The crash of the Union Générale or the Clericals' Bank'; the bank clerk was dressed as a priest and his assistant was a nun. This is the earliest such example I have come across. All the other towns were to gradually follow suit: at Lille, for the first time in 1887, there was a float decked out in red and a song entitled *The Well-being of the Workers* was sung (see *L'Avenir du travailleur*, 27 February 1887).

Saint-Quentin, Saint Louis's Day, which was the feast day of the weavers' guild, was 'turned upside down'. At the hour of mass, at which, according to *La Défense des travailleurs*, only a few 'country-folk' were present, the workers gathered at the Place Saint-Cloud and sang rude songs about the bosses to the tune of 'La Carmagnole'. In similar circumstances, the mayor of Graulhet forbade the 14 July parade, and the striking tawers took up the challenge and organised a march. With banners, a band and a bust of Marianne at their head, they 'marched through almost every street, every so often blowing on whistles and offering an occasional shout of "Down with Ferry!"'

Finally, we come to funerals, which were a major form of popular demonstration in the nineteenth century — though their political importance actually tended to decline as the Republic's skill at annexing them increased (from this point of view, Victor Hugo's interment marks the end of an era). In times of strikes, however, they regained all their old prestige. If the deceased was a striker and if his burial was a civil one, then a large crowd thronged to the funeral. They were generally silent and peaceful, anxious to show their cohesiveness by weight of numbers alone.[14] Only the burial of Eudes, the general of the Commune, which occurred right in the middle of the navvies' strike (he had died suddenly during a public meeting), stands in the great tradition of political funerals. There were violent exchanges at the funeral and *Le Cri du peuple's* headline read: 'Sixty Wounded. Shots Fired on the People. Beginnings of Civil War.'

Forms of Demonstration

Though diverse in their objectives, demonstrations were uncomplicated in their form. They consisted either of gatherings of people or

---

An old worker who died in the 1960s in Paris, where he was a *concierge*, an ex-Guesdist who had become a Communist, told me stories of his childhood as a weaver in Roubaix around 1890 and of the fun they had at these carnivals at which, hidden behind their masks, the workers were able to make fun of their bosses without fear of retribution.

14. Among the miners, funerals — particularly after accidents — were often the place where strikes began. During the long Decazeville strike, funerals were major events: thus on 7 and 8 May 1886, several hundred people attended civil funerals, which until then had been very rare events and delegations were sent from all over the coalfield (see Arch. préf. pol. BA 187). At Cours on 6 August 1889, there were 800 people in the funeral cortège of a striker who had died. Among the miners, the speeches made on these occasions usually provided an opportunity for attacking the companies: this was the case with Lepêtre's address at Anzin in March 1883 (Arch.

of marches. Indeed, the two were often combined: one gathered in order to march and one marched in order to be together, and the marches included stops at the most important places connected with the strike. However, the two varieties of action reveal certain morphological differences which derive in part from their respective functions.

Marches were predominantly demonstrative in their objectives, and the extent of ground covered was more important than the numbers taking part. The object was to carry news of the strike to the four corners of the town, to bring the strike to the towns-people's attention, to alert them without frightening them, by holding peaceful, joyful, disciplined processions, in which the group affirmed its cohesiveness — hence a preoccupation with spectacle and a kind of pomp which drew on both religious and military models. The weavers of Cours advanced 'in the most complete silence with a girl and a boy of some eighteen years of age at their head. The girl held an unfurled tricolour in her hand'. They also carried branches they had cut down when passing through the woods. The glass-workers of the Paris suburbs and the Decazeville miners 'marched in step as if to give themselves a military air'. Among the Roubaix weavers, 'sometimes as many as 15,000 gathered together; to control the movements of such a crowd, they blew on bugles brought along for the purpose'. There was in all this a clear concern for organisation, and even for stage-management, which was as much directed at the participants as at the spectators. By their very structure, marches revived hierarchies. They called for a leader. Every march had its Moses, a young and fiery one if action was in the ascendant (and we have seen above the preponderance of youth in the 'age pyramid' of demonstration leaders), or a wise old mentor if greater importance was attached to order. A march entailed a certain format which seemed as much functional as it was symbolic. At the head came the bands and flags, children, youths and women. Children like the urchins in *Germinal* — Jeanlin, Bébert and Lydie — or the lively, nimble ones in *Adalen 31*, were always running about at the head of the procession, ever ready to start throwing stones, and particularly ready to let rip against the factory windows. The women, often with very young children in tow, were no less ardent, making both a physical and a vocal contribution to the proceedings (in the Thizy town square, they

dép. Nord M626/1, pièce 3) and Lefèbvre's at Dorignies on 23 October 1888 (M626/18), amongst others.

'would not stop singing'), boldly haranguing the non-strikers and revealing themselves capable of the most extreme violence.[15] The presence of women and children at the front of marches may come as a surprise, as today's strikers would be more likely to keep their offspring out of harm's way, but these demonstrations were (at least in the early years) celebrations. We may say then that the strike procession was an organised society, with a marked family structure. It was socially homogeneous and relatively closed in on itself. Marches generally passed off without much incident. Once they had reached the end of their route, the marchers dispersed, having accomplished their objective, which was to spread a message.

As pressure groups were orientated towards action, static demonstrations sought to concentrate the greatest possible force at the precise places which were the sensitive points of a strike. Relying on numbers for their effect, the crowds that were gathered were open, egalitarian, fluid and shifting and exercised great powers of attraction. Hence the rapid swelling of their ranks, though these were anything but solid and the crowds could be quickly dispersed. At Lisieux on 9 July 1873, at 8 p.m., some 400 or 500 strikers assailed the manager of the Méry-Samson weaving-mill at the end of a day's shift; taking refuge in a nearby house, he was 'besieged by a furious crowd which, continually growing, soon totalled 2,000'; later, a gathering that had formed to wait for the delegates who were being received in the town hall, 'eventually reached a total of between 4,000 and 5,000 persons'. At Thizy, the gendarmerie managed to clear the Place de l'Hôtel-de-Ville, but at 7 p.m. there came a wave of workers from the factories to join the bands who had come down from the mountains, and the result was a stagnant flood of between 5,000 and 6,000 individuals. At Mehun-sur-Yèvre, to show solidarity with sixty strikers, meetings of between 300 and 700 participants, rising to 1,000 on the last day, followed one after another at the gates of the Pillivuyt factory.

Such crowds had a hybrid character. At Mehun the crowd consisted of 'first of all the larger part of the strikers, then a crowd of women and children and people with nothing else to do'. At Saint-Quentin, in the troop bearing down upon the Testart works, there were 'many people who had nothing to do with the factory'; a ragpicker from the town was later arrested, stone in hand. At Vierzon, in the demonstrations directed daily against the Société

15. At Cours they were present, 'carrying their children in their arms or holding them by the hand' (Arch. nat. F12 4653); at Fives-Lille, '500 women followed with children in their arms' (Arch. nat., F12 4661).

Française de Matériel Agricole in October 1886, there were fewer metal-workers taking part than glass-workers or workers from other trades. Such gatherings carried the debate out into the public arena. They linked the population to the strike and, more importantly, allowed them to give vent to that latent discontent (hidden resentment, repressed desire) which, when it is accumulated and then unleashed (in what Canetti would call the 'discharge') is at the heart of powerful demonstrations.

Number of Participants

In the period we are looking at here, it must be said that demonstrations remained modest in size. They reflected the strikes and the economic and demographic structures of a country which had no great conurbations. Below the percentages of different sizes of demonstration are listed according to number of participants:

Less than 100	20%
From 100 to 500	47%
From 500 to 1,000	15%
From 1,000 to 10,000	12%
More than 10,000	3%

The typical demonstration has only a few hundred participants: it corresponds in size to the workforce in a textile mill. Then come the 'gangs' of miners (500 to 1,000). The demonstrations with between 1,000 and 10,000 participants are the urban ones of which we have given a number of examples above, in which a lower-class public coalesces around an initial nucleus of workers. Gatherings exceeding 10,000 in number are met with only exceptionally in the great industrial agglomerations of the Nord and, particularly, at Roubaix, a town with a rapidly increasing population, which *Le Temps* called an 'American city'. In May 1880, between 12,000 and 20,000 workers marched through the streets, and there were as many as 75,000 on 3 May 1890, a figure which shows what resonance the first May Day had. Nevertheless, it is clear from these figures that the size of the crowds of French workers that were assembled towards the end of the nineteenth century remains modest. A *sans-culotte* would not have found the scene unfamiliar.

There was, therefore, perhaps an effort to compensate for lack of numbers by dynamism: overall, action and movement predominated. The authorities urged this upon the workers, knowing the dangers of leaving them standing still: 'I imposed on the strikers an obligation to keep moving', writes Paul Cambon of the Roubaix strikes of May 1880. 'Marching forces a certain discipline upon them naturally by compelling them to get into rows and sing in unison . . . it tires them and averts violence against either people or property by channelling their activity in a different direction.' Moreover, for these people who were accustomed to being shut up indoors, there was a sort of intoxication to be had from walking and from feeling free; sometimes they walked for hours, or even for whole days, pacing up and down the streets or through the country-side, like fresh-air fiends. It remains now to describe this noisy, colourful company.

Noise

Silent demonstrations were rare: the arrival of 600 weavers at Cours, 'in the most complete silence' was an exception.[16] Shouting, singing and even bands provide an indispensable background of sound. The chair-makers of La Chapelle-aux-Bois and the miners of Saint Eloy and Firminy marched behind their drum-bands. The wrought-iron workers of La Vrigne-aux-Bois were accompanied by the sound of the bugle; the dye-workers of Flers (Nord) marched 'with drums and bugles at their head', and to these the Doyet miners added the hurdy-gurdy. The Graulhet tawers commandeered the village brass band, while the weavers of Thizy brandished bucolic flageolets. Two hundred railway navvies from Commentry, driven from their work by a sudden feverish mood two days before May Day, went through the town 'in their working clothes . . . led by a musette; boisterous and bantering, they beat time with their great clogs.'

Most demonstrations broke into some kind of song, though we do not always know of what kind. The statistics given below have only an indicative value; they are derived from 164 demonstrations in which it is explicitly reported that there was singing:

'La Marseillaise'	64	(39% of the total)
'La Carmagnole'	36	(21% of the total)
Made-up songs	17	(10% of the total)
Other patriotic or revolutionary songs	13	

16. I have come across two others in which silence played a part: they were both women's demonstrations (the Bordeaux cigar-workers in April 1889 and the weavers of Notre-Dame-de-Bondeville in June).

Boulangist songs	4
Unspecified	30
	164

'La Marseillaise' remained the favourite song with strikers, the one they would strike up most spontaneously. The reader will, of course, recall the subversive character it possessed during the period of the *Ordre Moral* government. The workers marched to its strains in the great parades of 1880, but its dominance was subsequently challenged by 'La Carmagnole', which is first reported at Saint-Quentin in 1884. The importance of the latter song steadily grew to the extent that, between 1887 and 1890, twenty-three Carmagnoles are recorded, as against twenty-one Marseillaises! Moreover, Henri Leyret, writing in 1895, stresses the general loss of affection for 'La Marseillaise' in workers' sing-songs and the familiarity of the chorus of 'La Carmagnole'. Why did this song become popular? Was it on account of its rhythm or its imagery? Whatever the answer, it is interesting to register the persistence of the heritage of the French Revolution. By comparison with these two, the other songs are rather insignificant. At Vierzon and Mehun, they also sang 'Laissez Passer la Sociale'; at Cholet, the 'Chanson du Drapeau Rouge'; in October 1890, the glass-workers of Fresnes-Escaupont struck up Pédron's 'Chanson des Huit Heures'. Overall, the revolutionary repertoire of the streets was slow to renew itself, in spite of the activists' predilection for this form of propaganda.[17]

The improvised songs that are reported — without unfortunately always giving us anything of their flavour — were the work of local, and generally anonymous, poets. The miners were particularly keen on such songs. Calvignac relates that the course of the 1869 strikes at Carmaux 'unfolded to the strains of a song composed for the occasion by a young local man' and, in his *Mémoires*, he reproduces the first three verses. This served as a model; fragments of it are to be found in 'La Grève de Carmaux' of 1883, several thousand copies of which were printed and which was sung at every demonstration; they also survive in 'La Chanson de la Grève des Ouvriers de

17. In a pamphlet on *The General Strike* (Paris, Imprimerie Nouvelle, 1901), we read on p. 16: 'By this latter system, emancipatory ideas can be disseminated widely. We can sing in the workshops, at home with our families and at all our meetings'. The song and poetry columns held an indispensable place in the workers' newspapers. They are a rich source of material, and present us, through all their clichés and repetitions, with a complete world-view. J.-B. Clément, E. Pottier and, in particular, J. Jouy (in *Le Cri du peuple*) were the great song-writers of the labour movement at this period. There was no major strike they did not celebrate in song.

Rochebelle' of May 1890. These ballads of lament celebrate the 'togetherness' of the strikers and the rightness of their cause. They are scathing in their treatment of the managers and engineers, who, to the Carmaux miners of 1883, were 'that foul, accursed engineer', 'a ferocious tiger', 'that brazen Turk', 'accursed tyrants' and 'bigots'. For the men of Rochebelle (1890), they were 'a wild tiger', 'a fat bulldog and a stubborn old mule', and 'a terrible despot'. Their misdeeds are recorded, and they are promised retribution. We must, however, note a decline in the level of threats being made: in 1869, the colliers of Carmaux swore they would turn out their manager ('We'll see him off, His pack on his back. We'll follow him with cudgel blows') and pillage the château of the Marquis de Solages, which in fact they did. The 1883 song no longer includes this verse and ends on an invocation of France, the Republic and Jesus Christ. And at Rochebelle they sang: 'Let's be calm, good miners/ And lend each other a sure helping hand./Let's unite, arise and throw off that terrible despot'. At La Grand-Combe in 1881 and Anzin in 1884, strike songs are also reported, but there is no record of the words.

Weavers' songs were less elaborate. By contrast with the miners' songs, they generally took the form of songs sung to well-known tunes, with words improvised to a greater or lesser degree. They probably originated in the ranks of the demonstrators themselves or within the swirling movement of a crowd, and they lent themselves easily to being chanted in chorus.[18] At Saint-Quentin, to the tune of 'La Carmagnole', we find:

> Boca, and Testart swore a vow,
> They would lay the workers low
> But their plan was overturned
> Thanks to our standing firm
> We shall thrash them etc . . .

At Reims, the weavers sang:

> You can't buy bread on a weaver's pay.
> Oh, the masters are louses.
> We'll string them up
> Like rabbits today,
> In their own houses.

18. With the exception of five couplets, sung to the tune of *Curé de Pomponne*, written by a certain Léon Noël, a grinder of the montée Rey, who was 'born out of wedlock' according to the police records which were always attentive to that kind of information. This was a song about the manufacturers and workers of the Barral & Gacogne silk company, great 'poor-makers' of Lyon. Cf. Arch. nat. F12 4662, printed sheet, *La Grève des tisseurs*, 1884.

At Mazamet, the weavers alternately sang 'La Marseillaise' and another song written for the occasion having as its chorus, 'We want a living wage for our work. Pay the rate for the job or die!'. The verses sung by the Roubaix strikers seem to have had more notoriety and longevity, since they are still heard in 1890 as they had been in 1880, sung by thousands of workers both in the streets and in bars. A little poster reproducing the song was torn down from a factory wall by the police:

> If they won't give us more
> We shall wreck the whole place
> If they won't raise our pay,
> We shall cut their throats
> If the masters give no rise
> We shall string them up
> Our delegates are in prison
> With 6 million in the coffers

In all these texts there is one central figure, the master, marked out for every kind of retribution. If in practice very few were actually murdered, they were constantly being 'killed' in songs.[19]

Lastly, let us note the appearance in 1888–9 of a number of Boulangist refrains, both in the Nord and in Paris. These were particularly to be heard during the navvies' strike, though according to one report, they were 'without any political intention'.[20]

Mixed in with this singing were blasts on whistles, boos and shouts ('yells' was the term used by the chief constable of Château-Regnault in 1885), together with that 'enlevez-le',[21] which

---

19. Our documents report other made-up strike songs, though unfortunately they do not give the words. For example, at Hazebrouck in May 1885, 'a troop of 500 men, women and children . . . sang an improvised song about the strike in Flemish' (Arch. nat. F12 4661, gendarmerie report, 27 May 1885); at Boissières, the woollen-weavers at the Cattelain-Motte mills demonstrated for an hour to the strains of 'local verses containing threats against the masters' (Arch. nat. F12 4661), and the same thing occurred again in 1888 (Arch. dép. Nord, M625/57, pièce 85). In 1887 the songs sung outside the Pillivuyt porcelain works at Mehun 'were composed by the strikers' (Arch. dép. Cher, M16).

20. Arch. dép. Nord M625/57, pièce 85, s-préf-préf., 27 August 1888: apart from 'La Marseillaise' and 'Le Chant du départ', local songs and diverse popular and patriotic airs, the linen-weavers of Hazebrouck sang 'La Revue'. Towards midday on the 18 February 1889, the navvies of Saint-Souplet (Nord) 'met together, placed a red belt at the end of a pole and marched through the town' singing Boulangist songs and 'La Marseillaise' (Arch. nat., gendarmerie report, 19 February 1889). On 16 March the Halluin weavers 'set off through the streets of the town as was their wont, singing Boulangist songs' (*Le Progrès du Nord*, 17 March 1889).

21. According to the *Robert* dictionary, this is the equivalent of *Sortez-le!* (Out with him!)

was the classic threat addressed to the detested bosses and even, on occasion, real slogans, in which bread was a constant theme: 'Work or bread', shouted the Montjean miners; 'Bread. We're hungry. Work and bread' repeated the weavers of Le Château, massed for a whole afternoon outside the Palais de Justice; 'Poverty. Bread or lead. The masters are swine. We'll string them up. Long live '93! Long live the Social Republic! Long live the general strike', chanted their comrades from Fourmies in 1886. More modestly, the Vieux Condé miners wanted 'Eight hours' work. Five francs' wage.' The most common cries to fill the air were those of 'Down with' and 'Long live', the latter being in the majority. The people most subjected to catcalls were the employers — most usually by name — and the forces of law and order, the *cognes* (gendarmes) and the *sergots* (police). The army was spared such abuse, and weavers at Tourcoing in May 1890 were even heard to shout 'Long live the army!'. There were few political catcalls. However, the weavers of the Nord did not hesitate to assert their anti-clericalism. The cry of 'Down with priests' was heard at Roubaix in 1880 and again at Fives-Lille in 1885, where stones were thrown at religious establishments.

Cheers, however, were more common than boos. Acclaimed in this way were, first of all, quite naturally, the strike itself, followed by the Republic, a slogan so dear to the miners that the authorities used this commitment to the Republic as a means of putting pressure on them. The old 1848 expression *la Sociale* was employed time and again. 'Social revolution' was first invoked in the streets of Bessèges in 1882 by the miners, among whom there was great unrest at the time. 'Long live the Revolution. No more masters' was the clear message of the Reims weavers and the Paris shoemakers. From 1885–6 onwards, the two expressions 'social revolution' and 'revolution', which were apparently used interchangeably, or at least in the same milieux, took over from 'the Republic'. And yet, socialism was hardly ever acclaimed out in the open, and the Commune too was only rarely cheered. It took some audacity on the part of activists or a shock such as the death of 'General' Eudes to give the strikers the courage to pronounce such words out of doors.

. . . and Colour

Flags carried by young men, children or women, led the parades. The old guild banners had been put away and the tricolour dominated here (in about two-thirds of cases) even more than 'La

Marseillaise' dominated the singing. When it did appear, the red flag was almost always produced by some improvisation, some grass-roots initiative. It raised its head at Wattrelos in May 1880: 'I noticed', writes the chief constable, 'an individual carrying a sort of flag, made from a red handkerchief or scarf placed at the end of quite a long pole.' The embroiderers of Pontruet (Aisne), the Armentières weavers and the navvies from Saint-Souplet all wore a 'red belt'; the Decazeville miners sported a piece of scarlet cloth. We find red again at Bessèges in 1882, this time as a flag, together with the black flag and the tricolour. But it was May Day which institutionalised red by making it the colour of the workers' flag. It is no surprise to learn that this aroused the open hostility of the authorities. But we must also note the reservations expressed by some of the workers' leaders. At Decazeville, for example, 'a group of miners had stuck a red rag on the end of a pike. Having spotted them, Basly went over and urged them forcefully to desist from this form of demonstration, upon which they removed the seditious emblem from view'. And of course the controversy, stoked by Boulangism, which ranged the supporters of the tricolour against those of the red flag at the Bordeaux Congress of 1888, is well known.

The colour black appeared only rarely. Its appearance was almost always attributable to the activity of some small anarchist grouping, as at Bessèges in 1882, Paris in 1885 (anarchist tailors in the 'Panther' group) and at Vienne in 1890.[22] This influence is less easily discernible at Rimagne (Ardennes). On 16 May 1888, 400 slaters there 'with a group of drunken women, went around the district carrying black flags'. Black, the colour of mourning, 'an expression of sombre social misery' had a worrying, depressing effect. If the May Day march organisers regarded red as sacred, they avoided black completely. The workers' parties of today execrate it.

Violence in Strikes

A Statistical Approach

If demonstrations obeyed a certain order — as yet weak, though subsequently to be bolstered up as an organisational framework

22. *Procès des anarchistes de Vienne*, p. 33: 'The presiding magistrate asked . . . Martin what the significance of the red and black flags was. Martin replied that the red flag had always been the standard of those rebelling against all tyrannies and

developed — they were very largely free of violence. In only a third of them were there any disturbances. I have included in this category all collective, physical aggression against persons or property committed in the course of a strike. Fights among the workers themselves being counted separately, it is therefore principally violence against the class enemy (bosses, the authorities) which concerns us in this part of our study.

Only 3.6 per cent of strikes involved acts of this nature. This is a very small proportion; it is less, indeed, than the figures for brawls between workers (5.6 per cent). Strikes and violence seem then to be two quite distinct phenomena. Annual percentages fluctuate between 0.4 per cent and 10 per cent without any overall pattern of development emerging. The years from 1887 to 1889 are the stormiest, coming as they did at the end of a crisis period, when the long-run effects of poverty had become unbearable. As regards the various different trades and the differences between them, what was true of demonstrations also holds good here. The miners and the navvies are notable for their brutality (12 per cent and 15 per cent, respectively), while workers in the book-printing, wood and metal trades are notable for their affability. Although 17 per cent of violent incidents occur in the textile industry, the percentage rate for violence within strikes for this group is around the general average (4 per cent). Defensive strikes were more likely to give rise to disturbances (4.1 per cent as against 3.3 per cent for offensive strikes), but company structure was an even more significant influence, the rate for family businesses being 2 per cent as opposed to 6 per cent for joint-stock companies. The influence of the length and size of a strike on the figures is clear (Table 4). By contrast, seasonal factors do not seem to play a role. Lastly, it is noticeable that the theatres of violent conflict are not so much towns or cities as the little mining or textile villages which were the first staging-posts in the process of emigration from the land and thus in the formation of the working class.

How Violence Broke Out

Violence raised its head at various stages of a strike, but it was

against all forms of reaction. It flew at the storming of the Bastille and again in 1830; it was raised in 1848 by the revolutionary socialist people; lastly, it was also to be found in the hands of the defeated fighters of the Commune in 1871. The black flag is the expression of the sombre social misery which reigns in certain periods, as in 1831, when the workers of Lyon wrote on it *We'll live by our labour or die fighting.'*

Table 4: Percentage of disturbances in strikes

By numbers involved		*By length*	
Strikers	(%)	Days	(%)
1–10	0.9	1	2.4
11–30	0.6	2	2.3
31–90	0.7	3–4	2.1
91–270	2.8	5–8	1.0
271–810	6.7	9–16	6.0
811–2,430	22.0	17–32	5.0
2,431–7,290	17.0	33–64	10.8
More than 7,290	62.0	65–128	11.7
		129–256	22.0

particularly likely to occur at two points. The first of these was right at the outset. At Etricourt, for example, the seasonal workers in a sugar refinery demanded a wage rise; then, 'without waiting for a reply, they wrecked the Decauville railway which served to carry the beets from the silo to the washing plant, broke the lanterns and one of the factory windows and then threw beets at the workers who were replacing them'. But this brutal manner of registering a wage claim was rather exceptional. By contrast, many defensive strikes began this way, with a furious protest action, and were, in some cases, little other than such actions. Wage reductions were especially likely to produce reactions of this kind. When 250 cotton-weavers in the Berthet mill at Rouen learned of such a reduction, they went out into the yard, shouting, bawling and breaking windows. A similar situation was at the origin of the disturbances at Lisieux in July 1873, where the manager only just escaped being stoned. It was in similar circumstances that Watrin died, thrown from a window. However, the riotous strike, such a common occurrence in the first half of the century, was becoming quite rare. The figures for one-day strikes — which were generally turbulent rather than actually violent — have a below-average percentage of disturbances (2.4 per cent). The riotous strike was something to which only the most downtrodden, least organised workers had recourse. The prefect wrote of the Avesne-les-Aubert weavers that 'the workers are making up in violence for what they lack in organisation'. What was also usually required to produce this type of strike phenomenon was a long build-up of grievances which could be ignited by some final indignity. Though anger was certainly involved, the dominant sentiment behind such actions was exasperation.[23]

This explains why, as was increasingly the case, outbreaks of violence were particularly common in long strikes, especially in the final phases of such strikes (and the violence did much to hasten their end). At Roubaix in 1880, as at Reims, the most violent confrontations occurred three weeks into the strike and only a few days from its end. At Amiens in 1888, on the forty-ninth day of the strike, the velvet-weavers broke down the gates of the detested Cocquel factory, looted, burned and set up a barricade. On the fifty-seventh day of their strike, the Sommedieu chair-makers laid siege in the night to their employer's house; then, appalled perhaps by their own audacity, returned to work the next day.

At Anzin, the disturbances of 4 April 1884 occurred on the forty-fifth day of a dispute whose peaceful nature had until then surprised all observers. On the very eve of the troubles, Paul Cambon wrote: 'As it goes on, the strike shows no signs of anything other than a certain monotony', and he contrasted the wild strike movements of 1872 and 1878 with this one, which seemed made up of thoughtful men who were prepared to negotiate calmly. In passing, we may note that the sudden transformation which occurred here — which is connected with the development of a trade unionism based on negotiation — is typical of most miners' strikes. The early days were spent quietly tending the garden, looking after their potatoes, doing odd jobs and generally getting on with family life. In the evening, the workers dashed off with their whole families to the meetings at which their delegates reported back on the negotiations. The joy of rediscovered leisure and confidence in the 'rightness of the cause' combined to create a euphoric atmosphere. Then time passed, victory receded, and the negotiations marked time. The delegates, seated around the front table at the meetings, began to seem more and more like ridiculous stuffed dummies. Doubt crept in. Attendance at the meetings fell off. The strike entered a dull, melancholy, depressing period of waiting.

At this point the temperature began to rise in the mining villages,

23. The death of Watrin is a good example of this. All the files relating to the police investigations show it to have been the culmination of a suppressed hatred that went back over a six-year period. Watrin, the willing pawn of an ailing company's austerity policies had never ceased, since his arrival at Decazeville in 1880, to 'squeeze' wages by all the means at his disposal: by making jobs more onerous, lowering rates of pay, imposing fines of all kinds and even creating a company shop. Moreover, legitimist and intensely religious, he kept a constant pressure on the workers in both electoral and religious matters.

which had once again become decision-making centres. Faced with empty purses and empty cupboards, and bakers less and less willing to give credit, the housewives' anxiety grew. In the early hours of morning, a few timid, trembling forms set off furtively for the pit. Groups formed up along the way against these betrayers. Mocked, jeered, chased and attacked, these unfortunates provided a first target for a bitterness that was born of a feeling that they had been swindled. The gendarmes intervened to protect the 'right to work' and proceeded to make arrests, which stirred up the sense of solidarity. Secret talks took place in the night. Gangs formed up, moving towards the mines. They were led by fiery young men who were in the grip of a single obsession: they must stop the ventilators and cut the cables. And around the pits, with their military-style protection, the revolt was brewing.

This henceforth classic scenario — which of course provided the framework for Zola's *Germinal* — was repeated in many a long-drawn-out miners' strike and, with variations, in most of the strikes which failed. Negotiations presuppose a partner with whom one may talk: if that partner disappears, violence takes over once again — the more vigorous perhaps, and certainly the more deliberate, for having been bottled up. This delayed violence should not in fact be confused with the outburst at the beginning of a strike. There is less spontaneity in it; it is more a product of conscious decision. It is a fruit of bitter experience: the failure of the 'proper legal channels'. Then, as now, it was in that failure that a renewed recourse to violence had its roots.

This secondary violence, which occurred part way through or at the end of a strike, was neither fortuitous nor gratuitous. It resulted from encountering an obstacle; that is, first and foremost, the bosses' resistance. It was their refusal to negotiate, their intransigence, bad faith and volte-faces when they sensed the strike was beginning to weaken, that were at the origin of most of the disturbances. Their responsibilities in this regard are obvious and were frequently recognised by the authorities. I shall give only a few examples here to show how a process that can only end in violence was set in train.

At Anzin the attitude of Guary, the manager, caused the riots of 4 April 1884. On the 1 April the miners' delegates had a final meeting with him, which they had respectfully requested: 'We have been delegated by our *commune* to come and lay before you our proposals, which are simply that we should work as in the past and that our work-mates who have been dismissed for no good reason should be reinstated.' Guary refused both proposals, replying on the second point that 'the company had not sought to get rid of all the workers who were trying to do it harm, as there were at least 600 such workers at the mine'. The rumour then spread that there were to be further mass sackings. Anxiety grew and on the 4 April a crowd that had gathered at the station to welcome Roche went to the Renard pit to prevent the miners who had gone down from coming back up and to destroy the winding gear. The battle went on for the whole afternoon, and it took reinforcements from the gendarmerie and then a detachment of dragoons with a general at their head, to relieve the pit. There followed three days of serious disturbances throughout the coalfield.

At Saint-Quentin, where the weavers had been on strike since the 30 January 1886 for standard rates of pay, news came on the 4 February of the breakdown of negotiations. On the morning of the 5 February workers began to gather threateningly. In the early afternoon the workers broke windows in several factories and, around 5 p.m. they erected a barricade. At Le Cateau on the morning of the 29 December 1883, the closure of the Lempereur-Chantreuil mill produced some initial incidents. Between 200 and 300 workers stood around all afternoon outside the law courts, where the sub-prefect was in conference with the employers. When they learned that this attempt at mediation had come to nothing they charged the court building and looted the factory. At Roubaix in May 1880, not content with refusing to make any concessions whatever, the mill-owners demanded the workers pay a fine for not having given due notice of their action; this decision sparked off a number of attacks on the mills.

One final example gives some idea of this retaliatory, avenging violence which was tending to become dominant. After a three-day strike (11–14 February 1889) that had been legalistic in the extreme, the wretched linen-weavers of the Avesnois region (whose wages were less than 1 franc a day) won an across-the-board pay rise of 25 per cent, properly sealed and delivered and guaranteed by the signatures of the two parties. But in spite of the mayor's prot-estations, the manufacturers did not respect the agreement; indeed, they went further and locked the recalcitrant weavers out of the cellars where they worked. From that point on, the conviction grew among the workers that they would have to resort to drastic measures. 'Again and again you heard them say, "We shall burn and we shall loot if they don't pay."' On 13 March there was a planned and organised attack on all fronts: 'The workers . . . gathered in groups at around 9 p.m. At 9.15 p.m. gangs were organised and set off through the village streets singing "La Marseillaise". They stopped outside every house where one of the offending manufacturers lived and, after giving some thought as to whether or not it was appropriate to attack, they decided to smash everything.'

There is, in general, a certain relationship between aggressive bosses and violence on the part of the workers. The Boca, Testart and Gabréau establishments at Saint-Quentin, Rogelet at Reims, Cocquel at Amiens, Seydoux at Fourmies, and so on, were the epicentres of such violence. In fact, it was the arbitrariness of action even more than its harshness which sparked off movements of revolt. Other establishments — and by no means only the small ones — experienced no such clashes. The workers accepted that the game had to have rules: they had, in that sense, come into the industrial age. But they would not stand for chance factors interfering with their levels of remuneration. Aware of the risk they were running, the bosses became increasingly wary of employing such summary measures to protect their profits. If they did have recourse to them, it was doubtless because they had become routine, though they also used such measures on many occasions because they were absolutely compelled to. It would, in fact, be naive to seek purely psychological grounds for such an attitude; it is frequently rooted in a situation of relative economic inferiority. Stubbornness on the part of employers generally concealed a certain weakness. This mixture of high-handedness and impotence was tailor-made to produce a climate of violence.

The Pattern of Violence

We must now turn to an examination of the object, forms and degrees of violence perpetrated during strikes. To be schematic, we may say that such violence had the factory as its prime target, window-breaking as its major form and the stone as its principal weapon. At the outset, then, this locates the true level of violence: it is simple stone-throwing, doing little actual damage and having, in fact, an essentially symbolic value. It is a mock violence, and its object is to frighten rather than destroy.

Weapons

One thing which must be said right at the beginning is that the strikers were generally unarmed. Admittedly, what reports of armed incidents there are will seem strange to us today, since the

French working class is now totally unarmed. Readers will doubt-less make parallels in what they read here with the state of insecurity that prevails in American cities today. Amongst the miners who laid siege to the station at Anzin on 24 July 1872 to free their comrades who were being sent to prison, 'some [were] armed with pistols'. In 1878 at Raismes, among the bands bivouacking in the woods, 'only a few miners were armed with rifles'. The Montceau rioters of 1882 were 'armed with rifles, pitchforks and revolvers'. The reader will note the hotch-potch nature of this equipment and the restrictive formulations which appear in these various descriptions. There is no hint here of well-stocked arsenals.

Moreover, though they were always ready to brandish *the word* 'revolver' ('if [the soldiers] have rapid-firing rifles, then we have revolvers, which are more use than pikes', announced Tennevin proudly to the presiding magistrate at Vienne), they were less ready to use the real thing. The cases of shots being fired during strikes are so exceptional that we can draw up a complete list. The Anzin miners 'fired several shots at the troops . . . [who] fired back in self-defence. One miner was killed and two injured'. This is the only case of armed confrontation with the forces of law and order in the period. Furthermore, this account, which is too obviously aimed at justifying the killing which occurred, is itself somewhat suspect and does not match up with statements by other witnesses. The example of the young weaver Fournier has a certain symbolic value here. Firing on his boss, Bréchard, at point-blank range, (5 feet, we are told), he missed his target. This reveals a peculiar but symptomatic lack of experience with arms.

Gunshots were, by contrast, quite common in two sectors of industry. In the large factories of the Paris suburbs, which were characterised by extreme brutality, foremen and workers were quick to settle their differences this way, as can be seen for example in the incidents which occurred during strikes at the Raffinerie Parisienne at Saint-Ouen and at the Malétra chemical works at Saint-Denis in 1887. At Saint-Denis, Pierre Meubry, aged thirty-two and of Breton origin, fired three shots at the foreman held responsible for a cut in wages; it took the intervention of two brigades of gendarmerie to overpower him. At Saint-Ouen, a band of workers gave chase to a certain Geledts, another 'slave-driver', who was detested for having replaced the hourly wage by a piece-rate. '"Go on — let's get him." Geledts, without offering any response, crossed smartly over the Boulevard Victor-Hugo into the Rue Arago. However, there, one of Geledts's companions, a Monsieur

Dupré, was hit on the leg by a stone, whereupon he pulled out a revolver and fired a shot in the air. Their assailants immediately fired several shots, and one bullet only just missed Monsieur Geledts, who in turn fired back, though without wounding anyone.' It seems all these men carried revolvers in their belts and were as ready to draw them as cowboys on the range!

The railway navvies too were quick on the draw, particularly against foreigners. During disturbances in Haute-Marne in 1888 and 1889 for example, 'the French workers armed themselves with stakes, staves and even revolvers' to run Piedmontese workers off the site. Xenophobia, as we know, could override every last scruple.

In the immense majority of cases, however, strikers used less harmful objects, often taken from among the tools of their trade. Knives were drawn on several occasions: a number of non-strikers and two foremen received serious wounds in this way, and an Italian was killed. The navvies did not hesitate to wield their picks, while the carpenters brandished compasses and the shoemakers their awls; in one incident some women chased an overseer, scissors in hand, threatening to castrate him. In all these cases it was a matter of picking up whatever happened to be to hand on the site or at the work-bench. The miners never used their tools but had a liking for sticks. In the bands of weavers who roved around the Thizy area, 'most of the men carried pieces of wood of various sizes on their shoulders, apparently indicating by this sign that they [were] even prepared to use force to obtain satisfaction'. This is a perceptive comment; what was really involved here was a tactic of showing force in order to avoid having to use it. These sticks — more walking sticks than weapons — had a rustic air; they smacked of the copses they had passed through while wandering about the countryside; indeed, the weavers had 'cut them down in the woods they had come through'.

At the opposite pole from this weapon borrowed from nature, dynamite, invented in 1869, was starting out on its prestigious career. The Montceau insurgents used it in great quantities to blow up churches and wayside crosses. On several occasions, at Decazeville (1886) and L'Escarpelle, small charges exploded during the hours of darkness in renegades' gardens. The use of this substance remained principally the prerogative of miners, who could acquire it easily. However, in 1889, at Thizy and Cours, in an area where anarchism was rife, weavers placed a number of charges at the employers' houses. In all these cases the actual damage done was minimal, and the quantities employed were moderate, even timorous, when compared with the workers' apocalyptic predictions: 'with dynamite and melinite we shall finish off the bourgeoisie' was the cry heard at meetings in Paris, whilst the peaceable miners of Malafolie wrote to their mayor: 'If the company does not dismiss the manager, we are going to use explosives; we shall put dynamite to work.' There is no doubt that this particular substance modified representations of subversion: revolutionary action now came to be seen as 'blowing up the old world'.

But the universally employed projectile — an expression both of privation and improvisation — was the stone. This figured in both its urban and rural manifestations, as a pebble picked up from beside a country lane, a brick from a building site or a paving stone torn up from the road. Generally, all these pieces of ammunition were small enough to fit into children's pockets or women's aprons in large quantities, so that a 'hail' of them could be rained down on the adversary. The ancient act of stoning was the outlet popular anger instinctively sought. But even here instinct was tempered and organised, matching the projectile to the appropriate target. Bricks and paving stones were reserved for the gendarmes in the violent urban confrontations, whilst those lost sheep, the non-strikers, had only derisory objects thrown at them, such as mud, gravel, balls made out of bread or even, as at Mehun, apples. This was already a step along the road to the tomatoes, cooked apples, bad eggs or rotting pears of today's 'stonings'. This substitution of the soft for the hard, of the projectile which, rather than crashing into its target, is crushed against it, reveals a transition from destruction to derision, which would be worthy of a Bachelardian analysis.

Targets

The violence employed by strikers was as selective in its targets as it was in its form. It was directed more against things than persons and more against buildings than objects. The foremost among these was the factory. Hardly had the strikers left it, in that mass exodus which constituted the first joyful act of insubordination, than they returned to keep watch over it, to monitor the slightest noise or movement and, if need be, to take over the building again and re-enter it, though this time as victors. Something of the regret they felt at having left the enemy a free hand shows through here, the anxiety at losing their place, an irresistible attraction towards that space which constituted the workers' universe, the detested but indispensable factory.

The end-product of that psychological disposition was to be

factory occupation. For the time being, however, the factory tow-
ered over the daily horizon of the strike. It was an important
landmark on everyone's path, a stopping place on everyone's
travels. Moreover, seen from the outside, its face was changed.
Inside, it was an unbearable, suffocating prison; it generated an
irrepressible urge to escape. Seen from the outside, it stood like
some great Bastille, a symbol of bourgeois wealth and oppression,
and this impression was only reinforced by its being guarded by the
forces of law and order, a fact which lay bare the class nature of the
state. It was a Bastille which they no doubt dreamed of capturing,
though they did not really dare try. For although large, threatening
crowds gathered, with stones in their hands and oaths on their lips,
they thought twice about actually attacking.

I can find barely ten real sieges, almost all of them among the
weavers and virtually all of them products of an atmosphere of
deep, infuriating disappointment. Let me describe one such scene.
At Reims on the 31 October 1885 at 10 a.m., 1,500 weavers, angered
at having given up an entirely peaceful occupation without receiving
anything in exchange (the sub-prefect's efforts at mediation having
come to naught), attacked the Rogelet factory, demolished the wall
with pick-axes, broke open the gates and clashed with gendarmes
who were formed up in the yard. To the customary warnings of the
latter, they replied 'by insulting the police and gendarmes and
continuing to throw stones'. Eventually, cavalry charges and shots
fired in the air won out over their fiery spirits. Under military
occupation, then, the factory constituted an impregnable barrier
and, at that point, they began to talk of 'setting it on fire by
throwing inflammable materials into it'. The garrison inside then
had to be supplemented by day- and night-time patrols outside. The
workers went on to the offensive in this manner at Saint-Quentin,
Mazamet, Amiens, Fougères, Origny-en-Thiérache, Le Cateau, and
elsewhere, though they were almost always repulsed.

If, by chance, they managed, by their fervour or the effect of a
surprise attack, to break through the barriers set up against them
and get inside the factory, the records tell us that they 'looted'. The
word, however, requires some translation. Were they, for example,
taking property for their own individual use? Even in the very early
days of this kind of violent action, the workers involved took pains
to dispel such suspicions: during the Réveillon affair (April 1789),
according to the memoirs of an eye-witness, 'a barrier had been set
up and all the persons leaving were searched by the occupying
workers. It went badly with anyone who was caught carrying stolen

goods; he was first made to throw them on the fire, and he then received a beating commensurate with the theft he had committed'. A century later, the workers, though they repeated *ad nauseam* that their bosses were thieves, were almost equally as scrupulous, in spite of libertarian propaganda in favour of 'individual reappropriation'. At Vienne on May Day 1890 some anarchist militants, among whose number was Pierre Martin (known as 'the Hunchback'), led the workers to the factories to the strains of 'La Carmagnole'. At the mill owned by Brocard, an employer detested for his attitude during the great strike of 1897, they grabbed a 47-yard length of woollen cloth and, amid cries of 'Take it, it's yours', threw it to the crowd, who tore it up and took a piece each as one might with military trophies. With its intensely pictorial qualities — red and black flags flying, jubilant weavers and children — it was the kind of grandiose scene of collective appropriation and ritual destruction that might have inspired Eisenstein. The aim was not to take, but to destroy. At Amiens on 6 August 1888, the weavers knocked down the gates of the hated Cocquel factory, grabbed rolls of velvet, 'threw them into the street in front of the gendarmes' horses . . . and made barricades out of them. Within a few minutes, the factory had been ransacked'. While this was going on, others were setting fire to the tow workshops. What joy it was to wipe out the product of so many hours' work in just a few minutes and to see the mill-owner's profits go up in smoke. Here, that excessive expenditure or wastage, which is consubstantial with festival and whose place in precapitalist economies has recently been emphasised by sociologists, fulfils a quasi-magical function.

There can be little doubt that grandiose dreams of fire ran through the workers' minds; they at least haunted their language: 'We'll burn them', said the Cambrésis weavers, and we read that 'the strikers [of Roubaix] are in an excessive rage with their employers and are threatening to burn down their factories and their residences.'[24] In anarchists' discourse, fire became a theme to compete with dynamite: 'We have at our disposal the century's greatest innovation from the revolutionary point of view: the chemical match', said one of the defendants at Vienne, who also spoke of 'setting fire to the four corners of the town'. This weapon was, however, very little used. The incident at Amiens, which we have just described, was almost the only case. The Belgian example of

24. Arch. dép. Nord, M619/3. One poster stuck up during a strike at Armentières in 1887 (Arch. dép. Nord, M625/56 pièce 52), read: 'We must set fire too the fore corners of the town. That's the mane thing' [sic].

1886 was not followed. French workers in this period were not fire-raisers.

Neither were they Luddites. The decline in machine-breaking is significant. Only very rarely was the strikers' first act an attack on machines,[25] and as we have seen, workplace occupations were in fact respectful of plant and materials. It was, indeed, only at a later stage of the strike that these were attacked and then only in retaliation and with a specific object in mind; namely, to throw a spanner in the works, to prevent the factory from functioning and force the waverers to down tools. In the weaving mills, for example, a few drive-belts were torn off;[26] in the mines, burst boilers, severed cables and smashed ventilators[27] represented a means of intimidating fainthearted fellow-workers as much as — if not more than — the management. Overall, the machine was only the secondary and almost accidental target of acts of violence. Sabotage, of which Emile Pouget was to make himself the apostle, in no way signified approval of Luddite tactics: its enemy was production, but it was careful to do no real damage to the machines.

There was only a single case of Luddism in the classic sense in this period. This saw the slaters of Fumay in 1875 ranged against a mechanical saw which devoured work at a great rate, much as in bygone days, the weavers of Vienne had been ranged against the Great Shearing Frame.[28] The other strikes against the introduction of machinery (eight in all) passed off peacefully in what was vir-

25. There were only two cases in the period of such savage outbursts of anger: they occurred among sugar refinery workers at Etricourt (Somme) in 1890 and glove-workers at the Perrin company of Grenoble. Furious at having had their wages cut, the latter broke the needles in the sewing machines, according to *Le Cri du peuple*, 20 August 1888.

26. Arch. dép. Marne, 194 M12, s-préf.-préf, 29 October 1885: at the Rogelet mill 'work was still going on in the carding shop. The strikers burst into the workshop and tore off the drive belts so as to halt all work completely'.

27. Examples of such acts are legion: at Bert (Allier) in June 1873, 'some miners coiled up the wires from a boiler and caused an explosion' (Arch. nat. F12 4653, gendarmerie report, 18 June 1873). At Montceau on 28 February 1878 at 6 a.m., 'rioters burst the boilers . . . and cut the cables' (*Le Gaulois*, 4 March). At Firminy, after five days of peace and quiet, gangs formed and demolished a machine at the Lagrange pit (92 M16, pièce 25). At Bessèges in 1882 it was an attack upon a ventilator which provided the pretext for the military occupation of the coalfield.

28. Arch. nat. F12 4653, préf. Ardennes-min., 26 July 1875; the stoppage in June 1874, by fifty workers, was the first demonstration against the introduction of this saw. The following year, some 1,000 workers struck for twelve days; on the 13 July they set about the manager, who was molested, and the saw, which was seriously damaged. The rioters received severe sentences (thirteen of them, ranging from a fortnight to eight months in prison). The prefect commented: 'The working population of Fumay, who are at heart very good people, but have become overexcited by some deplorable economic prejudices, have not taken long to appreciate the wrong they have been doing themselves.'

tually an atmosphere of resignation. Under the influence of a complex range of conditions, the working class — or at least its highest stratum — had been won over to the machine. We would have to see the skilled workers at the Exhibitions looking over the new inventions, handling and comparing them to understand the fascination exercised on them by 'all this logic and all this certainty which make up the sovereign beauty of these beings of metal, this precision in power'. If delegates to workers' congresses deplored the disappearance of the craft system and the harsh effects of industrial concentration (increase in the pace of work, de-skilling, semi-penal factory discipline), they never attacked the machine; indeed, it was often glorified. A glowing tribute could be assembled from the comments of these delegates and the skilled workers (and in fact they were often the same people in this period). 'Marvellous devices, . . . instruments of progress', wrote the delegates to the Vienne Exhibition. 'Not only do we accept mechanical equipment, we recognise its immense advantages', declared the cabinet-maker Emile Chausse at Lyon in 1878. 'The machine represents progress . . . Our masters have them. We must seize them for ourselves and put our greatest hopes in them'.

For the Socialist militants — faithful in this respect to Marx — the revolution would only come about as a consequence of industrial development: 'The machine is the weapon which will emancipate the worker', we read in the Reims *Défense des Travailleurs:* 'He would do well to attack the person who has monopolised all of life's pleasures and has turned him into a machine of the machines, but he should never curse the machine itself'. And *Le Cri du peuple* waxed lyrical in celebration of Déprez's discovery: 'It is electricity which will strike the old society down by bringing light to the World.'[29] Such ideological statements were steeped in the great scientistic dream to which Berthelot would give expression in 1895.

The workers' attitude to the machine — which already reveals that 'workers' respect for their tools' that so starkly divided university and factory in May–June 1968 — shows that the labouring men were no longer fundamentally rebellious, but that they were in actual fact in the process of becoming integrated into the common model of productivity, into the bourgeois economy and 'scientific socialism'. Thus was formed the long-standing alliance between the workers' movement and economic growth, which has as its formi-

29. 1 August 1886. The headline reads: 'Important experiments. Transmission of power by electricity. An account of the problem. Harnessing the forces of nature. Tremendous consequences. Mechanics and Socialism.'

dable corollary the concept of a peaceful revolution, an idea which lies at the heart of one of the great controversies of our day.

Generally, once they had left the factory the workers could not go back. Reduced to plying their violence from a distance, they grabbed stones from the roadside, or sometimes used stones they had brought with them, and broke the windows. The total figures for broken window-panes are impressive: at Lisieux, while in pursuit of a manager, the rioters destroyed the panes of twelve windows in a few minutes; at Roubaix during the night of 12/13 May 1880 alone, some 300 were smashed to pieces. The gaping windows were like so many jagged wounds in the bruised façades of the factories. And the clatter of breaking glass, together with the eery reflections cast by the broken windows at sunset — for it was in the evenings that crowds tended to loose their fury on them — provided a kind of 'fireworks' for these workers' saturnalias.

Factories were not the only target; the employers' residences, which provided another focus of attention, were also attacked. In this period, the industrialist — or at least the provincial industrialist — far from hiding himself away, took pleasure in carving his success in stone. Opulent dwellings with lofty but open-work gates (an ostentatious construction, the nineteenth-century residence did not hide itself from view; in this it was precisely the opposite of the *galant* follies of the eighteenth century, that age of *douceur de vivre*, tucked away as they were in the friendly shadow of an English-style garden) symbolised a brilliant consecration of their wealth and were a mark of respectability, the indispensable foundation of nobility for a bourgeoisie passionately committed to property values and haunted by the aristocratic model. These chateaux, whose graceless silhouettes haunted the flat industrial landscape, stirred the workers' hostility. In their incendiary rhetoric, they spoke of these châteaux going up in flames along with the factories. Often situated off the beaten track on the fringes of the countryside, they offered a target for (preferably nocturnal) punitive expeditions, which re-called the Grand-Peur of the Revolution. At Avesnes-les-Aubert, the cellar weavers, who were in fact members of a semi-rural community, held secret meetings in the dead of night out in the fields far from prying eyes and then, when they had fixed upon a plan, would each leave home at an appointed time and go off to break up the homes of those they had chosen as their victims. On the evening of 13 March 1889, to the strains of 'La Marseillaise' and 'La Carmagnole', 'windows were broken by stone-throwing in thirteen different houses in the space of two hours'.

Elsewhere strikers broke down the fences around properties and attempted to enter them. At Carmaux in 1869 the miners ransacked the Marquis de Solage's chateau. Similar scenes occurred in the Roubaix-Tourcoing region in May 1880, and again in May 1890. On the evening of 4 May 1880, Desurmont, a rich industrialist, looked on as his furniture was broken up. During the night of 6 May 1890, 2,000 cotton-weavers surrounded the residence of another 'opulent' mill-owner, a certain Cordonnier, demolished the summer-house and advanced so threateningly towards the house that the servants in their panic fired into the air. Another night, at Sommedieu, about 100 chair-makers, enraged by their 'despotic' employer, van Weerssen, who had refused for over two months to enter into any negotiations, broke into his garden and were trying to break down the door of his house when the gendarmerie arrived. At Vienne on May Day 1890, the demonstrators planned, it seems, to attack Brocard's country house. There the strike took on tones of Jacquerie and anti-seigniorial revolt.

What impelled the workers to attack these residences and what conceptions lay behind their actions? The constant use of the term *château*, which had such significance in the popular memory, suggests it was perhaps the old feudal model. Indeed, were the capitalists not the new 'lords and masters', who held the workers in 'serfdom'? Speeches at public meetings were peppered with references to the theme of the 'new order' brought about by the 'barons of industry'. Furthermore, as the principal external mark of a wealth which had dropped its mask, these palaces were an offensive testimony to profit:

> Down with the tyrants! Down with the thieves!
> They shall give back these palaces
> Built from our sweat and blood!

And lastly, they were the tabernacle of the god. By committing the open sacrilege of desecrating them, the workers hoped in some vague way to reach a constantly elusive boss and, tearing the veil, force him to confront them face to face. Like the women of the Versailles market in October 1789 who demanded the presence of their sovereign, they wished to see their masters. This need for contact and this thirst for communication took precedence over, and arose prior to, homicidal fury. Gauging the reality of this and extricating it from the verbal inflation that was prevailed remains a delicate matter. In fact, cases of physical violence against the factory owners were rare. On several occasions managers were chased, besieged and attacked with stones, and overseers were molested. We can add several examples here to the ones already cited. A carpenter was seriously injured when he was attacked by three of his workers; at Trélazé, 'labourers, for whom there was no work, insulted the site managers and threw stones at them'. At Lecerf and Sarda, one of the capital's largest factories producing military equipment, a saddle-maker called Turgis stabbed a foreman in the stomach, then gave himself up, declaring to the police superintendant, 'I'm sorry I didn't kill him, for if he does happen to recover, he'll only begin his tyranny again'. In similar vein, a certain Fournier maintained in court that in attacking Bréchard, he was seeking to avenge himself and his long-suffering comrades 'against the man who', in his view, 'was the cause of the strike and the obstacle to their starting work again'.

However, serious injuries were the exception; there were cases of such injuries being sustained amongst most of the categories of lower managerial staff — the hated overseers — who were in fact the only men in direct physical contact with the workers. However, distance played an obvious role in determining who was or was not subject to this danger. Fournier's attack was an individual act and was disowned by the trade-union organisations. The murder of Watrin, his tragic defenstration in the tempestuous Aveyron department was a quite unique event. Indeed, even those who took part in the act were aghast at what they had done, as is evident from eye-witness reports of the stunned silence and panic flight which followed. The extraordinary repercussions produced by this event are double-edged in their significance. They both emphasise the uncommon nature of the event (had it been banal, it would have been ignored; every death of such renown is a unique one) and, at the same time, reveal what subterranean reserves of violence and hatred there were within the working class. The 'execution' of Watrin, which sent out a real psychological shock wave, aroused a great tide of admiration, as can be measured from the unrivalled success of *Le Cri du peuple*'s fighting fund. The Decazeville miners assumed the mantle of exemplary 'dispensers of justice' (as *Le Cri* called them), as heroes who had dared to break the great taboo. Watrin's already limp, lifeless body dropping down into the crowd represented a desacralisation of the bosses. The scale of the shock produced by that spectacle reveals both the obsessive power of a certain dream and how energetically that dream was repressed. But if the Watrin affair added new spice to the range of torments the workers promised their bosses and augmented the vocabulary of threats by one new term (the verb *watriner* entered the language at this point, though precisely how long it survived I cannot say), it was never actually copied anywhere else.

The Limits of Strikers' Violence

It is, moreover, difficult to establish the respective roles played by repression and self-restraint in this limitation of physical violence. The obstacle represented by the forces of law and order exerted a constraining power over the workers. It forced them, since their real target was out of reach, to content themselves with a secondary one that was more accessible. For want of being able to get to the bosses themselves, they attacked their homes. Since they could not always get at these, lost as they sometimes were in the anonymity of cities, they took out their anger on the factories. And where they were prevented from invading the factories, they threw stones at them instead. Window-breaking, that spectacular but superficial 'wound' which was the major form of damage committed during strikes, may have been a way of satisfying the desire for revenge, but it was also the mark of an impotent and somewhat puerile rage, a sign of the strikers being kept at arm's length in a way they could not willingly accept. The target of their violence was often simply a substitute for the real object. Speaking of the sharing out of the piece of cloth at Brocard's mill in Vienne, Martin le Bossu declares: 'It was as though they were fighting over and tearing up pieces of Brocard.' The transition to a form of ritual murder could not be better described. Unchecked, the workers would perhaps have gone further towards satisfying the murderous urges which their vocabulary starkly reveals, for the restrained nature of the actual violence contrasts markedly with the ferocity of their rhetoric.

In the final analysis, the violence committed by strikers was contained within narrow limits. Firstly, it was limited in its scope, being almost exclusively directed against employers. Confined principally to the factory perimeter, it rarely degenerated into street rioting. In twenty years there were barely half a dozen barricades to speak of. Paris saw only one of these, on 8 August 1888, the day of Eudes's funeral during the navvies' strike, on which so many Socialists thought they could sense the awakening of the drowsy capital.[30] The five other cases are attributable to the textile workers

---

30. Cf. Paul Lafargue to Engels, 8 August 1888, *Correspondence*, vol. II, p. 167. 'What is happening in Paris and in various places all over France at the moment is

of northern France: they occurred at Saint-Quentin in 1886 and 1889, at Amiens in 1888, and at Pérenchies and Neuvilly (Nord) in 1889. Furious at not being able to get inside the factories, the workers tore up paving stones, pulled down trees and overturned a wagon to protect themselves from the gendarmes. There were violent clashes, with stone-throwing on the one side, bayonet charges and shots fired in the air (though no less alarming for that) on the other. On many other occasions, for example at Anzin in 1872, 1878, 1884, at Reims in 1880 and 1881, at Le Cateau and Bessèges in 1882 and at Fougères, instead of dispersing as was usual, demonstrators squared up to the forces of order with the clear intention of putting up some resistance. At such moments the focus of the struggle was shifted. It broadened out to include the 'coppers' and through them the prefect and then the whole state apparatus, which was suddenly demystified. But such confrontations occurred only fleetingly and were normally the product of specific circumstances rather than planning. They were more an expression of anti-authoritarian feeling than genuine rebellion, and they were certainly not insurrectionary. 'The crowd is rowdy rather than warlike', noted Paul Lafargue on the evening of Eudes's funeral: 'They break windows and throw a few punches at the police, but they run off as soon as the bayonet comes out of its sheath. The crowd is unarmed'.

There were even cases, during the stormiest periods of unrest, of strikers seeking to preserve good relations with the forces of law and order. In two days of rioting at Lisieux, though certain public buildings were damaged, 'the gendarmerie was neither insulted nor threatened'. In 1888 at Trélys the miners cheered a gendarmerie lieutenant who had in fact refused to charge into the demonstrators as the managing director of the company had wanted: 'When the miners went back . . . a crowd made up of women and children some 1,000 or 1,200 strong gave this kind officer repeated ovations', reports the *Union des Travailleurs*, Socialist organ of the Gard. It goes on to comment: 'We wish our army contained many men like him in its ranks.' At Fougères, the shoemakers, venting their anger on the Houssaye and Rollin-Morel factories, 'publicly demonstrated their sympathy for the gendarmerie'. In May 1890 Roubaix weaving workers were heard to cry 'Long live the army!', whilst at Vienne, the anarchists themselves took pains not to attack the

phenomenal; we have seen nothing like it since the last century. Crowds invading the streets and clashing with the police: last century, before the Revolution, it was famines which roused them up; today, it is strikes.'

gendarmes: 'We have no axe to grind with you', Martin told them. 'Leave us alone; I am sure you will not prevent us coming through to go and see the masters.' The masters were the great — indeed perhaps the only — object of their resentment.

The restraint they showed in all this, which cannot be taken to represent a general rule, is an expression of the workers' spirit of Republican hope during this period. It reflects a faith in the mediating power of a state which has not yet been perceived as a class institution and which the strikers speak of with extraordinary indulgence. We shall see indeed how timid their political invective was. What is more, the Boulangist episode, which formed a backdrop to the incidents just mentioned, had confused matters where the army was concerned: it had in fact been possible, for one brief moment, for the workers to harbour illusions of a fraternal anticapitalist alliance with the army. The rude awakening at Fourmies doubtless dispelled any such illusions and contributed to converting the working-class electorate to socialism.

Limited in its field of action, strike violence was similarly moderate in its acts: one engineer killed and a few thousand windows broken form a rather meagre catalogue of destruction for a twenty-year period. The dominant impression is one of a constrained violence, more calculated than unbridled; it was not a blind, savage force but one that was tamed and channelled; it was not so much a raging torrent as a means of applying pressure. It is instructive to compare the cold anger of the semi-rural weavers of Avesnes-les-Aubert with the 'peasant furies' of bygone days, which were pure surges of physical force. The anger of the men of Avesnes was a considered reaction, carefully weighed up and almost planned stage by stage and raised to the level of grand strategy by an awareness of the economic conjuncture, an awareness which was pushed to such a point as to border on dangerously messianic hopes. Did these people not indeed affirm that 'these methods will be employed this year throughout the length and breadth of the country and that the Exposition Universelle will give them the opportunity to organise themselves, to stand up and be counted and act with such unity and suddenness as to thwart any who would resist them'?

One is naturally led to enquire what significance such a statement might have: was it a simple product of chance, a pause that can somehow be attributed to conjunctural factors or a break in historical development which could be easily explained by the Commune and its aftermath? Or, on a wider view, was it not a stage in a developmental process, the process of the domestication of the industrial proletariat and its integration into the triumphant industrial order? Doubtless, even if we admit that there is a meaningful question here, this study is too fragmentary and too localised in its concerns to provide an answer. For that we would need the much wider horizons of a long-term approach, together with fresh information on the everyday life of the urban working classes and such social symptoms as theft, crime, rape, brawling and vagrancy.

However, other works tend to show that in this *fin-de-siècle* period, the 'dangerous classes' were settling down, and French towns were becoming somewhat more peaceful. This is a major finding that is emerging from the current researches of Charles Tilly and his team, the first already extensive results of which he has kindly communicated to me. Urban violence was tending to decrease, to become less diffuse and more specific.

Why was this the case? The remarks which follow make no pretensions to being new 'Reflections on Violence', since this would clearly be most premature at this stage. Let us simply point out some features which strike us as important. The first of these is the repressive power of the bourgeois state, the only state to have won acceptance for the police and army by establishing them as national services in the name of public order, defined essentially in terms of peace on the streets. Secondly, and more importantly, there is the regulatory force of industrial civilisation, which is capable of harnessing all instincts (including pleasure-seeking) to its own ends, to the 'necessities of production'. One can do no other here than endorse the Freudian analyses and apply them to proletarian violence in developed countries.

In this perspective, trade unionism and socialism, as well as creating organisations for the defence of workers' interests, also seem to be instruments of adaptation to industrial society. In the period under consideration here, the trade unions' attitude to violence was quite unambiguous: violence originated outside their ambit, and they condemned it. At Decazeville, the trade-union officials Blanc and Carrié did everything they could to protect Watrin: 'My authority as a delegate was ignored', declared the latter, 'with the effect that some have asked whether I was not just as despicable as the others.' After young Fournier's failed assassination attempt at Roanne, 'fourteen of the former delegates — amongst them the three most influential, Epinat, Banquin and Delorme — went to the police station to protest vigorously against Fournier's action, which was, they said, an entirely personal act and not the result of a criminal plot'. When at a public meeting held on 26 March 1882 a quarter of those present (out of about 2,500) proclaimed Fournier honorary president, Epinat tendered his resignation. In Paris in 1888 the glass-workers' *chambre syndicale* went to great lengths to seek arbitration and condemned the brutal scenes which accompanied the return to work. At Roubaix in May 1890, 'Carrette and Lepers declare[d] that this sudden, ill-considered strike sadden[ed] them, and that they had been outflanked'.

As a broad generalisation, we may say that the trade unions took pains to prevent disorder. At Roanne, for example, the *chambre syndicale* took responsibility for policing the strike: commissioners were appointed for each area and given the task of ensuring that order was maintained: 'We shall never allow gatherings in the streets any more than we shall permit rude words against the owners ... or the members of the authorities.' At Lyon in June 1886 the strike committee dissuaded the glass-workers from attacking the factories as they were preparing to do after the arrival of 'blacklegs'. 'No violence' was the order of the day for the miners of the Nord-Pas-de-Calais region, as it was for those in the Loire, and the actions of men like Rondet, Lamendin and Basly contributed greatly to maintaining peace. The latter's change of attitude after his election to Parliament is particularly surprising. What a difference there was between the fiery young 'agitator' of 1884 and 'Monsieur' Basly, who in 1886 implored the Decazeville miners to fold away the Red Flag and begged the Vierzon metal-workers to remain peaceful, to the point where d'Harcourt, the correspondent of *Le Temps*, could write: 'M. Basly in particular has exerted a most favourable influence on the working people by his most prudent attitude and language. In yesterday's meeting at the Salle Boulard, distancing himself from the fanatics, he sought to concentrate the strikers' minds on the probable outcome of the strike.' It seems that the trade-union officials played a distinct role here; on many occasions they found themselves at odds with the mass of the workers, who were prone to sudden murderous and incendiary impulses.

Finding no outlet in action, violence flaunted itself in the workers' discourse. Perhaps this verbal insurrectionism was merely a mask concealing the men's actual submission.

8

The Collective Life of the Strikers: Meetings and Language

Whereas demonstrations were out of the ordinary, meetings were the norm. Everything converged towards their development, as an indication of the role of the strike as part of the negotiating process. Meetings took various forms and ranged from workplace gatherings held in quiet corners of the workshop before coming out on strike to the great set-pieces of public meetings with outside speakers, which were publicised with posters and reported in the press. This second type of meeting, by which strikes acquired political significance, will be dealt with separately from strike meetings proper.

Strike Meetings

These were held often. They took place daily, or even twice daily in small localities. In Reims in 1880 the loom-workers congregated every evening, at 6 p.m., on the 'Champ de Grève', while the Cholet weavers met twice daily but, they said, 'without really knowing why'. In Paris or Lyon, meetings were less frequent, partly because of the distances involved but also because the union organisation was more efficient. In 1876 the Paris carpenters met once a week, then twice, on Mondays and Thursdays. However, workers tended to demand more frequent meetings as they were keen to exercise their rights of control.

Meetings were also well attended. On each occasion that it was feasible (and local police reports are fairly informative in this respect), I calculated the maximum rates of attendance at meetings (by correlating the maximum number of those present with the maximum number of workers on strike). The figures were very high, of the order of 80 per cent or more, and often exceeded 100 per cent. Indeed, when a strike affected only a limited number of workers in a union (such as only those employed in one workplace or only one category of workers), their comrades, who were concerned by the dispute and its consequences, often attended gatherings and, at any rate in the provinces, frequently came with their families.

These gatherings, then, had genuine powers of attraction, which may be surprising in view of the sense of weariness they often generate today. The same can be said of election meetings, which were lively and crowded during this period in the nineteenth century, though today they are often deserted. In addition to the fact that public meetings and the spoken word had few rivals as means of communication, the right of assembly was a recently acquired right (conferred by the law of 1868) and corresponded to a desire which had not yet been fully satisfied. In Paris in particular, the era of the political clubs at the end of the Second Empire and at the time of the Commune, vividly portrayed by Auguste Vitu and de Molinari, was still alive in people's minds. There was an enthusiasm for public meetings, a belief in their virtues and power, and an appetite for direct democracy which, at times, the events of May 1968 were able to revive but which before were much in decline. In this way, audiences of several thousand workers crowded into packed halls. During the navvies' strike in Paris in 1888, the *Bourse du Travail* regularly failed to accommodate between 1,000 and 2,000 people, who were left outside clamouring at its doors in a noisy crowd. It is important to remember this when considering the size of audience reached by the language of strikes and how widely it was spread.

On other hand, these numbers were very fickle. Except for some cases of well-disciplined strikes (in Roanne, in 1882, for instance, the audience of weavers was kept stable at around 2,000), they showed disturbing variations and reveal the enthusiasm or despondency of the strikers. The attendance curves would seem to reproduce — in accentuated form or, in some cases, in anticipation — the highs and lows of the corresponding strike. The move to return to work first showed itself in falling attendance at such meetings; by the same token, their power to make effective decisions was reduced.

Meeting Places

Originally, as a result of the need for clandestine action, open-air meetings enjoyed support, particularly amongst miners and weavers in the small towns, for whom the fields and especially the woods

189

were a traditional place of refuge and secrecy. In Cours in 1875 and 1889 the blanket-makers met there, just over a mile outside town, occasionally in one spot, then in another, as though to allay suspicion. In the linen-making cantons of the Cambrésis hand-loom weavers held 'secret gatherings, at night, in the middle of the fields, far from prying eyes'. The miners in Noeux (in 1877), Anzin (in 1878), and Montceau (in 1878 and 1882) did the same; they served as models for Zola's *Germinal*. In 1887 the Vicoigne miners met in the Raisme woods, at a place called 'Rebels' Sanctuary'. In the empty lands of the Cévennes the miners of the Gard fixed meeting places in the countryside, changing them from day to day. They marched there in procession, led by a brass band or drummer, and singing. In the woods around Robiac, on 14 May 1890, 5,000 of them listened almost religiously to the fiery words of an impassioned young woman who brought tears to their eyes.

In towns, any waste ground in the faubourgs, or public gardens, fair grounds or squares served as *ad hoc* venues for public meetings, which were always under threat from the police who were ever quick to react. The gendarmerie dispersed 150 weavers congregating on the outskirts of Nonancourt to draw up and sign a petition. In May 1880 the weavers in Reims met every evening on the military exercise ground, christening it the 'Champ de Grève' and marking the ceremony by the planting of a tricolour and of a tree of liberty adorned with a banner proclaiming 'Long live the strike in Reims'. Their anger was provoked by the army closing the site. At the same time, their fellow workers in Roubaix flocked to the exposed areas near the border, to Le Ballon, to listen to the Belgian socialists and to receive their support. Lacking enough space in the Café Serre, Tarare weavers regrouped in the Rue de la Pêcherie; a speaker standing on a table exhorted the strikers not to return to work; and, at midday, at another public meeting in the Place d'Armes, a representative from Lyon promised support. Being refused the use of the school yards in the villages they had come through, the Thizy strikers invaded the town-hall squares. But, more generally, the authorities, who were worried that open-air meetings might too easily lead to demonstrations, channelled workers towards covered areas, which were much easier to control and to keep under surveillance.

Cafés, taverns, bars and cheap eating-places, and their like, all these pre-eminent places of proletarian leisure and society were the natural setting for small meetings. Weavers and glaziers in Lyon congregated in the Boule d'Or, and the Cholet loom-workers at the

Boeuf Couronné, while in Paris the tailors met at the Boule Noire, and the saddle-makers of Clichy at the Libre-Échange, and workers in Bordeaux in the Café de la Russie, and so forth. Worth mentioning, too, were the cafés of the Nord, with their picturesque names: the Brasserie Humanitaire, much liked by the Armentières anarchists; the Ouvrage in Pérenchies; the Grand-Saint-Esprit, the home of Lille free-thinking; or the Ermitage of the Denain miners. For Rasseneur's drinking shop in *Germinal* (the Avantage), Zola drew on Basly's XIXe Siècle and the Cantinière in Anzin.

These places offered the possibility of secrecy, which was at times sought quite systematically, and during the period of the *Ordre Moral* a bunch of flowers placed on the table in full view would suggest some union banquet. Over the same period, the 'communal kitchens' of the Parisian curriers, which were a kind of consumer cooperative that had developed after 1848,[1] were the hub of all the *coalitions* of these workers, particularly the one in the Rue Lafayette, under the leadership of Pastoureau, which was a 'proper club' and which the police considered closing down. Many strike leaders, having been dismissed from their workplaces, carried on their careers as activists from behind the bar (like the figure of Rasseneur in *Germinal*, who was in part copied from Basly) and, on the pretext of keeping count of the rounds of drinks, served as treasurers and secretaries to the early unions whose offices were in their cafés. Naturally, the authorities kept close watch on them and, by bribing the café owners, attempted, with some measure of success, to enlist them as informers. In that way Victor Capart, a café-owner in Mont-à-Loeux, and subsequently in Tourcoing, 'operated' for almost fifteen years amongst the Guesdists and succeeded in becoming a full-time official in the Nord Federation. The department archives provide much evidence of his reports to the police and his claims for expenses.[2]

But the advent of Republican civil freedoms and the increases in

1. *A.P.O.*, vol. II, p. 194. These kitchens developed hand-in-hand with mutual societies known as *gourmandises* because the sharing-out of financial balances was done at meal-times and, on occasion, in the form of feasts. The curriers in a *quartier*, or even in a workshop, would organise communally for the buying and cooking of provisions. The kitchen in the Rue Lafayette ran from 1873 to 1887. Another one, in Les Gobelins, continued from 1887 to 1891, and closed with the workshop it served.

2. One example is worth quoting: Arch. dép. Nord, M 625–56, p. 129: 'Nobody is better informed than I am about what is happening at Carette's. I am on all the committees and am present at all the decisions. The police informer in Roubaix is known to us and is not allowed in. I've noticed that he often made things up to appear better informed. Yesterday, I was at a meeting at Carette's and was appointed a delegate to the central committee. That proves I am at the centre of things, and that involves me in a fair amount of expense.'

numbers made it necessary to find larger premises. Only with reluctance did strikers request halls in schools or town halls and more readily turned to dance halls (like the Bal Cérès or the Bal des Romains in Reims, which were regular meeting places for the weavers) or to theatres and circuses, like the Alcazar in Lyon, Amiens and Saint-Quentin, or the Fernando Circus in Paris, the scene of the verbal jousting much favoured by Radicals and Socialists in the 1880s. In the capital, many former dance halls became the venues for public meetings but kept their original décor, like the famous Salle Favié, the lair of many sessions of the clubs at the end of the Second Empire and during the Commune, which 'with its tempera paintings, its chandeliers, and even mirrors, had an aristocratic air'. Similarly, the Salle Graffard in Ménilmontant, where Gambetta held tremendous meetings under President Mac-Mahon at which Guesde and Longuet clashed, hosted, many a strike gathering till its closure in 1884. Jean Béraud used it as the setting for a popular painting, *The Sovereign People*.[3] And there were, too, with various former uses, the Salle Lévis, and Salle Pétrelle, or the Salle des Mille Colonnes (in the Rue de la Gaieté), the Rivoli (in the Rue Saint-Antoine), the Elysée-Montmartre, and the Tivoli-Vaux-Hall. After 1887 the setting up of the *Bourses du Travail* made better accommodation available for workers' meetings. This gave rise to much animosity from hostile opinion: 'Striking malcontents . . . treat the *Bourse du Travail* as the Hôtel de Ville of strikes', wrote *Le Figaro* during the coachmen's *coalition* in 1889; 'it gives the strikers an air of respectability which can only add to their arrogance. A strict government would not hesitate an instant in closing this establishment . . . It is quite repugnant that we, the tax-payers, should have paid for a building designed to harbour the schemes of men who wish to oppress us'.

The Course of Meetings

The arrival in the hall emphasised a ritual borrowed from parliamentary procedure. First came the indispensable nomination of the 'committee', even in open-air meetings. In Reims, on the Champ de Grève, it sat behind a small table and had a little bell. Each day in the woods around Robiac, the miners elected a fresh chairman and

3. 'Suspicious-looking individuals surrounded by pipe-smoke, with drunken women sprawling on the platform or on benches', was how *La Bataille* saw it, on 6 December 1884, while retracing the history of the Salle Graffard on the occasion of its closure.

even a secretary for the meeting. Women could figure on the committee but rarely presided over meetings. At times an 'honorary president' was appointed, a well-known activist, the choice of whom would not go without discussion. While the Brassac miners acclaimed Rochefort by unanimous agreement, the Parisian joiners, in 1879, rejected Pindy, a *communard*, who was judged to be too compromising, and the Roanne weavers, as we have seen, were much divided at the suggestion of Fournier. Anarchists tried to resist this hierarchical bourgeois procedure, refusing to occupy any seat on the platform and attempting to have it done away with.

The committee would enforce discipline and respect for the standing orders. It coordinated the various activities of the meeting, distributing financial assistance, selling newspapers, handing out leaflets and pamphlets, all aspects which were to grow with the development of competing workers' parties but which were still embellishments to the essential ingredient of verbal exchange. Delegates reported on the situation of the dispute, correspondence sent or received was read out, reports were made on the financial situation, and so on. All this was interspersed with constant reference back to the audience.

Voting played a major role. Everything was subject to a vote: the list of demands, the action of delegates, the accounts, motions (of condemnation, thanks or congratulation) and, of course, the continuation of the strike, the initial decision for which, in prepared *coalitions*, was put before a preliminary assembly. These votes were taken by acclamation (simple Yes or No) for uncontroversial issues, by standing or sitting, or show of hands with a count for the more important options. To avoid any challenge, some unions used written ballot papers. The Paris distillers, to determine the nature of their strike action (whether it was to be limited or general), circulated two lists, and those present signed their names to the one or the other. Tailors used open voting slips which were signed: 'So that nobody', it was said, 'could refrain from stating their view, everyone was sent out into the garden. The strikers then returned into the hall and dropped their voting slips into a hat.' The point therefore was not to safeguard freedom but to involve the participants more closely.

Secret ballots, which were supported by the employers and the authorities, were much disliked by activists as a concession to individualism, as an obstruction to clear decisions, or as an inducement to cowardice. A secret ballot was called for by those who wanted to return to work, but was often rejected, and accepted only when a strong tendency to give up the strike showed itself. Workers would try to record the vote while respecting sensitivities, like a veil thrown over a shameful act.

Without doubt certain ballots by show of hands were ambiguous and volatile. Parisian navvies, many of whom mouthed privately the idea that they should return to work 'because the women and children have nothing to eat', voted in two quite contradictory ways at two minutes distance. The first, unanimous vote was in favour of the continuation of the strike, while the second, which was almost as overwhelming, called for the ending of the strike. Between times a speaker had drawn attention to the shortage of funds, and had provided the dimly sought after pretext.

Decisions were taken by a majority of those present. The question of some kind of quorum was never raised. The general meeting of workers considered itself representative, and sovereignty rested with the meeting, whatever its attendance. Few workers challenged this customary right. When they disagreed, they abstained from coming, and when they were determined to return to work, they would desert meetings rather than confront them. Often meetings would have to acquiesce, by a somewhat meaningless vote, to an already existing situation.

Disagreement, moreover, was difficult within these fairly intolerant meetings, which were more disposed to exclude than to listen. The faint-hearted were shouted down, traitors were loathed, and employers, if any came, individually, to explain their actions, were ejected, and any who disagreed were thrown out. 'A speaker from the Church wished to speak', said one report, 'but he was insulted and thrown out'. At the Boule Noire, where there were 600 tailors, no sooner was a strike-breaker identified than he was beaten up. A general brawl ensued during which the platform was overturned. Admittedly the responsibility for these last incidents belonged to the members of the Aiguille or the Panthère, who were firm believers in strong-arm tactics. In a general way, the involvement of anarchists in meetings after 1882–5, particularly in Lyon and Paris, markedly changed their atmosphere, which became more tense and almost feverish.

Gatherings were seldom places for discussion or study. Despite constant reference back to the audience, their function was less one of decision than of communion. It was not that the audience was passive; on the contrary, it demonstrated its approval or dissent noisily, but it did so collectively. Shouts of Yes and No, clapping, booing, yells, more varied and bolder in substance than those heard in the street, punctuated the selfsame words of regular speakers, whose purpose was less to explain than to celebrate or disparage. It was a people's mass alternating between priest and flock, soloist and chorus, in which the final cry — more and more often a vibrant 'Long live the Social Revolution!' — resounded like the 'Ite, Missa Est'.

The Diversity of Audiences and Styles

The composition of the audience, which varied according to the professions and areas involved, did however have some influence on the style of meetings. In Paris the leading position of male-dominated and highly qualified trades gave gatherings a more narrowly guildlike character and as a result made them more functional. Careful discussion of the strike demands occupied the major part of the time and took a more technical turn. Those present were quick to show their distrust of everything which departed from these issues and tried to lead them into the unnatural paths of 'politics'; they mocked utopians and dreamers and did not believe everything they heard.

In the provinces, meetings easily turned into family evenings, especially in the textile trade, as a result of the static nature of the workforce, and in the mines because of the strong family ties. Women came, and from their numbers and their attitude, the leaders (as well as the local police, who were very alert to their presence) gauged the combativeness of their troops. These audiences, who were less experienced, were at times silent, as though they were intimidated. In Anzin, observes one report, 'everything takes its course in perfect calm. There is nothing of the stormy atmosphere of anarchist meetings, but women attend in small numbers. The audience observes total silence. There are no objections or recriminations'. In other cases the audience behaved like a group of young people. In Reims the women gossiped and the men called out to one another: 'The committee kept order with imposing sternness. Not even shouts of Yes! or No! were tolerated. At the slightest word, the bell was sounded and the chairman shouted, "Be quiet! You are out of order".' These audiences were more malleable, more credulous and easier to manipulate. Public figures knew this and used their influence unashamedly. The mayor of Villars boasted of having induced the miners to return to work: 'I asked', he recounts, 'for the vote to be taken for the ending of the strike, and achieved this to the repeated cry of "Long live the

Republic".' Congregating at the Saint-Etienne *Bourse du Travail*, the mine-workers appeared quite attracted by the prospect of a general strike. Then Girodet, the mayor, made his entrance. 'He was given a standing ovation', writes a report, 'and all removed their hats.' Girodet showed that those who were for a general strike were 'the enemies of the Republic', and the motion was lost. And Léon Bourgeois, the prefect of the Tarn, brought about the return to work in Carmaux in much the same way. He got the delegates to stand on the platform by his side, harangued the meeting, then, he records, 'I asked the workers to support the motion [to return to work] by a show of hands. There was a moment's hesitation which was very uncomfortable. Only a few hands were going up, when one of the delegates, preaching by example, took the whole meeting with him as though it was only awaiting his signal'. Truth to tell, direct democracy demands much maturity of mind and a critical awareness.

These simple and trusting assemblies were the chosen place for popular rhetoric, moving, emotional, somewhat nostalgic (as in the case of Richebourg in Armentières, or Armandine Vernet in Robiac), but also violent, threatening, vengeful and prophetic. It was the Revolution made Word.

Lectures and Public Meetings

In public meetings, whose sole function was one of propaganda, indoctrination and communion, words were paramount. Some 129 strikes (representing 4.4 per cent of the total in this period) were the occasion for such gatherings, which were also called, especially at the beginning of the period, by the more old-fashioned and didactic term of 'lecture' (*conférence*). Of course, the number of public meetings was far in excess of this figure. When a strike became protracted it was transformed into a forum, and speakers of different shades of opinion were keen to be heard, and while there were certain established strongholds — the possibilists held sway in Cholet; Clément and Allemane had control in the Ardennes, and the Guesdists in the Allier — elsewhere there was obvious rivalry. The Roanne weavers were invited on 13 February 1882 to hear Allemane and Trinquet, who had been sent by Malon. On 19 February it was the turn of Guesde, and on 12 March of Clément. In 1886 the steel-workers in Vierzon, in addition to Vaillant, the area headman, welcomed Basly, Camélinat, Guesde, Furet (of *Le*

Radical), Massard, Goullé, Boyer, Clovis, Hugues, the deputies Planteau and Michelin, and so on, who, it is true, took part in workers' meetings more than organising separate ones. Parisian workers in particular had many calls made on them, and in addition to the daily meetings at the *Bourse du Travail*, public meetings competed daily for the attention of the navvies, who in the end had had quite enough of them. Tables 5 to 10 summarise the most significant statistics relating to strikes with public meetings.

1. The growing number of public meetings after 1879–80 (1.3 per cent in the first decade, rising to 5.3 per cent (in the second) is a sign, under Republican freedoms, of a tendency for strikes to become politicised, and of their convergence with socialism.

2. The nature of the strike (whether offensive or defensive) had little influence.

3. On the other hand, the duration of the strike and the numbers of workers involved played a determining role. Public meetings were the result of major disputes.

4. Strikes involving women were an inhibiting factor (3.4 per cent). This perhaps accounts for the relatively low level of strike activity in the textile trade (4 per cent). But the correlation with

Table 5: Annual percentages of strikes with public meetings (absolute figures in paren.)

1871	4	(2)	1881	4	(10)
1872	0.6	(1)	1882	5	(15)
1873	2	(1)	1883	3	(7)
1874	1	(1)	1884	5	(6)
1875	0	(0)	1885	3	(4)
1876	0	(0)	1886	5	(11)
1877	1	(1)	1887	6	(13)
1878	0	(0)	1888	8	(16)
1879	4	(4)	1889	7	(14)
1880	3	(6)	1890	4	(17)

Table 6: Nature of strikes with public meetings

Offensive strikes	1,847	81	strikes with meetings	4.3%
Defensive strikes	1,056	48	strikes with meetings	4.5%
Indeterminate strikes	20			
	2,923	129		4.4%

Table 7: Duration and size of strikes with public meetings

Duration		Numbers involved	
Days	%	Strikers	%
1	0.3	1–10	1.8
2	1.0	11–30	1.5
3–4	0.0	31–90	2.0
5–8	3.0	91–270	3.0
9–16	4.0	271–810	8.0
17–32	8.0	811–2,430	14.0
33–64	21.0	2,431–7,290	29.0
65–128	23.0	7,291–21,870	50.0
129–256	44.0		

Table 8: Strikes with public meetings, according to strikers' wages

Wages	% of strikes with public meetings (absolute figures in paren.)	
Less than 1F	0.0	(0)
Between 1 and 2F	3.6	(6)
Less than 3F	5.1	(22)
Less than 4F	5.6	(21)
Less than 5F	4.3	(15)
Less than 6F	9.2	(15)
Less than 7F	10.2	(9)
Less than 8F	8.0	(7)
8F and more	13.0	(6)

Table 9: Percentage of strikes with public meetings, according to industrial groups (absolute figures in paren.)

Farming	0	(1)
Mines and quarries	7	(17)
Food industries	5	(4)
Chemical industries	1	(1)
Printing industries	1	(1)
Leathers and hides	5	(13)
Textiles	4	(41)
Wood	3	(11)
Metal	5	(20)
Glass and porcelain	9	(12)
Building (stone)	3	(3)
Transport	6	(5)

Table 10: Strikes with public meetings, according to department

Department	Number of strikes	Number of strikes with public meetings	%
Seine	380	31	8.0
Rhône	257	14	5.0
Nord	431	8	1.8
Ardennes	62	8	12.0
Cher	41	7	17.0
Aisne	55	7	12.0
Bouches-du-Rhône	121	6	5.0
Loire	166	6	3.0
Maine-et-Loire	45	5	11.0
Gard	50	5	10.0
Allier	22	4	18.0
Isère	69	4	5.0
Gironde	84	4	4.0
Marne	74	3	4.0
Aube	29	2	
Loire-Atlantique	42	2	
Somme	76	2	
Alpes-Maritimes	17	1	
Aveyron	19	1	
Corrèze	6	1	
Ille-et-Villaine	29	1	
Indre-et-Loire	17	1	
Pas-de-Calais	51	1	
Sarthe	12	1	
Seine-Maritime	97	1	
Seine-et-Oise	17	1	
Seine-et-Marne	11	1	
Haute-Vienne	14		

wage groups is even more evident. Public meetings were for the more comfortably off; the Gospel was proclaimed to the wealthy.

5. The numbers of meetings for different professional groups were subject to complex influences. There were no public meetings for farm-workers, very few for those in the chemical industry, printing, or building (wood and stone). They were more numerous, however, in the case of glaziers, porcelain-workers, miners and transport-workers. But within the professional groups influences tend to cancel each other out. To obtain a true picture, it is necessary to look at individual trades. Mechanics (23 per cent), casters (16 per cent), porcelain-workers (17 per cent), coach-men (10 per cent), metal-workers (8 per cent), clothing tailors (8 per

cent) were clearly in advance on the others.

6. After the Allier (18 per cent), the Cher (17 per cent) and the Ardennes (12 per cent) show higher ratios. These were followed by the Aisne (12 per cent), the Maine-et-Loire (11 per cent) and the Gard (10 per cent), while the more militant departments show lower percentages (the Seine, 8 per cent; the Rhône and Bouches-du-Rhône, 5 per cent; the Nord, 1.8 per cent). The geography of public meetings was highly concentrated. Only twenty-eight departments were affected. The distribution coincided to some extent with those areas where socialists were firmly established, which they often were already.

Organisers

An examination of the organisers of public meetings does show that the impetus for them came just as much, if not more so, from socialist groups, social-study circles, and so on, than from the unions or strike committees, in a proportion of between 60 and 70 per cent. These socialist organisations, especially via the activities of this or that activist, largely coincided with workers' organisations but were not identical with them. Thus, in Saint-Ouen (in 1881), the Cercle d'Etudes Sociales invited Joffrin and Labusquière to come to speak to the striking mechanics, while in Montluçon, the Cercle des Travailleurs organised a lecture by Guesde to the miners. In Roanne, the group Travail et Progrès invited Allemane and Trinquet, while the Drapeau Rouge did the same with Guesde, who in 1883 was called to Tours by the Avant-Garde and to Le Mans by L'Egalité. The Blanquists were active through their 'revolutionary socialist committees', both in the Cher and in Paris. However in the Ardennes, the *chambres syndicales* became direct members of the (possibilist) Socialist Federation of the department, as did many Parisian *chambres syndicales* which joined the Federative Union of the Centre (which was also a possibilist body). Both these organisations were of the labourist type put forward at the Marseilles Congress and advocated first by the possibilists and then by the Allemanists as a step towards the creation of a workers party based on the trades unions. Guesdists and Blanquists, who were more suspicious or more aloof towards the unions, sought conversely to set up separate bodies which in their view (and particularly in the eyes of the Guesdists) were more important. The relations between the working-class movement and socialism, seen in the context of strikes, were revealing themselves to be extraordinarily intricate.

Speakers at Public Meetings

Public meetings were a show. The choice, as was frequently the case, of a Sunday, the charging for admission (which cost between 20 and 50 centimes, with reduced rates for ladies), and smartness of dress, the hall itself (a dance hall, theatre, or circus) with decorations,[4] were all factors which underlined this aspect. The main ingredient, however, was the speaker, or rather speakers, for a series of contributions, with a well-chosen platform and reasonable length of time, was much preferred to the single lecture. If it were too short, the meeting would be too slight and would fail to achieve its purpose. Local activists were present as support for the leader from Paris, who was the main attraction and enjoyed top billing. Out of the 120 public meetings for which we have detailed information, 130 names of speakers can be noted down and categorised as follows:

1. According to geographical origin:

— Local speakers: 67
— Regional speakers (from neighbouring areas or departments, like Pédron from Reims, Epinat from Roanne, Dormoy from Montluçon and Ménard from Trélazé, who all travelled within a certain radius from home): 6
— National speakers (from Paris): 57

Amongst this last group, the most active (times cited in public strike-meetings), in descending order, were:

— Vaillant: 16
— Clément: 14
— Guesde: 12 (though Guesde, because of illness, disappeared from view between 1888 and 1890)

4. The symbolism of socialist decorations is a subject of great interest. This was how one observer described the Salle des Folies-Bergère — where the Marseilles Congress was held on 20 October 1879 — in the *Compte rendu*, p. 19: 'Behind the platform . . . a bust of the Republic, surrounded by a clasp of flags. Insignia giving the names of the town represented at congress or affiliated to it, were fixed around the room. The following Socialist slogans, like "Liberty, Equality, Solidarity: No rights without duties, no duties without rights", or "The land to the peasant, the tools to the workers, work for all", or "Science, Peace, Unity, Justice", written on a red background, adorned the walls. Beneath the platform was the speaker's rostrum, decked in red velvet like the platform itself. An inner circle had been reserved for congress members, and two large tables, placed on either side of the speaker's rostrum, had been made available to members of the French and foreign press'. It goes without saying that public meetings organised for strikes were infinitely less elaborate.

— Allemane: 11
— Basly: 8
— Chabert: 7 (Chabert was responsible for the first lectures of this type, in Vienne and Rennes, in 1879; after 1883 he disappeared from sight)
— Joffrin: 6
— Dumay, Féline, Langrand, Louise Michel, Simon Soëns: 5 times each
— Camélinat, Chauvière, Dalle, Fournier, Gambon, Labusquière, Roche: 4 times each

2. According to political grouping (number of appearances), taking into account only the speeches of national leaders, as the classification of local speakers is too hazardous:

— Possibilists: 45
— Blanquists: 44
— Guesdists: 31
— Independents: 19
— Radicals: 3
— Anarchists: 3

The anarchists, who had a deep distaste for personality cults, had no major national figures, and their lack of a centralised organisation restricted the involvement of their activists to the regional or even local level. The notoriety of Tortelier, for instance, did not reach beyond Paris, and the reputation of Ludovic Ménard, say, remained confined at the time to the Maine-et-Loire (and even so, he was never invited to Cholet). The possibilists had available a whole string of well-known leaders, who were often called upon by workers (and included Chabert, Clément, Joffrin, Allemane, Soëns, Dalle, Labusquière and others), and the most forceful of whom were moreover to go over to Allemanism. But the high-water mark of possibilism was between 1882 and 1889.

Conversely, the Radicals, whose deputies or local councillors continued to play a fairly important part in mediating in disputes, were little used by the workers, who viewed them as rather remote 'Messieurs'. Similarly, Rochefort, who had formerly been very popular, undertook only one public strike meeting, in the Ermitage in Denain on 21 March 1884.[5] As a group, the working class

5. But it was a tremendous meeting. See Arch. dép. Nord, M 626/14, document 513, Valenciennes police, 21 March 1884. There were 4,000 people in the hall and 1,500 outside. Speeches were by Rochefort, and by a certain Talleyrand, who, it was said, had been a miner in Chile and who gave the strikers 5,000 francs. A balloonist

remained deaf to the Radical message, though individually many of them persisted (and would do for some years to come) in voting for them.

Public meetings were announced by leaflets or posters,[6] stating the subjects to be discussed. The following are some of the titles which appeared:

Subjects of public meetings

1879

10 June (Vienne). Chabert: 'Industrial Crises and Their Remedies'.

11 Sept. (Rennes). Chabert: 'The Emancipation of the Workers'.

November (Lyon). Roussel, Berjon and Arnel: 'The Crisis and its Causes'.

1880

November (Denain). Lefèbvre: 'The Social Question and the *Chambres Syndicales*' (cancelled).

1881

15 Oct. (Paris). Clément, Rouzade, Guesde and Chabert: 'Political and Economic Action of the Proletariat'.

1882

13 Feb. (Roanne). Allemane and Trinquet: 'The Strike in Roanne and the Workers' Union'.

12 March (Roanne). Clément: 'The Strikes in Bessègues and La Grand-Combe and the advent of the Fourth Estate'.

2 April (Saint-Denis). Brousse, Paulard, Lissagaray and Allemane: 'Class Struggle. Parliament and the Strike'.

11 June (Rouen). Piéron: 'Strikes and Trades Unions'.

October (Paris). Labusquière, Chabert, Joffrin, Allemane and Clément et al.: 'The Furniture-Carvers' Strike and the Bosses' Coalition'.

4 Nov. (Paris). Louise Michel, Digeon, Gotard and the Daniel Woman: 'The Strike in the Faubourg: Actions of the Magistrates in Montceau-les-Mines. International Workers' Solidarity'.

1883

4 March (Bessèges). Guesde and Chabert: 'The Social Question'.

---

from Paris said he had wanted to inflate his balloon for a demonstration in Denain, but that the authorities had refused permission. To the cries of 'Long live Rochefort', 'Long live Basly', and 'Long live the Republic', the crowd acclaimed unanimously the continuation of the strike.

6. In the small localities in the Ardennes, J.–B. Clément acted as town-crier, though the local authorities refused him permission, and he went about with a saucepan and a fire shovel.

13 Jan. (Limoges). Chabert: 'The Bourgeoisie and the Proletariat'.

16 Jan. (Limoges). Chabert and various local speakers: 'The Workers Federation'.

11 May (La Ferté-sous-Jouarre). Chabert: 'The Strike, Its Aims and Consequences'.

28 May (La Ferté-sous-Jouarre). Labatière: 'The Usefulness of *Chambres Syndicales*. Strikes and Their Consequences. The Workers Party.'

1884

11 June (Le Mans). Guesde: 'Strikes: The Separation of the Classes'.

19 July (Tours). Bertrand (the editor of *Le Tours-Journal*): 'The Expulsion of the Jesuits by the Pope and the European Monarchy in 1773'.

20 July (Saint-Quentin). Langrand and Roche: 'Strikes. Free Trade. Socialism'.

1886

4 April (Paris). Boulé, Gambon and Combomoreil: 'Labour and Poverty. The Hunger Markets of the *Quartier* Marbeuf'.

22 Sept. (Vierzon). Camélinat and Vaillant: 'Syndicalism and Socialism'.

16 Oct. (Bourges). Guesde: 'The Strike in Vierzon and the Bourgeois Police and French Workers'.

1887

11 March (Bessèges). Labusquière: 'Society before and after 1789. The Crisis. The Corn Laws'.

14 March (Mehun). Clément, Baudin and Gambon: 'War. Capital and Labour. The Corn Taxes. The Need for a Workers' Government'.

15 March (Vierzon). Gambon and Clément: 'Capital and Labour'.

Sept. (Nouzon, Ardennes). Faillet and Soëns: 'Class Struggle'.

23 Sept. (Cholet). Dalle: 'Rich and poor'.

1888

15 May (Paris). Dumay, Lavy and Walter: 'Workers' Solidarity against the Bosses' Coalition'.

26 May (Paris). Roche and Vaillant: 'Priests, Exploiters and Politicians'.

30 July (Cholet). Dalle: 'The Need for Political Reform'.

1889

2 June (Firminy). Colombet and Crozier: 'Socialism, Trades Unions and the Fatherland'.

12 July (Paris). Basly, Chauvière and Vaillant: 'Exploitation by the Employers'.

1890

8 September (Combrée, Maine-et-Loire). Ménard: 'Socialism and Trades Unionism'.

The subjects advertised were left intentionally vague and were more social than political, as though to avoid scaring people. The term 'strike' was a common one, and the idea was to start from the immediate situation of the workers in order to interest them and draw them in.

Audiences

That audiences showed reservations, the reasons for which are difficult to evaluate, but which could be due to the fear of being singled out or of being dismissed, is clear from the numbers of participants at such meetings. They were almost always less numerous than those on strike, while attendances at workers' meetings proper, as we have seen, often exceeded these. In theory public meetings, which were directed at the whole population and had much larger halls and publicity available to them, ought to have been better attended. In Le Mans, where 600 cobblers were on strike, only 150 of them went out of their way to come and hear Guesde. In Cholet, whereas more than 3,000 loom-workers took part in the daily strike gatherings, only 600 were in attendance for Soëns and 300 for Dalle. The socialist group in Grenoble, on the topic of 'Exploiters and Exploited', attracted an audience of only eighty compared to the 300 at the workers' meetings, and so on. Of course, there were counter-examples. In Roanne, Guesde addressed an audience the same size as that attending the general-strike gatherings, while Vaillant, in the Cher, always had a full house.

Audiences at such public meetings were slightly more varied and motley than at workers' meetings proper. The tendency to make them into family occasions, which has already been mentioned, became more pronounced, and women made up up to a third of those present.[7] In Rimogne, Clément made a special effort to invite them, and in Bessèges Labusquière congratulated them for being there. 'Contrary to Christianity', he argued, 'which spreads its ideas

---

7. According to the police reports, which often try to put a figure on the number of men or women present, there were a third women in Saint-Denis out of the 500 (who were mechanics in the main) come to hear Joffrin and Louise Michel, the same in Le Mans to hear Guesde, a fifth women in Rouen, for Piéron, a tenth in the flower market with the Paris cabinet-makers, 'a half made up of women and children' in

through men in order to get more women, socialism must first of all recruit women to its cause in order to win men over to its beliefs.' On Sunday afternoons children were brought along, and in Lyon on 29 April 1890 in the brasserie Gruard, writes one account, 'there were even fathers carrying babies on their shoulders'.

In the small towns, dominated by 'industrial feudalism', in the popular *quartiers*, shopkeepers mingled with the workers. In Saint-Amand (in the Cher), Vaillant and Camélinat addressed an audience of 200 workers, 100 wine-growers, fifty tradesmen, as well as commercial employees and people with private incomes. 'The first 300', says a report, 'belonged to the Socialist Party. The last fifty were Conservatives or moderate Republicans and began leaving before the lecture was over'. Outside elements sometimes came to raise objections, as a certain Morel, in Le Mans, who was a member of La Petite France, who protested against Guesde's attacks on the national flag. In the Ardennes, employers came to interrupt Clément, who 'invited the workers to clap as loud as they could while the masters were speaking and to observe total silence while he spoke himself'. Nevertheless, the room for debate was small. Workers filled the benches, overwhelmingly from the unions on strike, to the exclusion of other groups of workers. There was a compartmentalisation of social life which strikes managed to break down only on rare occasions.

Generally, audiences tended to be fairly passive and became involved only by clapping and shouting, and showed their enthusiasm by making generous donations, the results of which were usually modest. The 800 francs collected by Guesde in Roanne, from a hall of 2,000 people, were a mark of exceptional fervour. Reactions to the socialist message were various and differed according to milieu, area, the extent of earlier campaigns, and familiarity. Despite the simplicity of what was said, some members of the audience professed they could not understand. In Montluçon, when called before the judicial inquiry into the activities of Guesde, Lafargue and Dormoy, several witnesses avoided questions by using this as an excuse, though it was perhaps only a dodge.

Others were resistant to theoretical arguments. In La Ferté-sous-Jouarre, the millstone-workers, who had come in great num-

---

Combrée for Ludovic Ménard, and 'many women', we are told, in Limoges (1883, porcelain-workers), in La Ferté-sous-Jouarre (1883, millstone-workers), in Cholet (1888, weavers) and Chambon (1889, file-makers), and so on.

bers (there were about 700 of them to 180 on strike) to hear Chabert, then Labatière and Joffrin, declared their disappointment; they were expecting financial support and were unimpressed by propaganda. Similarly, the Combrée slate-quarry workers thought the 12 francs handed to them by Ludovic Ménard an insult. They listened impassively to words about Christ as the forerunner of socialism, and about Saint-Simon and Fourier, and only departed from their sluggishness to applaud a tirade against the employers: 'Let me tell you that if I, as a quarryman, was condemned by M. Picherit to work for eleven hours at the bottom of a pit, without light and liable at any moment to be flattened by blocks of stone, sooner than dying of hunger, I'd more likely kill him', asserted the meek Ménard. This was the sort of rhetoric the workers enjoyed.

In Roanne, Guesde had major success when he called on the employers to 'submit to a night of the 4 August. Let them give us back the means of production they have stolen from us. At that moment we shall disarm; before, never'. 'Political tirades', observes one report, 'and calls to violence were much applauded.' Conversely, in Le Mans, states another, 'except for a group of about twenty workers, the majority disapproved of the recourse to violence'. Guesde received applause only when he predicted that 'when the German proletariat abolishes the monarchy, they will restore Alsace-Lorraine to us'. In Limoges a number of porcelain-workers, as they left a public meeting on the subject of the 'Workers' Federation', during which the speakers jeered at the Radical deputies of the department, 'thought', we are told, 'that there was too much politics'.

In Saint-Amand, noted one observer, 'the wine-growers and workers welcomed avidly the brilliant promises they were made, and fell into ecstasy at the infinite perspectives they were given a glimpse of'. But Parisian cabinet-makers were very sceptical at the anarchist vision. When one speaker asserted, 'we revolutionaries want no more laws, our ideal is to live in freedom without rules or regulations', several members of the audience burst out laughing, and interjected, 'that's stupid. We need laws'. And when Louise Michel described the society of the future, some were heard to say, 'I'll believe it when I see it', and she provoked general hilarity by crying, 'there will be room for everybody at the feast of life'.

In this way, working-class audiences offered some resistance to the new message. Overall, they appeared uninterested in doctrines, and distrustful of what they called 'politics', which they distinguished from 'socialism', as well as being responsive to violence and unwilling to accept pure anarchy. Audiences were profoundly workerist. They expected speeches to be about them, to deplore their conditions and the exploitation they were subject to, or to attack their most feared enemies, the bosses and to promise them a better future, without going into too much detail about how this might be achieved. The public meeting had to bring hope and spread the gospel of salvation. Aspirations such as these had an inevitable influence on the language of strikes, and it is this that I now want to examine.

The Language of Strikes

The level of expression reached by the working-class movement during this period, corresponding no doubt to the general cultural situation, would seem to be characterised by three things: by the retreat from action, the growing attraction of written material, and the prime importance of the spoken word.

The Importance and Functions of the Spoken Word

The spoken word took on, at the very least, four different functions. Firstly, it acted as a safety-valve, as a means of letting off steam, which explains the proliferating vocabulary of threats and insults, as well as the raciness, compared to which the language of workers today seems bland, watered down, academic almost. Secondly, it was a means of communication. Information circulated by family or professional contact or via travel. 'Workers', wrote Audiganne, 'much prefer verbal communication, where much more is said in less time, to accounts by letter.' It was by word of mouth that those 'networks of imitation' were formed, whose role in spreading strike demands, especially with regard to the settling of wage rates, we have already mentioned.

The images and ideas which make up the consciousness of the working class at a given period were spread in much the same way. 'The present notions of the workers', wrote Gustave Le Bon, 'are fixed in their cafés, by assertion, repetition and contagion.' As for Renan, the 'socialist workers spreading their ideas from café to café' recalled the memory of the early founders of Christianity. Indeed, from the formal viewpoint, the growth of socialism was comparable in many ways to the process of evangelisation. The arrival of some great leader on the occasion of a strike had a missionary goal, and the message of socialism was like a 'sermon'.

During these times, when the socialist press was irregular and had a limited circulation, the spoken word remained the main instrument of innovation and propaganda. The prestige of a leader, at every level, was due to his physical presence and, particularly, his skills as an orator. A figure such as Guesde, and later, though in a very different way, Jaurès, whose very silences were 'full of words to come',[8] owed much of their popularity this ability. Moreover, speeches were an important source of written material. Distributed in the form of pamphlets, they made up a major part of socialist literature. Conversely, the majority of Guesde's articles were written like speeches, and similarly, reports to congress, which were the basis of working-class reading material, were designed to be delivered aloud. During this era of eloquence, the boundary was a thin one between the spoken word and the written text, itself often composed, in Montaigne's phrase, 'on the paper as from the lips'.

The prime importance given in this way to the spoken word places the working-class movement in the same category as classic popular movements or movements in rural societies, where the proverb, the saying, or the simple rhyme predominate. But in the case of the latter, the spoken word is, in addition, a means of conserving the past. The oral tradition stores up and passes on memories of all sorts — comical, heroic and meteorological — and takes on the role of a collective memory. In the working-class environment this function seems, however, to have lapsed. Studies in contemporary sociology have shown a tendency to forget and the poverty of workers' historical awareness. And while in the summer of 1969 the lock-keepers of the Burgundy canal did, after a few drinks, strike up the song of 'La Butte rouge', they professed no longer to know what the song was about.[9] Admittedly, in this context it is impossible to take words at their face value, and properly guided introspection can bring to the surface things thought to be lost for ever and which are perhaps simply unspoken and deeply buried.[10] We are unable to say what forgetting means for a society and how the collective memory works.

Confining ourselves to words, which are for times long past our

8. According to Jaurès's own expression. See *Mouvement social*, April–June 1962, special Jaurès number, p. 8. Descriptions of Jaurès's skills as a speaker figure centrally in all the accounts of him assembled in the volume.

9. As was ascertained by J. Ozouf.

10. A television producer, who wished to look into the 'memory of Belleville', contacted local people, and discovered that 'some of them had memories reaching

only recourse, we can note the sparseness of references to the past in speeches or writings. This is the case at any rate for references to national history, more so than to the history of the working class, which does not seem to be perceived as having a particular history of its own. The events of 1889, or especially 1893, which embodied the true popular revolution (and in the argot of *Le Sublime*, 'faire 93' is to begin the revolution), were cited more often than the Commune, which was no doubt concealed beneath self-censorship. On the more humble plane there were few allusions to earlier disputes, to the strikes of yesterday, for instance, the lessons from which appear lost as though everything had always to be rediscovered. In Paris in 1876 an elderly carpenter boasted about how well organised the *coalition* of 1845 had been, and in Vienne in 1890 people flocked to Brocard's because his stubborn resistance in 1879 was held against him. The death of Watrin left more visible marks, but how long did these last? Does Decazeville today still remember him? It was unusual for such memories to be spelt out. The mobility and intermixing, which were characteristic of the urban proletariat and which disturbed the structure of the *quartiers*, the rapid turn-over in leaders as their energies were spent, their youth, the lack of prestige given to predecessors in the working-class world, all these were factors which made it easier to perceive breaks in tradition more than continuities. And yet, while there was nothing to equal 'peasant lore', that product of centuries-old expertise and wealth of ethnographic understanding, it is possible to see in people's behaviour the accumulation of experience (such as the awareness of the present, which is so subtle), passed on in everyday conversation.

The Growing Prestige of the Written Word

However, the monopoly of the spoken word was loosening its grip, while the prestige of writing grew. Some 22 per cent of strikes used a range of written material in the following numbers:

Letters to employers	295
Press releases	290

---

back as far as the Commune'. 'The true history of a country, or city', he concluded, 'is not to be found, as I see it, in monuments, but in the cumulative weight of ordinary days. This is why the oral tradition is so important' (from an interview with Gérard Chouchan, in *Le Monde*, 3 October 1969). The multidisciplinary interest of such experiments hardly needs to be stressed.

Posters and leaflets	121
Correspondence with other workers	120
Letters to the authorities	72
Petitions	48
Others	41

These writings were in part handwritten texts, letters, placards or graffiti, and so on, and in part printed, including leaflets, posters, press releases and circulars. The recourse to the printed medium reflected a striving for publicity, but this ought not mislead us, since it was intended almost exclusively for the workers for whom the vast majority of appeals and bulletins were meant. 'We are well aware that the wage-earner can only turn to his fellow-worker to find support', began one subscription list, and there were few appeals to public opinion, as though nothing was to be expected from that quarter or because they did not care much about it. It was first and foremost the working class who had to be informed and rallied. The written text did not leave the family circle; it retained the informal tone which made it a substitute for the spoken word.

Difficulties in Studying the Language of Strikes

This close relationship between the written and the spoken word makes it possible to consider them jointly as sources for studying the language of strikes, though it is important to remember how artificial it is to unite them in this way. While access to the written word is direct, the knowledge we have of the spoken word, except for those speeches by leaders which were published in the socialist press (but which occasionally lack the unwritten asides or other remarks improvised in the heat of the meeting), is usually deferred, mediated by the local police, who, having neither tape recorders nor even stenographers at their disposal, only give a truncated version, and one perhaps altered by their own understanding of it. The words which are reported are reproduced in three different ways: by summary, as when we read 'Delorme mouthed threats against the masters. He spoke of the English workers, mentioned Marx, the events in Roubaix, and pot-bellied employers'. Alternatively, they are given in indirect speech, or in direct speech, in inverted commas. In the present discussion, which focuses on vocabulary as much as content, attention will be paid particularly to the fragments of speech authenticated in this way.

A second difficulty results from the diversity of speakers and the different levels of speech involved. It seems legitimate to distinguish three separate layers:

1. Language at the grass-roots level, coming from anonymous authors who had no mandate, and expressed in the most rudimentary forms of spoken or written language, ranging from cries, graffiti, unsigned handwritten placards to fragments of conversation which are valuable remnants of everyday language. Language on this level was unrehearsed, but ought, however, not to be taken as a purely spontaneous outburst. As we shall see, much self-censorship and tradition entered into this language, which was perhaps, on the contrary, a place for clichés and stereotypes.

2. The language of the activist. This was the language of the local strike leaders, who spoke and wrote less in their own name than in the name of the bodies directing the dispute. This accounts for the major part of what was said in meetings or written for them and also means that the activists' speeches and writings are the best represented in the documents available to us. The language of the activist was a strategic language, functional and intentional, and had its own models and its own yardsticks.

3. Finally, there is the language of the speeches held at public meetings by outside speakers (journalists or politicians) and which had its own aims and import. Strikes provided an opportunity and a pretext for preaching a gospel. Followed attentively by the local police and transcribed by them in lengthy extracts, often reproduced in the socialist press, which based articles on them, these speeches are the best known and have been closely studied by historians of socialism and of politics. We shall linger less on them here. They mainly did no more than put forward a message. The problem is to know how this was received.

Admittedly, all these different sources do not make up a single homogeneous corpus, as do, for instance, the *Cahiers de doléances*, or *Le Barodet*, particularly in view of the length of time involved. Twenty years, or even ten (and most of the documents analysed belong to the second decade), is too long, particularly when linguists tell us that nothing renews itself more quickly than political vocabulary (the social vocabulary, it would seem, is more resistant to change and is less of a day-to-day phenomenon). And at the same time, language does not conform so readily to the aims a speaker might want to fix for it, and may largely escape his control. 'It is not I who speak, but language which speaks in me.' But these voices were the voices of one and the same language, the language of strikes over this period.

I have, of course, been guided in my search for contrasting or identical terms and fields of verbal association by the lexicographic and semantic model put forward by Jacques Dubois. But I cannot do otherwise than invoke this model except as an example inadequately followed for lack of the necessary sophistication.

Language at the Grass-roots

This peremptory language, crude and picturesque, was full of insults and threats, acclamations and jeers, and afforded some refuge for violence, withdrawing more and more into the earthiness of words.

Insults and threats

The bosses and their 'acolytes' were the favourite target. Hatred for them was spread over walls, burst forth in cries and songs, and provided material for conversation. The popular vocabulary was rich in pejorative expressions or terms of abuse, to point out oppression and to condemn it. *Dummies*, *red-skins*, or *scum* were among the more anodyne. Animal imagery, as is often the case, was a rich source of invective. Overseers, or other such *slave-drivers* or *whip-masters*, were *lapdogs*, *pigs* or *boors*; employers were *bulldogs*, *tigers*, *swine* and, of course, *apes*. *Layabouts* and *good-for-nothings*, these *Messieurs* were most frequently *tyrants* and *thieves*. 'Down with the masters, down with tyrants!', one could read on the walls of Vaugirard, in red chalk, during the joiners' strike; or in Roubaix: 'Our good-for-nothing masters, those grasping thieves.' Another placard ended with: 'Our cry will be: death to thieves! Long live the Social Revolution!' One hand-bill, attacking a certain Despret, the manager of a mirror works in Jeumont, had no less than five terms of abuse for the man: 'A Watrin, a Bismarck . . . that despot . . . that tyrant . . . that Jew.' This last term was unusual for the period in working-class speech. But when they wished to personify capital, workers often mentioned the Rothschilds. One handwritten appeal to the 'slaves of the Bouchez works', signed by the 'Reimsdort Committee' (the naivety of the sub-prefect was such that he made inquiries to see if there was anybody of that name at the factory!) vituperated: 'Your exploiter, tyrant and thief . . . your master, who is no better than a scoundrel . . . Come on, workers, can't you see that your master is trying to rob you?.' 'All our brothers are battling against the swindlers who have exploited them to this very day', asserted one anonymous worker on the walls of Decazeville. This theme of robbery and theft recurred like a leitmotif in the most elaborate speeches.

The bosses, those *starvers*, were *bloodthirsty*, drinking the workers sweat. A whole series of pronouncements spoke of the misdeeds of 'those vampires who claim to be your masters'. 'Messieurs the masters of the Solesme weaving-mill', said another, 'you are thirsty for the blood of the workers'. Others went further: 'We must strike down these bloodthirsty vampires and not allow ourselves to be bled dry', 'Rid yourselves of that heap of rich men and priests who are sucking your blood and bones dry', 'Free yourselves from those who are sucking your blood', those *parasites*, *leeches* or *lice*. Animal imagery was still present, and the boss class was a beast 'devouring' labour and working people, a *predator* or *vulture*, 'feeding off the workers', holding them in its grip and 'growing fat'. 'Speculation is an open-mouthed monster ever swallowing the workers up with frightening appetite', one reads in one place, while the workers were smothered by 'capitalists like octopuses with countless tentacles'. The theme, magnified by Zola in *Germinal*, of a 'sated god', feeding on human flesh, linked into popular imagery: the workers felt obsessively they were being *gobbled up*, *emptied* of their life's strength to feed their *gorged* and *overfed* bosses. Employers were fat, *bloated*, *obese*, *swollen*, *gorged*, *paunchy*, *fat-bellied* or *pot-bellied*. This last term was a very common one used to describe the 'exploiters', what Denis Poulot called 'the savage ventrocracy' (*la ventrocracie farouche*). The same image was used for capitalists in the cartoons of the period, which made the belly the very symbol of wealth.[11]

Those *bandits* deserved to die, and this was the fate popular language reserved for them. 'That rogue of a manager has brought us to Bousies to die of hunger. He must be killed within the week or we shall perish', one read on the gates to the weaving mill in Seydoux. ... 'Arm yourselves then with daggers and revolvers. Time is short to kill our masters and managers and, most of all, those great layabouts of overseers. Kill-kill-kill, Shoot-shoot-shoot', exhorted one handwritten placard posted up at the Dulac factory in Armentières. Another implored: 'Why not kill a thief like

---

11. Arch. nat., F 12,4661, préf-min, 19 February 1884. A handwritten placard in Leers read: 'Our masters, to puff up their bellies and their fortunes all the more quickly.'

that?', and a further one, at the Motte weaving-mill in Leers, stated: 'We'll find a way to kill our masters.' At times workers made so bold as to send threatening letters to their tyrants, like the Firminy miners to their manager: 'Monsieur Monistrol . . . Watch out. Instead of sending workers down the pit you might drop in it yourself quicker than you think. You've got to go or the Lachaud pit might go instead.' The Solesmes weavers wrote in the same vein: 'Messieurs our masters . . . we, your workers, we're warning you that if you cut wages any more, we'll ruin your mills for you.'

Militant anarchists enjoyed much success in exalting this kind of physical violence. At meetings they spoke of little else than 'stringing up the masters and burning down the factories'. 'Strikes', said one, 'will only be effective when strikers turn up in the exploiter's workshops and smash everything and, if needs be, burn it to the ground.' During their strike, Lisbonne attacked the cowardice of the striking navvies: 'We need', he said, 'to hang three or four of the masters from the streetlamps . . . Arm yourselves with saw-files, clubs and staves, and smash them all in!' But the anarchists had no monopoly on threats. In the streets thousands of workers became elated with revenge: 'The masters are swine, we'll hang them all', sang the Saint-Quentin weavers. In Roubaix the call was the same: 'If they don't want to give us a rise — We'll butcher them. If the masters don't give us a rise — We'll hang them up by their feet!' 'We need blood before there's an end to it', murmured the Chambon file-workers. In the canton of Thizy, for instance, 'as the workers marched past the masters' homes, the men in the procession yelled for a long while, crying they were sharpening their blades or that they'd cut the yarn from their looms to make nooses to hang the masters up with'.

It is worth noting that the fate reserved for the bosses was first and foremost hanging, the age-old punishment of the common man. Neither the guillotine nor firearms supplanted the medieval and rustic gallows. In earlier times they had wanted to have the aristocrats 'hanging from the street-lamps', in the words of the Revolutionary song, now what they wanted was to see the bosses swinging from the gas-lamps.[12] A picture by the Roubaix weavers, *The*

---

12. In addition to the various documents already cited, it is worth recording these words of Laroche, a journeyman carpenter, at a meeting on 12 October 1884 in Lyon, Arch. nat F 12 4662: 'Let us not be deceived by our masters or executioners, and, rather than letting them profit from our sweat and get rich at our expense, we shall see them hanging from the gas-lamps.'

Factory Owners' Road, showed that road leading straight to the gallows. The glove-makers in Céton (Orne), rebelling against their manager, enjoyed the luxury of a multiple hanging, just as, in the past, the rioters of the Réveillon affair had done, following in the most unadulterated of traditions: 'Three stuffed dummies were made', a report recounts, 'representing La Maniette (the manager), his faithful wife, and his niece. They were wheeled about through all the streets in the town. There was a reading of the list of charges they were accused of, then they were hanged and burnt.' After 1886 there was much talk of *watriner* and of *watrinage*, and defenestration rivalled hanging as a punishment, without however overtaking it.

Such preferences may well appear surprising, coming at the end of the nineteenth century, on the part of city-dwellers who had experienced, either at first or second hand, the shootings of the *Semaine Sanglante* and who knew the power of modern weapons. Hanging was, *par excellence*, a peasant death, and in the Normandy countryside of Maupassant's stories, as today in some cantons of the Auge, where individuals will 'string themselves up', there was no other form of suicide except by the rope, the rustic weapon of the pauper. Hanging, in addition, provided the most infamous of ends, the one most likely to produce the most collective impact and the most durable pleasure. The guillotine had something underhand about it. In its very speed (the executioner Samson boasted of needing only a minute per victim), it already made a concession to the remorse felt for shocking the eyes. The image of a hanged man was an object of contemplation, horrible yet pleasurable, like a vestige of a time when executions were a spectacle. But it is also possible that this old-fashioned representation masked the lack of any real bloodthirsty intent and was, after all, merely a form of words.

Cries

Demonstrations and meetings were interspersed with identical cries which, in addition, marked their culmination. No gathering was concluded without some cheering, like a final moment of communion, or a sharing out of provisions prior to dispersion. Generally, street cries were less bold and less varied than those heard at meetings. On the streets workers kept themselves in check, in a typical example of self-censorship which shows the limits of spontaneity. Inside the meeting they felt at home. But also, cries did not have the same function. On the streets they accompanied crowd movement by providing a rhythm for people's marching, and they were simple, traditional and unanimous. In halls they became charged with greater intensity and purpose, in tune with the enthusiasm generated by the speaker, or else active minorities tried to get their own message heard, like the anarchists calling out: 'Long live dynamite', 'Death to robbers' or 'Long live the violent Revolution'.

The marching or litany-like cry gave way to the cry as slogan or profession of faith. This led to diverse reactions. Thus, in 1882, 'Long live the Social Revolution', which was still a recent coinage, brought protests from Parisian strikers in various gatherings. Amidst the tailors' cutters, Couchot proposed this cry, 'but the majority preferred 'Long live the strike'. In a meeting of cabinet-makers, one worker, says a report, 'galvanised by the speech of citizen Bacheley [the president], cried out: "Long live the Social Revolution!" — Protests were heard'. Asked to explain himself, he replied: 'I believe it's only by revolutionary means that you'll be able to free yourselves from . . .'. He was interrupted by shouts and laughter, and told to be silent. He 'disappeared from the platform amidst general hilarity'. The scenes are interesting ones in that they suggest how recent the message was and the resistance it encountered. They also show how the language of the grass-roots becomes domesticated.

The Language of the Activist

The language of the activist covered three main registers. It deplored the condition of the workers, attacked the employers and glorified working-class struggle and its various forms. The first two of these themes were fairly traditional and gave rise to a wealth of commonplaces such as those found in the language analysed previously. As for the third area, here differences became visible, which opened up onto plans for the future. The language of the activist was a hybrid form. It had the violence and verve of popular language, as well as the forward-looking energy of socialist evangelism, of which it was often a simplified form.

'Working people' as seen by themselves

Firstly, what words did they use to refer to themselves? Speaking directly to their fellows, workers most often used the terms, *working people* or comrades; or else it was *brothers* (this was generally qualified, as in *brothers in misery*, *brother producers* or *brothers in*

217

suffering)[13] or *citizens. Companions, companions in misery* and, in more solemn appeals, *people* are also found. *Colleagues* was rare, and *workers* is almost never found on its own, but only specified either in terms of place or professional group.

Within the normal run of documents, descriptions, and so on, *working men* (*travailleurs*) is by far the most frequently used term, more so than *workers* (*ouvriers*), which Marxist terminology was later to establish and which predominated at that time only as an adjective (as in *classe ouvrière* or *solidarité ouvrière*). It can be noted that in the singular the *worker* was used in the more sordid depictions of proletarian life: 'The worker', as in one instance, 'is condemned to witness the death throes of his dear ones', or 'the worker who produces cannot satisfy his needs.'

Producers, which was widely used — and which, after a period in which it was used only in a limited way, took on, according to J. Dubois, a Saint-Simonian sense — retained in working-class speech its restricted sense of 'working men'. These are a few examples of its use:

— 'a workers' party which . . . will seek the practical means of improving the lot of the producers' (1880)
— 'working men, the sole producers and creators of public wealth' (1880)
— 'We are the producers . . . and when our hands are not busy at their labour, capital will fall' (1879)
— 'one class, that of the producers, continually in a state of wretchedness' (1881)
— 'Is it just to see the producers of public wealth vegetate and languish in wretchedness?' (1882)
— 'You, the producers of public wealth, who receive in exchange only the strict minimum so as not to die of hunger' (1884)
— 'We, the mass of producers, having long contributed to the wealth of the authorities, see ourselves forced to walk the streets and end up dying in the workhouse' (1890)
— 'Men are divided into two camps: those who produce and those who do not produce . . . The result is not only that the

---

13. On the religious origins of *brothers* and its secularised usage in the nineteenth century, see J. Dubois, *Le Vocabulaire politique et social en France de 1869 à 1872* (Paris, Larousse, 1982), pp. 81ff. Dubois notes a decline in its use and its gradual replacement by *comrades*. In strike documents for the period from 1871 to 1890, however, *brothers* was still very widely used.

producers see themselves forced to share what they have with the unproductive, but also that they must dispossess themselves of nine-tenths of the product of their labour' (1890)

The idea of production works in three different semantic contexts: that of privation as opposed to wealth (by far the most obsessive contrast); that of the utility of the producer as opposed to the superfluousness of the unproductive; and that of the power of the producers versus the fragility of capital. In the main, more emphasis is laid on the lot of the producers than on their function or power, more on the social or moral aspect than on the economic. Nevertheless, this last aspect, which lay at the heart of the notion of the general strike, underwent a major boost in the years following 1888–90, notably in the year of May Day actions, which for many were a trial run. As one activist put it, 'if the producers cease producing, the march of social order will be halted and mankind will stop in its tracks'. Capital only survived with the aid of the labour of the workers.

The predominance of a vocabulary of exploitation is quite manifest, however, in the fondness for the oppositions between *exploiters* and *exploited* (which became particularly repetitive), *oppressors* and *oppressed*, *masters* and *slaves* or *pariahs* or *serfs*. The terminology of the penal colony was also much used, as in *hard-labour convicts*, *galley slaves*, *slave-drivers*, or the vocabulary of frustration: the *disinherited* or *dispossessed*. Workers were 'the oppressed . . . the pariahs of the age', 'sheep . . . shorn at will', 'the disinherited who only know of life the suffering it can bring', 'the serfs of the capitalist', 'ever more enslaved and wretched'. Wage-labour was little better than slavery: 'Slaves yesterday, exploited today', 'paid slaves', 'paid workers that we are, that is to say the slaves of the capitalist minority who own everything'. The bosses treated their employees like 'chattels', like 'tools maintained as cheaply as possible and thrown away as they become too old'.

Relatively speaking, the vocabulary of class (*proletariat, working class*) was comparatively less frequent, with a slight preponderance towards the former, which was always linked with the idea of struggle or solidarity. The *proletariat*, to some extent, was always the working class in action, conscious of itself and organised.

The condition of the workers (the term used was more often their *lot*) was therefore defined by enslavement and poverty, and poverty which was getting worse and becoming more acute. This theme of deterioration, linked to the 'rapacity and ever-growing demands of the bosses', who were 'more and more idle and greedy', recurred constantly, with the feeling that things could not be tolerated much longer: 'Today', in the words of one activist, 'the situation has arrived at such a point that it could not be more strained. The rope must break.'

The terms used to depict this condition belonged to the classic arsenal of pauperism: in addition to *wretched* and *wretchedness*, which were much used, more so than *poor* and *poverty* (which, in spite of all, faded away from workers' language), there were *sufferings*, to *suffer*, *tortures*, *hunger*, *cold*, *death*, and so on, all constantly contrasted with the *luxury* and *opulence* of the capitalists. As one worker put it, 'An end to the wretchedness we are made to bear. No more torture'; and in the words of another, 'we, the workers, are dying of hunger and wretchedness'. The worker could not 'live by his labour', he possessed not even the 'bare necessities', a 'crust of bread', to feed his family (this was another constant reference; as has been said, the worker defined himself as a 'family bread-winner') or to make provision for his old age. On many occasions, the backward-looking character of working-class grievances has been stressed. From this point of view there was little change over the whole period. Documents representing very different shades of opinion made in this respect much the same noises.

'Most of the time we have only rags to clothe our children with, while we are dressed decently, but wretchedness lies hidden beneath these noble tatters', said Louis Richebourg, a weaver in Armentières in 1880. 'When old age comes and takes away our strength', he added, 'we are cast from the workshop just as the sea casts out its jetsam. Our only recourse is to beg . . . We do not have enough to live on, nor enough to give a crust of bread to our children . . . Is this situation tolerable? We do not think so, seeing our faces gaunt and the muscles of our features stiffened by undue labour.'

Comparing their children's lot to that of the boss's children, the Carmaux glass-workers cried: 'Of what account are a worker's children to them . . . just so long as their own [the bosses'] go to fine places, have warm feet in winter and a good vintage wine to cheer their bellies, while our own walk barefoot in the snow and drink a glass of water to calm the cramps of hunger.' 'The night-shelters are becoming too small, there are too many people in the bread queue', one reads in a May Day leaflet; 'the horror of it! one sees men who for thirty or forty years have produced for the good of the capitalists, go singing for their supper in courtyards, then turn to house-breaking and die exhausted, like old nags, finishing up on a hospital

slab or on heaps of stones by the side of the highway . . . Working
men, you are no better than beggars! Beggars for work, beggars for
food . . . Famine and a slow death have us in their grasp.'

In all these documents a dual obsession recurs, that of childhood
and old age (the law on pensions in 1910 was to be a response to a
public demand), the fear of the workhouse and the dread of *death*
(as fate or as threat), one of the key words of this vocabulary.

The boss-class as 'exploiters' and 'tyrants'
The *boss-class* forms a linguistic pairing with *proletariat*. The terms
and epithets applied to it are the antithesis of those used for working
men, just as the description of its condition reverses that of its
counterpart.

Our *masters* or *bosses* are found more or less equally, the former
having a more precise, localised sense and the second a more general
meaning, as in these instances: 'in view of our masters' (*patrons*)
stubbornness in wanting to reduce us to wretchedness and to
submission, and desiring us to capitulate', or 'the bosses (*patronat*),
the sworn enemies of the proletarian classes'). Most of the time
these expressions were used without distinguishing the capitalists or
the managers in a firm. All the same, some documents introduce a
slight nuance, and the *masters* refers most of all to the men who are
in direct contact with the workers, and talk is of 'those implacable
enemies of ours, the *bosses* at every level and the capitalists'.

Following on from these came the cohort of *overlords* (*maîtres*,
always preceded by a possessive), *oppressors*, *exploiters*, *tyrants* and
despots (the last two were more often used in popular speech).
Exploitation was denounced as morally wrong, as for instance in
such statements as 'the capitalists who exploit us so shamefully', or
'those who exploit us unworthily', or 'their vile exploitation'.

Capital, used on its own, had a more narrowly economic context
of reference. In 'labour creating capital', 'capital' referred to money
in opposition to working *hands*. As an object complement (as in:
'the demands of capital', 'those who own capital', 'the despots of
capital who wanted to trample on the workers'), it was equivalent to
capitalists, which was very common even on the most humble lips.
'You can see these great capitalists are beginning to undo the
worker', one read on a 'proclamation to the people', posted up in
handwritten form at the Dulac weaving-mill in Armentières. Speakers at meetings constantly took issue with the 'capitalists', and
spoke of them as a 'handful of individuals', 'a tiny minority', 'a
small fraction' of people who nevertheless 'owned everything' and

'imposed their law on working men'. Many documents, notably those in favour of a general strike, emphasised this numerical contrast, which was the source of the proletariat's strength, and spoke in terms such as these: 'We, the mass of producers', 'we are the mass', 'we are fearfully many', or 'the producers are infinitely more numerous than the unproductive'.

Capitalism was a more recent coinage and was used infrequently; while words like *monopoly* or *monopolist* were in retreat. The words *bourgeoisie*, and to a greater extent *bourgeois*, which always had a pejorative sense, even to the point of caricature, were heavily used, as were the corresponding adjectives (as in: 'bourgeois press', 'bourgeois Republic', 'bourgeois starvation'). They were equivalent to 'capitalist' and were found in the same broad context, particularly coupled with 'getting rich, exploiting, profiteering'. It is worth noting, however, that the term 'profit' (*profit*) still had not penetrated into the vocabulary, nor had 'profiteer' (*profiteur*). As for *surplus-value*, it was not used.

The word for 'profits' was *bénéfices*. It was used in phrases such as these: 'Your bosses and masters, not content with the *bénéfices* levied (i.e. stolen) from your meagre wages', or 'the *bénéfices* of the merchants increase day by day, and the bourgeoisie takes advantage of them to subsidise its theatres and cafés'. These *bénéfices*, the spoils of exploitation, had been accumulated long ago and passed on by inheritance. In the words of one worker, 'to us are due the *bénéfices* they are hoarding away, just as they owe our fathers the capital left them by their forerunners'. The phenomenon of capitalist exploitation was perceived as having been in existence for many years. One document speaks of 'this accursed bourgeoisie which has exploited us for so long', and another states it thus: 'When one thinks that for a thousand years and more the product of the labour of millions of human beings has been gobbled up by a mere handful of individuals', while another document mentions 'your chains which you have carried for twenty centuries'. Words such as these imply a historical continuity in which wage-labour appears as the direct descendent of slavery and serfdom, with no social mobility at all. But other documents emphasise the importance of the French Revolution as laying the foundations for bourgeois domination, by substituting the 'lords of finance' for those of the land. This theme of 'capitalist' or 'industrial feudalism' was a constant leitmotif in the speeches of those political leaders who sought to demystify the 'bourgeois Republic'.

In sum, the language of the activist went little further than grass-roots language in its economic description of capitalism. The very use of the word *bénéfices* for 'profits', a prime example of vagueness and of a word avoided by economists, is just one instance among many. Capitalism was denounced for essentially moral reasons, and it was its injustice that was constantly emphasised, as in these words: 'Brother producers, is your conscience not outraged by so much injustice?'. Born from an act of crime, from a theft committed in the depths of time, capitalism was equivalent to constant robbery, and an organised act of banditry. Speculation was its major object, and its motive force was 'the loathsome passion to get richer', 'the hunger for gold', gold being the very symbol of wealth.[14] Capitalists were 'millionaires',[15] rotten with corruption. Their physical portrait and way of life were contrasted point by point with those of the workers. They were 'opulent' and 'idle' and did 'little else than eat, drink and sleep while we labour'. These men, whose 'barns and cellars are overflowing' and whose 'vast fortunes are an accumulation of tears, wretchedness and deprivation', squandered public wealth on sumptuous luxuries, like *châteaux*, 'opulent *salons* exhibiting riches which break our hearts'. These 'sensualists' 'wallow in the most shameful orgies'.

At the Marseilles Congress, Tranier, one of the tailors from Toulouse, described 'the princely lives of these so-called saviours of the people. One Republican lord', he said, 'for we can call him that, who couldn't afford a square meal in 1868, now spends 60,000 francs solely on his dinners. Just thinking of these nameless orgies fills you with anger.' One leaflet condemned the celebrations held to commemorate the centenary of the Revolution: 'It was the

14. Compare *L'Egalité*, 12 May 1880, from an appeal from the Reims strike committee: 'The hunger for gold, this leprosy whose only outcome is murder.' And one speaker at the Marseilles Congress depicted capitalists in terms such as these: 'Messieurs who have the monopoly . . . , all you need to do is to mop your brows with your bent fingers to catch a little of the sweat and blood which is flowing from our mutilated bodies and you will find enough there to pay for your daughters' dowries' (*Congrès de Marseille*, p. 467).

15. The theme of millions, and of millionaires, was one which already reached back a long way, as shown by J. Dubois (1962, p. 888) and by the documents he cites. The following are some examples drawn from the strike documents which are the focus of this study: Arch. dép. Rhône, M. Grèves, 1888–91, from a leaflet of the *chambres syndicales* and workers' groups in Paris', May 1890: 'There is no more hope for the working man, even small businesses are overwhelmed by the joining together of the capitalists' millions . . . The capitalist class . . . without producing anything, exploits the workers with the help of the millions it has stolen from them.' Arch. dép. Rhône, M, dossier du 1er Mai, includes an appeal from the *chambre syndicale* of Paris cabinet-makers: with the general strike, 'the man who owns millions would be just as unable to live as the man who doesn't have a farthing in his pocket'. Arch. dép. Nord, M 628/3, the Carmaux glass-workers: 'These Messieurs and their millions'.

greatest celebration ever seen by human eyes, with parties upon parties, opening ceremonies, firework displays and unthinkable orgies, and while 18,000 town mayors were getting drunk on tax-payers' money, at the Palais de l'Industrie, thousands of men and women who had worked all their lives were dying of hunger.' What was scandalous, for the people, was this inequality in living conditions, the contrast between luxury and need. Bed and board, these were the things that stood out. And still today, the man in the street will get angry at the news of official receptions, which are still for him the most obvious cause of the budget deficit.

The *monopolists*, these *heartless* men, had no notion that the worker was 'made of flesh and blood just like them'. He was treated as belonging to an inferior race. The bosses were hard, self-centred and arrogant. Not content with exploiting the workers, they despised them and 'want to have nothing to do with the men who bring them their livelihood and meet their desires'. For them, 'those who produce are not even worthy of interest'. It was not enough for them to enjoy themselves, they also had to dominate, to triumph over their servants and 'trample them to the ground'. On top of their tithes, they wanted homage to be paid to them too.

Workers' Struggle

Hand in hand with this denunciation of capitalist exploitation went a glorification of the workers' struggle. It expressed itself in the following ways.

Its description

Worth noting first of all was the absolute primacy of the term *struggle*. *Fight* or *war* were less frequent. The term 'struggle' itself was sometimes used in a very general sense, as in 'the struggle has begun. Till today, the struggle has been difficult, if not impossible, because of the lack of understanding and cohesion amongst us'. At other times, it was used more specifically, and the antagonists were identified: 'In this struggle between the exploited and the exploiters', or 'our struggle against the masters', 'the struggle between the employers and the wage-earners', 'the real struggle of labour against capital'.

The expression *class struggle*, which was common in the mouths of socialist leaders, was less frequent on the lips of grass-root activists. 'We need to carry on this class struggle', said the appeal of the Bessèges miners, but Eugène Fournière had a lot to do with drawing up this manifesto. The Anzin miners declared that their strike was 'only the prelude to this class struggle', but, as the sub-prefect pointed out, 'you can see in this pamphlet the hand of citizens Roche and Quercy'.

Struggle was presented as an awakening, a revolt against a situation which had been allowed to last too long, and as a refusal to endure further sufferings. Enough was enough, as many documents put it: 'We have suffered long enough', 'an end to the wretchedness we are made to suffer', 'is it not time we threw off the terrible yoke which bears down on us and bends us to the whiplash of capital', 'enough of being slaves. It is time to call an end ... We cannot suffer that any longer', 'companions in misery, it is time to stop', and so on. Waiting was perilous, 'because if we are not very careful, workers, we shall soon have no strength left to react against the present situation, given all the sacrifices of every kind we are forced to make'.

To struggle was primarily to stand up, to lift oneself, to stand erect, to rise up in the literal sense of the word. These metaphors had military as well as religious overtones. Similarly, strikers were presented as standard-bearers, and the strike as a battlefield, where the important thing was not to 'retreat' but to 'advance', and if one fell, to do so gloriously. The Revolution was a long march: in the words of one worker, 'the time will soon have come when we shall march all together on the Social Revolution bearing a red banner with the words: "Live by our labour or die fighting"'. There was talk of 'taking the capitalist Bastilles by storm' (especially in speeches at public meetings), of 'planting the standard of the Fourth Estate amidst the ruins of the Old Society', or of 'levelling the masters to the ground'. Evoking bodily combat, Boulé, in a speech written entirely in military terms (it was entitled, 'A Review of the Building-Site: A Guardsman's Report'), wrote: 'Our supreme consolation and hope is that, by falling in a just cause, we shall demolish our implacable enemies, the bosses at every level and the capitalists.'

Every strike was an episode in an unending struggle, in the 'economic war being waged continually between wage-earners and wage-payers, which will end only when the masters have disappeared'. A failure was only a temporary truce. The Anzin miners 'agreed to lay down their arms momentarily', while others proclaimed: 'When the moment has come, we shall declare war on the capitalists.' The struggle had to be waged 'to the last', 'to the bitter end'. It was a struggle to the death which would end only with the physical elimination of one or the other of the opposing camps.

'Bread or death' was the slogan of the Nord miners in 1878. And twelve years later a poster stuck to the railway bridge in Lens swore: 'Vanquish or die.' Many other documents identify what the alternative was: 'We must kill him [the manager . . . or we must perish', 'victory or emptiness at our backs'. The famous watchword of the Lyon silk-workers recurred like a refrain, unchanged, or with modifications which sometimes altered its meaning: 'Companion Marquis from Dijon said, as he died, that he preferred a violent death to slowly vegetating away'; 'it is better to die without working than die by working'.

What was at stake in the struggle?

On this point, speakers diverged, language hesitated and became uncertain and, though the hope of a final solution asserted itself increasingly, there remained much shadow and light, and a contrast between immediate demands and the grandiose but vague prospect of the coming of the Revolution. Wages, which were 'puny, shocking, insulting, meagre and insufficient', as well as being perpetually under threat and being whittled away, had to be 'proportionate to the cost of food', 'the demands of life'; in short, they should represent fair payment for the job. But wages, which were the cornerstone of *coalitions* and, as we have seen, at the heart of three-quarters of the disputes, played a secondary and almost shameful role. It was only incidentally that protest developed into a technical analysis of the situation and presented a series of specific demands. What counted was the repeated and general assertion of the 'rights' of the workers, the claim that their *demands* (or *claims* or *grievances*) were fair and 'legitimate', 'those of all the workers', and were in fact quite modest. The 'right to idleness' was not at issue, and the need to work was hardly ever challenged. 'It has never occurred to us to avoid working', declared the glass-workers of the Seine in a May Day leaflet in 1890, and joiners said much the same: 'Our tyrants have no more the right than we have to live in idleness.' It was merely a case of 'claiming the right to exist by working', of 'obtaining the means of living by work'. 'We are the ones who work, we are the ones who must live by our labour . . . It's our right to live by our work,' repeated endlessly a handwritten poster placed at the gates of the various weaving-mills in Reims.

What was at stake, then, was the 'right to work', in terms at times very reminiscent of those of 1848, but there was also the 'right to happiness'. In this respect, what a century earlier had been for the whole of Europe a 'new idea' had now become one for the proletariat. 'It's our turn to enjoy life', they said. 'Death to tyrants.' The happiness they sought was a simple one. 'We do not envy our masters' prosperity, all we ask is for labour proportionate to a man's strength, and our share in the joys of family life', explained in sober mood the workers of the Reims woollen industry. It was a happiness shared, they said, 'we want our seat at the feast of life', 'our place in the sun', 'our share of happiness'.

Reversing their present lot, this hoped-for happiness reflected three fundamental aspirations: the satisfaction of material need; the hunger for respect (like Beckett's Vladimir in *Waiting for Godot*, the workers suffered from not being acknowledged); and the desire for freedom, which was especially dear to the anarchists. Various quotations illustrate these aspirations: 'In the near future', said one worker, 'the workers will be something and will no longer die of hunger.' In the words of another, 'we will be able to eat something different from boiled potatoes and beaten milk'. The women of Vienne wanted to 'live free and happy by our work'. 'These parasites must disappear, and we must live like men . . . and be free', demanded another group of workers. 'We want no more masters', proclaimed proudly a leaflet signed 'the Miners' Revenge', 'we all want to be free, we all want our share in happiness'. The dream of a future society beckoned in the distance, like a garden of Eden where everyone would eat their fill, where equality, justice, and unity would reign, and where there were no bosses, a society without masters, 'without hornets', but not without work. The workers' dream was not a hippy vision of the world.

The 'Social Revolution' and messianic language

But how was this promised land to be reached? Through the Social Revolution, ran the answer, 'that is to say, a place in the sun for the whole proletariat'. 'Short of social revolution', it was said, 'we shall never find salvation.' These words, voiced increasingly at rallies, are found in many documents. At times they were replaced by words such as *emancipation, liberation, social renewal*, or *social transformation*, or more religious-sounding paraphrases, like 'the hour of deliverance', 'the moment of triumph', and so on. However that may be, after 1880, in the majority of speeches or writings (and if I had to give a figure, I would say in between 70 per cent and 75 per cent of cases), the idea was present that strikes were only an episode in a greater struggle in time and in space whose inevitable end would be the coming to power of the proletariat. The common nature of strike demands and the fact that strikes were taking place simul-

227

taneously gave obvious strength to this conviction, and the great surges of the 1880s and 1890s were particularly favourable to its dissemination: 'What consoles us in our wretchedness', it was argued, 'is that everywhere workers are rising up against their masters and the hour of the Revolution is growing nearer with every day that passes.' 'The movement is general in France', commented one speaker, 'everywhere workers are making the same demands as you and before long the workers will be a force to be reckoned with.' From 1886, social unrest in Europe (mainly in Belgium, where in the spring of that year violent strikes and riots were rife in the Charleroi basin) and in the United States broadened perspectives which till then had been confined to developments within France. 'London trembles, while Berlin waits . . . Saint-Fargeau is ablaze, and Liège and Charleroi are on the move', declared an unsigned placard posted up in Decazeville during the night of 23/4 April 1886. The international character of the May Day action in 1890 widened the frame of reference of activists' speeches, and there is little doubt that at this level what was taking place was the rebirth of a formula which had remained dormant for twenty years.[16] But it is difficult to ascertain what impact these events had on the broad mass of workers who were still swayed by nationalist concerns.

Moreover, their more progressive conception of history, which was that of an age which thought more readily in terms of continuity than of breaks, led workers to think of the Social Revolution as being a French phenomenon, and as something which would 'finish the work of the Revolution of 1789'. The very expression, the 'Fourth Estate', implied a right of succession, almost as an inevitable process.

Inevitably, the Social Revolution was felt to be in gestation, and very close at hand, even imminent, as the following extracts make clear:

— 'The hour of social renewal will not be long in coming, and . . . it would be foolhardy to resist its arrival'[17]
— 'The hour of deliverance is not far off, and . . . it may be that

16. Here are some examples of a theme which recurs often in the various local appeals made for May Day: Arch. dép. Loire, 10 M 87, document 109, in a poster signed by 'the workers' groups joining the Demonstration': 'The Proletariat will accomplish something unknown in the annals of the world. In all civilised nations it will defend one and the same principle by the same means. The working men of Saint-Etienne, bent beneath the same yoke as their brothers in Europe and America.' Arch. dép. Rhône, dossier of May Day 1890, in a leaflet by the Paris cabinet-makers union: 'Already in Germany and Belgium changes are afoot.'

one day, perhaps soon, the distance between the proletariat and the class which forces it to sell its labour cheaply will be insurmountable'

— 'We must prepare ourselves for the great day of the Social Revolution. We must all be ready and armed for this longed-for day'

— 'The time will soon come when we shall all march together in the Social Revolution'

— 'Patience, the time is close when we will make the bourgeois pay for the sufferings they have made us endure'

— 'The Revolution is advancing'

— 'Everywhere, in France, the Revolution is getting ready to stake its claim';

— 'The Social Revolution is imminent', cried the Marseille curriers as they left their meetings

— 'The People are rallying together at last. The Great Day has come'

Some were bold enough to make predictions. 'Within six months a great upheaval will take place', said one. Louise Michel asserted that '1889 will be the workers' awakening'. The power of anniversaries, at times elevated to the status of fateful days, is well known, and the centenary of 1789, combined with the nearing of the end of the century, played its part in creating a climate of millenarist expectation which echoed through all the levels of the activist 'hierarchy'. Speakers like Guesde or Lafargue were fond of such prophecies.

The messianic nature of such beliefs rested not only on the fervour and conviction with which they were held (for if one faith was shared it was that in the 'inevitable and imminent Social Revolution') but also on the notion of an event which would happen with all the suddenness of a thunderbolt from heaven. 'I will come like a thief in the night', said Christ, and similarly the Revolution 'comes', and 'bursts forth'. Its power was irresistible, it would overwhelm its enemies and no one would be able to resist its victory. From ideas such as these came the expectation that the Revolution would be sudden. It would be a 'day', an 'hour', an

---

17. Arch. dép. Seine-Maritime, 14 M, document 122, a pamphlet by E. Piéton, *Étude sur la corporation ouvrière*, 2nd edn., 1872, pt I. Its author draws extensively on Lamennais: 'What then is about to happen? The world is trembling, spectres are in the air, a dim glow is enveloping everything. Is this a dawn? Is it an evening twilight?'.

'instant'. Discussing how long the general strike would need to be to bring about the collapse of capitalism, the *chambre syndicale* of the Paris cabinet-makers opted for the shortest period: 'How long', they asked, 'do you believe that a situation like that could last? At the most three days, four at the outside. It would be enough for all producers to cease production, at every point, and all at the same time, to bring about the final debacle and to force the bourgeoisie and capital to capitulate and thus win in one fell swoop their right to existence. Would there be suffering? Yes, there would. But what are three or four days?' 'What if on one single day we were all to cease producing?', echoed another group. 'On that day the bourgeoisie would be dead and the Revolution would have already begun.'

The ease with which the Revolution would come was a consequence of the feebleness and decadence of the 'obese' bourgeoisie, which in any case represented only a tiny minority who were unable to support themselves or survive without labour. Images of collapse were common in this context ('When the hands cease work, capital will fall'), as were images of crumbling ('People, arise and you will see them fall to dust'). Shorn of its supply of blood, the vampire of capital, like Dracula, would fall to dust. A whole conception of capitalism lay behind this language. Capitalism lived on unearned income, was idle, parasitic, totally superfluous, incapable of innovation and of direction. Nothing was more remote from the working-class world than the Saint-Simonian or even Schumpeterian conception of the entrepreneur. The strength of 'hands' was enough to make a factory work.

'Scientific' socialists spoke much the same language. Lafargue or Guesde had only sarcasm for the incapacity, the 'imbecility' of the ruling classes, who were as immoral as they were inefficient. Two additional arguments swelled the indictment: the crisis (an 'economic battle of Sedan') in which many saw the death-throes of the system, and the drop in the French birth-rate, which statisticians, like Bertillon, attributed mainly to the middle classes. Not only was it useless, the bourgeoisie was impotent into the bargain, dried up, worn out by pleasure and by orgies, literally bastardised. It was responsible for France's decline. 'France will be Cossack or Prussian within a hundred years', predicted Guesde, who saw in the healthy fertility of the proletariat the proof of national recovery. Making the racial-class theory of Boulainvilliers or Augustin Thierry their own, socialists were not far from seeing in the proletarian revolution the revenge of the Gauls.

As for the army, it was said, 'they will not shoot at the People'.

'The army is entirely on our side', asserted an unsigned placard in Lille. Boulangism made this prospect of a new army more credible and left its mark on Guesde's words in Vierzon in 1886, where he expressed the following view: 'The behaviour of the army has been praiseworthy . . . The soldiers haven't stirred. The army today is no longer as it used to be; the soldier knows that he was himself a worker yesterday, that tomorrow he will be a worker again, that he is the son of a worker.' In Bourges the theme was the same: 'The army . . . is beginning to come over to socialism.'

The 'means' of revolution

As a result, there was relative silence concerning the revolutionary process itself, which was relegated to the vagueness of the word *means*, which was much used, though admittedly in different combinations, such as: 'legal means', 'practical', 'violent', or 'revolutionary means' and especially in the expression 'all possible means', which was almost always used in an extremist sense.

Admittedly, after 1880, calls for *organisation*, for *groupings* or *federations*[18] became more widespread in meetings. The main support was for *chambres syndicales*, while in the minor industries there was a strong current of opinion in favour of producers' cooperatives, which would be 'designed to emancipate the workers from their bosses and bitter enemies'. On the other hand, around this period, within the speeches of activists, there was little mention of a *workers' party*, and the extracts which follow show the ambiguities which surrounded the term. In 1880 the metallurgists' *chambre* in Grenoble launched an appeal to all the unions in the industry with the statement that 'faced with political parties which increasingly fail to carry out their promises, it is necessary, indeed it is indispensable that we create a workers' party, not a political party, but a socialist one, which, leaving by the wayside those who want power for its own sake, will seek practical means to better the

---

18. The word *federation*, another key term, would merit lengthy semantic analysis, if only on the basis of the speeches of the Marseilles Congress, 1879. These are some examples of its use: in *L'Egalité*, 24 March 1880, Biesse, a shoemaker from Blois, put forward 'the federation of all productive forces'. In Arch. nat. F 124662, Federation of the *chambres syndicales* of building-workers in Lyon, we read, in the preamble to its statutes, in 1881, that 'the federation of the *chambres syndicales* will be, in a word, the *coalition* of all the workers against all parasites'. Arch. dép. Loire, 92 M 19, document 29, from a weavers' meeting in Roanne, 11 February 1882: 'We must learn, form ourselves into a federation, group ourselves together and meet unceasingly.' The Bessèges miners in 1883 spoke of 'federating themselves'. On the strictly working-class notion of the federation, see the *Congrès de Marseille*, p. 814.

lot of the producers'. At the same time, Dolland, of the Paris wheelwrights, put forward the idea of a federation of *chambres syndicales* which were to have the aim of 'appointing ourselves our own candidates for Parliament with a settled and binding mandate'. Conversely, in the appeal of the miners of La Grande-Combe (of 1881) the Workers' Party took on the appearance of an organised revolutionary avant-garde: what they foresaw was for 'the Workers' Party, solidly constituted and conscious of its goal, to tell all the exploited: Brothers, arise, onwards to social emancipation'.

Two further terms were little used, too, in the type of document which has been quoted up to now: *socialism* and *socialist*, which were otherwise quite widespread. But it seems the workers were distrustful of them, and when they use such terms, they made attempts to define them, as though they wanted to avoid certain of their senses. One appeal, from the dockers in the port of Marseilles, makes clear that 'it is not our role, respectable workers that we are, to be revolutionaries. Socialism, for us, is fraternity'. 'We are all socialists', proclaimed Eglen, a delegate from the Lyon glass-workers, 'and the enemies of those who exploit us, and we are not afraid to say so, in spite of the police being here.' Such statements suggest there was a desire to retain the wider significance of the term *socialism*. And in the appeal of the Grenoble metal-workers the marked opposition between *politics* and *socialism* will have been noted. Many offered silent resistance to the embodiment of social-ism in a party.

Politics did not enjoy a good reputation. In this respect the examination of vocabulary is extremely revealing. The word *politics* was almost always used in a pejorative sense, closer to 'political scheming'. This is clear from the following extracts: 'The assembly has decided that politics will be excluded, without exception, from its debates'; 'the majority of workers withdrew, protesting against the introduction of political issues into the strike'; 'we refuse to become involved in your political intrigues'; 'the present movement is outside of politics . . . Let us take care it does not become confused with other things'; 'we are not here to play politics but to defend the interests of our union organisation'; 'we acknowledge that sectarianism and politics have taken up too much of the workers' time and create divisions. All our efforts will be devoted to bringing the struggle back into the economic and union domain'. Politics corrupted and divided, as opposed to economic or social concerns which united. Thus it was that the strongly Guesdist National Federation of Unions could declare, on the subject of the

May Day action, that 'we trust there is no need to tell you that this action is solely a working-class affair, in the broadest sense of the word, which can and must unite all wage-earners above and beyond all political or electoral rivalries'. For their part, the Bordeaux delegates to the same Federation asserted: 'Economic-peaceful-legal: such must be the May Day demonstration.'

The strength of the Revolution lay principally in its logic. to go on strike was to 'support the rule of law'. The workers were struggling in 'a just cause', 'a sacred cause', even 'a holy cause'. They had justice on their side, whence their confidence: 'Right triumphs always', they believed. The moral rightness of the fight, in sum, guaranteed its success. The vision was a Manichean one, in which good would always necessarily triumph, and is reminiscent of many popular movements, like that of the Puritan farmers in the American West. This was the reason for the importance, in action, of moral qualities, like courage, energy, perseverance, unity and solidarity, which were repeatedly exalted, while cowardice and weakness were condemned. Many slogans bore this out: 'Let us be united and act decisively, and victory will everywhere be ours'; 'On our energy depends our success. Let us struggle through to the end!'; 'no compulsion! But courage! Courage!' Such formulas were repeated constantly. They reflected the voluntarist conception of social struggle which was to be the driving force behind revolutionary syndicalism. In the eyes of the anarchists, the 'brutalisation' of the proletariat was the main cause of its exploitation. The appeal to *solidarity*, much more so than to *fraternity*, which was a term in decline, as J. Dubois has noted, was expected and demanded, mainly in subscription lists, which gave it more concrete relevance. In speeches not directly concerned with fund-raising, the word was mainly *unity*, and the call to unity had a vague, at times almost mystical ring to it: 'Let us unite to fight this accursed bourgeoisie', was one phrase; 'to vanquish our oppressors, we must all be united', was another.

Permanence and Change in the Language of the Activist

Much more, no doubt, could be gleaned from an even more elaborate analysis of speeches read at congresses. It is worth considering, in particular, how much a lexicographic, semantic and statistical study could draw from the fat volume of material relating to the Marseilles Congress. Strike literature itself, pressed by time as it was, and by the need to act, constrained by the limitations of leaflets and posters, and emanating from simple men who were little given to theorising, was brief, empirical and cursory, and made much use of the same expressions and the same repeated images. For this reason it was easy to caricature.[19] But my decision to concentrate on this material has, I hope, been justified, for its language was a mass language, which, precisely because it is usually so inaccessible, was worth exploring in detail, even at the level of banality.

It was a language which had its notable permanent features. In it a whole story of exploiters and exploited was unfolded, changing little in its themes or forms. There were strong religious overtones, and activists modelled themselves on the images, and even the vocabulary, of the Christian tradition (which weighed so heavily in the nineteenth century as a whole), at times spontaneously, without even realising it, and at times deliberately, following the process of transposition often employed by the zealots of a new faith. Speaking in the *chouan* country to an audience of Combrée slate-quarry miners, Ludovic Ménard invoked this Christian tradition, and argued that 'the founder of the Catholic religion was a socialist . . . but in the mystical rather than economic sense. He wanted to free humanity from its suffering'.[20] In Roubaix, activists distributed the *Prières du socialiste*, *Les Dix commandements* and *Le Pater et la foi*, which, as an informer recounts, were read out aloud in public in the course of a 'Bacchic evening'.[21] Waiting for the emancipation of the proletariat, presented as a captive and chosen people in a modern

19. *Le Temps* for 23 October 1890 described a socialist speech in the following terms: 'A revolutionary socialist speech is composed of a series of antitheses: capital versus labour; employers versus employees; bosses versus wage-earners; bourgeois versus proletarians; exploiters versus exploited; and robbers versus the robbed. The two are contrasted and the epithets changed every minute. The lowly, damp and insalubrious workshop is set against the palaces where idle bosses lie sprawling; or the slums where proletarian misery reigns against the rich apartments of the bourgeois oligarchy. Workers whose heads are not turned by revolutionary ideas are "traitors". Overseers are the servants of "apes" living off the sweat of the people. Next, the vocabulary contains a few simple expressions, like "grasping bourgeoisie, capitalist class, or class of starvers", or longer phrases, like "raising high and firm the banner of the proletariat" and "greeting the delegates of the working world to the true workers' parliament. After this, there are some plays on words which try to impress: the workers have calluses on their hands, and the masters calluses on the heart. Lastly, to end up with, there is the call to social revolution and for the emancipation of the workers by the workers themselves.'
20. Arch. dép. Maine-et-Loire, 71 M 2, document 243, lecture given on 8 September 1890.
21. Arch. dép. Nord, M 154/59, document 34. This was the Lord's Prayer drawn from this remarkable text: 'O Socialism, thou who was announced to us long ago, reach down to us, may thy kingdom of equality and justice prevail on this earth. Give us today the total product of our labour, suffer not that our Masters take from us the daily bread that we produce, bring us not into wretchedness, but deliver us from wage labour, for thine is the strength and thine is the future — it's very urgent.' The Creed was in a similar vein: 'We believe in labour, the creator of all riches and

variation on millenarist thinking, took the place of waiting for the Messiah.

The changes in this language were produced by the vocabulary of action. After 1880, action became more violent and aggressive. The setting up of the bourgeois Republic, as an indispensable first step, seemed to introduce a new stage in the struggle, and terms like *federation, workers' party* or, in particular, *general strike*, which, if not new ones, had been little used till then, became more wide-spread. In the language itself a certain revolutionary commitment was beginning to take shape.

The Language of Public Meetings: the Socialist Message and Its Impact

A study of the semantics of socialist speeches, in these times of fresh horizons, would be an interesting one. But it would be impossible to confine it to an examination of what was said on the occasion of strikes, which, though they were important, were not the only, or even the most central platforms for socialist leaders, since only slightly more than 4 per cent of strikes led to the calling of wide-spread public meetings. A proper analysis would have to widen its scope, and be based on the systematic use of the press, whether socialist or not, since it was there that long extracts, and at times whole speeches, were reproduced. Over this period, in this prov-inces, at any rate, public meetings constituted an event which gener-ated a wide response. Picking out the lexicological structures of the language of Guesde, Vaillant or Clément, analysing the shifts in that language and dating the appearance of new terms would tell us more than many painstaking accounts of events. That would be a worthy task for political 'science'. But it is not something I can undertake here, not because it is not worth doing but because the exhaustive approach which would be needed would fall well outside the scope of my present purposes. To give a fragmentary account would just be to impose my own arbitrary choices, and in this case discretion is the better part of honour.

---

products of labour on this earth, which are the product of the labour of our hands, by the sweat of our brow, which are dragged from the workshop to the house of the rich man, then come to the shops of our masters, to be exchanged into gold and vanish into the capitalists' coffers, coming then down to us in the form of humiliating charity; we believe this is unjust and that therein lies the cause of our wretchedness, of our sufferings and the ignorance of our children, our domination by the wealthy and the uncertainty of our existence; we believe in the vengeance that will come.' The parodies of Paul Lafargue (see his *La Religion du capital*, 1887) had their antecedents.

The remarks which follow, then, are merely empirical ones. Their purpose is to look at the ways in which the language of the leaders resembled or differed from the language I have considered up to now and to examine what new elements it brought to the debates. The language of the leaders was a language of circumstance, which put much emphasis on social issues. This was true not only of the titles of speeches but also of the way speeches were developed. They painted the contrasting picture of workers' conditions and exploitation by the employers in terms closely resembling those which have already been noted. Greater stress was put on 'class struggle', thought of in the same dualistic terms as those of the *Communist Manifesto*, by which the bourgeoisie was set against the proletariat with no mention of the 'intermediary' social strata or of the peasantry.[22] All the major speakers, from Chabert to Guesde, were at one in predicting social revolution, which acted as a kind of melting pot for language and beliefs, and of which Guesde, in particular, became the passionate advocate.

The differences lay in the way the leaders gave these issues a political dimension. Workers were reluctant to confront these questions and used words like *socialism* or the *workers' party* in vague ways, as though they were afraid of falling hostage to them. Public speakers, on the other hand, enjoyed criticising the government, 'which did nothing for the working man', political parties, career politicians, who were mere opportunists (Gambetta was 'that well-known clown', while Ferry was ridiculed as 'Ferry-the-famine' or 'Ferry-the-cholera-outbreak'), as well as the Radicals. The problem of political power lay at the heart of their preoccupations. Where workers tended to dissolve their own history into that of the eternal exploitation of the pauper by the rich man, the socialist leaders had a more detailed time-scale and were concerned in particular to demonstrate the bourgeois nature of the Revolution of 1789, to which their vocabulary made constant reference; they spoke, for instance, of 'taking the bourgeois Bastille', or of inaugurating the reign of the Fourth Estate. They exhorted the workers to 'direct their own affairs themselves', and to form a workers' party having clear electoral objectives. But their economic analysis remained extremely rudimentary. One theme, however, which was voiced was that of the need for 'collective control' and for

---

22. At the end of *Capital*, Marx sketches out the threefold theme of the classes: capitalists, landowners and wage-earners, at the same time as he puts forward the idea that the notion of the source of income is inadequate for a definition of the classes. The theme is a fine one, though one sadly broken off like *The Art of Fugue*.

'nationalisation', though what might be understood by these terms was left undefined.

When they addressed audiences of strikers there was little to distinguish between the various competing groups which divided the socialist movement in France at the time like the rival sectarian bands. However, the possibilists seemed more legalistic and more electoralist to their audiences, and affirmed, during the period of Boulangism, their commitment to the Republic. In Vierzon, re-counts an observer, Clément and Gambon 'preached revolution, not by violence but by the ballot-box, and argued that when the representatives elected by the people were all socialists, the revolu-tion would take place of its own and without a blow being struck'. In Cholet, Dumany and Dalle, in one account, argued that 'an electoral battle must be waged against all the bourgeois parties. It is for the workers to direct their own affairs themselves'. The essential thing was to vote for workers. Guesde, on the other hand, by the vigour of his criticisms and views of the future, was at times closer to the anarchists. The line he expressed was that 'we must organise the Workers' Party, which will fight by the vote until it is time to fight with something else. Classes will only set themselves free by the use of force and violence'. 'We will use', he said, 'all possible means, including force'. He went on, leaving far behind him the language of libertarian progress, to outline the prospect of the dictatorship of the proletariat: 'We are accused', he declared, 'of being authoritarian . . . Make no mistake about it, we are authori-tarian, yes, and when we are masters of the situation we shall respect no single freedom. We will wage war on the property-owners and capitalists without pity nor mercy.'

Strikes and socialism

It is worth repeating to what extent it is impossible to gauge the amount of contact between workers and socialism solely on the basis of public meetings, which were too short as encounters. But between the different groups there were many other types of contact, some of which, in the context of strikes themselves, were far more efficient. The most important of these was the press, which provided an open platform for the grievances and fears of the workers, whose bulletins it published, and for whom it organised financial help, unconditionally, and without expecting anything in return. As a direct result of this, socialist newspapers increased their audience quite spectacularly in the affected areas. The strike of May 1880 in Reims gave them a readership of 3,000, where before virtually no papers had been sold. The support of *Le Cri du peuple* for the workers in the major disputes of 1886–87, especially in Decazeville, took its circulation to the highest point it ever achieved. In the Aveyron there were not enough copies to satisfy demand, and we read, 'the vendors selling *Le Cri du peuple* were set upon by a crowd of workers who all wanted to buy a copy of the paper'. The same was true further afield. In the Nord, which was seemingly quiet to the point of indifference, sales of copies went from 200 to 2,500 in the Roubaix-Tourcoing-Armentières conurbation. The surge was short-lived, it is true, and once the events had passed, curiosity and enthusiasm dwindled and the paper, a daily, lost circulation so rapidly that it closed in 1889. Such impermanence was typical of the whole socialist press during the period and is indicative of its shifting and unassured foundations. The question remains an open one as to how much of an impact it left on its readership.

The arrival on the spot of Socialist leaders, no longer simply as speakers stopping off between trains to hold sway just for an evening, but as resident activists, constituted a second tangible form of support. Fournière, who was the first to do this, in La Grande-Combe in 1881, followed by Duc-Quercy and Roche in Anzin (in 1884) and Decazeville, by Dumay and Dalle in Cholet, Féline in Amiens (in 1888), Lachize in Cours and Thizy, Vaillant in numerous *coalitions* in the Cher, or Clément in many similar ones in the Ardennes, were active not only as reporters or mediators but also as real advisors. They presided over the daily meetings, drew up statements, suggested courses of action, gave an impetus to organisation and became personally involved, even to the point of being imprisoned for 'inciting citizens to violence and to civil strife'. The thin figure of Fournière, leading a miners' demonstration, on 22 February 1882 in Bessèges, and standing up to the sub-prefect, no doubt did more to establish socialist ideas than many speeches. For the mine-workers his face was that of a 'young man aged between twenty-four and twenty-five, with a wan and weary look', while for Goblet, the Minister of the Interior, he was a 'travelling revolutionary' and one denounced as 'the real instigator of these strikes'. By comparison, the Radicals, who were shouted down in the Gard for their laughable attempts at mediation, appeared like 'pompous fools'. The workers had a great need for leaders who would stand out as figureheads of their struggle.

Daniel Halévy saw this involvement in strikes by journalists and politicians as a trait characteristic of the underdevelopment of the

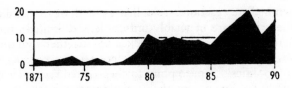

Figure 6:   Political involvement by journalists and politicians

French trades-union movement. Indeed, it may be noted that such involvement most frequently was the case in the areas which were the most backward in this respect: amongst the semi-rural weavers in the Lyonnais, or around Cholet, and the miners on the edge of the Massif Central or amongst the Amiens dyers. Even so, in all these instances the local activists and leaders who were called in to give support, worked closely together. Disputes led almost entirely by outside socialists (and there were very few of them) came about amongst the most deprived groups. In this way the possibilists directed the *coalition* of the Parisian refiners in 1882, while the Blanquists did the same for the women workers in hide-dying on the Boulevard Arago, or for labourers and women in general. These workers did not refuse this type of patronage, which was rejected, at times vehemently so, by their comrades in higher-status jobs. The skilled workers in the metal industry, or in the glass, wood, leather or building trades needed nobody, and did not tolerate others giving them advice, and if they welcomed leaders, it was as allies and on an equal footing with them. In the thorny problem of the deep-rootedness of socialist ideas, sociological factors ought not to be underestimated. The examples of Guesdism, and of the French Communist Party between the wars seem to suggest that authoritarian-type parties value political innocence.

The reception of the message

Strikes, then, made contact with socialism more widespread. But the question which needs to be researched is that of the long-term impact of these actions and temporary 'missions'. What would be more interesting is how this message was perceived and received by its audience. Various questions arise. What images did these words give rise to? How were they passed on and communicated? In the last analysis, did they create new attitudes, and in particular, since this was the explicit goal pursued by the leaders, did they bring about electoral change?

The immediate reactions of audiences (and we are dealing here with clues which are inevitably unreliable and limited), their reticence in terms of the words they picked up, together with the strong emotions created by certain terms and the pejorative associations of the word 'politics', seem to point to deep-seated resistance on their part. The list of symptoms of this could be extended, particularly with reference to Paris. The cabinet-makers, for instance, debated at length the question of whether they should accept the funds raised for them by *L'Egalité*. 'We must remain solely within the confines of the strike movement', said one speaker, 'and enter into no agreements with revolutionary socialists . . . Workers can accept money from nobody except from workers in their own union organisation without compromising themselves.' The piano-makers refused to underwrite two shares in *Le Prolétaire*. As for the gas-workers, they turned away Chauvière, who was a Blanquist, with the words, 'we did not want M. Chauvière to lecture to us, nor did we want the assistance of the several revolutionary committees who wanted to offer us their support'. In Lyon and Saint-Etienne, socialist activists were jeered at. 'Enough is enough! Come to the point! We are not here to play politics', said the Lyon carpenters. 'Down with agitators! No more of them', shouted the Loire miners. Elsewhere, anarchists preaching violence were shouted down.

But the resistance encountered ought not to be interpreted in a single way. It came from a strong desire for autonomy, without it being necessary to see this testy *ouvriérisme* as having a revolutionary or corporatist intent. It was perhaps in the main a defensive reaction, expressing a fear of being led in a different direction, enlisted in some other cause and diverted from the only battlefield workers knew, that of their struggle against the employer. To this extent it was a rudimentary but crucial form of the self-consciousness not found at any level in the working classes of Western countries.

As for the role of the strike in laying a basis for socialism's electoral support, it might be possible to see this by comparing the workers' votes (which would mean finding areas which were socially homogeneous) in precise parts of the country affected by a strike, before and after the dispute. If research were carried out into this question, it would be possible to get some understanding of the importance of strikes as a factor in political change. In my own view, this remains an issue of considerable obscurity. On the one hand, the combativeness of workers can be expressed both in strikes and in voting patterns, without there necessarily being a relationship of cause and effect between the two. Moreover, the fact that one of these may predate the other, as a simple effect of time-tabling, cannot serve as an explanation. In Bessèges-La-Grand-Combe, for instance, the electoral swing to the Socialists was already under-way in the legislative elections of August 1881, *before* the *coalitions* of December and February 1882. For a large body of opinion, these were the result of collectivist propaganda. Had the elections taken place in the summer of 1882, no doubt the contrary argument would have been put.

On the other hand, major social activity can at times be ac-companied by traditional political options (let us remember, for instance, the election results in June 1968), because there is not necessarily any direct correspondence, any close matching between these two levels of expression. They exist rather like two different languages, each internally coherent and largely independent. This is why the economic, social and political history of the working class (no doubt in the same way as most other social groups) does not present a neatly stratified cross-section of staggered layers but, on the contrary, a somewhat unclear picture of overlapping and con-flicting strata. But I am beginning to stray here from the question of language.

In this chapter, burdened as it is with quotations, I hope to have given voice to this language, not with the aim of winning plaudits but simply to give others the opportunity of feeling what the language was like. But as soon as the task becomes one of interpret-ation (and this is impossible to avoid), a whole host of fresh questions arise. How, for instance, are we to evaluate the impact of the words used? Or how are we to draw the line between the thrilling moment at which a word is coined and that moment when it hardens into a habit, a mere formula and a cliché? One would like to know, too, how much real obsession, or didactic intent, or simple unthinking banality enters into the repetition of words. Perhaps there is something beyond language; or perhaps it is wiser, as Michel Foucault ('this happy positivist') suggests, to limit oneself to mere statements. No doubt the contrast between words and atti-tudes, between language and action, can reveal much. Events pos-sess a discriminating potential. But to give them too much weight is also perhaps to accept like some decision of fate the failure of the many latent possibilities events exclude.

Freed from the often sterile study of literary movements and sources, the *nouvelle critique* has not rid itself so easily of the question of interpretation. At the very least it invites us to listen

241

patiently to the text it has rediscovered. Blinded by the descent into the Hell of erudition, may the historian, if any manage to return, rediscover, too, the keen pleasures of reading.

9
How Strikes Ended

From this point on, we shall be concerned with how strikes ended, and in looking at this question we shall have to divest ourselves of a number of contemporary notions. Tripartite negotiations at the national level, as symbolised in France in the names of Matignon, Grenelle and Tilsitt, reflect what are in fact quite recent conceptions of the roles both of trade unions and the state, conceptions produced in an economy where everything is integrated and interdependent. And the outcome of today's strikes is affected by the impact of popular opinion, as is seen for example in the famous French Electricity Company strike of November 1969, where, in an unprecedented move, the unions ordered a return to work after hostile demonstrations by consumers, or in the French miners' strike of 1963, where the public's active support for the strikers caused the government to propose a compromise.

Things were very different at the end of the nineteenth century. The lack of organisation among the contending forces (particularly on the national level), the local and fragmentary character of the disputes which were confined to the industrial centres alone, the watchdog state's principle of non-intervention and the habitual indifference of a poorly informed public that was little affected by strikes in its daily life all meant that the ending of a dispute generally depended solely on the relationship between the two parties involved. These parties were of course the workers and the employers, and the context of their relationship was a factory or, at best, a town. However, if the government remained aloof, the political conjuncture caused the local administration — particularly at department level — to intervene increasingly, and not always in the unilateral direction one might imagine. Something akin to an arbitration function was developing, and the Act of 1892 was to mark a significant milestone in that process. Classical liberalism was shipping water on all sides. The worker–capitalist duet of the class struggle was on occasion replaced by a more subtle capitalist–worker–administration triangle.

It would be naive to think of these three terms as being simply self-contained. Each one is set in a social environment and connected to forces which inform its conduct and its attitudes. Although labour disputes seem more circumscribed and isolated than in our day, where everything is interrelated, each one weaves a knot of complex relations which any account necessarily simplifies by dividing out its constituent elements.

Strikes have effects, then, which reach beyond their own particular sphere. One should no more judge a strike's repercussions by its immediate results alone than one should take the workers' express demands for the causes of a strike. However, it is these immediate results — the only quantifiable ones — which we must first assess. The statistics speak quite clearly for themselves, so we shall limit ourselves to a brief commentary.

An Assessment of Strikes: Analysis of Immediate Results

For greater convenience, we shall argue only on the basis of the strikes where we know the outcome, since the rest represent only 8 per cent of strikes, 3 per cent of strikers and 1.9 per cent of strike days. Following the distinctions made by the Office du Travail (and by most available statistics), I have distinguished three types of result: total success (S), compromise settlement (CS) and total failure (F). 'Compromise settlement' here denotes the satisfaction of part of a demand or set of demands.[1] For an overall appraisal of the results — the profit-and-loss account, as it were — it seems reasonable to compare successes and settlements against failures alone, since strikers often asked for more than they hoped to get and a compromise at least represents some measure of gain.

On this calculation, although there is a solid block of failures, the balance in favour of strikes is mildly positive: there were successful outcomes for 50.2 per cent of strikes, 53 per cent of strikers, 58.7 per cent of person-days lost and 52.6 per cent of strike days. The differences in percentages between the various headings show that it is the largest (on average 394 workers per strike), longest (average length, 15.8 days), most intense (on average 4,586 work-days lost per strike) and most extensive strikes (average number of establish-

---

1. On condition, of course, that this concession was not cancelled out by some compensatory measure completely nullifying its effects. In fact, many compromise settlements were booby-trapped. I have therefore endeavoured to assess each of them qualitatively as far as the documents allowed.

ments affected, 7.1) which were completely successful. Smaller, shorter, less intense and less extensive strikes were more likely to end in failure. Thus the length of a strike, its size and extension weighed in favour of the workers in this period. For them, holding out over a long period and spreading the movement were guarantees of success. The owners' resistance wore down more quickly than the workers' patience.

This was only true up to a certain point, however, as is shown by the way in which the results vary as a function of the length of disputes and the numbers involved. The percentage figure for S + CS grows as the numbers involved grow, until it reaches a maximum threshold of 64.5 per cent (between 811 and 2,430 workers involved); beyond that point it regresses. The findings are the same for the length of strikes (maximum S + CS = 57.2 per cent for 17–32 days). There are therefore optimum conditions for success which work out as follows:

Complete success	91 to 270 strikers	5–8 days
Success and compromise settlements	800 to 2,400 strikers	17–32 days
Complete failures	1 to 10	1 day

It would have been desirable to investigate the statistics even more closely to arrive at a more precise definition of these ranges. Unfortunately, I omitted to ask the computer to map the outcomes of strikes against the actual figures for the duration of strikes and the number of participants. Neither duration nor level of participation are, of course, isolated factors; they are always combined within a total context.

If we may say that, where strikes were concerned, trade-union strategy was not preoccupied with determining the optimal conditions for success, or at least that it did not do so explicitly, or in statistical terms, the abandonment of the strike-by-rota (*grève tournante*) tactic (striking in small contingents) in favour of the generalised strike (*grève généralisée*) and the support subsequently shown for the idea of the general strike are evidence of a preference for mass tactics (references to numbers as a measure of the workers' power recur obsessively in their speeches) and, beyond that, of a vision of the struggle in which the revolutionary armies are unleashed, as they were on the battlefields in the second year of the French Revolution. Strike strategy today is based on quite different principles. The targeting of key sectors of the economy and the limiting of action to short periods of time — all of which have made the short stoppage seem preferable to the strike[2] — derive from a more technical, less lyrical conception, one that is more rational and not so subversive, in which the desire for effectiveness takes precedence over all other considerations.

The results of strikes vary considerably according to the situations of the strikers:

1. They vary by level of skill: women, young people and labourers suffered a particularly high failure rate (65.75 and 68 per cent, respectively); 'semi-skilled workers' (and we must remember that miners, spinners and weavers were put in this category) weigh in with 54 per cent, whilst for skilled workers the figures are reversed. They had a 38 per cent failure rate, scored 61 per cent for S + CS and won total victories in 39 per cent of cases. In its early years it was principally the skilled craftsmen who 'profited' from the emergence of the labour movement. Labourers derived but little benefit from it, and it seems possible that one of the first results of struggle was to increase wage differentials further and to widen the gap between the various levels of workers.

2. The relationship between strike outcome and strikers' wage levels in part overlaps with the preceding section. At less than 3 francs per day, failures predominate; between 3 and 6 francs, the success rate grows steadily. However, beyond 7 francs, failures are again in the ascendant, as if the restricted strikes in which these privileged workers engaged in their small professional groups collapsed for lack of support.

3. We find these influences again when we examine the overall situation trade by trade. The industries that registered most victories (S + CS) were:

Wood	63.0% (including 33 per cent total success)
Glass and porcelain	62.6%
Food	59.0% (due to the success of the bakers)
Building (stone)	54.0% (a hybrid group; although the skilled building-workers — masons, painters etc — enjoyed great success, the labourers were correspondingly unsuccessful)

2. Cf. *C.G.T. Congress* 1963.

The most mediocre results are to be found amongst the following industries:

	S + SC (%)	F (%)
Agriculture	36	63
Printing	39	60
Chemicals	41	58

whilst the following hovered around the average levels:

	S + C (%)	F (%)
Warehousing/packing	45	54
Mining	45	54
Textiles	46	53
Metals	50	49

The mediocre results achieved by certain groups, in spite of being skilled, quite well paid and organised, may seem surprising, as for example in the case of the metal-workers. But other factors come into play here, such as the content of demands. The bosses gave in more easily to claims that were purely concerned with wages; those relating to working hours aroused bitter resistance and the reaction was even fiercer when trade unionisation was at issue. Of strikes in defence of trade unions, 66 per cent failed; conflicts with the overseers ended in 77 per cent of cases with the workers backing down and the offending individual keeping his job. There could be no compromise over the principle of authority. Where these differential degrees of resistance are concerned, the type of employer involved also emerges as an important factor. Proprietors of family businesses were more ready to meet demands or to negotiate than private companies:

	S (%)	C + S (%)	F (%)
Family businesses	23.5	28.9	47.4
Companies	15.3	27.3	57.2

Apparent here is one of the reasons for the numerous defeats suffered by the miners, who were up against powerful and unyielding companies. Moreover, the effectiveness of the resistance mounted within the different industries owed more to the particular situations of those industries than to the degree of collective organisation. Trade unions, which were still rudimentary defensive bodies, were not able to favourably influence the outcome of strikes.

The nature and conduct of a strike also influenced its outcome.

1. Offensive strikes were more likely to succeed than defensive ones:

	S +CS (%)	F (%)
O.S.	56.6	43.4
D.S.	39.7	60.3

2. Strikes that were *prepared* and declared beforehand were much more likely to be effective than sudden ones:

	S + CS (%)	F (%)
Strikes with advance warning	68.1	31.8
Sudden strikes	34.4	65.5

3. Strikes with a clear set of demands had better chances of success than those with only a single objective:

	S + CS (%)	F (%)
Strikes with single demands	47.2	52.7
Strikes with multiple demands	59.6	40.3

4. There is a clear connection between a willingness to negotiate and the achievement of compromise settlements. To a lesser degree, resorting to arbitration — particularly to the prefect and his officials — weakened resistance on the employers' side and improved prospects of a compromise. In the short term, such arbitration proved beneficial.

5. The efficacy of financial solidarity can also be seen:

	S + CS (%)	F (%)
Assisted strikes	57.4	42.5
Non-assisted strikes	48.0	52.0

6. Outbreaks of violence, on the other hand, coincide with higher failure rates:

	S + C (%)	F (%)
Strikes without incident	53.5	46.4
Strikes with violent incidents	37.1	61.4
Strikes with acts of violence	49.4	50.5

7. Organisation guaranteed the workers better results and the assimilation of this experience doubtless explains the increasing part played by trade unionism in disputes and the progressive elaboration of a strategy to supplant the old trial-and-error methods. However, trade-union intervention remained as yet insufficiently developed to affect the overall success rate in any real way. This

continued to vary very erratically from year to year and seems to have been mainly subject to the necessities of the general economic situation. The subsequent development of trade unionism was to eliminate some of the more violent swings in these results by adapting strikes to the prevailing market conditions. Between 1890 and 1914 fluctuations in the success rate were to decrease in intensity.

The immediate results of strikes therefore depended on a range of economic, political, sociological and psychological factors. The will and judgement of the workers certainly played a cardinal role, though they were not simply able to achieve anything they wanted. The outcome of a dispute did not depend entirely on them, any more than that of a revolutionary movement depends on those who support it. This is an obvious truth, yet it is one that historians of social movements always tend to forget, as though such attacks unfolded in a space devoid of all enemies, as though the capitalist 'Bastilles' were deserted fortresses.

Strikes: the Employers' Reactions

Methodological Difficulties

Strikes give us only a selective and, in some respects, arbitrary view of the employers, since we see them only at the moment of conflict. It is their hard, tensed, steely side that is highlighted, the side that is under attack and showing resistance. Strikes could not give us a full picture of the normally serene course of the employers' domination in what was still for them a golden age, nor of their overall attitude to workers' demands. To grasp that attitude fully we should need, for example, information on what the German statistics (which, in contrast to the French equivalent, recorded such data) called 'wage movements' — *coalitions* that were still-born because their claims were swiftly met — as well as on the extent of rises 'spontaneously' granted by the employers and the thinking which lay behind such calculations. It would be wrong to assume from the outset that the employers were simply acting out of fear or reacting to pressure, and that they did not indeed have a more developed wages strategy, which was part of a general company policy or reflected their thinking on the 'dictates' of the market. These are all things which hardly show up at all in the tense situation of a strike.

249

A separate study would be required here. Company records, chamber of commerce minutes, responses to boards of enquiry, such as those of 1872 or 1884, and the business press would be the sources that would allow us to see what the nineteenth-century French enterprise and entrepreneur looked like. While I cannot provide such a picture here, a description of the actual wrestling between bosses and workers is not without some interest, since it is so rarely described elsewhere.

There is a second difficulty here, which arises from the unsymmetrical nature of the source material produced by strikes themselves. The strikers are exposed to the full glare of publicity, since it is they who are the troublemakers. We are told a great deal about *them* and *they* speak loudly to us. We see the bosses through their impassioned eyes and yet theirs is an hallucinatory vision, distorted by the gigantic figure of the exploiter, whose massive, abstract, changeless form filters out individual features. This noisy and colourful seizing of language by the workers stands in sharp contrast to the silence in which the employers cloak themselves. These latter were content to remain aloof from any public exchanges, walled up in that best of defences, a lofty silence. As in Kafka's castle, the employers remain as much hidden from our view as they were from the workers'. When they do speak, it is in a stiff, icy manner. The declarations — posters, letters — in which they set out their case are couched in that measured, conventional language which is designed to conceal the real motives for their actions. If the employers reveal their official façade to us on the one side, on the other their internal dealings remain hidden. The professional indiscretion of chief constables or police informers provides us with thorough accounts of the workers' deliberations; those of the employers, which take place far from any prying eyes, are beyond our grasp. Even the minutes of board meetings only give us an expurgated version of what happened; they were clearly designed for public consumption. Moreover, apart from the fact that such documents are rare, most of the factories affected by strikes had no board of directors. Nothing remains and nothing can be known of the family discussions or personal conversations in which an entirely empirical and purely oral managerial policy was thrashed out.

However, there are some gaps in this wall of silence. For one thing, the extensive heterogeneity that is concealed beneath the term 'employers' produces a few discordant notes. In this period, as we know, a sprinkling of small businesses provided the humus of French industry. The modest employers who ran them had neither the power nor the means to maintain an anonymous aloofness. Whether they were jolly or irascible types, history records them. Thus it records, for example, the textile-factory owner who rang a bell every morning and posted himself at the factory door like a school-master to await the workers' daily surrender. A whole host of small family business proprietors kept this 'captain of the ship' style of management alive, and they are visible — and audible — in the records.

Our second opportunity to glean some knowledge of the employers derives from the intensity of political passions. In this transitional period, these broke down old class solidarities and, on occasion, even permitted the authorities a degree of objectivity. As we have said — and we shall have more to say on the subject — though the government services were often accommodating to capital, they were not servile; dissension and even resentment between the monarchist directors of the major companies (particularly the mining companies) and the new Republican personnel from the ranks of the 'new strata' caused the old pact of silence to be broken. It is those prefects, sub-prefects and police chiefs who were annoyed at being snubbed whom we have to thank for the best pieces of critical information we possess.

Averting Strikes

We should note at the outset that between 1871 and 1890, approximately 16,000 establishments of five employees or more were subject to strikes, whilst the 1896 census shows that there were 85,560 such establishments. In other words, over a twenty-year period, only 18 per cent were affected. Though, in view of uncertainties surrounding the figures, the statistic is only approximate, it nonetheless suggests that there were broad swathes of the country in which social peace was the norm. This was the case for most factories; while some were hit frequently by strikes, four-fifths of them escaped any action whatever. At the Gabréau factory in Saint-Quentin there were some ten strikes in this period, whilst at the Baccarat, Peugeot and Saint-Gobain works, strikes were not even mentioned. Certain firms remained free of strife even though they were situated at the centre of areas of wide-scale conflict. At Reims, for example, the Isaac Holden carding mill, the town's largest enterprise, stood apart from the rest; though Montceau was in ferment, Le Creusot remained unmoved, and the passivity of the workers in the great Schneider company astonished contemporaries.

Present-day sociology of work tends to emphasise workplace relations as factors producing integration or dissatisfaction, and in my own material I can often see the impact of such relations. There is patently a relationship between aggressive bosses and worker violence, most of which indeed is produced by the workers' resistance to such bosses. At the other end of the scale, workers who are paid and treated better than their fellows in neighbouring firms are less easily roused to action. The Parisian tailors, who were always ready for a fight, were not able to carry with them their colleagues in the big clothing firms (Belle Jardinière, Pont-Neuf, Godchaux) since these latter enjoyed more regular work and other appreciable advantages.

The practice and psychology of the great Lorraine factory-owners (e.g. Baccarat, Roechling, de Wendel), revealed by their replies to the 1872 board of enquiry as being so different from the general run of company heads, goes some way towards explaining the more pleasant atmosphere prevailing within their firms. However, in emphasising the importance of 'good atmosphere' they were alone in what was otherwise a chorus of lamentations.

When it came to combining the concession of paralysing material advantages with preventative repression, Schneider had no equal. It was something he did with consummate skill. Jules Huret, to whom we owe a life-size portrait of the great ironmaster worthy of those one finds today in *Enterprise* magazine, wrote: 'It is common knowledge that, under his management, the accord between capital and labour is being tested out in relatively satisfactory conditions.' Wages were relatively good at Le Creusot, particularly for metalworkers; unemployment was rare and the workers had a range of institutions at their disposal that was quite exceptional for France (training schools, social security, pensions, accommodation). The management were concerned to keep to the law, and they did not reject innovation out of hand. The firm was one of the first to approve and put into practice the election of workers' delegates who were to be given responsibility for presenting all complaints to the head of the establishment each week. Though many other employers denounced this procedure as a threat to their authority, Schneider saw it as a means of averting conflict. The same flexibility prevailed in political matters. Though he had been a notorious Bonapartist, Schneider transferred his allegiance to the Republic when it became clear that it was bound to come, and he went on to pursue a political career with a thoroughly Anglo-Saxon pragmatism. He was very different in this respect from certain mine-owners who were more ideological and backward-looking. Whilst many of his peers were more than unfriendly towards the representatives of the new regime, Schneider made a point of receiving them with courtesy. The prefect of Saône-et-Loire, who complained bitterly at the rebuffs he received from Chagot, pronounced himself delighted with the manner of his welcome at Le Creusot. Schneider apparently came out to meet him 'spontaneously' (*sic*) and guided him on his tour of the workshops without however preventing him from talking to the workers ('All of them seemed to show a friendly deference towards M. Schneider'). The prefect spoke highly of 'the relative liberalism of his economic and political opinions' and went into raptures over the fact that a majority of the engineers were Republicans. How then, when Montceau was in flames, could we doubt that the surprising peacefulness of Le Creusot was a result of the workers' satisfaction? 'The comfort [the workers] enjoy makes them seem disinclined to follow agitators.' Ten years later, an overseer interviewed by Jules Huret was to exclaim in a similar vein: 'Why have strikes. They do everything for the workers here!'

He did, however, add that 'you mustn't be heard to complain', as a subordinate of his nonetheless did when he spoke out against the fear that prevented him from voting freely. 'To begin with, the place is full of informers and woe betide anyone who tries to get up to something.' At the municipal elections of 1878 the Gambettiste *République du Morvan* denounced the overt pressure exercised by Schneider, who was also the local mayor, and his officials. This extended right into the polling stations, which were entirely without individual polling booths.[3] In the years which followed, Schneider's grip on the workers was to take on a more insidious character in the town and a more highly developed one within the company. In 1882 the *commissaire spécial* wrote to the sub-prefect of Antun (and it will be evident here how greatly his comments differ from those of the prefect): 'It is quite certain that everything which is Republican or tends towards the extreme is subject to the special surveillance of agents employed by the factory; this surveillance is . . . thoroughgoing and continuous.' The 'suspects' were transferred to less

---

3. Issue of 13 January 1878. Though there were no opposition candidates, the three polling stations were presided over by managers from the factory; in the first of these, Henri himself was in charge. 'The voting papers were issued by a man standing just inside the door of the town hall, dressed in the livery or uniform of the factory management's office boys, which bore the initials S.C. . . . the two others, also in company livery, stood outside. Beside each of the men handing out papers stood a guard dressed as a fireman, together with clerks and security staff from the factory, not to mention other persons who were there as observers.'

rewarding work and were led in this way 'as a result of perpetual harassment, to ask for their cards themselves'. This is a procedure that has since become standard and was in fact recently denounced in a work by M. Lesire-Ogrel. Whenever an election was announced or when there was a strike in the region, the surveillance effort was stepped up, and if necessary, there were purges to clean up the atmosphere. When a few rebels, doubtless in liaison with Jean-Baptiste Dumay, founded a *chambre syndicale* ('La Métallurgique') in 1882, the management was swift and harsh in its response: some thirty militants were dismissed without any reason being given.

Generally, however, the sheer dead-weight of the institutions was enough to stifle any initiatives on the workers' part. These institutions bound them into an immobilising network of obligations, such as the *épargne-logement* system which prefigures the servitudes of modern credit: 'Ah this accursed house we have to pay out for every month! It's these forty francs that are killing us!', groaned a worker interviewed by Jules Huret. And then there is the very layout of the sites. By sharp contrast with the earlier rebellion-breeding dispersion through wooded terrain, the ordered concentration of housing along lines initially conceived by Ledoux made surveillance easy. The very grouping of the living space, laid out beneath the eye of the master like the outbuildings of a château, suggests what a heavy price was paid for the extinction of pauperism: it was achieved at the cost of freedom. Having seen the Société Métallurgique de Normandie's factories on the outskirts of Caen operating on similarly Schneiderian lines, I have no difficulty in understanding the complex set of causes underlying Le Creusot's peaceful record.

Internal company relationships remained as yet, however, too inorganic for them to provide a general explanation of this phenomenon; similarly, 'company spirit' was unable to stem the effects of the general currents running through the working class. As the 1893 Enquiry into Wages and Working Hours shows, most firms had no institutions for their workers, or, if they had, they were so alien in spirit to real workers' institutions, so hectoring, moralistic and laden with restrictions on workers' freedom as to constitute more a source of bitterness and tension than anything else, and to engender more disputes than they averted. Hence the mining companies' cooperatives and relief and pension funds, which were regarded as supplementary means of oppression, aroused particular hatred. To dissuade the workers from action, the first recourse of these large companies was to repressive measures: checks on whom they hired, constant surveillance, the expulsion of ringleaders. In their attempts to nip any emergent demands in the bud, they employed what was in effect a police force of lower supervisory staff, whose disciplinary tasks were as important as their technical functions. The Anzin company used pit guards, among whom there were a number of former policemen who kept up contacts with their ex-bosses, thus performing spying functions for two masters. The awkward types amongst the workers, those who attended socialist or trade-union meetings or who showed any kind of resistance, ended up being sacked with or without good reason being given. In the townships that bordered on Cambrésis, where underemployment was endemic, the bosses stamped out any unrest by dismissals accompanied by threats of closure at the first sign of hostile action. In 1885 Fevez-Senez carried out one such preventative lock-out, during which they set about rehiring a whole new workforce.

And when management was unsuccessful in isolating the unrest, it issued dire threats, either orally or in writing. In one large glass-works in the Paris region, 'the director forbade anyone to speak of politics and, most importantly of all, of strikes, on pain of dismissal'. In the Cail factory at Denain, where, as at Lille, the metal-workers were seeking a ten-hour day, the director informed them that if they asked for their *livrets du travail*, their names would be passed on to all the Cail factories. Seydoux, a major manufacturer, senator and owner of several establishments in the Fourmies region, sent each of his workers a letter which was a classic of the genre. In it he protested that, a month before, the company had been operating simply in order to employ labour: 'In these conditions, should you, in all conscience, really be putting us in such a difficult position? Well, of this you may be sure: (1) We shall not accept M. Richou's resignation; (2) If you strike, we shall not listen to any of your proposals.' In the short term, such manoeuvres were often successful. But repressive employers ran the risk of attracting the most violent counter-attacks.

A quite different way of averting strikes was to head off the wage claim. The action of the Paris saddle-makers Lecerf and Sarda in 1887 offers one example of this. 'The factory which had an important order for military equipment to fulfil, and anticipated a wage claim, raised its ordinary prices and offered ... the workers new rates.' Perrin of Cours provides another example. Faced with a 'nonchalant' workforce and feeling 'pressed for time', they offered a bonus of 10 centimes per blanket, which sparked off a strike in other companies where the bosses refused to follow suit. The chief constable calls this 'a rather bizarre case of a strike being caused by a thoughtless employer', thereby emphasising the unusual nature of the occurrence.

Does all this, however, warrant our speaking of 'spontaneous' rises? It is clear that in both the above cases a calculation was being made in which the fear of a strike played the same role as a strike might have done in reality. This fear was based on past experiences either of a personal or a collective nature. Pressure from the workers was exercised in a latent manner; one might say it had become part of the atmosphere, part of an accumulated social memory.

Moreover, behind a number of rises that were presented as being 'spontaneous', one can detect effective pressure. At the Perrin mill, the 'nonchalance' of the blanket-weavers was in fact a kind of 'go-slow', a practice that had doubtless not yet become systematised. The Office du Travail informs us that in the Parisian tawing shops, 'after the war, the wage was raised to 5.50 francs without there having been any need for recourse to a strike'. In fact, the police files mention a small strike in 1871 at Sayer's in the Rue du Fer-à-Moulin (XIIIe), in which the employers feared they were seeing the prelude to a generalised stoppage on the scale of the 1869 strike, the memory of which was so painful to them. They gave in quickly, and the wage rate was everywhere raised to 5.50 francs.

Wage increases granted by factory-owners in the wake of successful strikes in their colleagues' establishments are part of the same process; they throw some light on the 'mechanism' of the wage-rise which economists attribute so coldly to the harmonious marriage of supply and demand. Thus the coalitions of 1864, which caught the employers unawares, brought about a wave of preventative rises. The same process was repeated in 1872, between 1880 and 1803, and in other years. Expressing his pleasure at having won an extra 10 centimes after a strike at the Hotchkiss works, the secretary of the Paris Mechanics' Union said, 'what we have gained may seem very small, but when you take into account the fact that fears of a strike have led to an increase in the hourly rate in most workshops, we have achieved all we set out to do'. The Fourmies strike of 1886 similarly had the effect of producing a general rise in pay-rates throughout the whole area. And the miners' strike, which hit many companies in the Nord/Pas-de-Calais region in 1889, caused the Mine-Owners' Association to grant a 'spontaneous' 10 per cent increase.

Strikes do not then have only their own individual impact at the precise points where they break out, but have repercussions on a much wider scale by virtue of their psychological effects. The most perceptive observers did indeed recognise the fear of strikes — the impact of which today's economists are fond of emphasising — as an important factor even in this period. 'Strikes', wrote P. Leroy-Beaulieu, 'achieve their effects through the fear they inspire . . . They may ruin the strikers for a short while, but the fear of provoking a strike is a necessary brake on the factory-owners. The preventative effect of the right to strike has done the working class more good than the disturbances and costs brought about by strikes have done it harm.' And Piquenard writes, 'fear of strikes produces more results than strikes themselves'. As in nuclear strategy, expectations of how the other side will act — the subtle calculations of deterrence — come to count for more than the action itself.

However, a large fraction of the owners could not or would not play this game. The reaction of company chiefs in the face of workers demands was determined empirically, on a day-to-day basis by the state of the economy — which remained the most important factor — by the political situation, and by their own personal position. A study of the outcome of strikes reveals almost equal tendencies towards victorious resistance on the employers' part and to (enforced) conciliation. We must now study both of these outcomes more closely.

Negotiating

The tendency to yield (in whole or in part) to the workers' demands is, by a small margin, the dominant one. Our study of the outcome of strikes has shown it to be influenced by diverse factors. The only thing that will concern us here is the negotiation process. If we look at the relationship between the length and the result of disputes, we may learn something of how that process began. There were several ways of capitulating:

1. It could happen rapidly and without any negotiation, though usually also without any guarantees. The idea here was that the bosses should deal with the immediate problem and yet stay ready to go back on their word once the danger was past. This is how the pragmatic and none-too-proud management of the small firms behaved; they did not make it a matter of honour to resist, especially when it was only wage rates that were at stake. However, this type of attitude was that of a minority only. One-day strikes generally had the highest failure rate, which is evidence of a domi-

nant tendency for the workers' demands to be rejected out of hand.

2. As strikes increase in length, so too does the proportion of successes (S + CS), at least up to a threshold of one month, beyond which it falls off again slightly. *Coalitions* lasting one week achieve the highest rate of outright successes. After that point, a tendency towards negotiated settlements develops; the longer strikes last, the more the part played by negotiation increases. The many and varied forms of mediation which then intervene push the parties towards the negotiating table. Negotiation and compromise settlements are connected:

	S	CS	F	S + CS	F
Negotiation	206 (36%)	304 (53%)	53 (9%)	89%	9%
Refusal to negotiate	19 (7%)	46 (18%)	182 (73%)	25%	73%

The main thing, then, for the strikers, was to get negotiations going. This explains the absolute refusal of aggressive employers to let themselves be drawn along this dangerous road.

In all, 575 strikes (19.6 per cent) ended with a genuinely negotiated agreement; in 252 cases (8.6 per cent), we find a categorical refusal. This latter figure is higher for limited companies than it is for family businesses, which were more ready to enter into discussions. Company size and the structure of power played a role here; they were in part responsible for the particular form in which authority was exercised within an enterprise:

	Total	Negotiations	Refusals to negotiate
Family employers	2,180	466 (21.3%)	177 (8.1%)
Companies	552	86 (15.5%)	61 (11.0%)

Negotiations were sometimes conducted indirectly, through the good offices of the municipal or, more often, the prefectoral authorities. Exercising their function as mediators, they passed proposals and counter-proposals between the various parties involved, and strikes were on occasion settled without the two sides ever having met. This procedure avoided offending the bosses' susceptibilities, but it was slow and fraught with the danger of possible misunderstandings. In fact, it actually disguised a refusal on the part of the employers to recognise the workers as legitimate negotiating partners. This is why the latter preferred face-to-face encounters, as did certain bosses who were reluctant to go to arbitration.

Direct negotiation (which was the most common form overall)

posed the problem of deciding who was a valid negotiating partner. Most employers would only agree to have discussions with their own workers. Fearful of the considerable knock-on effect of granting representative power, certain of them even advocated a Caesarist type of relationship in which the head of the enterprise, as the sole holder of power, would converse with 'all the workers *en masse*'. However, given the practical difficulties such a procedure presented, the bosses had to allow delegates to be appointed. On occasion, they asked for this themselves, showing a preference for the 'most influential' workers, by which they meant the 'longest-serving'. In certain factories, these latter were invested with a quasi-permanent function. The bosses were loath to enter into discussions with workers who were too young or too recently appointed. They were even less willing to talk to workers from outside their establishment mandated by a strike committee; those representing a trade union received an even frostier welcome. The bosses feared two things. Firstly, they were afraid of finding themselves up against a common front of workers calling for the dreaded general standardisation of working conditions, since 'divide and rule' was one of their main weapons. Sensing the dissolution of the great movement of weavers at Reims, Poulain, the president of the Employers' Federation, wrote to the prefect, 'we are only up against detached segments now, which we have to prevent from coming together . . . It is better to let each employer sort things out with his own workers'. Secondly, they were even more fearful of having to recognise trade-union power and to legitimate it by entering into negotiations with the unions. This was what lay at the bottom of many a dispute; it was the principle obstacle to negotiations: 'No employer must seek to reach a settlement with any workers other than his own' became the golden rule. There was something of a paradox here, in that as a response to the rise of the trade-union threat, many employers clung to the principle of the election of workshop delegates as a solution of last resort.

The location chosen for negotiations posed another problem. The factory was the usual setting for the initial meetings, at which certain employers showed a great deal of high-handedness, receiving the workers out in the yard, as if trying to indicate that they could not possibly sit down at the same table with them. For genuine negotiations, others demanded premises of their own choosing. The Roanne Manufacturers' Union offered its headquarters: 'The workers have to get used to coming to us when they have a problem . . . We are here to judge and to restore harmony.' These industrialists rejected the offer of an administrative building: 'The workers have received backing from the town hall and the prefecture. We would be their inferiors there'; the *conseil des prud'hommes* had been adopted by Parliament, but after much discussion, at the last moment, these employers bypassed it. Increasingly, however, some kind of neutral building became the norm — especially in the provinces. The presence of a third party (mayor, sub-prefect, prefect or public prosecutor) — in theory in a mediating role — also became standard. A few moments before the defenestration of Watrin at Decazeville, the negotiators were seated around the municipal table in an arrangement which is exemplary in the way it reveals the accepted hierarchy: in the centre was the mayor, on his right Watrin and two engineers, on his left two town councillors and at the lower end of the table, ranged on either side, the ten miners' delegates.

Sometimes, prominent local personalities were present at these meetings. At the town hall at La Grand-Combe, the gathering instigated by the public prosecutor comprised, alongside the manager of the mine and the workers' delegates, the parish priest, his two curates and the Protestant minister. According to the *Radical de la drôme*, 'the priest referred to the workers in ill-mannered and unseemly terms. This holy man even insinuated that the strike had been organised by drunkards; he was deservedly booed for this. The minister's comments were no better received'.

The tone of the meeting depended on the impartiality (or otherwise) of the mediating third party. On numerous occasions, particularly where the workers felt intimidated, the public official simply added his might to that of the employer, and the talks turned into a ticking-off session. At Lourches the twelve miners' delegates, dumbfounded by a dual harangue from Schneider and the subprefect, withdrew. Many delegates, lacking self-confidence and embarrassed by their inability to express themselves, allowed the employers to get the better of them.

Such proceedings were clearly no more than a caricature of negotiations. In other circumstances, notably when dealing with semi-skilled workers, the employers found themselves dealing with equal partners in dialogue. These discussions, which were often courteous in tone, were detailed and technical in content. The workers would arrive laden down with figures which the bosses would contest, especially where geographical comparisons were being made. 'Competition, competition' was their eternal cry. At the end of these sessions, minutes signed by the two delegations would summarise the points of agreement and disagreement. As for the workers' delegates, they were under an absolute obligation to refer everything to those who had mandated them and the negotiations were interrupted by the workers taking proposals back to general meetings.

This type of practice initiated a new style of social relations, in which strikes were no longer considered a personal affront to the employers, but as a 'perfectly natural occurrence affecting the labour-market' and 'one of the forms by which the freedom of labour was expressed and asserted. We must remember that at no point did the employers give in to the temptation, that had been so strong in 1872, to seek to have the 1864 law repealed.

Resistance

Bastions of resistance
We must first identify who it was who resisted. All the reports and statistics are in agreement here that it was the big industrialists who, given their anonymity and high levels of industrial concentration, were the most able to curb the appetite stoked by the economic situation and to afford the luxury of defending the principle of their right to govern. These big industrialists have a place in the history of strikes that is out of all proportion to the position they occupied in the country generally. They show a higher rate of categorical refusals to negotiate and were also more successful in strikes. Though the average length of strikes in joint-stock companies (8.9 days) was lower than that found in family businesses (12.6 days), the workers' failure rate in such companies was 57 per cent (as against 47 per cent for family businesses). The disputes also took a particularly violent turn there (Table 11). In 20 per cent of cases the forces of law and order intervened. Sure of protection and secure in

Table 11: Strike incidents, according to type of business

Type of business	% of strikes with incidents	Demonstrations	Disturbances	Intervention of gendarmerie or army
Family businesses	18	8	2	6
Joint-stock companies	28	15	6	20

261

the knowledge of their monopoly grip on the labour market, and the wide variety of means for exerting pressure open to them, the big industrialists took a tough line. The most hard-fought and intense disputes in these twenty years took place in the joint-stock companies — particularly in the mining sector.

The harsh line followed by the latter has a variety of causes. Some of these are economic: the importance of the wage bill within overall costs explains why there was greater unwillingness here than elsewhere in industry to raise wages and a constant temptation to reduce them. Some still consider that in this 'highly labour-intensive industry' the safeguarding of profit can only be done by squeezing wages. In badly managed companies the initial reflex was to 'squeeze' them or to seek the remedy to insufficient productivity levels in increasing the yield from human labour.

The political rationale for the attitude of the joint-stock companies is no less coherent. As has already been indicated, the problem of power was posed at every level: in the enterprise, the municipality and the state. The advent of the Republic represented a setback for the directors of the traditionally monarchist large-scale companies who had hitherto held both the municipal and parliamentary seats and had been used to exercising such complete domination that they assumed it to be in the natural order of things. The wage reductions introduced in 1878 may have had some economic justification, but how could they possibly appear to the miners, and to the freedom-hungry *petit peuple* that supported those men, as anything other than a punishment for having voted for the wrong candidates? Petitjean, the manager of the Decazeville mines, ousted from the town hall by Dr Cayrade (a man the miners consulted before going on strike), Chagot of Montceau, a friend of the Jesuits (defeated by another doctor), Jeannin, and Baure, the Allier representative of the Chatillon-Commentry Iron and Steel Company and a 'militant Bonapartist', were all said to be satisfying base desires for revenge, for which they were unanimously denounced by the officers of the prefecture of police, who had been charged with a special investigation into the matter. According to the Doyet miners, who were involved in violent confrontations with the police at the time of the October 1877 elections, the *coalition* had been provoked by a group of *blancs* — bogus miners in the pay of the management who were re-employed after all the real militants had been got rid of. These strikes look like the settling of old scores; the employers' arrogance was rooted in their feeling that the legitimate order had been flouted. The 1878 disputes are undoubtedly of great significance. But most miners' strikes in this period had more or less visible political implications.[4] Almost a whole generation would be required for this type of leader, whose style was distinctly aristocratic, to adapt to the new political conditions of parliamentary democracy. This was something the iron-masters learned more quickly and more thoroughly than the mine-owners.

Lastly, the very structure of power in the coal companies — an unconscious replica of feudal models, in which each level of the hierarchy felt it had personal prerogatives over its immediate subordinates — made resistance easier, as did the decision-making process peculiar to large companies (in which those who really held power never came into direct contact with their petitioners) and the kind of anonymity which made it so easy to pass the buck. The lower management grades took refuge in the claim that they were not responsible for decisions; they were merely carrying out orders. The middle management, those engineers embittered by a process which was tending to reduce them to a purely instrumental role, and who were always made to carry the can for austerity policies, took their revenge by being increasingly aggressive. Reduced to the status of mere NCOs, they behaved as such. Feeling generally done down, they themselves became oppressors; hoping firmness might win them promotion, they became unnecessarily strict. At Mont-sou, Villard, the general secretary of the mines, and Mathey, the first engineer, behaved even more vindictively than Chagot himself. At Doyet, although Baure, the manager, was willing to accept modifications to the statutes of the company insurance fund, the engineers who had a financial interest in its management stood out against any. At Carmaux, Fayol, the principal engineer, rejected all the workers' demands out of hand without referring the matter to his superiors, and forbade any contact with Liénart, the new manager, with whom the workers sought to communicate by way of very respectful letters. Things came to such a pass there that the *commissaire spécial* informed the prefect that: 'One may thus assert that the provocative attitude of the principal engineer is the sole cause of the strike.' Hatred for the engineers, as we have seen, was at the root of many a dispute.

The managers, who were more distant and consequently less of a target for the workers, would be hidden from our view were it not

4. Or religious implications, the two being naturally closely linked. The disturbances at Montceau in 1882 provide an example of a revolt against the politico-clerical system of the company as personnified by Chagot.

for the fact that they took part in the discussions with the prefects and the mining engineers, who for their part acted with all the severity of hard-nosed civil servants and badly paid technical staff. Some of the managers were more like landowners than modern businessmen and practised a sort of absentee landlordism, only intervening from afar in distraught, solemn messages, moralistic in tone, which generally did nothing but exacerbate the situation. This was the case with men like Jacques Palotte at Lavaveix-les-Mines and Chevalier at Montjean: 'I call on those people who, like me, wish to see the restoration of the working family that willingly cooperates with its employers.' By contrast, others who had risen through the ranks from their former position as engineers, freely indulged their taste for giving orders and behaved like suspicious potentates. The unpopular Blanchet, at Epinac, a 'very severe' man, was one such; his volte-faces scuppered all attempts at mediation. There were others too, such as Brun at L'Escarpelle in 1889, a brusque, haughty man who refused any concessions on principle, and Aniel, known as 'Iron Face' (Gueule de Fer), a brutal and whimsical man, described in 1877 and again in 1889 as 'cordially detested by all'. Veldurand, the prefect of the Pas-de-Calais was eloquent in his condemnation of Aniel: 'From the first engineer to the last miner, all are of one voice in protesting against his abrupt manner and the harshness of his actions . . . he allows no-one to answer him back, even if they are trying to apologise. At present his voluble recriminations are directed against the refusal of the authorities to collaborate with him in the desired manner (their refusal, in other words, to beat down his slaves). He rails too against the laws permitting strikes and against his workforce, who for their part can stand him no longer.' Moreover, Aniel, who in 1877 received an annual salary of 50,000 francs, plus 2,000 francs travelling expenses — a very tidy sum at the time (engineers' annual salaries in this same period ranged from 2,500 to 15,000 francs) — nurtured aspirations of running the whole show. In spite of the *lois sociales* and, it seems, without the authorisation of the shareholders, he subsidised a Catholic private school from the coffers of the insurance fund, arguing that 'the employers' position of responsibility makes it their duty to give their workers' children an education that is more in keeping with the dictates of morality and religion than that which is imposed by the state system'. Many managers who were more political than technical animals, took an equally moralising and clericalist line, as if mining — a noble activity bound up with the soil and a substitute for agriculture — crystallised a whole aristocratic mentality. Chalmeton at La Grand-Combe, an advocate of 'remaining continously by the workers' sides', to 'make oneself their leader and tell them the truth, so that others do not lead them to their ruin', and Chagot at Montceau, both of whom were imbued with a strong sense of duty, were classic examples of the type of employer-patriarch dreamed of by such as Albert de Mun and Léon Hamel.

These managers themselves were aware of being closely monitored by boards of directors, who held power over them. The intransigence of the latter increased in direct proportion to their distance from the place of work (they were never exposed to any physical threat: indeed, the workers hardly even suspected their existence). To reduce wages seemed only natural to them, and they considered disobedience scandalous. On many occasions they decreed even harsher measures than the local managements. In 1878 in the Allier, Paris supported the engineers — who were hostile to concessions over the question of the *caisse de secours* — against the manager, Baure. At Epinac, where in 1886 wage-rates had been reduced for a period of twelve months, the board of directors opposed any restoration of wage levels on the grounds that no dividend had been distributed to the shareholders. In the same year at Vierzon, whilst Monteil, the directeur of the Société Française de Matériel Agricole, proposed to reduce working hours rather than lay workers off in response to the crisis, the board, presided over by the senators Louis Arbel and Jacques Palotte, 'observed that since there were a large number of workers ill-disposed towards the firm, these should be identified and a hundred of them dismissed. Only those who were loyal to the company would be retained'. In the Decazeville strike the board, chaired by Léon Say, provided the core of the resistance. They despatched Desseiligny, Schneider and Raoul Duval into the Aveyron to stiffen the resolve of Petitjean, who had become more moderate; the three men decided, against the advice of the prefect and the minister of the interior, to put up notices announcing that the strikers had been sacked, a decision which moved *Le Petit Journal*'s correspondent to write, 'the company wants the strike'. Furthermore, the board scuppered the mediation attempt by Laur, which the workers themselves were prepared to accept. When consulted on the subject by Petitjean, the board replied by telegram: 'The company can only accept the intervention of an arbitrator on one simple question, the verification of the equivalence of the pay-rate set on 26 February with the preceding rate.' Petitjean, having assured himself of Basly's cooperation, made one last attempt to persuade the men in Paris to grant a wage rise: a majority of directors still refused. It was to require the concerted pressure of the manager (who in desperation threatened to resign) and Baihaut, the minister for public works, to bring them round.

The foregoing remarks apply to the mining sector. The other industries — the glass industry in particular, where, between 1886 and 1890 the employers were engaged in a full-scale war against rapidly expanding trade unionism — would supply many a portrait for the industrial despots' hall of fame, with all the various nuances which accompany the different forms of organisation in the various branches of industry and in specific firms. In the metal industries, social relations seem to have been less tense and the employers, who took greater pains to explain their actions, seem to have been more ready to negotiate. The smaller part played by wages in total costs in this sector, where the major outlay was on machinery, and the need for a skilled workforce, which was difficult to replace and which a higher level of education made more capable of bargaining, together with more technically inclined managerial staff, who occasionally expressed the opinion that it was wrong for the defence of profit to be pursued too often by way of 'the deplorable route of wage reductions', were all factors tending to produce a different, freer, more contractually based climate. The social psychology of the ironmasters and the big building contractors deserves a detailed study in its own right. There is no doubt that the entrepreneur, in the Schumpeterian sense, flourished here more than elsewhere.

The humdrum, vulnerable world of textiles, by contrast, teemed with medium-scale mill-owners, ever ready to fall back on wage reductions and to seek to increase productivity by calling for ever greater efforts from the workers (e.g. by two-loom working, which pursued its unstoppable march in the weaving trade). These men managed their businesses as they did their households, supervising everything themselves, irascible and yet intrusive, willing to go down on to the shopfloor in person to rant and rave at their workers. At Armentières, Dulac, having refused to make any concessions to his 700 workers, reopened his factory and planted himself on the threshold, not fearing the workers' anger. To three weavers who asked for their *livrets*, so they could go off and find work elsewhere, he retorted 'loudly, in such a way as to be heard by everyone, that the workers should give the agitators a sound thrashing, that they were cowards for not doing so and that it was only when the army made an appearance at Armentières that the workers would start work again because they would see then that they could not achieve their ends'. This good Republican, the chairman of the Armentières Manufacturers' Association, had money distributed to local police officers and was astonished to receive rather a curt refusal of his favours from the chief constable.

In most textile districts, a single establishment — usually one of the most important — formed an epicentre of resistance to the workers' demands and, consequently, also an epicentre of revolt. At Reims it was Rogelet; at Roanne, Déchelet and Bréchard; at Amiens, David and Huot, manufacturers of worsted in the suburb of Hem;[5] at Saint-Quentin, Boca, Testart and Gabréau — the latter the archetypal 'satanic mill', with its long hours (in 1880 between thirteen and fourteen hours a day, and until midnight on a Saturday), its ever-contested wage-rates and its despised 'slave-driving' overseers.[6] The Fourneau and the Sans Pareille mills at Fourmies (owned by Jacquet and Rennesson), where there were repeated disturbances, and at the Pochoy & Bruny factory at Voiron provide examples of those silk manufacturers of the south-east who unashamedly exploited young peasant women, kept regimented in convent-like establishments, feeding the record of social conflict with endless disputes, which were generally rather defensive and very violent in nature (there were as many as seven at the Gabréau mill between 1880 and 1890, one of which, in 1884, lasted for seventy-two incident-packed days). Mention of these strikes is made on almost every page of this book.

The heavy industrial concentration of the Nord region conceals individual physiognomies beneath the surface of more coherent groups,[7] who were doing reasonably well out of an expansion which was tending to turn Roubaix into what was at the time called an 'American city', where the employers had a reputation for being among the most innovatory. According to *Le Temps*, 'the big manufacturers are . . . the natural allies of the workers and both

5. In 1888 they tried to put pressure on the women strikers in the carding shop through their husbands and fathers, by calling on these latter, 'on pain of dismissal to invite their wives and daughters to resume work'. Annoyed at the refusal this move met with, the owners had the *prud'hommes* hand these workers their cards: 'Given their refusal to resume work, we have decided to break off all relations with these rebellious workers, and we consider them as no longer forming part of our workforce' (cf. Arch. nat., F12 4664, préf.-min., 1 September 1888).

6. In 1890 an overseer named Hartmann, the *bête noire* of the Défense des Travailleurs, forced the weavers to shop at his grocer's store and victimised them if they did not. Most reports on this company emphasise the brutality and arrogance of the staff, the general tone being set by the owner.

7. At Roubaix it is difficult to single out any one particular factory in this regard. Let us merely note that there were six strikes in twenty years at Wibaux-Florin, almost all of them against wage cuts or the very strict staff.

have an identical interest in the fight against unacceptably low wages . . . If the masses are to become prosperous, what are required are high levels of production and low-cost products.'[8] One only has to think of the intense poverty of the back alleys described by the Bonneff brothers — that 'weavers' hell' — to see what a rosy view this is. It is, however, true that Roubaix — though it was the strike capital of France — no longer held the record for violence, and that in this period the disputes there (which were to some degree a product of prosperity) were often successful offensive strikes.

By contrast, the west, where industry was weak and thin on the ground (and where the recession had, in fact, set in train a long-term process of decline), was a stamping ground for small-town despots, exhausted, bitter and resentful at seeing a hitherto docile workforce in rebellion.[9] One example is a certain Frémont at Flers-de-l'Orne, the owner of a mechanised weaving-mill with 400 workers, the lord and master of his prices and his wages, which he himself always deemed adequate. As soon as any new article came into production, he would lower wage rates, arguing that conditions were now more favourable for making money, and forcing the other mill-owners to follow suit. In 1880 he extended the working day to eleven and a half hours at the very moment when workers were campaigning throughout France for the ten-hour day; he also introduced two-loom working and set the rate per metre at 10 centimes instead of 15 centimes, since the workers were now producing at a faster rate. 'What seems to me primarily designed to stir up the workers', commented the local mayor, 'is the reasoning of those employers who claim to be laden down with stock, yet lengthen the working day and increase production as a result.' In 1888, on the pretext that the heavier cotton now being used reduced the time required for unwinding, he knocked 50 centimes off the wages; the winders, who had found difficulty up until then to earn 1.40 francs, now saw their wages fall to 80 centimes a day! In both cases, strikes with violent incidents ensued. 'The workers' hatred of Frémont is so great that I should not in the least be surprised to be called out some day or night to find he has been killed or seriously injured', wrote the local chief constable to the sub-prefect. Naturally, Frémont was stub-

8. 26 May 1880. At the time of the great May strikes, *Le Temps* conducted a very interesting survey of Roubaix industry. The newspaper made much of the innovative and progressive role of the large firms, and pointed out that the smaller companies sought to compete by keeping down wages.
9. This has been described and analysed in C. Fohlen, 1956.

bornly set against the authorities and conducted a running battle against them in the local press. He was also opposed to the Republican town council, which he accused of bias.

Not far away at Saint-Pierre-du-Regard, the firm of Baron & Son, whose owners had themselves only recently risen from the ranks of the workers, juggled the wage-rates so arbitrarily as to prompt the sub-prefect to intervene: 'Monsieur Baron has announced both to his workers and to myself that he would prefer to close his factory rather than enter into any arguments with the workpeople. He declared that he wanted to be master in his own house,' notes the sub-prefect, who stresses by contrast the 'calm and respectful . . . attitude of the workpeople.' In the neighbouring town of Condé-sur-Noireau, the authoritarian Lehugeur completes a trio of despotic textile bosses in this dying corner of Normandy.

The man dubbed the Master of Cholet, Pellaumail (his factory employed 260 wage-labourers in mechanised production, and he also had workers who toiled in their own cellars), resembled the Normandy bosses like a brother; he fought against civil funerals and against the union and railed as they did against his over-conciliatory colleagues. One strike poster accused him of 'wishing to turn his workers into serfs and drive them with a whip'. In these outlying areas of Brittany, the manufacturing bourgeoisie had in fact taken over from the old squirearchy of days gone by.

To varying degrees, then, the large enterprise — whether joint-stock company or family business — appears as a site of multiple conflicts. It was not that it particularly lowered the standard of living; in many ways, by making work more regular, it guaranteed the workers a more stable income. But if it did not produce immiseration, it certainly produced subjugation, frustration and a veritable castration in terms of freedom. And it is this sense of lost independence which lies at the heart of the wage-earner's consciousness.

In small and medium-scale industry the situation was identical: in strikes involving more than one company — a type that Paris knew so well — the 'big firms' always formed the most solid bastions of resistance. These large companies could afford to sit the strike out; they even hoped to take advantage of the dispute to strengthen their grip on the market. At Cours, it was said that 'the largest firms, those with plenty of stock and capital, viewed without particular displeasure the perpetuation of a strike that would irreparably ruin their less fortunate fellow manufacturers'. They meant to show who was boss and a number of them acted like medieval lords. To one meeting of the Paris carpet-weavers, Krieger — without himself condescending to attend — sent along his representative, who announced indignantly: 'We now know that we cannot count on the solidarity of our fellow manufacturers. We shall find a solution of our own for our own difficulties and when you, in your turn, are blacklisted, as you doubtless will be in the near future — for you will all be sooner or later — you will not be surprised to receive no support from us.'

Among the 'little men', however, such situations produced a general stampede. They were not financially sound enough to be able to let such a favourable moment pass them by. Often recent recruits themselves to the ranks of the employer class, they gave free rein to their hatred of the 'big shots'. What a marvellous opportunity it was to get back at them, to show them they were not all-powerful by spiriting away those of their clients who could not afford to wait for the strike to end. And it was a chance to win some easy popularity among the workers by showing them who their real enemies were. Sometimes the beginnings of alliances were formed. At Vrigne-aux-Bois in the Ardennes, the mechanisation of nail-making led by the main manufacturer, Manil, encountered violent and staunch opposition from the workers in alliance with 'the rivals of Monsieur Manil, who are fearful of not being able to compete against him'. During a *coalition* of bookbinders and gilders in Paris in 1881, a small employer from Auch sent a letter to the trade union that was read out at their general meeting, in which 'he proposed the federation of all the workers and small manufacturers of France . . . The higher the workers' claims, the more the big firms who can engage in unfair competition on account of their machines, will be forced to raise their wage-rates, which will allow the small employers to survive'.

Ruthless competition, accentuated by the economic crisis, increased these divisions and split what was in any case an impossible common front among the employers — whence the defections from meetings, the difficulties involved in promoting association, in 'keeping up' a lock-out. Though most of the time it remained below the surface, the employers' mutual dislike occasionally came out into the open; for example, after the dyers of Roanne had subsidised the strike of the workers at Thizy to combat the difference in wage-rates between the two districts, their fellows in Thizy soon repaid them in kind. In 1889 the Armentières industrialists gave financial backing to Belgian strikers in their struggle for standard wage-rates, and so on.

Thus the notion that the employers were united is shown to be completely erroneous. 'Between two bosses', writes Roger Priouret, 'it is antagonism that is the natural condition and solidarity that is a secondary state.'

Forms and techniques of resistance by employers
These varied according to the type of employer involved, the style of strike adopted (thus the lock-out was an exact counter to black-listing by the workers), the extent of the dispute and the prevailing economic conditions, and so on. The multi-centred strike gave rise to the necessity for temporary or permanent concertation on the part of the employers. However, association between employers was a response to an offensive on the workers' part; it neither preceded it in time nor in importance.

Refusal is the most elementary form of resistance and it takes a variety of forms. Certain employers reacted to workers who put their demands in writing, with a simple, 'systematic' silence, a total mutism, not deigning to respond to their invitations or even to those of the authorities. This explains the workers' preference for sending delegates to *talk* with them.

But delegates sometimes came up against closed doors; the employers argued that they had no mandate and represented no one, especially when they came in the name of the union. When they were allowed in, they ran the risk of a harsh, scornful or even insulting welcome, followed by immediate expulsion. 'These gentlemen would not listen to reason', wrote the young women silk-weavers from the Pochoy & Bruny factory in Paviot to the prefect of the Isère, 'and they dismissed us with scorn, refusing to hear any of our arguments. What is more they tore up the written request we had presented to them and threw it in the mud.' Such harshness was not reserved only for women. At the ironworks in Joinville-le-Port, where unemployment was rife, the workers proposed working one fortnight per month so as to employ everyone and received the curt reply from the manager, Debert, 'you only want to work a fortnight. Alright then, don't work at all. Get out of here!'. At Molières a miner named Pascal submitted a set of demands to Chalmeton, the manager, who, having read the demands curtly ordered him to collect his cards — and to do so within twenty-four hours. Subsequently addressing the workers, he told them that if they wished to go on strike, they should do so immediately. To the slaters of Pont-Malembert near Trélazé, 'when a man with a family pointed out that he could not meet the needs of his household, he

271

was told that there was grass growing in the fields'; the Mayssant brothers, the quarry owners, famed for their harshness, called in the armed forces and ordered the workers' tools to be thrown into the meadow.

If such brutality seems astonishing — today it is reserved for immigrant workers — we should not forget that employers did not hesitate to take up arms against their workers. At the Salins-du-Salat salt-works a striker died as a result of such action; another was wounded on the Unieux railway building-site in the Loire; at Lyon the glassworks owner Mesmer armed his staff and had them fire on the advancing workers. In the very centre of Paris, in a large printing-works, one owner threatened a militant worker with a pistol he kept in his drawer. These were doubtless historically residual events and ones that met generally with disapproval, as is shown by the fact that history records them and that they had therefore been noted at the time; they were unpleasant reminders of capitalism's inherent brutality, which was, however, tending to become veiled in these latter years of the nineteenth century.

An alternative to refusal pure and simple was reasoned rejection. Quite a number of employers showed some concern to explain their reasons for rejecting the workers' demands. They did this by posting up notices in the workshops, by sending out circular letters ('To the workers', 'To our workers') or, seeking also to convince public opinion, by using the local press or by putting up posters in the town. This literature, which was varied in its tone (running from technical refutations to moralising harangues), was quite uniform in its general lines of argument: the economic situation, it was claimed, did not allow the bosses to accede to the workers' demands; they were having to meet growing foreign competition (English in the case of the mining companies or the mill-owners, and German in most other cases), a competition based on the lower wage levels, longer hours and greater productivity of those countries. 'Any increase in prices will benefit the Prussians', wrote Martin of Tarare in a letter distributed to his weavers. From there to seeing the 'hand of the foreigner' in strikes was only a single step and one that was easily taken. According to the manager of the Bessèges mines, 'Fournière could well be the agent of the English companies who today have numerous offices in Marseilles and are seeking to capture the Mediterranean market to the great detriment of the companies of the Gard.' The weaving bosses of Moirans denounced one militant as 'a man who is doing the Germans' job very well for them'. In these conditions, to strike was to commit an act of treason, and to put it down, a duty to the nation. Phrased in these xenophobic terms, the employers' arguments hit home with the public, a fact which the conservative newspapers did not fail to make use of for their own ends. From time to time this produced some uneasiness among the workers themselves, who, in their heart of hearts, feared an industrial Sedan and were tempted at times to join forces with their bosses against free trade, in defence of the nation's industry, as is shown by the success of the protectionist campaigns conducted in textile circles in 1878 and 1879, which followed on from those at the end of the Second Empire.

Alternatively, the employers could try to break the strike; and in adverse economic conditions it was sometimes possible simply to let it fizzle out of its own accord. A strike could even have favourable effects from the employers' point of view. It could offer them an opportunity to reduce production, cut stocks and reorganise the labour force. They would quite happily countenance a strike at such junctures, and would sometimes even provoke one: 'I'm not sure the company doesn't need a strike to get rid of our surplus labour', wrote Paul Cambon of the Anzin company. A second possible option was intimidation. When the workers downed tools, the bosses would reply with dismissal notices. After a certain date, those who were still out would be deemed to have resigned. The period of notice given was usually as little as twenty-four or forty-eight hours.

Enterprises with a solid network of company institutions had a large number of ways of putting material pressure on their workers. Company shops, housing and schools that had been dangled in front of the workforce like pieces of bait had now become traps. At Noeux-les-Mines, the company 'made moves against, and even issued threats against, miners who are tied to the land': at the same time, they sent all the children belonging to striking families home from school. Mesmer at Lyon provided housing for about fifty glass-workers, and when they came to pay their rent, he gave them notice to hand in the keys to their apartments or, if they refused, they would have 18 francs stopped from their wages. The convent-like silk factories of the south-east treated the young peasant girls who worked for them like naughty schoolgirls, sending them back to their homes, where they were often badly received. Nonetheless, this politics of feudal domination was tending to disappear in two sectors in particular: provisions and schooling. In respect of the latter, the Ferry Acts had had a particularly liberating influence.

During long strikes, the employers would resort to scaremongering against those they called 'the true instigators' of strikes, the agitators and socialists, who, they said, were growing fat at the workers' expense. Increasingly frequent attempts were made to appeal to the workers' better natures. In those areas of countryside that had remained fervently religious, the clergy, who now leaned for support on the factory, as they had in the past on the château, spared no effort in this regard. At Decazeville, 'the *curés* went from house to house, exhorting the miners to go back to the pits'. In their sermons they equated striking with sin and threatened the strikers with hell fire and damnation. 'A *curé* in the Cholet area informed his flock that those who stayed out on strike would not go to heaven.' It is difficult to measure the effects of such remarks: a sense of sin remained long after any formal links with the church had been broken. In the minds of women especially, saturated with guilt as they were, such threats had every chance of finding their mark.

But the most effective means of forcing the workers to go back was to continue production without them. By having goods manufactured outside the factory, in the works of sympathetic colleagues in the provinces or in rural locations, the bosses could gesture towards the possibility of fulfilling their much-feared threat of moving the centres of production. In Paris, in particular, in the rapidly changing wood and leather industries, the bosses took advantage of those changes in order to install machines that could be operated by a new workforce, trained on the job. Thus, in the tanneries every strike brought about an advance in mechanisation. It accelerated a de-skilling process which had causes extending far beyond the effects of strikes but which was associated with the strikes in the minds of the workers.

One last possibility we should consider here is the employers' option of taking on new workers, those who were soon — amid popular opprobrium — to be baptised 'blacklegs' (*jaunes*). They were, in general, provincials, foreigners, seasonal migrants desperate for earnings, labourers, women, rural labourers from Belgium who derived a half-conscious satisfaction from hitting back at the factory workers, and hardworking home-workers. These were the classic batallions of the industrial reserve army; always reluctant to strike themselves, they represented a pool from which strike breakers could be drawn. Wherever they existed as a source of pressure, it was difficult for the workers to win their demands; they were to be found mainly in the less skilled trades, which did not require long apprenticeships, and in underdeveloped and overpopulated regions. Once again, the general economic situation had a determining effect here, full employment alleviating these difficult conditions, unemployment exacerbating them. However, dialogue between groups of workers could on many occasions reduce these tensions. The exchanging of information permitted the workers to prevent the arrival of new employees, and sometimes, by persuasion or threats, they succeeded in getting them to go back whence they had come. In the metal-working and glass industries, counter-attacks of this kind proved to be effective. And yet, the exploitation of divisions among the workers remained one of the employers' trump cards. Had the employers been better organised, they might have turned these divisions even more successfully to their advantage, but before Japy's day, the employment of blackleg labour was practised on a purely individual, trial-and-error basis.

Indeed, the employers were far from keen to organise; they saw it as a last resort, a humiliating length to have to go to, a sign of weakness, if not of total collapse.

	Strikes with organisation	Strikes without
Employers	15%	85%
Workers	59%	41%

The record shows no fundamental change of attitude on this matter during the period. In 1890 there was no organisation whatever among the employers in 93 per cent of disputes. The erratic growth of this kind of organisation in the period from 1880 to 1882 seems then to have borne no long-term fruit. It nonetheless merits attention on account of its implications. It occurred in favourable economic circumstances; in the face of a vigorous workers' offensive, the employers felt the need to arm themselves to resist. That need was all the more acutely felt during this period, since the establishment of the Republic and the reservations of the administration and government towards the employers obliged them to rely more on their own devices. Such organisation most often took only temporary and *ad hoc* forms:

Temporary organisation	446	9.6%
— with lock-out	92	(3.1%)
— with fighting fund	13	(0.4%)
Pre-existing permanent organisations	138	4.1%
Permanent organisations emerging from the strike	26	0.9%

These temporary forms consisted primarily of meetings in which the company heads laid down rules of conduct, where necessary arriving at these by a vote. These were then often incorporated into written agreements, signed by all parties, which carried fines of varying severity for non-compliance. In these agreements the signatories undertook to respect existing pay scales (wage-freeze), to apply the various agreed counter-measures or, on occasion, to refuse to employ strikers.

The employers' fighting funds that were formed — principally in Paris — were made up by the payment of an equal sum by each or by a levy proportional to the size of the establishment concerned: at the time of the *coalition* of furniture carvers, the fifteen main manufacturers involved paid 100,000 francs each into a fund of this kind; the second- and third-order industrialists paid 15 francs plus 10 centimes per worker. The Lille mill-owners had an arrangement whereby each had to pay 25 centimes per spindle per week; the indemnity to be paid was set at 15 centimes per spindle per week.

The lock-out, the most radical means of depriving the workers of employment, merits particular attention, though such action was taken in only 3.1 per cent of disputes (I have counted ninety-two over a twenty-year period). The 'bosses' strike', which was common practice in Germany and Great Britain, had only recently arrived in France (at the end of the Second Empire); its application remained sporadic, as did the use (and spelling) of the term. In 1882 *Le Citoyen* expressed its 'reluctance, in a popular newspaper, to use foreign words that are not understood by the population at large'. It nonetheless adopted the term, emphasising its onomatopoeic qualities: 'Two words are all you need. Get out, dog! proletarian! . . . Out! Heraus! Lock! Clunk! There, you're locked out.' The lock-out, however, soon became a naturalised French phenomenon (in 1883 Pottier devoted a poem to it), especially in the years from 1880 to 1883, though it never exceeded a maximum level of 5.9 per cent (1882). The following regions account for most of the total in what was a closely grouped distribution: Paris (twenty-two lock-outs; 5 per cent), Lyon (fourteen; 5 per cent); Cher (three; 7 per cent); Loire (five; 5 per cent); Nord (sixteen; 3.7 per cent). Certain industrial sectors were totally unaffected by lock-outs, whilst for some trades they occurred in more than 10 per cent of strikes: moulders, porcelain-workers, glass-workers, cabinet-makers, tailors, hatters, all highly skilled trades and, with the exception of glass-working, barely subject to industrial concentration. In effect, the lock-out was used mainly by small, family proprietors with small-scale workshops.

Family businesses	71 lock-outs	3.2% of strikes
Companies	14 lock-outs	2.5% of strikes

Though its effects were felt in numerous establishments, the lock-out remained, then, a relatively small-scale phenomenon, the record number of workers locked out being 10,000 in the Parisian cabinet-making trade (20 September to 12 October 1880), 7,000 in the tailoring trade (15–22 July 1882). Except in times of economic recession, the length of lock-outs rarely exceeded one or two weeks. This is explained by the fact that then, as now, the lock-out was essentially a retaliatory measure. The bosses never used it first, nor spontaneously, but as a form of reprisal or indeed a last resort, against forms of organisation and modes of action they deemed particularly damaging or intolerable: joint workers' committees, workshops for the unemployed, unions and, above all, strikes-by-rota; 19 per cent of these latter brought this response, and 29 per cent of lock-outs were aimed at neutralising the strike-by-rota system, which was based on the methodical exploitation of divisions among employers and the subsidisation of strikers by fellow workers still remaining at their posts.

The employers' hesitancy where the lock-out tactic was concerned is explained by the practical difficulties involved and also by its limited effectiveness: it had virtually no effect of the eventual outcome on strikes:

	Outcome of strikes with lock-outs	*Without*
S + Cs	50.5%	51%
F	49.4%	49%

There are several reasons for this. Firstly, there was the extreme difficulty of maintaining a united front among a large number of diverse industrialists between whom there were latent rivalries. The lock-out brought all these contradictions into the open. The German model — which involved closing down large factories — had an altogether different degree of solidity. The rarity of such a tactic in France can be explained by both economic and social factors (industry was not so highly concentrated and employer organisation was relatively backward). And lock-outs could also backfire badly on their perpetrators; where the workers were well-organised, use of the tactic could simply stir up more solidarity, with indignation transforming locked-out workers into highly motivated strikers. When the factories were subsequently reopened it

277

was quite usual for none of the workers to turn up. Who indeed would dare to? The whole of the workforce would then lend their support to the group of workers or the shop that had originally come out alone. Far from weakening the workers' resolve, it actually strengthened a resistance which was now raised into a matter of honour.

Lastly, the lock-out was unpopular. And that unpopularity was not restricted to the workers, who quite naturally saw it as a particularly malicious and evil act, or to the Socialist or Radical Left, where one finds general and apparently sincere indignation together with an emphasis on the novelty of the practice: *Le Citoyen* called the lock-out of the Paris cabinet-makers in 1880 'an unheard of measure'; 'this is a disgraceful thing to happen in a Republic where the worker is supposed to be the equal of the employer', echoed *Le Mot d'ordre*. The practice was also unacceptable to a broad swathe of moderate public opinion, which (though it is difficult to gauge these matters exactly) was opposed to extreme measures and to the kind of speculation which lay behind this manoeuvre by the 'big barons', and was shocked also by the injustice of a factory closure which punished both strikers and non-strikers indiscriminately. The authorities themselves condemned this dangerous, arbitrary and extreme measure: 'There were workers involved who had worked thirty years for the same master. They had made no demands.' To sum up then, a section of the public did not accept the industrialists' argument that they had to 'fight fire with fire', nor the related definition of the lock-out as an 'employers' strike'. They instinctively saw it as something much more scandalous and, indeed, as an almost immoral act of oppression against the workers. The image of French industrialists as men who would starve out the workers (what memories the word *affameurs* is laden with), together with a commitment to the idea of the right to work, explains an aversion to the lock-out which is today enshrined in French law, where the practice is considered a crime committed by the employer against each of the workers affected.

In only 4 per cent of cases did associations of employers predate a strike. The figures vary greatly according to the industries and occupations under consideration. From 1 per cent in mining, they rise to 12 per cent in the wood industry, 11.2 per cent in glass and porcelain, 9.6 per cent in the garment industry (tailors, hatters). The leading role played by the building trades here is clear to see: entrepreneurs in the joinery and cabinet-making trades score 16 per cent, painters plasterers 13 per cent, and carpenters 12 per cent. Moreover, the figures for trade unionism record the existence of numerous entrepreneurs' federations, both in Paris and the provinces. This relatively high degree of organisation is no doubt to be explained by the early existence of labour organisation in the same sector. Many years of *compagnonnage* activity had forced the employers to find an adequate response.

If we break the figures down geographically, the same conclusion is reinforced. The highest percentage of strikes involving employers' federations are found in the regions with long-standing labour traditions. Thus:

Paris	12.0%
Rhône	6.0%
Loire	7.0%
Cher	12.0%
Nord	0.9%

There is little correlation between these figures and the degree of industrial concentration. The big employers had no need of an employers' union or federation to defend themselves; they saw it as a weapon of the weak. Nonetheless, strikes did spur them into organising: the greater part of the twenty-six federations formed in such circumstances belong to large-scale industry. The textile federations of Reims, Lille, Armentières, the Vosges and Cholet (1887), those in metal-working (Lille, Bordeaux, Nantes, etc) and the glass-masters' federation, which was able from 1886 onwards to put a firm brake on the workers' demands, were born in the wake of important *coalitions* as attempts to prolong the '*bureaux*', the employers' committees formed at the time. They had, moreover, a markedly anti-strike style; their statutes include clauses making provision for lock-outs and the blacklisting of strikers: one secret article in the Cholet statutes declares that 'no worker who has been on strike may be employed again for several months'. The merging of several slating companies at Trélazé, decided on after the strikes of 1890, was accompanied by a concerted effort to uncover the 'ringleaders'.

Employers' federations behaved more as (primarily defensive) organisms of social struggle than negotiating bodies. One could apply Tocqueville's phrase to them that 'most Europeans still see association as a weapon of war, which you hastily cobble together before going out to test it immediately on a battlefield'. The labour movement, though it had not been the initial cause of this phenomenon, became a powerful added stimulus to its development. It would play a major role in the birth of the first CNPF. However, the threat posed by the workers had not yet reached a level where it became truly compelling. The employers infinitely preferred the system of individual relationships — which arose out of free competition and which was so well suited to the operation of clandestine pressure groups — to the dismal necessities of association. They preferred to act on the state apparatus.

The Role of the State

'No magistrate should make himself the workers' man nor the masters', for that would be to adopt a very dangerous course of action and to assume the gravest of responsibilities. It is therefore important that you avoid this trap for the unwary, which is all the more redoubtable in that by being seen to abstain when they are being pressed on all sides to accept the role of arbitrator or judge, the public authorities give the impression of failing in a part of their mission at the very moment when they are fulfilling it most faithfully.These instructions have been communicated to me by the Minister of the Interior', wrote the prefect of the Nord to the mayors in February 1849. Two and a half years later, the police minister reiterated the golden rule of *laissez-faire* liberalism to the same prefect: 'The authorities must never become involved in questions of wages, even if the interested parties were to solicit their intervention. Wage levels always necessarily express the relation that exists between supply and demand. They cannot be set by administrative rulings.' There were many prefects in 1880 who still took refuge in the old theses of non-intervention expressed in these texts, as a cover for their own inertia. Ministers persisted in opposing the myth of the liberal state — as the neutral guarantor of a neutral order — to the criticisms of an 'interventionist' Left.

But actual practice was at variance with such pronouncements. The state did intervene, and it did so in two ways. As the guardian of order, it exercised a repressive function. And in a mediating role it attempted to arbitrate in a certain number of disputes. The first function was traditional. The second was, for a bourgeois regime, more novel. Admittedly, arbitration remained clumsy, timid, rarely impartial and usually confined to the spheres of local administration: the government ordinarily kept its distance. And the gentle, subtle pressure it maintained on the employers was not exactly comparable with the presence of troops at the factory gates. These contradictions nonetheless highlighted liberalism's disarray and opened up a breach through which Radical and Socialist critiques were able to enter. Within that breach there also lurked a corporatist nostalgia: this was a flickering flame, but one that was constantly kept burning and one which was to have new life breathed into it half a century later by the difficulties of the democracies.

Liberal theory itself was running out of steam. Who still believed in it? Who in this period of the Great Depression, the rise of international competition and the first evidence of the decline in the birth rate would dare to underwrite the optimism of a J.-B. Say or the serenity of a Bastiat or a Charles Dunoyer, apart perhaps from academic economists.No one, however, was looking to these latter for innovation. The confidential cabinet circulars — from Waldeck-Rousseau to Jules Siegfried — suggest quite a different picture. An empirical 'interventionism' was developing which sooner or later would spell the end of classical liberalism. It was a slow death, with many remissions, and it was subject to the ups and downs of the political situation. The practice of Thiers, the *Ordre Moral* and early Republican governments were all different — as much for circumstantial as for biographical reasons. The flexibility of Waldeck, the demagogy of Boulanger, the recantations of Allain-Targé, the hesitancy of Floquet and the firmness of Constans — all play their role in a history that has been related by Seignobos. Having described the winding paths of that political trajectory elsewhere, I shall not retrace them again here, but shall concentrate rather on the underlying lines of force.

Keeping Order

The observation of dangerous milieux, the first duty of governments, is performed in two ways: police surveillance of individuals and social enquiries into the condition of the masses.

Police surveillance, though it took care to include records of 'states of mind', was more concerned with describing the life of fringe political groups or the acts of individuals and detecting agitators. In such work the building up of files was considered the principal objective, the supreme achievement, and even at this early stage it became an obsession. This was the permanent mission of the police. Since, however, they were unable to conceal themselves completely, they were supplemented by informers. Indeed, there was a whole network of informers in Paris, where a special budget had been put aside to pay them. In the provinces, where there was less money for the task, judging by the complaints made by prefects dissatisfied with the resources placed at their disposal for such work, they were more isolated. Very variable in quality, to judge by their reports, which filled box after box at the Paris Prefecture of Police in particular, these informers were sometimes very well placed.

It comes as a surprise to the historian to find that a man known as an active — indeed respected — militant, was in fact a 'copper's nark'. The researches of Marc Vuilleumier have enabled him to identify several informers among the ex-Communards who had returned from exile, and Jean Maitron has located a number of black sheep in the ranks of the anarchists. We must certainly be extremely cautious in making such identifications. We shall guard against succumbing to the mixture of spy fever and extraordinary naiveté, that prevailed on the extreme Left in this period and which Jules Romains has described so well. There were on occasion some spectacular purges. In 1884 a solemn jury made up of the editorial staff of *Le Cri du peuple* denounced as informers Druelle, Bausan (=Brice), Ernest Lefèvre (=Gontran), Plisson (=Félix) and Hérivaux (=Hilaire), the latter being an active collectivist. The informers, who did not actually know each other, tended to see fellow informers everywhere. One of their number thought that he saw in Émile Pouget's incitements to action a sign of his role as an *agent provocateur*, a piece of speculation for which there has never been any evidence. Most often, all this was mere gossip, and it is not to be trusted without serious investigation, if indeed we should attach any value at all, beyond the merely anecdotal, to such seedy stories. Clandestinity begets suspicion; that is its particular stigma, its specific malady. The historian will, however, mistrust that suspicion, just as she or he must also guard against the deep-seated prejudice of the 'organised' militants against the anarchists, who were always suspected of playing a double game.

Persons are of less interest here than the procedures by which the police insinuated themselves into working-class milieux. They made systematic use of concierges and café-owners, the sympathetic listeners of the faubourg. Victor Capart, who kept a bar at Le Mont-à-Loeux, was able in this way to be secretary of the Workers' Party for many a year without attracting particular attention. At the time of the Anzin strike, the police established contact with a door-to-door salesman whose business travels enabled him to make wide-ranging observations; a member of the Progressive Circle of

Denain, he had the confidence of Basly and Fauviau; he even became secretary of the local union and signed his police reports with an 'F'. At Roanne the sub-prefect prided himself on having been kept informed of stirrings among the anarchists 'thanks to a rather clever secret agent', to whom he paid 70 francs a month. This was meagre remuneration and was only likely to tempt a few poor wretches. The case of Jules Romains's Quinette, seduced more by adventure than money, may be credible, but it is infinitely rarer at this level.

Though the activities of the Paris Prefecture of Police were in theory restricted exclusively to the capital, officers were sent elsewhere on special assignments when major disputes so demanded. Thanks to these officers, the Paris archives contain important files on the miners' strikes of 1872, 1877, 1878 and 1886 (Decazeville) and that of the metal-workers at Vierzon (1886), amongst others. For their part, the local authorities approached them for officers to do tailing work. Lastly, in these cases, they sought and obtained direct and prior communication ('in such a way that no telegraph clerk could know of the existence of these communications') of all the telegrams sent by or to the strikers. Thus the sub-prefect of Valenciennes was the first to know of all the despatches that Duc-Quercy sent to *Le Cri du peuple* from Anzin. The press correspondents' reports figure in all the dossiers for major strikes.

The Ministry of the Interior demanded from the prefects regular reports on the 'material and moral' state of the areas for which they had responsibility. Constans (1889–92), in his anxiety, would seek to substitute monthly reporting for the previously annual accounts (circular of 30 March 1889). Social agitation, by increasing the ministers' anxiety, made them in effect more demanding: they wanted reports on trade unions, *coalitions*, relationships with foreign workers, the workers' reactions to certain specific events, May Day preparations, and so on. Most often formulated in general terms, these requests were sometimes made in the form of genuine questionnaires: 'the confidential enquiry into the conditions of the workers' of August 1882 included thirty-three questions, nine of which related to strikes.

These enquiries certainly had a practical intent: knowledge-gathering in order to avert action or repress it. 'Was there a police commissariat in the industrial centre or nearby? Were there gendarmes? Were there troops in sufficient numbers?', enquired the 1882 questionnaire.'If there were no armed forces on the spot or if there were not enough of them, where could they be brought from?' The employer appears in all this as the privileged informer. In Paris the Cail factory was connected by a special line to the Ministry of the Interior. In March 1890 Constans told the prefects: 'I advise you to contact the managers of the industries situated in your region, to invite them to communicate to you all the information they possess on the manoeuvres reported and to enquire of them at the same time what means they intend to employ to deal with the consequences of a general strike.' Waldeck ordered the prefects to stay 'in constant relations with the managers of the industrial establishments'. Conscious of the criticism that this interventionism would unleash, he added, 'It cannot in effect have escaped the leaders of industry that if they wish to reserve the right to call on the authorities to intervene in certain cases, they first have a duty to render them able to take such measures as the situation may necessitate'. These are ambiguous texts which reveal both the class nature of the state and the precautions it has to take in a democracy.

Repression

On the ground, the forces of law and order — police, gendarmes, army — protect[ed] the right to work' when called upon to do so by the prefects or municipalities. Governmental instructions as to their use underwent enormous variations over this period. The unmitigated harshness of Thiers and the *Ordre Moral* gave way to much greater circumspection. The fledgeling Republic could not afford to massacre its supporters as it had in 1848. To the right-wing press, which made great play of the frequency of strikes, which was as great as it had been under the Empire, the Republican press riposted that at least there had been neither a Ricamarie nor an Aubin. The Waldeck-Rousseau circular (of 27 February 1884) recommended that the security forces be employed discerningly and that the gendarmerie alone should be used; calling out the troops should only be countenanced in 'exceptional circumstances' and the minister would have to be scrupulously informed of these.

It was, no doubt, Republican thinking on the 'new army' which underlay this separation of roles. It would be impossible to call on the defenders of the national frontiers to preserve social order, given both the Left's opposition to calling in troops at any time, a key theme in their parliamentary speeches, and also a certain visible distaste for such action on the part of an army humiliated by defeat and far from keen to increase its unpopularity by strike-breaking. Even under the *Ordre Moral*, generals resisted excessive demands on them from civilians: in 1873 General Bourbaki told the prefect of the Loire, who was requesting his intervention, that the facts did not seem to him to warrant it. At Bessèges in 1882 the troops had to be cajoled into action. Elsewhere, officers refused to charge into the strikers as the employers wished. Moreover, gendarmerie reports were, very generally, free from any animosity against the workers. On several occasions prefects complained of the 'unreliability' of the troops: at Montceau-les-Mines in 1882, 'in the battalion of chasseurs, there were said to be a certain number of locally born soldiers who could not be relied upon'. Elsewhere the workers made attempts to fraternise with them, some of which bore fruit: 'Workers engaged the men in conversation singly or even in groups, and took them into local bars and inns, bought them drink and food and found them girls, and so on. Once picked up in this manner, the soldiers fraternised with the workers, called them their brothers and got all the socialist pamphlets and papers from them that are always hawked around in the mining villages.' The situation had reached a point where the troops had to be confined to barracks. There was a mood of great agitation 'even among the NCOs'.

The Boulangist episode is an example — indeed, the pinnacle — of this attempt to bring the people and the army together. If the General's celebrated declaration in the Chambre des Députés of 13 March 1886 on the attitude of the troops at Decazeville brought the opprobrium of the Right down upon him, it won Boulanger great goodwill among the workers and aroused the enthusiasm of many Socialists, who saw it as a symptom of the new times. Boulanger himself vouched for the good relations between the soldiers and the workers: 'How could it be otherwise? Our army is the nation of today. Could our workers, who are yesterday's soldiers, have anything to fear from our soldiers of today, so long as they, while exercising their rights, respect their duties to society?' The army had only been sent to Decazeville 'to protect the miners against themselves'. The soldiers 'are therefore . . . immobile, their guns by their sides; they are not partisan; they no more act today for the company against the miners than they would act tomorrow for the miners against the company. It has been said that there have been as many soldiers as miners at Decazeville.This is clearly an exaggeration, but I tell you: do not lament this fact, do not reproach yourselves for it, for it is possible that at this very moment, every soldier is sharing his soup and his bread ration with a miner'.

In their intervention at Vierzon too, the troops showed moderation, to judge by the opposing commentaries of the various factions. Whilst for *Le Figaro, L'Autorité* or *Le Matin*, Boulanger was now merely 'General White Flag!', *Le Cri du peuple*, while criticising the government's constitutional right to send in the army, wondered if there was not perhaps some way of 'creating such relations between the workers and the military as to remove for good any possibility of a future clash between them'. And, after having condemned the 'invasion' (26 August), Guesde praised 'the remarkable attitude of the troops'.

Did Boulanger initiate a whole tradition? A few months later, his successor at the War Ministry, General Ferron received the saddlers' delegates from the Lecerf & Sarda Company (military equipment), who had come to put their claims to him, with unusual cordiality. According to *Le Cri du peuple*, which hailed the 'workers' victory', 'the minister began by apologising for having kept them waiting and declared that, as a worker's son himself, he could not remain indifferent to the situation which had caused the delegation to be sent'. He acceded to their proposal that representatives of the workers' trade unions should be included among the experts ('Well, yes indeed. That seems a good idea to me'). Finally, by applying pressure, he obtained the requested wage-rise ('Monsieur Lecerf said that he had only met the strikers' demands because he had been forced to do so by the minister of war'). Though shortly afterwards the minister had to beat a hasty retreat before the fury of the employers, his initial impulse is nonetheless evidence of the popular face the army was trying to give itself at the time.

The instructions of the Lille central chief constable to his subordinates on 14 November 1885 echo this moderation. Looking ahead to what he expected to be a hard winter, he wrote: 'We are at the beginning of winter, and the industrial crisis which weighs heavily on France is probably going to mean that industrialists generally will have to reduce the working day or cut wages and thus place the working class, so worthy of our attention, in an extremely difficult situation.' Strikes were to be expected. 'We must rigorously see to it that order is kept, the right to work upheld and property respected. So long as an assembly does not take on an aggressive character against persons or property, let us place ourselves in the midst of the workers; if we speak with them in a fatherly manner, there is every chance we will be listened to and that we can give them good advice and help them to be aware of the misery strikes always bring in their wake. Besides, our presence alone may perhaps be enough to prevent them from becoming overexcited and to keep any dangerous counsellors away from them. However, as soon as the strikers begin to engage in any reprehensible acts, let us be energetic and move in the greatest possible numbers . . . If it becomes necessary to disperse an assembly, we should not forget to give the three warnings required by law, each one preceded by a roll on the drum and, after each drum roll, to exhort the workers to disperse.'

Overall, the level of intervention in disputes by the forces of law and order was relatively moderate during this period. It is not, however, very easy to draw up a complete balance-sheet. In 1872 at Anzin the army killed one or perhaps two people with their fire, though these deaths were carefully covered up. During the demonstrations to commemorate the *Semaine Sanglante* in May 1885, *La Bataille's* headline ran: 'The murderers of the Père Lachaise, 87 wounded, 3 dead.'

Under the Republic, the orders were to avoid the use of firearms. Cavalry charges with swords drawn were the major tactic employed to disperse assemblies and gatherings. These mainly left men injured: 'a severed arm, an eye put out, a forehead split open' was the balance-sheet of one clash during the navvies' strike. The workers replied by rolling marbles under the horses' hooves to make them slip. The task of occupying factories, mines or building sites was allotted to the infantry. Where there were serious disturbances, these occupations could become quite prolonged. In July 1873 the 20th Infantry Batallion was garrisoned for a month at Lisieux, where there were plans to erect a permanent barracks.

The brief period of détente we have looked at here, which was based partly on the hopes for peace that had been vested in the Republic, was soon dissipated by a new wave of major disputes and by the development of socialism and anarchism. In 1888 the navvies' strikes saw some quite serious clashes. From 1889 onwards, the instructions of Constans, the new minister of the interior, became more harsh. May Day 1890 produced what was in effect a mobilisation, if not indeed a state of siege, marking a return to the earlier climate of fear. May Day 1891 brought Fourmies and with it an end to all illusions.

The *Comptes de la justice criminelle* allow us to gauge the vigour of this repression with some precision. There are two figures to be considered. Firstly, the rate of repression or the relation between the annual figure for strikers and the number of persons convicted annually. This reveals with some clarity the relaxation of repression under the Republic and, at the same time, highlights the importance of the political conjuncture in this regard. When it comes to repression, not all regimes — not even all bourgeois ones — are the same;

Secondly, the conviction rate, or relation between the number of persons charged and the number convicted, is interesting because it gives us some indication of how the courts behaved. Between 1864 and 1890 this ratio varied from 70 per cent (in 1883) to 100 per cent (in 1868 and 1885); that is, within quite narrow limits, as though there were, if not norms, at least certain customs in this domain. The courts rarely showed any indulgence, nor did they show much initiative. They seem to have been relatively conformist creatures of habit, finding overwhelming numbers of those brought before them guilty and leaving only very limited scope for leniency. In sixteen years out of twenty-six, the conviction rate exceeded 90 per cent. During the July Monarchy the poverty of the workers exercised the minds of presiding judges and even state prosecutors; by bringing the severity of the Penal Code to public attention, several of them played a role in the promulgation of the law of 1864. After the Commune, this type of liberal, enlightened magistrate became rarer, as if fear had strengthened the ties between the legal world and the established order. What written records there are of preliminary hearings and court proceedings and the small number of items of administrative correspondence that are to be found in the archives, confirm this impression. The magistrates show themselves only too inclined to collaborate with the bosses. At Decazeville, statements were taken from the accused at the company's own offices; at Vierzon, the justice of the peace conferred with the industrialists every day throughout the two months of disturbances and spoke in favour of taking repressive measures. At Rouen, the state prosecutor, Pellerin, admonished fifteen weavers accused of taking part in a demonstration at Bolbec: 'What temerity to put in jeopardy this shower of gold that is falling upon you and the source that feeds it! What would you put in its place if it were to dry up? You have oppressed and violated the property, the homes, the social conventions, the labour and the persons of your fellow citizens.' The state prosecutors received workers' delegates with much more harshness than the prefects. The Republic's prosecutor replied to the Anzin miners who had come to lay their demands before him 'that the law would take its course and sought to demonstrate to the strikers the inanity of their pretensions'.

These too fleeting impressions should properly be backed up by a thorough study of a reliable historical source. Unfortunately, *La Gazette des tribunaux* is much less interested in strikes — the small beer of criminal law — and merely gives a brief account of proceedings without any record of the hearings. The disappearance of the reports of the state prosecutors (BB 18) for our period is equally regrettable, for they would have permitted us to make a better assessment of the psychology of lawyers when confronted with the workers and their world.

Interventions and Mediations

Caught between the employers, who were their natural allies and often their friends, and the workers, who were strangers, the prefects were subject to contradictory and differently weighted influences.

The relations of employers and workers to the state

The employers had a spontaneous tendency to consider the authorities as their personal servants and to demand from them protection and the repression of the workers, according to 'that rather common state of mind' denounced by Léon Bourgeois, prefect of the Tarn, 'which makes the powerful companies confuse their own individual interests with the public interest and leads them to call on the authorities to be in all circumstances the defenders of the company against their workers'. If, by chance, anyone resisted them in this, they were surprised and irritated, as though it were a breach of their prerogatives. This can be seen, for example, in the extremely curt letter Liénart, the manager of Carmaux, addressed to the same Léon Bourgeois, who had turned down his request for troops: 'I feel duty bound to protest strongly to you, Monsieur de Préfet, against this flagrant violation of the right to work and against the absence of any intervention by the police and the municipal authorities. Quite recently in Paris the government openly proclaimed its right to disperse assemblies which form on the public highway. I cannot but imagine . . . that you esteemed it opportune to avail yourself of this same right at Carmaux.' Identical conflicts arose each time a member of the authorities chose to keep his distance from the industrialists or took it into his head to interfere.

But more often the employers had reason to thank the authorities for the exercise of their good offices. 'We wish to express our sincerest thanks to you for the speedy aid you afforded us during the recent strike among our tawing workers', wrote a certain Monsieur Fortin to the chief constable of the Rochechouart district of Paris. 'It is by virtue of this aid that we were able to give effective protection to the workers who had not deserted their posts.' After the Roubaix textile strike of 1880, the president of the Chamber of Commerce, Delfosse, praised the prefect (Paul Cambon) for his assistance: 'You have, Monsieur le Préfet, made a powerful contribution to this result [the ending of the dispute] by the fair and firm tone of your remarks to the strikers' delegates. You reminded them of the rules which dictate the duties of every man and, at the same time, you advised them that they should resume work immediately. It was from that moment on that we began to see a considerable increase in the numbers returning to the factory. For this, we thank you most sincerely.' Guary, the manager of the Anzin mines, addressed a similar letter of appreciation and 'congratulations' to Jules Cambon. These messages serve as transparent illustrations of the employers' collusion with the administration.

For their part, the workers cherished great hopes of the state, at least after the triumph of the Republic. Conscious of the fact that they had brought the new regime to power, they expected to derive some benefit from it. When requesting the intervention of the prefect, the Carmaux miners reminded him that they had resisted all the reactionary pressures applied by the company in 1877. Above all, though, the workers believed the Republic had it within its power to improve their lot. Like the hero of Flaubert's *Sentimental Education*, they thought: 'The Republic is proclaimed! Now we shall be happy!' These expectations, as we have seen, in large part explain the great strike wave of 1878–80; these were strikes of Republican hope.

For similar reasons, the workers turned willingly to representatives of the state for help. It was to the prefects and sub-prefects, rather than to the mayors, that they sent their delegations and addressed the letters or petitions describing their 'sorry condition' and requesting their intervention as an arbitrator. These were respectful, almost affectionate (if sometimes ingenuous) letters, some of them redolent of the days of the *commissaires de la République*. In May 1880 the cotton-weavers of Tourcoing wrote to their 'Dear Fellow Citizen', beseeching him to come and see for himself a spinning workshop where the temperature remained at between 32 and 36 degrees centigrade, 'and even a bit more': 'You were meeting [sic] there old men of fifty . . . We believe we are following the proper course by writing to you, for we do not wish to be disruptive, we know you are a good citizen and have a kind heart. You will come and protect us.' Similarly, the miners of Carmaux assured Léon Bourgeois of their 'admiration and deep respect'.

Women, who were more vulnerable, and the miners, who felt bound to the state by their legal position — the state in French law being the master of all things subterranean — adopted such an

approach more often than other workers. By contrast, direct recourse to the government remained the exception. Paris was a long
way off (you had to write) and silent, as the miners of Pontgibaud
learnt to their cost. Having sent two petitions to the Minister of
Public Works in the approved manner, duly authorised by the
mayor, and still having received no reply after forty-eight days on
strike, they repeated the message by telegram, 'reply paid'. This was
no more successful.

And yet what naive gratitude the workers expressed when they
felt someone had listened to them! The women cigar factory workers of Marseilles sent the prefect a bouquet, the miners of St-Etienne
passed a motion congratulating him and the Roanne weavers de-
fended their sub-prefect against the malicious dealings of the employers: 'We know the sub-prefect is Republican . . . we have
confidence in him . . . he will not have any reason to reproach
us . . . we know that at this very moment the masters are bringing
pressure to bear in Paris for him to be moved from Roanne. If they
succeed in making him leave, things could be different here.' The
tawers of Graulhet feted the authorities on the occasion of a *conseil
de révision* which came shortly after one strike: 'The whole population — men, women and children — came out to meet us with flags
waving and a band playing. They had wanted to come like this to
thank us for the way we had acted with them during the strike.'
These *images d'Epinal* illustrate the simple faith of the Republican
people, a faith always there waiting to be reborn, a chain of age-old
loyalties so easy to revive.

This attitude was not only an expression of their Republican
faith, but of their belief in the primary importance and, indeed, the
omnipotence, of political factors, which led them to seek the key to
happiness in a change of regime and to interpret all economic crises
as a product of political machinations. In 1878 the miners saw the
lowering of their wages as an act of revenge on the part of companies beaten in the elections and nostalgic for the monarchy. The
Vosges and Normandy textile-workers attributed the unemployment of 1879 to the ill-will of an anti-Republican employer class.
Posters on buildings in Bolbec and Lillebonne declared: 'Mister
factory-owner . . . there are men of your sort who say they are not
selling because they wish to bring down the Republic, because they
don't like the Republic. In this you are making a big mistake, for the
workers will support it as long as they can . . . We want the
Republic. *Vive la République* for ever!'

The depression of 1883–4 naturally stoked such speculations.

Some unemployed workers' demonstrations attacked employers paying 'starvation wages' and priests, and even went so far as to blame aristocrats and monopolists. The serious *chambre syndicale* of gun-metal workers condemned 'the economic crisis created by the capitalists, the enemies of the Republic, who have stopped all the orders currently being fulfilled with the clear goal of making all the workers disaffected with the present regime'. As a response to this situation, the button-workers called for 'the revision of the constitution and great vigilance regarding the pretenders to the throne'. Workers had been dismissed, they said, and 'certain people are saying that these dismissals are not unconnected with politics and that the manufacturers believe they can seek to lay the responsibility for these wrongs at the government's door'.

Prefects, sub-prefects and strikes

Particularly after 1878, the conduct of the members of the government service regarding strikes became more nuanced and complex. The aristocratic personnel of the Republic of the Dukes, as portrayed by Albert de Broglie, knew nothing of the urban world, 'the incoherent and subaltern' crowds of workers.[10] But the corps of prefects underwent a thorough political overhaul at the time of the Republican victory. Dufaure proceeded at that point to transfer eighty prefects and remove forty-six from office: 'In one month, the whole administrative physiognomy of the country was completely transformed.' After this, prefectoral stability seems to have been reconstituted; the ministers who subsequently flitted across the scene in quick succession hardly dared attempt any further changes: the ambitions of Waldeck-Rousseau during the *Grand Ministère* from December 1881 to January 1882 stand in marked contrast to the restraint he was to show between 1883 and 1885. The body of men which was thus installed, as a veritable breeding ground for the new regime — their posts constituting stepping-stones to the highest office — was to ensure the smooth running of the Republic for many years to come.

But who were these new prefects? And was this process also one of social renewal? In Jean Lhomme's opinion, this was not simply an administrative change-over, as an effect of some type of spoil

10. Daniel Halévy, *La République des Ducs* (Paris, Grasset, 1937), pp. 10–11: 'The crowds milled around; they seemed strange, indeed more than strange, and, in their distant agitation, presented an incoherent and subaltern spectacle. Incoherent and subaltern was how Albert de Broglie would always regard city dwellers, Parisian intellectuals, crowds of workers; they were simply great masses of people who knew nothing of the laws of life.'

system, but a process of dispossession of the upper bourgeoisie, a class which was on the way to losing political power. Should we accept as he does that 'political posts, and the administrative posts that were clearly dependent on them at the time, belonged hence-forth to the middle classes ... to the members of the middle bourgeoisie'? Was the umbilical cord which connected the prefects to the great property-owning bourgeoisie severed, or was it simply stretched — and if so, to what extent? Can we detect in the more detached tone of certain reports towards the local potentates, sus-pected as they were of clericalism, the voice of Gambetta's 'new strata'?

It is true that a new type of prefect was taking shape. These new men were more distant from the manufacturers, freer in their judgement (often seeing through the employers), capable of resist-ing the seductive social power of the manufacturers and, with solid backing from Paris, eager to pursue an interventionist line. Men of this type were certainly not simply a product of the Republic: many prefects under the Second Empire had already expressed the need for 'a protective authority' that could provide a counterweight to the omnipotence of the employers; but now these men began to impose themselves, to become freer and leave behind their earlier stiffly respectful manner. They were now more frequently critical of the employers' obstructiveness, harshness and short-sightedness. In 1879 the prefect of Saône-et-Loire attributed the tension prevailing in the Montceau collieries 'to the difficult character, authoritarian acts and lack of tact of certain members of the company's senior management'. During the 1882 disturbances, he denounced the management for its clericalism: 'There can be few who have shown themselves so intolerant in religious matters; this organisation seems to have been set up with the sole aim of dominating the workers and forcing them to observe the practices of the Catholic religion'. For his colleague in the Loire department, 'it is well known that the Firminy company ... is very harsh towards its workers ... Constant annoyance, continual harrassment — es-pecially from the pit deputies and their assistants are designed to have that effect'. A great number of reports contrast the workers' moderation with the 'absolutely reactionary' and sometimes provo-cative attitude of the employers. 'You would think that the employ-ers were committing one blunder after another on purpose', wrote Frémont, the sub-prefect of Roanne, who accused the factory-owners of trying to spark off an incident, 'hoping thus to bring troops in to Roanne and to bring the workers to heel by fear and by force'.

This question of calling in troops was a thorny one. The employers, who tended to think of the army as their own personal militia, always called for it to be sent in quickly: 'The management would welcome such an act on my part and as early as yesterday morning M. Fayol, the company engineer, came to request the stationing of several brigades at Carmaux. I felt that I had to refuse', said Léon Bourgeois. At Roanne in 1882 the sub-prefect himself vouched for the peaceful conduct of the workers, who had expressed their confidence in him and allowed them to organise the policing of their strike themselves, a move the industrialists considered scandalous. At Villefranche in 1881 a similar refusal saw them once more up in arms, demanding 'more effective protection than they had so far received' from the authorities.

The Waldeck-Rousseau circular of 27 February 1884 recommended to prefects that they should intervene, without however laying down any arbitration procedure. This latter in fact consisted of 'meetings with the representatives of the interested parties in which sources of misunderstanding were brought out into the open and where it became easier for each of the parties to see what basis there was in fact for certain grievances and what was the legitimacy of certain claims'. Certain prefects made an honest attempt to perform such mediation; they invited the two parties to explain their points of view, suggested concessions and sometimes brought about real face-to-face negotiations between the contending forces. As a general rule, however, contact was established through the prefect. In actual fact, when employers and workers could agree to meet (i.e. when the former agreed to see the latter), they talked directly, not through intermediaries. This is the reason, indeed, why many of these prefectoral attempts at arbitration failed, being generally unable to have much effect on the natural course of events; they developed too late or in hopeless cases. The law of 1892 was later to attempt to develop a preventative arbitration procedure, or at least one that came into effect at an early stage. Most of the time the prefect only managed to limit the damage, particularly the number of dismissals, which the employers made a classic sequel to strikes. At Trélazé, Decazeville, Carmaux and other strikes, the prefect tried to avoid any victimisation, though not without difficulty. Having obtained a return to work, Léon Bourgeois turned to the company: 'It was said . . . that the management intended to lay off about 200 workers. I called in the manager at the end of the meeting and initially received the most unfavourable of replies from him. I announced very firmly that all the workers had to be taken back without exception, and that this was an absolute condition of the return-to-work motion which had just been passed. The manager continued stubbornly to insist on the company's rights in this regard, and it required an almost dictatorial attitude on my part to obtain a solemn commitment from him to take everyone back.'

When intervening in this way, the prefects complained of the mistrust and even the duplicity of the employers. Félix Renaut, prefect of the Loire, deplored 'the bad grace shown by the mining companies when it comes to providing the authorities with the information required to facilitate our work of peace-making and reconciliation . . . The company is unhappy to see the authorities becoming embroiled in these strike questions and seeks to fight against them'. At Vierzon in 1886 his colleague Berniquet expressed doubts about the claims made by the board of the Société Française de Matériel Agricole, whose chairman was Arbel, a powerful figure and a senator: 'I am not sure that in presenting their grievances — which they doubtless tailor to the audience they happen to be speaking to — the directors are not playing a double game.' 'They are perhaps exaggerating.' During a cotton-weavers' strike at Cornimont, the sub-prefect was angered by the manufacturers' lies: whilst they claimed not to be able to survive the crisis without lowering wages, research conducted personally by the sub-prefect ('since the employers are refusing . . . to produce their books and put figures on the real extent of their wealth') led him to suggest they owned some 4 million francs of capital, 2 million francs of it in fixed assets. The sub-prefect concluded that 'it was therefore easy for them to cope with the crisis until more favourable commercial conditions were restored'. They had also lied about the wages they were paying to the workers: 'You will naturally understand how offended I was to discover these deceptions.' Such was the virtuous and naive indignation of a provincial civil servant! His words exude that bewilderment born of longing and frustration which a thrifty, 'fair-minded' petty-bourgeois feels when he contemplates those fabulous, unimagined shores which will remain for ever beyond his reach. There are certain tones that are unmistakable.

Aware of all the dangers intervention by the authorities might bring, the employers mounted vigorous resistance against it. They politely declined such intervention or refused it angrily where they were being asked to make concessions. The sub-prefect of Cornimont, who suggested to the employers that they should reduce the workers' hours rather than their wages, received from 'these gentlemen' the reply 'that they did not wish to hear of conciliation, that they would listen to no offer of negotiations, either from the workers or from me. They said the masters were the masters and the workers the workers. The former, they said had a duty to command; the latter could obey or leave. Moreover, they announced that they were resolved to dismiss at least 250 of them as soon as the men returned to work'. All of this certainly put the sub-prefect in his place.

The employers also sought to stir up support in the reactionary press. And they attempted on occasion to appeal to the government in Paris, which was more detached from local affairs, against municipal authorities, which they saw as caught in the trap of universal suffrage. The *Journal des débats*, the newspaper of Léon Say, a member of the board of the Decazeville Mining Company, developed this argument during the great strike of 1886: 'The prefect, who doubtless is not greatly concerned about the interests of the company, cannot help but notice that weight of numbers is on the miners' side. He therefore concludes that the management is wrong not to yield and reserves his harshest words for them.' During the anti-clerical disturbances at Montceau, the prefect was accused of having allowed a secret society to develop among the workers. At Marseilles, during the dockers' general strike (1883), Poubelle came under a fierce attack from the *Gazette du Midi* which denounced his collusion with the strikers; he had to answer for his actions to the *conseil général*.

Rarely, however, can the conflict have been more open than it was at Roanne, where the sub-prefect, Frémont, with the support of his prefect, Thomson, made the manufacturers dance to his tune. 'They cannot accept', he exclaimed, 'that the workers be given access to the sub-prefecture and the town hall and that the same welcome should be given to them there as would be accorded to any citizen. They would like the authorities to join in some form of coercive action against the workers. To allow them to act, discuss their interests and organise themselves, so that we, the authorities may give them support, seems to these gentlemen quite criminal. They are from another age.' Whilst *L'Avenir roannais* and *Le Moniteur de la Loire et de la Haute Loire* conducted a fierce campaign against him, three employers went to Paris to the Ministry of the Interior to obtain his transfer. The prefect had in turn to go to Paris to defend himself. As for whether the government allowed itself to be intimidated in such cases, it must be admitted that, most often, the civil servants involved were transferred to another post after the dispute. This was no doubt essentially a peace-making measure, but it could be used as a way of giving certain individuals spectacular promotion. In October 1883 Poubelle was appointed prefect of the Seine, where he acquired a reputation which survives to this day!

Those prefects who were inclined towards arbitration did, however, remain the exception. There were more of the traditional type who preferred the comfort of abstention to the trials and tribulations that mediation and enquiries might involve. And though they were now perhaps less common and their activities more veiled, there were still a great number who, either by elective or social affinity, behaved as the employers' allies — if not their doubles. They aligned themselves with the bosses' positions, reproduced their explanations word for word (Victor de Girardin, the prefect of the Gard, was content merely to transcribe the words of Chalmeton, the manager of the coal company, verbatim), sang their praises, extolled the merits of the industrial paradise they had brought into being and refused to see strikes as anything but a product of deliberate disruption, the sinister work of some agitator. For men like these, the development of the labour movement and the more frequent involvement of socialist and anarchist militants in disputes removed their last lingering doubts and left them with an easy conscience. Though some new emphases would be introduced, in general terms, the anthology of conformism was simply to become more voluminous and repetitive.

Certain members of the administration, unhappy at having to parley with the workers and gainsay the industrialists who were often their friends and hosts, countered the interventionist desires of Paris with the forces of provincial inertia, with barely disguised disapproval or even with vigorous protests. I shall give some examples of this here. One of the causes of the 1884 Anzin strike was the company's dismissal of a number of miners. Since every attempt by the authorities to secure compensation had been rejected by the employers, Waldeck-Rousseau proposed that the government take these workers into its care: 'It seems to me that the state could, without departing from the reserve which it is duty-bound to maintain and without leaving itself open to recriminations, substitute itself for the company and bear the transport costs of the miners whom other employers would be willing to take on.' The prefect, Jules Cambon, dissuaded him from doing anything of the sort: 'It would mean creating a dangerous precedent in a region where strikes are always accompanied by workers receiving their cards.' And the matter rested there.

In the same year, the women who worked in the Pochoy-Bruny factories at Paviot (Isére), a typical south-eastern silk industry boarding institution, went on strike, seeking at least to have the law of 1848 observed. Though this limited the working day to twelve hours, they actually worked thirteen or fourteen. The minister of trade then charged the *inspecteur divisionnaire du travail* of Grenoble, Delattre, with an information-gathering and conciliatory mission. This latter, a courageous and hardworking official, who had for some time been recording these abuses in his annual reports, investigated the matter and concluded unambiguously that the employers were entirely to blame. He found them guilty of imposing inhuman and illegal working conditions. This was not, however, the opinion of the prefect, who sketched an idyllic picture of the silk factories and supported the employers' argument: 'There is no spontaneity in the strike, no general consensus. The factories were closed down one after the other under the influence of certain ringleaders.' He went on to stress the part played by a local councillor from Moirans, who, he thought, might well be an agent of a foreign power. He wrote of this man: 'It is not known on whose behalf he is acting.' The employers by contrast simply accused point-blank 'the man who is doing the Germans' job so well for them'. But the prefect railed above all against Delattre's mission, which he found offensive and inflammatory. Was it not dangerous to give the workers the impression that the government supported them? It would have been much better, in his opinion, 'to leave the strikers to ponder on matters for a few days and . . . when the time was ripe for it, to let them have some sound advice'. Not long afterwards, he obtained Delattre's recall to Grenoble. In similar fashion, in 1880, his colleague from the Nord, Paul Cambon, was astonished by the arrival of Barberet in the name of the new Bureau des Sociétés Professionnelles, that had been formed within the Ministry of the Interior: 'Disarming the government against the lay associations' he said, 'means disarming it also against the religious congregations'. Having heard it said that Barberet was a man who had in the past been convicted of political crimes, he declared, 'This is inconceivable!'

Government can never have come under more criticism for its initiatives than it did in the Denain miners affair in 1880, in which Paul Cambon was ranged against Constans. The latter saw the system of bonuses granted to the overseers by the company 'in inverse proportion to the cost of coal', as the major cause of the reduction of wages and therefore of strikes. 'Such exploitation is odious', he wrote, 'and cannot be condemned too strongly'. The minister of the interior expressed his regret that this point had not been seriously broached by the prefect in his discussions with the representatives of the company. He invited him to intervene once again: 'The surest way to pacify the workers and win them over again — and their honesty and moderation are tried and tested — seems to me to be to put an end to these lamentable, disgraceful abuses. It is not a matter of benevolence, but of what is necessarily entailed in observing the rules of common justice.' His tone here is evidence of the goodwill of the young Opportunist Republic. However, the prefect's reply shows up its illusions. Paul Cambon curtly refused to intervene, on the pretext that the government was supposed to be committed to a *laissez-faire* position. In the process he gave his own definition of the role of the authorities: 'I know I can speak my mind to you, Monsieur le Ministre. Moreover, as this letter is not an official one, I can permit myself to give my opinion quite freely. Well then, it seems to me that you are following a quite erroneous conception of the part that can be played in strikes by a member of the public services. We are neither arbitrators nor dispensers of justice. We are policemen, and it is our task to ensure that everyone can exercise their freedom. It is just as contrary to our principles to impose working conditions on an employer as it is to impose them on a worker.' He accepted that things were not equally balanced between these two parties but added, 'you must not take it upon yourself to redress the balance. To take that course would mean going quicker and further than you wish, for I imagine that a liberal spirit like your own has little taste for the economic fantasies of a Louis Blanc . . . If ever you adopted any other line of conduct, you would quickly incur everyone's mistrust . . . The best thing is to keep your reputation intact. A liberal government must be moderate in its actions and its words'.

This is certainly a fine text and one that is surprising for the free and easy manner in which the prefect addressed the minister. Doubtless Paul Cambon, whom Casimir-Périer called 'my dear friend', had a somewhat exceptional personal position, and yet in these, the apprenticeship years of the parliamentary Republic, in which the responsibilities of power were shared by young men who had only recently been students together, there was no hierarchical rigidity in the higher échelons of the civil service; there was not much distance on occasion between a minister and a prefect who would himself very soon be a minister. And on how many occasions did an ephemeral executive — with all its fragility — run up against the stability of the civil service! Constans had been a minister for six months and was to remain so for twelve more; Paul Cambon had been prefect of the Nord for three years and was to remain so until 1882, when he would be replaced by his brother Jules, who was to hold the office from 1882 to 1887. The two Cambon brothers 'held' the prefecture of the Nord for ten years and saw thirteen ministers come and go. Moreover, the influence of prefects on ministers is there for all to see. The change in Waldeck-Rousseau's position during the Anzin strike and the hardening of his attitude reflect to a certain extent — though he was never to go as far in his repressive actions as the prefect of the Nord desired — the changed stance of the prefect, who had moved from an initially understanding attitude to one of irritation and anger.[11] Similarly, by his alarmist daily reports, Camescasse, the Paris prefect of police, caused Waldeck-Rousseau to fear social upheavals.

The influence of the prefects, who acted at times as observers of social reality and reformers and, at others as brakes on progress and transmission belts in the hands of the employers, thus appears ambiguous. Through these various clashes of ideas, contradictions and uncertainties, a new practice was, however, emerging. One might argue that this was in fact a form of casuistry, but does not every casuistry suppose a certain sense of sin? Since it was now the case that the employer could be judged and even, at times, condemned, the days of his 'divine right' employer were now drawing to a close.

It only remains now to assess the influence of the public on the outcome of strikes, an apparently limited influence in the period and one for which we have almost no source material. Apart from the fact that the notion of 'the public' is vague and needs to be further specified and, no doubt, broken down into its elements, there are few documents to tell us how opinion reacted in particular

11. On the changing attitude of Jules Cambon himself, the archives contain a lengthy correspondence (Arch. dép. Nord, M626/13): 'The brutal conduct of the company has caused me to be deeply out of sympathy with it', he wrote on 26 February 1884 (pièce 116). However, the failure of his personal attempt at mediation and the indifference with which he was received at Denain during his visit of 21 March and the time Basly took to go to the town hall to meet him greatly annoyed him. On 2 March he wrote: 'It is intolerable that a large number of people should be oppressed by a band of fanatics and self-seekers' (pièce 10). On 24 March we read: 'The time for negotiations is past and today if this strike does not end, public opinion will put the blame on the weakness of the authorities' (pièce 3). On 8 April he proposed arresting the leaders in order to 'decapitate a movement which has ceased to be simply a severe economic problem and has become a revolutionary movement . . . I insist that a means be found, by whatever legal channels may be open to us to carry out these arrests' (pièce 347, *au min.*, 8 April).

cases. Most often, the newspapers expressed the traditional position of the political 'families' they represented, and they most often did this in general and conventional terms. Furthermore we do not know how much importance the principal actors — employers, workers, public authorities — attached to public opinion in framing their attitudes and decisions. The answer seems to be that they did not accord it very much, at least not explicitly. The employers appealed more often to the national interest, which they considered their own property. The workers, by contrast, addressed themselves almost exclusively to the labouring masses and, except perhaps in Paris, where the City imposed its presence and its diversity, they behaved with a certain indifference towards any possible third party. The social vision which emerges from their statements was dichotomous. They saw two antagonistic classes pitted against each other — bosses and workers, capital and labour — and they ignored the others. But their discourse conceals as much as it reveals. Does not the workers' reluctance to resort to violence, showing great restraint and amounting to virtual self-censorship of their actions, suggest that they were taking into account a spectator-judge, to whom they wished to project the expected reasonable and reassuring image.

The nature of economic relations with the public also plays a role. The 'producers' — weavers, miners or glass-workers — walled up in their factories, faubourgs or housing estates felt they had almost no connection with the consumers, with whom they indeed had no direct contact. On the other hand, service workers, such as those in local transport for example, could not afford to ignore the users of those services. Here the case of the Paris coach-drivers is very revealing. They called on their clients to be witnesses to their lot and on occasion managed to turn them into allies. In 1878 public opinion supported their strike, condemning the Compagnie Générale des Petites Voitures for its monopoly, its exclusive concern for profit, its relative unconcern for the quality of the service provided and, especially, for the feeding of the horses. Reports attributed the negotiated settlement achieved to the pressure put on the company by ordinary Parisians.

By virtue of their functions, the authorities gave greater attention to local opinion, which for electoral reasons they had to handle carefully. It seems reasonable to put forward the hypothesis that the strike success rate in Republican areas would be better than it was in politically conservative ones, but there are few ways of verifying this. The figures for strike outcomes in individual departments are generally not based on a sufficient number of cases to enable us to draw any clear conclusions from them. In any case, a department is too large an area to allow us to make correlations with political opinion; to do that we would need figures at *commune* level. Lastly, there are a great number of other factors that come into play, in particular the nature of the industries involved. Departments where negative strike outcomes predominate are also those in which the major textile disputes occurred (Nord, Aisne, Aube, Somme, Marne). The poor showing of Paris (54 per cent failure) will surprise many — Lyon, which was a 'depressed area' fared better — but the case of Paris provides quite a few surprises in this period.

However, though it was a classic method of the early years of political sociology, the direct comparison of statistical data for a specific geographical area would be quite inadequate here, even if correlations could be established. We would need to back up such data with a thorough and detailed study of decision-making processes, examining how, at a time when pressure groups were still informal associations, the various currents of opinion or interest exerted their influence. Did they seek to shape the attitudes of members of the government services — and did they succeed? I simply pose the question here without attempting to offer any answers. On this point the documents do not 'speak for themselves' (if indeed they ever do!). We should need to approach them with a much greater awareness of this specific question than I have been able to, since I only formulated this line of enquiry when my work was at quite an advanced stage; we should also need to research other sources.

Beyond the specific involvement of particular individuals, the public, ordinarily little affected in its immediate interests by strikes, its daily life insulated by factory walls from the limited, enclosed world of industry, exerted a general pressure on the situation by virtue of its underlying ideological world-view. The workers' condition ('the horrible life of the workers' — Daudet) provoked in them a reaction that was a mixture of fear, reproof and pity, which generally made them a force advocating arbitration. French society being profoundly rural and attached to the values of the soil, had not really accepted industrialisation, the failings of which were emphasised in the nineteenth-century sociological and novelistic literature on pauperism, where various archaic remedies were also advocated. Decentralisation, the organisation of work on a family basis and a return to the land were the main chapters in this search for time past. The Rousseauist rejection of the town and a Ruskinian distaste for factories, together with an extreme mistrust of monopolies and the barons of industry, were all aspects of a resistance to modern capitalism.

Industrialisation, experienced as a traumatic episode, a loss of substance and identity, provoked a sense of shame. And it was this bad conscience as much as any greater wisdom which gave rise to the movement for reform, the progress of which, at the end of the nineteenth century, was registered in Radical and Socialist electoral victories and in considerable achievements in social legislation. This collective sense of remorse, which affected both industrialists and prefects was one factor militating in favour of compromise settlements. Indeed, it may perhaps be true to say that strikes owe part of their success to this factor.

Strikes and Society

It is not enough to assess strikes by their immediate effects alone. Beyond the many and varied stages on which they were acted out, they exerted a general influence on the working class and on society as a whole. Their effects were not limited to the precise spot where they were taking place. These were in fact multiplied in at least two ways. Firstly, solidarity between workers and the increasingly tightly-knit fabric of the economy meant that every success was broadcast far and wide and took on an exemplary and normative status. This can be confirmed for wage-rises and also, to a lesser degree, for other types of advance; once these had been won in one place, they were soon claimed and, sooner or later, granted elsewhere. History provides many examples of this process, which economists call an 'imitation effect'.

Secondly, an attendant phenomenon produced by strikes is the fear of strikes. This is a powerful deterrent which modifies the attitudes of the employers. In a period of expansion, to nip a threatening wage-offensive in the bud, the employers may 'spontaneously' raise income levels. In times of recession, foreseeing resistance, the dangers of which they recognise from experience, the bosses may hesitate to reduce wages and seek other means of safeguarding their profits. From the 1890s onwards, the public more or less accepted the idea that 'you do not lower a wage-rate'. This fine achievement can be attributed to the workers' resistance. The effect — both defensive and offensive — of strikes on wages and, generally, on the workers' condition was thus broadly positive.

From the end of the nineteenth century onwards, liberal economists (e.g. Paul Leroy-Beaulieu) acknowledged their influence, which contemporaries (cf. Hicks, *The Theory of Wages* and, nearer to our own day, Tiano, Lhomme, etc.) fully incorporated into their wage theories.

At the same time, the attitudes of the 'social partners' were thoroughly transformed — particularly the attitude of the employers, who were now forced into a position where they had to calculate and plan ahead, limit their arbitrary rule and rationalise and increase their productivity. Strikes, like wars or economic crises, stimulate innovation and growth, both by the purchasing power they create and by the research and development they impose. By making it less easy to produce profits, they transform capitalism itself. The socialist countries are quite wrong to reject strikes: in doing so they are depriving themselves of a powerful stimulus.

If the influence of strikes is not limited to the individual framework of a single private company, it is not confined either to the sphere of industrial relations. Through the channels of Parliament and the civil service, it reaches the whole of the state and forces change upon it. Between 1880 and 1882, to cite but one example, certain prefects in the most strike-affected departments condemned the state's liberal attitude towards the unions and called for a clarification of the legal position. Nevertheless, they saw association between workers as a guarantee of social peace. During the most notable disputes — in 1882 (Bessèges), 1884 (Anzin), 1885 (Château-Regnault), 1886 (Decazeville and Vierzon) and 1890 — great parliamentary debates raised the question of the workers' condition and the employers' abuse of power, notably in respect of political and trade-union matters. Radicals who would not dream of questioning the capitalist system as a whole, nonetheless took advantage of the miners' strikes — which were the most spectacular and those that gripped public opinion the most — to attack the companies' monopoly, to bring up again the question of the state's ownership of underground resources and raise the question of nationalisation.

The number of statesmen conscious of the danger of social upheavals and advocating reforms was steadily growing. At Toulouse in 1886 Freycinet declared: 'The Republic must study ways of rendering the worker's lot less precarious and putting an end to that antagonism which is currently surfacing everywhere, an antagonism which is nothing but the unconscious and yet profound sense of an as yet unresolved problem.' A little later, Charles Benoist wrote: 'We shall not save ourselves by force alone.' After 1880 it would be impossible to find anyone daring to argue there was no social question! Certain laws were the direct result of workers' campaigns for better wages and conditions. The law of 1884 on trade unions was a product of the great *coalitions* of 1878–80, which finally succeeded in persuading Republicans that it was necessary to permit combination. Agitation in the collieries, which was so lively in 1890, hastened the passing of the law on miners' delegates and safety in the mines. The law laying down a system of conciliation and arbitration in labour disputes (1892) ripened in the days that followed May Day 1890. The overall legislative achievement in this period remains, however, modest, being perpetually held back by the dead-weight of the rural representatives who were the masters of the Senate and, indeed, of the Republic. But a process was set in train which carried within it, ultimately, the seeds of liberalism's destruction.

By their sudden eruption, the impact of which was not yet dulled by familiarity, strikes imposed the worker's view on a society which wanted nothing better than to forget the evil of industrialisation. In spite of deep-seated resistance, the troubling spectre of the strike insinuated itself into artistic and literary representations. The 1880s marked an important breakthrough in this regard. At the end of the Salon des Indépendants of 1880, Huysmans exhorted his contemporaries to promote 'an epic nationalism', taking as its subject 'the imposing grandeur of the beautiful factories'. In 1889 Maximilien Luce founded a Club d'Art Social, which brought together a great number of politically committed artists such as Pissarro, Meunier, Signac, van Rysselbergh, Valloton, and so on. Their works were confined to relatively minor genres — engravings, drawings, posters, caricatures — but ones that had a wide audience. In the Salons a few paintings gave evidence of the penetration of the world of work into the heart of peaceful genre or historical scenes: one of these was Roll's painting, *La Grève des Mineurs* (The Miners' Strike), of which Robert Mitchell, the art critic of *Le Gaulois* wrote: 'This is an epoch-making event . . . the subject is the most important episode in the annals of contemporary life, one that we encounter again and again, every year more grandiose and more lugubrious. That subject is unemployment, poverty and despair; tomorrow, it may well be revolt and civil war'. However, painting generally — both that of the Impressionists and the *fin-de-siècle* 'Aesthetes and Magicians' — remained hermetically sealed off from industry (which the Ruskinian canon deemed ugly by definition) and exclusively devoted to depicting the countryside.

Literature was infinitely more open to new influences. The image of the modern worker gradually emerges out of that of the 'lower classes', that 'world beneath a world',[12] where it was veiled by those of the artisan, nostalgic witness of a bygone era, the cut-throat, dangerous prowler around the town gates and the domestic servant. In this slow penetration, strikes play a role for which the genesis of *Germinal*, the story of a strike, provides a fine example. The social agitation at the end of the Second Empire had led Zola to plan a novel 'of the workers' in his Rougon-Macquart saga. The Commune spurred him to add to the description of the proletarian's condition the description of its revolt. But the Parisian worker, so singular in his 'sublimism', for a long time masked from him the new world of work. The great strikes of 1878–80, and notably that at Anzin in 1878, which he knew through the reports of his colleague on *Le Voltaire*, Yves Guyot, finally made Zola aware of the existence of heavy industry. He then chose this as the framework for his book, though the 1884 strike at Anzin was in fact to add numerous new elements to his initial conception.

These are symptoms of the vast upheaval strikes were to impose on society as a whole, an upheaval I would have liked to have been able to describe more fully. Their repeated thrusts produced cracks in the social edifice and suggested it might not be as solid as was thought. They contributed to fuelling the pessimism of the ruling classes and their belief that 'a world was coming to an end', the obverse of the revolutionary hope of the workers. This pessimism stimulated the revival of reactionary ideologies, but it also encouraged the development of a social third party committed to compromise, and this has transformed the style if not the nature of social relations in Western societies. In this decisive transformation, the part played by strikes, where the pressure applied by the workers is at its most visible, has clearly been very considerable.

As actions by workers to transform their destinies, strikes were both effective and limited. They produced not so much revolutionary upheavals as modifications, which in turn had reciprocal effects on the labour movement. On the eve of the First World War that movement showed marked reformist tendencies, and the feeling among many observers was that an English-style trade unionism

---

12. The Goncourt brothers, *Germinie Lacerteux*, 1864, Preface. On this celebrated preface, see the critical commentary by Erich Auerbach in *Mimesis* (Princeton, NJ, Princeton University Press, 1968), pp. 493–524.

was developing. Events were — those perhaps only apparently or temporarily — to thwart such predictions, by one of those irruptions of 'chance' into the fabric of necessities, which are perhaps the motor of all evolution (including the biological) and which pose such a formidable obstacle problem for the social sciences to contend with.

Conclusion

As this book draws to a close with a consideration of how strikes themselves end, we should ask what we have learnt, both about strikes and about the workers to whom they were supposed to lead us. What has been the value of taking this route? What has been the value of our object of study and the method adopted?

It is certainly not easy for an author, unless he or she is a little schizophrenic, to pass *truly* critical judgement of his/her work. She needs a little time to acquire the degree of distance that is necessary for detached assessment. She may from the outset perceive the limits of her work and the gaps within it, but by identifying too strongly with the research object, she remains unaware of her own presuppositions. What is 'hidden' in her work, what remains 'unthought' is for others to discover.

This final survey of the research has no other ambition than to discern, beyond the confusing tangle of details, the broad outlines of a classic landscape encountered in industrial societies — the terrain of the strike. It is a young landscape, with slender growths as yet, and a landscape of clashes and contrasts. The history presented here is that of a period of adolescence, about which little has been known until now. After the Commune, the succession of strikes, perceived in a fragmentary way from 1864 to 1870, was totally hidden from view; for this reason the Commune appeared to mark a sudden break. By an exhaustive labour of information-gathering, we have attempted to arrive at the most complete list of industrial disputes possible. Quantitative analysis has allowed us to highlight the major upsurges — 1864, 1869–70, 1880–82, 1889–90 — and to break them down into their component parts to show both the trades involved and the demands that were put forward. The liberating effects of the law of 1864, which ushered in the era of the modern strike, the extent of the pressure applied by the workers' movement at the end of the Second Empire, its truly proletarian character as well as its predominantly economic direction, the vigorous revival of that pressure as early as 1872 — the sign of a combativeness that was still intact (at least in the provinces); the relative decline of the movement under the *Ordre Moral* government, and above all, the extent of the social explosion that followed the triumph of the Republic and the wave of emotion aroused by the first May Day, are all events on which not only traditional histories, which have eyes only for the cut and thrust of the political battle, but even histories of the labour movement, are silent. Those histories, fixated on the polarised situation which trade unionism produces, unsure of their bearings where there are no stable institutions to latch on to and operating with models derived from contemporary practices in which institutions dominate and have a determining influence, tend to neglect this invertebrate period, which has seemed to us by contrast possessed of a great richness of expression and a genuine inventiveness. As far as is humanly possible, men and crowds appear without masks in this period; we see their true faces. Their speech is hesitant, wavering and improvised; it has the charm of youth.

Beyond the simple recovery of this chronicle of events, we have been interested in the strike as a social phenomenon and have been concerned to extract regularities rather than singularities from our material, dominant structures rather than individual details. Devotees of monographs or regional studies — necessary genres, but different from our own — will obviously not find satisfaction here. How indeed could a Parisian, a stranger to village life, ever hope to emerge victorious on that terrain? Knowing too little of the subtle interrelations which characterise and mould geographical behaviour, I have preferred not to venture into this field. I did not set out to write either a history of battles or a local history, but rather, if I may use the term, a work of historical sociology.

The aim dictated the method, which has consisted in a rigorous work of social statistical research. The object lent itself to such an effort, as did the historical moment itself, in which the computer made its irresistible entrance on the scene. The time has now come to take a critical look at this method. Let us note here at the outset, to dispel any possible misunderstandings, that there is nothing very sophisticated about the quantitative approach employed. Continuous series, double-entry tables, correlations, co-variance and percentages constitute the classic arsenal to which an inadequate training as well as the relative paucity of data, reduce historians. And not only historians. After all, percentages remain for the time being the simple but essential unit of measurement in the 'social sciences'.

Limited as it is, this attempt at quantitative analysis seems to me to have beneficial consequences. It requires vigilance and attention to detail in the making of observations, and it roots out mere approximation. From this point of view the use of punched cards, with their abhorrence of a vacuum, imposes a constraint that cannot be evaded: they dictate an unrelenting quest for information. By increasing the volume and reinforcing the resistance of an object which the passage of time has removed from our view, the quantitative dimension gives the object greater presence, imposes its necessity, even its objectivity and, in so doing, removes it from the uncertain, reversible and tortuous paths of ideology. By making it impossible for us to write in a random fashion, by multiplying the obstacles to arbitrary judgement, by sifting our first intuitions and making us think 'against ourselves', numbers impose a discipline which we should not need to praise here, were it not for the fact that they are so decried and contested in our field.

The intrusion of nuclei of hard data into the soft fabric of an uncertain text has, moreover, the added advantage of highlighting contrasts; ripping into that fabric, they reveal the fragility of the interconnecting threads which constitute the tissue of historical discourse. At the same time, this method has a number of consequences which constitute in turn a whole series of objections to the method itself. By focusing on one fixed point, it makes the surrounding area appear vague by comparison; we are compelled inexorably to consider that point wrenched out of context. It leads to an *in vitro* observation which is first and foremost concerned to discern the internal textures of an object withdrawn from its normal environment. This type of laboratory procedure is a (distant!) cousin of structural analysis, which seeks to extract models that are defined as ensembles of coherent and interdependent characteristics — models designed to give an optimum account of the real without that account itself being taken for the real. What we gain here in intensity, we lose in scope. We step outside the broad avenues of 'total history' and the royal road of the 'long term', concepts which have obsessed historians over the last thirty years but which, though they can be both stimulating and fruitful, are in many ways mystificatory and more poetic than operative. The modesty and attention to detail of ethnological, sociological or linguistic observations (to speak only of the 'human sciences'), which are ordinarily very limited in their scope, should be a lesson to the historian, that conjuror of time. Given that the past places an additional obstacle in the path of knowledge — the virtues of historical distance are not what they are made out to be — how can the historian claim to have access to everything which has occurred over the centuries?

It will doubtless also be claimed that using quantitative methods means primarily establishing the banal, sketching out the solid areas of dominant characteristics while paying less attention to the exceptional; it means preferring the neutral, sombre shades of resemblance to the lively tonalities of difference; in short, describing the grey history of repetitive events. But apart from the fact that it is repetition upon which human societies — and doubtless all organised bodies — are based, quantitative methods also allow us to discern which tendencies are becoming weaker and which, by contrast, are growing stronger. To the historian who is attentive to change, marginal behaviour is as interesting as the actions of the majority, and the sense of changing trends as important as sheer quantitative measurement. Even over a brief time-span, changes occur; I have tried to identify them. Furthermore, the assessment of minority phenomena also poses a number of delicate problems. If the times under consideration are past (and their meaning therefore revealed), the historian can evade these problems by resorting to simple assertion: death, as we know, transforms everything into destiny. But this *ad hoc*, retrospective procedure, from which we derive no capacity for future prediction, provides no guide for the present. The contemporary disarray of historians when confronted with the phenomenon of small groups or sects (in the broadest sense) shows how necessary it is that some thought be given to this topic.

The final objection will be that the extension of quantitative methods to social history is based on a dubious analogy between economic and social facts, which are in reality different in nature. The former are said to be much more homogeneous than the latter, where there is a much greater problem of assessing the 'value' of specific phenomena. There is, for example, a relative identity between two pounds of potatoes, but not between two strikes. Each of the latter forms a complex set of differently ordered elements. Certain disputes are weightier than others. In only 4 per cent of strikes was there violence, but these strikes had far greater repercussions. Decazeville or Anzin were much more important than a hundred little routine *coalitions*. Accumulating social statistics does not provide an answer to every question. The hermeneutic power of such a method is limited. Its descriptive value is great, but not great enough.

We are, then, thrown back on to the qualitative, on to literary and subjective evaluations, and on to the fluidities of the text! Throughout this work, texts have increasingly drawn our attention, both as sources and as modes of expression. We shall not deny the pleasure we feel in meeting up again with these old friends, whom we have perhaps neglected a little but never actually abandoned — though we remain of the opinion that an abundance of words are in fact the signs of a certain infirmity, the mark of a difficulty we experience when we try to encompass the real; they are, in short, the garrulous mask of our ignorance.

After so many detours and pointilliste touches, I should now need the pencil of an Urs Graf to sketch with a sure hand the physiognomy of the strike, its shape and movement. In the period studied here, when a dying liberalism still refused to countenance collective agreements, the strike retained a flamboyant supremacy. It was an offensive weapon as well as the defensive cordon cast around the workers' condition; its effects were multiplied by the fear it inspired. Its influence on the employers, on the state and on society as a whole, both directly and indirectly, was decisive.

Modest in scale, but often lengthy in duration, strikes had a markedly proletarian character. Neither confined to the labour aristocracy nor to the marginal, they drew their vigour from the middle strata of the working class, who were the worst victims of industrialisation. The prime territory for strikes was neither the large factory, with its interlinked departments (the large-scale metal industries remained outside its sweep), nor the small company (whose role, though it persisted was no longer dominant), but the medium-sized factory with a few hundred workers that had often not been established very long. Here, with mechanisation, the division and specialisation of labour continued, spawning the unskilled worker, that pariah of modern times. It was workers in the weaving trade, where wage differentials were not very great, who were pushed to the front of the stage by their greater propensity to engage in agitation, They were behind the most spectacular disputes and those with the greatest impact. It is to them that the Nord owes its place on the map of disputes, where Roubaix — the French Manchester — rivals Lyon and Paris, the failing or fallen capitals of the French labour movement.

The nature, objectives and style of a strike varied according to the nature of the strikers. Young people, women and foreigners did not hold the same kind of strikes. In each different trade, one can discern different temperaments, made up of a combination of particular traits. Here, the type of occupation counted for more than regional factors. Collective forces fashioned industrial disputes, to the extent even of suggesting the style of their expression and prompting them in their language. And yet the strike phenomenon cannot be dissolved into a sociology of strikers, no more than a town can be reduced to the sum of its various districts, nor any complex whole to the elements which make it up. The strike is not an empty form. As a social process, it has its own life, its rules, its custom and practice to which everyone bends, its overall movement and its specific course.

The rapid growth of the strike phenomenon illustrates its popularisation, its generalisation, and its irresistible extension to all categories of the working class and, already, to other social strata. In a society based on the regularity of work, stopping that work constitutes the only riposte, the great trump card of the producers. By the beginning of our period, the workers had long since discovered the power that 'downing tools' could represent, but the illegal character of such stoppages prevented them from turning that power to good account. By leaving them free to do so, the law of 1864 created the conditions for the modern strike: once legalised, it advanced by leaps and bounds. The prodigious rise of this social practice was accompanied by its ideological valorisation. The theme of the general strike, later theorised by Georges Sorel among others, was not the product of the theorists' imagination: it was something which welled up from below; it was based upon a lived experience.

In this first period of growth, the strike phenomenon underwent more or less regular fluctuations. The short-run fluctuations were particularly regular. Seasonal, monthly and weekly in character, they reveal a coherent and ordered distribution, which suggests the operation of a certain necessity. In the short term, the triggering of strikes appears to be to some degree externally determined; spring and the start of the week or beginning of the month were favoured moments. Economic and psychological factors provide explanations for a statistical distribution that lies largely beyond the play of chance. This statistical recurrence removes the dimension of chance from strikes and confers upon them the eminent, dignified status of being 'social facts'.

Yearly oscillations and the alternation of high and low periods present a more complex problem. The influence of the economic situation can be the more clearly seen if we make a distinction between offensive and defensive strikes, which are two divergent and almost symmetrical sides of the same phenomenon. The former are positively correlated with prosperity; the latter, by contrast, accompany recession. The two are opposed both in their origins and in their patterns; the graphs which represent both of them together therefore have a hybrid character. When the Great Depression considerably increased the number of defensive strikes, the consequence was a disturbance of the economic harmonies.

Economic crises also made their mark on this history. They created internal tensions within the workers' universe, which weakened class consciousness. The strike, with its unifying force, began to be supplanted by tendencies towards disintegration: movements of unemployed workers, torn between anarchist fury and meek recourse to the authorities, and xenophobic demonstrations giving vent to a vigorous nationalism aroused by the wounding awareness of a double defeat — both military and economic — dissipated the energies of the movement for better wages and conditions.

But the economic conjuncture could not alone explain the extent of some retreats, nor the scale of certain offensives. Political circumstances weigh very heavily and provide the key both to the quiet periods and to the major upsurges of activity. If fear serves to repress desire, the hope raised by improved political perspectives fuels a very active ferment of demands, both at the national and local levels. Having dislodged the companies' monarchist representatives from the municipal councils in 1887–8, the miners rebelled against the companies' economic despotism; the strikes of 1878 sounded the charge of the movement for revenge and were as much a veiled settling of electoral scores as a refusal to accept lower wages. The general political climate played a very important role. Conservative governments, by the real or potential repression they exercised, stemmed the tide of strikes, whilst this tide actually swelled under liberal governments. 1830–31, 1840, 1864, 1869–70, 1888–90, 1905–6 and, above all, 1936 provide repeated examples of upsurges in social agitation born of hopes for a better government. Thus, though very rarely political in their objectives, strikes in this period frequently had political origins. This is evidence of the power with which the workers credited government and, particularly, the Republic, which they saw as the key to happiness. These economic and political factors allow us to understand the causes of many strikes and their principal articulations, but they cannot account for every aspect of the phenomenon. They cannot explain the underlying curve of development, nor the vigour of certain unforeseen outbursts, which even in retrospect seem astonishing. To understand these one is forced to appeal to the magical resources of social psychology, if not indeed to the secrets of the 'collective unconscious'. These are convenient terms, but perhaps too vague; they both indicate and yet conceal certain events which remain impenetrable; they are, without doubt, realities, but ones which, for the moment, leave us disarmed. At a more modest level, the strike, analysed not as an abstract mechanism but as an instance of human decision-making, leads us to enquire into the psychology of the actors. A lively political sensibility, the exercise of which was stimulated by those troubled times, combined here with an awareness of the economic conjuncture, which remained the essential tool of daily decision-making. The choice of the 'right moment' on a day-to-day basis was a function of that economic assessment. The workers showed themselves particularly gifted in this regard, though the gift was unequally distributed between different occupations and different types of enterprise. Older trades which moved at craft rhythms and small workshops subject to the fluctuations of the market, provided the best conditions for a sense of timing to develop; large-scale industry, by contrast, was not conducive to that development. The building-workers and the miners, the 'look-out posts' of the working class, both displayed outstanding talents, but they did so very differently. The building-workers represent an example of a traditional awareness of the economic conjuncture, which was a function of the transparent nature of seasonal rhythms and the fact that the number of 'hands' needed and the number set on could be clearly seen. The miners, faced with the opacities of modern capitalism, took account of stock-levels and prices — not to mention profits — though they did not derive a model for their own action from these considerations. That action remained relatively empirical and marked by old habits (namely, the miners' strikes in the summer).

The domain of the strike is not totally governed by rationality. Insofar as they were the product of a great number of isolated, individual decisions, strikes lay largely beyond the grasp of reason. Crude and sudden, liable to erupt violently under the influence of emotions of anger or desire, they retained to some degree the vigour of the spontaneous strikes of times past. This spontaneity, while it reduced their instrumental dimension, was the key to their richness of expression. Naiveté — albeit relative naiveté — is often more valuable to us than calculation, which masks what is actually occurring, and discipline, which renders everything uniform. There can be no doubt, however, that such spontaneous strikes represented recessive behaviour. In fact, strikes had already become highly domesticated, and even before the days of trade-union 'government', the leadership of which was already beginning to form and assert itself, they were sobered down and civilised. Accumulated experience handed down from earlier generations was channelled into the running of the strike; this was an element of that working-class 'custom and practice' which constituted one of the pillars on which the class itself was founded.

What I have termed the 'domesticated profile' of the strike can already be identified in a mature state in the widespread use of advance warnings and even of preliminary negotiations, which deprived strikes of their aspect of romantic insurrection and gave them their modern character as a means of applying pressure within an ongoing bargaining process. This profile became more clearly delineated with the increasing part played by organisations, which gradually substituted their fund of wisdom for the passion of fiery if somewhat transitory 'ringleaders'. It became even more pronounced in the course of a strike's development, which followed an ordered, sometimes even ritualised scenario in which violence, rarely initiated by the strikers, only broke out exceptionally. In actual fact, the use of quantitative methods provides a sharp corrective to the literary vision of strikes. *Germinal* is more an epic poem than a naturalistic novel. It is an arbitrary bundle of real characteristics, but the model it presents has only a limited application.

Restrained and modest in its means (the great disarmament of the working class had begun), controlled in its actions and narrowly directed in its objectives (the *Patron* as the eternal enemy), violence on the part of the strikers withdrew into a sanguinary discourse, which we must not allow to deceive us by its aggressiveness. Words have to be compared with deeds and vice versa. It is when there is no violence that the shouting is the loudest; it is when there is no revolution that people talk about it so volubly. Discourse, like dreams, has a compensatory function and allows the release of pent-up emotion. Hence the difficulty one has in simply trusting what is said; for it conceals and mystifies as much as it reveals. This is without doubt the greatest objection that can be raised against the 'positivist' method of simply recording 'historical facts'.

Discourse — or at least those commonly repeated phrases which make up the relatively durable communications network of a class — lags behind the real. It keeps alive antiquated images that are pure fictions. The representation of the worker as classic pauper and the capitalist as feudal lord, the portrait of the bourgeois as idle and bloated pleasure-seeker, the vision of an inevitable revolution that was both just, by virtue of the rights of succession of the Fourth Estate and necessary, by dint of the total decadence of a bourgeoisie, emptied of its substance and incapable of initiative or even of procreation; all these recurrent themes go to make up the incantatory song of the strikers, the great fresco of the exploited, the dream of a better world.

This discourse co-exists, on the other hand, with a thoroughly realistic attitude towards immediate claims on the employers. The central plank of these claims was the question of wages, or, more precisely wage-levels. For a working class resolutely concerned with money income, as yet not particularly aware of the effects of the cost of living on real incomes, the principal objective lies in increasing nominal rates of pay. Calls for a reduction in the working day, a typical demand of prosperous years and one much heard at the end of the Second Empire, were now less frequent, both as a result of a relative (and provisional) level of satisfaction and, more particularly, because of unemployment, the natural enemy of leisure. Meanwhile, internal tensions within companies were increasing, giving rise to conflicts with supervisory staff, confrontations over regulations or fines, and trade-union struggles. The crisis made the rigours of factory life even harsher; it produced new sources of dissension and led to a somewhat illusory extension of the range of workers' demands. This was, however, the result of an increase in the number of grievances rather than of the development of more detailed programmes. Once expansion returned, wages recovered their position of primacy, their magnetic power of attraction. With the exception of the miners, the workers turned out to be little concerned with other matters. All they asked was that they should earn a little more. The modest nature of their desires and the limited character of their expressed needs indicate a standard of living that was still very basic, only one step removed from the fear of hunger. As far as other matters were concerned, they put up with them as they were. Against those factories where harsh conditions prevailed — factories which were truly detested — their belligerence, though endlessly reiterated, remained overwhelmingly verbal in nature. Whether they liked it or not, the workers bowed here to discipline. Indeed, the patience they showed seems more surprising than their violence; their tendency to accept situations — and even to become resigned to them — is as striking as their rebelliousness.

Rebellion is not instinctive. It arises out of action and out of unity in action. In this respect the strike offers a remarkable propaedeutic, an antidote to isolation, that icy wind to which the division of

317

labour exposed the workers. With its leaders, meetings, demonstrations, language and sometimes even financial organisation, a strike creates a community with Rousseauist aspirations, deeply committed to direct democracy, avid for pure, untrammelled relationships, for communion. This was all the more true in our period, since strikes went on for such·a long time (on average ten times longer than today).

This characteristic differentiates them fundamentally from today's disputes, whose aim is size coupled with brevity. The length of nineteenth-century strikes is all the more remarkable in that strike relief, like workers' savings, was very small, a weakness that was not greatly offset by the fact that they often lived closer to the countryside, giving access to farm produce. In certain interminable disputes, the asceticism of the workers, who were elsewhere described as prodigal and improvident, surprised all observers. Inured to penury, poor societies have unsuspected reserves of resistance when hope sustains them; they also enjoy a greater degree of freedom *vis-à-vis* a capitalism which does not as yet beset the popular classes with the perfidious snares of credit.

Strikes, then, even if they were becoming rationalised in their conduct and their objectives, were not purely functional. They were an experience, a piece of history, an event. Experienced as a liberating force, capable of breaking the monotony of the daily round and counteracting the power of the employers, they gave form to an ephemeral and often much lamented counter-society. Nostalgia for the strike carried within it the seed of its rebirth.

In the light of strikes, the world of the workers of the 1880s seems extraordinarily complex and ambiguous, shot through with diverse currents and contradictory aspirations. Neither marginal, nor primitive, it seems to be in the process of adapting to industrial society, shaped to its rhythms, ruses and values — work, money, machines, family, nation — sufficiently integrated to show some skill at playing 'by the rules of the game' and to accept compromise solutions. This process was, in turn, aided by the fact that an analogous tendency towards compromise was developing in the ranks of those with whom they had to negotiate, and even among their enemies.

From another point of view, however, this proletariat, camped at the gates of the city, reveals itself as permeable to contagion, quick to be stirred to action, open to change, hungry for freedom. These people are reminiscent of semi-nomads; they are on the way to permanent settlement and yet they remain ever ready to strike camp. They are to some degree settled, but theirs is an unstable condition. Secretly, they are tormented by the desire to be travelling. Even given all due caution about the effects of language, it seems revolutionary speeches had a real resonance among the workers, that they were truly capable of spurring them to action. May Day 1890, the first bourgeois panic since the Commune, sent out a shock wave of expectation. Like so many others at the end of the century who believed 'the world was coming to an end', the workers awaited the revolution that would, it seemed, inevitably come in peace and serenity, the simple fruit of a slow process of maturation, of a necessary evolution. Children of Darwin and the steam-engine, they were unable to step outside the collective representations of their period — a period that was both a time for putting down roots and an age of hope.

Select Bibliography

A detailed bibliography can be found at the end of vol. II of the original publication, *Ouvriers en grève* (pp. 735–844).

Sources

1. The sources for this study are mainly *manuscripts*, to be found in:
— *Archives de la Préfecture de Police de Paris*, a gold-mine for this period (especially series B A);
— *Archives Nationales*: series BB 18, BB 24, BB 30, (Parliamentary Archives), F 7 (Police), F 12 (Commerce and Industry), F 22 (Labour and Social Security);
— *Archives Départementales*, systematically catalogued: series M (consists of the accounts of the Préfectures) and U (judicial proceedings).

2. *The Press*, from Paris and the provinces, by workers, radicals and socialists, has contributed a number of elements. Particularly important: *Le Cri du Peuple*, founded by Jules Vallès (1883–9); *Le Rappel*, indispensable for the years 1871 to 1880; and the little socialist journals of the *Départements*, like the northern *Le Forçat* and its successors, *La Défense des Travailleurs* in Reims, etc. These journals published, during most of the time, 'Revues des Bagnes' ('Around the Works'), very detailed.

3. *Official publications*, especially those of the *Office du Travail*, created in 1891 as a body to carry out sociological inquiries. Particularly useful: *Enquête sur les salaires et la durée du travail dans l'industrie française (grande et moyenne industrie)*, Paris, Imprimerie Nationale, 1893–7, 5 vols. and 1 vol. of statistical data; *La Petite Industrie*, 1893–6, 2 vols.; *Les Associations Professionnelles Ouvrières*, Paris, Imprimerie Nationale, 1899–1904, 4 vols.

Bibliography

Gérard Noiriel, *Les ouvriers dans la société française, XIXè–XXè siècles*, Paris, 1986 (the most recent and best survey to date; lists 364 titles. To be published by Berg Publishers in 1988).

Two major dissertations

Yves Lequin, *Les ouvriers de la région lyonnaise (1848–1914)*, Lyon, 1977, 2 vols.
Rolande Trempé, *Les Mineurs de Carmaux (1848–1914)*, Paris, 1971, 2 vols.

In English on the strikes

Edward Shorter and Charles Tilly, *Strikes in France (1830–1968)*, London, 1974 (a quantitative survey applying the methods as developed at the University of Michigan, Ann Arbor; indispensable).
K.G.J.C. Knowles, *Strikes. A Study in Industrial Conflict with Special Reference to British Experience between 1911 and 1947*, Oxford, 1952 (a classic).

On the lives of French workers, some recent American studies

John Merriman, *The Red City. Limoges and the French Nineteenth Century*, New York/Oxford, 1985.
William M. Reddy, *The Rise of Market Culture. The Textile Trade and French Society (1750–1900)*, Cambridge/New York/Paris, 1984.
Joan W. Scott, *The Glassworkers of Carmaux*, Cambridge, Mass., 1974.
— and Louise Tilly, *Women, Work and Family*, New York/London, 1978.
William H. Sewell, *Work and Revolution in France. The Language of Labor from the Old Regime to 1848*, New York, 1980.